Context and Consciousness

Context and Consciousness

Activity Theory and Human-Computer Interaction

edited by Bonnie A. Nardi

The MIT Press
Cambridge, Massachusetts
London, England

Second printing, 1997

The book was set in Sabon by Asco Trade Typesetting Ltd., Hong Kong and was printed and bound in the United States of America.

Library of Congress Cataloging-in-Publication Data

Context and consciousness : activity theory and human-computer interaction / edited by Bonnie A. Nardi.
p. cm.
Includes bibliographical references and index.
ISBN 0-262-14058-6 (alk. paper)
1. Human-computer interaction. 2. Computers—Psychological aspects. I. Nardi, Bonnie A.
QA76.9.H85C68 1996 95-10974
004′.01′9—dc20 CIP

Contents

Figures and Tables vii
Preface xi

I Activity Theory Basics 1

Introduction to Part I 3

1 Activity Theory and Human-Computer Interaction 7
Bonnie A. Nardi

2 Activity Theory as a Potential Framework for Human-Computer Interaction Research 17
Kari Kuutti

3 Computer-Mediated Activity: Functional Organs in Social and Developmental Contexts 45
Victor Kaptelinin

4 Studying Context: A Comparison of Activity Theory, Situated Action Models, and Distributed Cognition 69
Bonnie A. Nardi

5 Activity Theory: Implications for Human-Computer Interaction 103
Victor Kaptelinin

II Activity Theory in Practical Design 117

Introduction to Part II 119

6 Designing Educational Technology: Computer-Mediated Change 123
R. K. E. Bellamy

7 Applying Activity Theory to Video Analysis: How to Make Sense of Video Data in HCI 147
Susanne Bødker

8 Tamed by a Rose: Computers as Tools in Human Activity 175
Ellen Christiansen

9 Joint Attention and Co-Construction of Tasks: New Ways to Foster User-Designer Collaboration 199
Arne Raeithel and Boris M. Velichkovsky

10 Some Reflections on the Application of Activity Theory 235
Bonnie A. Nardi

III Activity Theory: Theoretical Development 247

Introduction to Part III 249

11 Activity Theory and the View from Somewhere: Team Perspectives on the Intellectual Work of Programming 257
Dorothy Holland and James R. Reeves

12 Developing Activity Theory: The Zone of Proximal Development and Beyond 283
Vladimir P. Zinchenko

13 Mundane Tool or Object of Affection? The Rise and Fall of the Postal Buddy 325
Yrjö Engeström and Virginia Escalante

14 Epilogue 375
Bonnie A. Nardi

Contributors 381

Index 383

Figures and Tables

FIGURES

2.1 Mediated relationship at the individual level 28
2.2 Basic structure of an activity 28
2.3 Hierarchical levels of an activity 30
2.4 Examples of activities, actions, and operations 33
2.5 Potential ways of supporting activities by information technology 36
2.6 Activity theory areas corresponding to the defined levels of research objects 38
3.1 Expansion of the subject matter of HCI: three dimensions 48
3.2 Computer tool as an extension of the internal plane of actions 52
3.3 Computer-mediated group activity 59
5.1 The "information processing loop" of human-computer interaction 105
5.2 Two interfaces in human-computer interaction 111
6.1 Cole and Engeström's analysis 124
6.2 Application of Cole and Engeström's activity analysis 126
6.3 Typical screens from Dinosaur Canyon 133
6.4 Screen from Media Fusion 138
7.1 Engeström's model 151
7.2 The object is present only in the artifact 152
7.3 The object exists as a physical object 153

7.4 The only object is physically co-present outside the artifact 153
7.5 Characteristics of the system, tool, and media perspectives 154
7.6 A breakdown using a report generator 156
7.7 An overview of VIRK 162
7.8 Generating a report 164
7.9 The objects and focuses involved in report generation 166
7.10 Using the page numbering form to insert page number 167
7.11 Screen 167
9.1 A fragment of *Earth* by Guiseppe Arcimboldo 206
9.2 General design of the joint attention study (experiment 1) 207
9.3 General design of the joint attention study (experiment 2) 209
9.4 Two connective personal views of Arcimboldo's painting 211
9.5 Sample protocol of the Repertory Grid Technique 221
9.6 Common view of networkers 223
9.7 Common view of system administrators 224
9.8 Diagram of cooperative modeling 226
12.1 Convertibility of the internal and external forms in human subjects 293
12.2 One chronotope 294
12.3 One node of development 302
12.4 The vertical axis of development 305
12.5 The ontological and phenomenological aspects of development 317
12.6 Visualization of one possible development case 318
12.7 Space for the creative conceptual efforts of interested readers 320
13.1 Postal Buddy kiosk 326
13.2 Postal Buddy network 341
13.3 Postal Buddy network extended 343
13.4 The problem with the fax 354
13.5 Finger used as a remediating tool 357
13.6 Another customer used as a remediating tool 358

13.7 Activity system of Postal Buddy Corporation 366

13.8 The local post office identified as a missing link in the Postal Buddy network 369

TABLES

6.1 Analysis of Dinosaur Canyon 134

6.2 Analysis of Media Fusion 139

9.1 Matching methodology of process level 228

13.1 Key persons interviewed 329

Preface

There is a fundamental need for a theory of practice in human-computer interaction studies. This collection offers readers a chance to become acquainted with activity theory as a means of studying practice. Activity theory is a psychological theory developed over the course of some 70 years in the Soviet Union. It is concerned with understanding the relation between consciousness and activity and has labored to provide a framework in which a meaningful unity between the two can be conceived. Activity theory is pertinent to technology design and evaluation for a large number of reasons elaborated in this book, but fundamentally among them is an emphasis on *artifacts*, of which computers are a particularly interesting example, as crucial mediators of human experience.

The contributors to the book have varied backgrounds but all have used activity theory to illuminate issues of human-computer interaction. Some contributors are eminent activity theorists, others new enthusiasts. All share a concern for excellent science and humane technology.

The book is divided into three parts. Part I introduces the reader to activity theory. Part II illustrates the use of activity theory in practical design. Part III contributes to the theoretical development of activity theory.

I wish I could say that this book resulted from an intensive exciting workshop in which the contributors hashed out issues of activity theory and human-computer interaction. But in fact I have never even met some of the contributors to the book, not in person anway (though I hope to remedy that situation when I can). Instead of a workshop, we instigated a special-purpose virtual community for the creation of the book so that we could complete it in as timely a fashion as possible. Inspired by

Susanne Bødker's book, *Through the Interface*, in which she introduces activity theory to the human-computer interaction (HCI) community, and recognizing that the moment had come to provide a further look at the work of a variety of activity theory researchers, we "just did it." Our virtual community worked well, and the book was conceived and gestated through upwards of 700 e-mail messages, from the first message I sent to Kari Kuutti, on September 7, 1993, to the time I shipped the papers to MIT Press on Halloween, October 31, 1994.

ACKNOWLEDGMENTS

Our first acknowledgment then, must go to the Internet, without which we could not have assembled this book. Working in six countries, in differing research traditions, across academia and industry, the technology linked us together for the accomplishment of our common purpose.

It was a privilege, and I do not use that word lightly, to work with the contributors to this book, most of whom have much longer acquaintance with activity theory than I do. Any edited collection is a fragile craft, especially one plying the virtual seas, but the contributors proved sturdy and resourceful sailors. It has been a deep pleasure to learn from and work with them.

At Apple, I thank my manager, Jim Miller, for his continuing support of my work. I enjoyed stimulating discussions with many of my Apple colleagues about activity theory and design, and I thank Rachel Bellamy, Tom Erickson, Charlie Hill, Matthew Holloway, Don Norman, Dan Rose, Dan Russell, Mike Tschudy, and Jenny Watts for their interesting perspectives on activity theory. At the Apple Research Library, Lorin Hawley kept me well supplied with reference materials and citation checks, and I am grateful for his timely and probing search efforts.

Several people commented on individual chapters; we profited from the generosity and thoughtfulness of Olav Bertelsen, Michael Muller, Vicki O'Day, Robert Szulkin, Steve Whittaker, and Jay Zimmerman.

Bob Prior and the proficient staff at MIT Press gave full support to this project, and I thank them for their advice, enthusiasm, and practical help.

Many thanks go to Nicolas Spomior, who supplied the English translation for Vladimir Zinchenko's chapter.

Bran Boguraev, my colleague in the Intelligent Systems Program at Apple, supplied the language-based domain modeling software used to automatically generate the index terms for book. My thanks to Bran for help with this burdensome task!

I am very grateful to Victor Kaptelinin who provided help at every step along the way of compiling this book. Victor answered my questions great and small, provided much practical help in communicating with Russia, and never failed to offer encouragement and sound advice. I am very much in Victor Kaptelinin's debt.

My family, as always, provided love, support, and good times. I lovingly acknowledge my husband, Chris Darrouzet, and my children, Anthony, Christopher, and Jeanette.

And finally, the contributors and I acknowledge activity theorists and their predecessors in the cultural-historical school in the Soviet Union who worked, often under extreme duress, to provide us with a way of looking at things that is expansive and enriching and will continue to animate and motivate our efforts to understand human activity. This collection is dedicated to them.

I

Activity Theory Basics

Introduction to Part I

In part I, basic concepts of activity theory are explored with respect to human-computer interaction (HCI). I begin this part by outlining in chapter 1 some themes of activity theory and their relation to HCI studies.

Next, in chapter 2, Kari Kuutti motivates the current HCI interest in activity theory: the laboratory-based research paradigm has been "unable to penetrate the human side of the interface." The perspectives of Carroll (1987, 1991), Bannon (1991), and Grudin (1990) are used as a backdrop for a consideration of HCI and its discontents and the ensuing struggle to change and reformulate the basis of HCI research. Kuutti discusses the historical roots of activity theory and its terminology. He provides an overview of basic activity theory notions: activity as the unit of analysis, history and development, artifacts and mediation, the structure of an activity, and the levels of an activity. Kuutti incorporates some of the Scandinavian extensions to activity theory in the overview. He concludes with a discussion of the potential advantages of activity theory for HCI studies.

Victor Kaptelinin (chapter 3) notes the discomfort we feel when we think about extending the purview of HCI studies to include the messy, intractable world beyond the laboratory, beyond the human-machine dyad. This "explosion" of our subject matter is potentially a "powerful expansion of the object of study," but it also "creates a feeling of confusion." Kaptelinin discusses the ways in which activity theory can help to provide conceptual anchors to deal with the greater compass of our interests. He summarizes key activity theory notions—functional organs, internal plane of actions, levels of activity, and development—and argues that "computer-mediated activity," rather than "human-computer interaction," is a fruitful way to define the scope of our research activity.

One of the key points Kaptelinin makes about a strength of activity theory is the importance of its integrating framework linking a set of theoretical principles—rather than what we often get in HCI, which is an insight here and an insight there. Kaptelinin provides an example of the power of a larger theoretical framework, comparing Norman's (1991) notion of "cognitive artifacts" and activity theory's notion of tools. Cognitive artifacts are on one level almost identical to tools, but in activity theory, the notion of tools draws on principles of mediation, internalization, and functional organs, leading to very different conclusions about the nature of tools, as Kaptelinin details. Finally Kaptelinin discusses some of the limitations of activity theory.

In chapter 4 I compare activity theory, situated action models, and distributed cognition. Each research framework is considered with respect to unit of analysis, the categories that support a description of context, the extent to which each treats action as structured prior to or during activity, and the stance toward the conceptual equivalence of people and things. The chapters in this book are tied to the themes in this chapter, providing at least one orienting framework for considering them as a whole. An argument is made for the theoretical richness of activity theory while visiting highlights of situated action and distributed cognition. Methodological implications of activity theory are summarized. This discussion anticipates the practical tools of activity theory analysis described and applied to empirical work in the chapters in part II.

Victor Kaptelinin in chapter 5 contrasts some of the key notions of cognitive science with activity theory. He discusses the fundamental project of activity theory, which is to understand the "unity of consciousness and activity." Basic principles of activity theory are described: object-orientedness, the hierarchical structure of activity, internalization/externalization, mediation, and functional organs. Kaptelinin notes the continuing links between cognitive science and activity theory, observing that activity theory "does not reject the experimental results and techniques accumulated within the cognitive tradition."

Those well versed in activity theory will find that we include a great deal under the activity theory umbrella; that is, we include the foundational roots of the work of the cultural-historical school founded by Vygotsky, the activity theory of Leont'ev and his students, as well as the Scandinavian extensions to activity theory of more recent vintage (though individual authors may make finer distinctions in their chapters). Purists be warned! My own view is that the concerns with consciousness and mediation that are so important for technology design are common to the cultural-historical school and activity theory. Zinchenko (1995) discusses the differences between cultural-historical psychology and activity theory, calling them "two strands of research." He notes that cultural-historical psychology has been more concerned with the problem of meaning, while activity theory has contributed a focus on object-relatedness. The cultural-historical school emphasized mediation by language, while activity theory has concentrated on mediation by tools (explaining its attractiveness to those of us concerned with technology). However, there is nothing incompatible in the two "strands"; rather, they reinforce one another, and I concur with Zinchenko (1995) that we should "look at [the strands] as mutually amplifying one another ... [each] enriching the other."

REFERENCES

Bannon, L. J. (1991). From human factors to human actors: The role of psychology and human-computer interaction studies in system design. In J. Greenbaum and M. Kyng, eds., *Design at Work: Cooperative Design of Computer Systems* (pp. 25–44). Hillsdale, NJ: Lawrence Erlbaum.

Carroll, J. M. (ed.). (1987). *Interfacing Thought: Cognitive Aspects of Human-Computer Interaction.* Cambridge, MA: MIT Press.

Carroll, J. M. (ed.). (1991). *Designing Interaction: Psychology at the Human-Computer Interface.* Cambridge: Cambridge University Press.

Grudin, J. (1990). The computer reaches out: The historical continuity of user interface design. In *Proceedings of CHI '90.* Seattle, Washington.

Norman, D. Cognitive artifacts. In J. Carroll, ed., *Designing Interaction: Psychology at the Human Computer Interface.* New York: Cambridge University Press.

Zinchenko, V. P. (1995). Cultural-historical psychology and the psychological theory of activity: Retrospect and prospect. In J. V. Wertsch, P. del Rio, and A. Alvarez, eds., *Sociocultural Studies of Mind.* Cambridge: Cambridge University Press.

1

Activity Theory and Human-Computer Interaction

Bonnie A. Nardi

What is activity theory, and how will it benefit studies of human-computer interaction? This book addresses these questions. Many HCI researchers are eager to move beyond the confines of traditional cognitive science, but it is not clear exactly which direction to move in. This book explores one alternative for HCI research: activity theory, a research framework and set of perspectives originating in Soviet psychology in the 1920s. Just as HCI research is concerned with practical problems of design and evaluation, activity theorists from the outset have addressed practical needs, applying their research efforts to the problems of mentally and physically handicapped children, educational testing, ergonomics, and other areas. Following the lead of dialectical materialism, activity theory focuses on *practice*, which obviates the need to distinguish "applied" from "pure" science—understanding everyday practice in the real world is the very objective of scientific practice.

Activity theory is a powerful and clarifying descriptive tool rather than a strongly predictive theory. The object of activity theory is to understand the unity of consciousness and activity. Activity theory incorporates strong notions of intentionality, history, mediation, collaboration and development in constructing consciousness (see Kaptelinin, chapter 5; Kuutti, this volume). Activity theorists argue that consciousness is not a set of discrete disembodied cognitive acts (decision making, classification, remembering), and certainly it is not the brain; rather, consciousness is located in everyday practice: you are what you do. And what you do is firmly and inextricably embedded in the social matrix of which every person is an organic part. This social matrix is composed of people and artifacts. Artifacts may be physical tools or sign systems such as human language. Understanding the interpenetration of the individual, other people, and artifacts in everyday activity is the challenge activity theory has set for itself.

Unlike anthropology, which is also preoccupied with everyday activity, activity theory is concerned with the development and function of individual consciousness. Activity theory was developed by psychologists, so this is not surprising, but it is a very different flavor of psychology from what the West has been accustomed to, as activity theory emphasizes naturalistic study, culture, and history.

The chapters in part I explain what activity theory is. They, along with the seminal article, "The Problem of Activity in Psychology" by the Russian psychologist Leont'ev (1974) (widely available in English in university libraries), form a primer of activity theory.

Activity theory offers a set of perspectives on human activity and a set of concepts for describing that activity. This, it seems to me, is exactly what HCI research needs as we struggle to understand and describe "context," "situation," "practice." We have recognized that technology use is not a mechanical input-output relation between a person and a machine; a much richer depiction of the user's situation is needed for design and evaluation. However, it is unclear how to formulate that depiction in a way that is not purely ad hoc. Here is where activity theory helps: by providing orienting concepts and perspectives. As Engeström (1993) has noted, activity theory does not offer "ready-made techniques and procedures" for research; rather, its conceptual tools must be "concretized according to the specific nature of the object under scrutiny."

As we expand our horizons to think not only about *usable* systems but now *useful* systems, it is imperative that we have ways of finding out what would be useful. How can we begin to understand the best ways to undertake major design projects, such as providing universal access to the Internet, effectively using computers in the classroom, supporting distributed work teams, and even promoting international understanding in ways both small (e.g., international video/e-mail pen-pals for schoolchildren) and large (e.g., using technology to find new means of conflict resolution)? Laboratory-based usability studies are part of the solution, but they are best preceded in a phased design process by careful field studies to ascertain how technology can fit into users' actual social and material environments, the problems users have that technology can remedy, the applications that will promote creativity and enlightenment, and how we can design humane technology that ensures privacy and dignity.

Recently a major American journal of HCI rejected a set of papers that would have formed a special issue on activity theory. The concern was that activity theory is hard to learn, and because we have not seen its actual benefits realized in specific empirical studies, the time spent learning it would be of dubious benefit. The chapters in parts II and III of this book speak to this concern by providing empirical studies of human-computer interaction developed from an activity theory perspective. In these pages you will meet Danish homicide detectives, a beleaguered U.S. Post Office robot and its human creators, disgruntled slide makers, absent-minded professors, enthusiastic elementary school students, sly college students, and others. These people and artifacts, and the situations in which they are embedded, are analyzed with concepts from activity theory. Several interesting ways to structure an activity theory analysis are provided in these chapters, so readers are offered substantial methodological tools to support practice.

Throughout the book we have tried to "compare and contrast" activity theory with other techniques and theories to make it "easier" to learn (if indeed it is truly difficult). Thus readers will find that as they read the chapters, they may think about activity theory in relation to cognitive science, GOMS, Gibson's work on affordances, Norman's cognitive artifacts, situated action models, distributed cognition, actor-network theory, and other social scientific artifacts. Bannon and Bødker (1991) have compared activity theory to task analysis and user modeling elsewhere, so we have not undertaken that task here. Briefly, they argued that these approaches are very limited in that (1) task analysis provides a set of procedural steps by which a task supposedly proceeds, with little attention to "the tacit knowledge that is required in many skilled activities, or the fluent action in the actual work process," and (2) user modeling considers user characteristics (e.g., is the user an expert or a novice?) but says little about the situation in which the user works or the nature of the work itself.

Activity theory proposes a strong notion of *mediation*—all human experience is shaped by the tools and sign systems we use. Mediators connect us organically and intimately to the world; they are not merely filters or channels through which experience is carried, like water in a pipe (see Zinchenko, this volume). Activity theorists are the first to note that activity theory itself is but one mediating tool for research (as are all theories!) and that like any tool, its design evolves over time (see Kaptelinin, chapter 3, this volume). Activity theory is certainly evolving and growing; it is not by any means a static end point.

Activity theory has a tremendous capacity for growth and change, an intellectual energy that is being realized in research efforts in Russia, Europe, North America, and Australia. I think perhaps this is because of activity theory's rich philosophical and scientific heritage and because it permits such wide scope of analysis. Activity theory provides ample room in the intellectual sandbox for adventure and discovery and leads to the work of philosophers, psychologists, anthropologists, linguists, educators, and others whose thoughts have influenced activity theory. The chapters in part III of this book push on the frontiers of activity theory, expanding its conceptual base.

Let's talk for a moment about the most concrete practical benefit we could expect from activity theory in the near term. The most immediate benefit I hope for is the dissemination of a common vocabulary for describing activity that all HCI researchers would share. Activity theory has a simple but powerful hierarchy for describing activity that could be common coin for all HCI researchers. This hierarchy (described in several of the chapters in this book) has a superficial resemblance to GOMS but goes beyond GOMS in essential ways, especially in describing dynamic movement between levels of activity rather than assuming stasis.

The development of a common vocabulary is crucial for HCI. As we move toward ethnographic and participatory design methods to discover and describe real everyday activity, we run into the problem that has bedeviled anthropology for so long: every account is an ad hoc description cast in situationally specific terms. Abstraction, generalization and comparison become problematic. An ethnographic description, although it may contain much information of direct value for design and evaluation, remains a narrative account structured according to the author's own personal vocabulary, largely unconstrained and arbitrary. Ethnography—literally, "writing culture"—assumes no a priori framework that orders the data, that contributes to the coherence and generalizability of the descriptive account. This leads to a disappointing lack of cumulative research results. One would like to be able to develop a comparative framework, perhaps a taxonomy as suggested by Brooks (1991), that would help us as we pursue design and evaluation activities. It would be desirable to be able to go back to previous work and find a structured set of problems and solutions. Activity theory will help us to achieve this goal but not until its concepts become part of a shared vocabulary.

Let us look briefly at a few of the main concerns of activity theory: consciousness, the asymmetrical relation between people and things, and the role of artifacts in everyday life. Each of these concerns (and others) will be considered at length in this book, and I introduce them briefly here to anticipate some of what the reader will encounter.

A basic tenet of activity theory is that a notion of consciousness is central to a depiction of activity. Vygotsky described consciousness as a phenomenon that unifies attention, intention, memory, reasoning, and speech (Vygotsky 1925/1982; see Bakhurst 1991). Does HCI really need to worry about consciousness? The answer would seem to be yes, as we have been worrying about it all along. A notion of consciousness, especially one that focuses on attention and access to cognitive resources, permeates HCI discourse. When we speak of "direct manipulation," "intelligent agents," "expert behavior," and "novice behavior," we are really positing concepts in which consciousness is central. The notion of consciousness has continually snuck in the back door of HCI studies, as Draper (1993) has pointed out. We use the word "transparent," to describe a good user interface—that is, one that is supportive and unobtrusive, but which the user need pay little, if any, attention to. We have borrowed the concept "affordances" from Gibson, which practically dispenses with the notion of consciousness but still implies a particular stance toward it. We speak of "skilled performance," implying a kind of mental ease and access to certain cognitive resources peculiar to experts who have become very good at something. "Novices," on the other hand, consciously labor to perform actions that will later become automatic, requiring little conscious awareness. Their less able performance is attributable to their need to focus deliberate attention on task actions while at the same time working with fewer cognitive resources than they will have available later as they gain expertise and experience in their tasks.

Even in the earliest HCI work we find concern with the user's consciousness. In 1972 Bobrow wrote that a programming technique "can greatly facilitate construction of complex programs because it allows the user to remain thinking about his program operation at a relatively high level without having to descend into manipulation of details." This is a succinct statement of the interdependence of the "how" and the "what" of consciousness: the user's attention is at stake, and at the very same time, so is the content of what he thinks about as he programs.

Consciousness is still with us: Carey and Rusli (1995) argue that simply observing users does not tell the researcher enough; it must be discovered what the user is thinking. They give an example, asking, "Was a switch in search tactics the result of abandoning an unproductive attempt, or the result of gaining knowledge from the last few actions?" There are very different implications for technology design depending on the reason for the switch. Looking back more than a decade at Malone's (1983) classic paper on office organization, we find that Malone noted that users' behavior cannot be understood without reference to intentionality: is a user organizing her office so that she can find something later, or so that she will be reminded of something? The observer sees the same behavior but cannot know what it means without asking the user. Malone observed that finding and reminding are quite different functions, equally important for users, and that we cannot understand them if we do not take account of the user's intentions.

The unstudied use of a notion of consciousness will continue to crop up in HCI research, and rather than dealing with each new instance piecemeal, in a new vocabulary, as though we had never heard of it before, an overarching framework prepared to deal with the phenomenon of consciousness will be useful. Draper (1993) talks about "designing for consciousness," and it seems that this is exactly what we should be doing when we discuss the possibility of, for example, "intelligent agents." The notion of agents suggests that the user direct conscious awareness toward the user interface rather than that the user interface disappear "transparently." In a direct manipulation interface, on the other hand, cognitive content concerns the nitty-gritty of one's task, with the interface ideally fading from awareness.

Thus we see from this brief excursion into the difficult subject of consciousness that already we have gained two insights: (1) we must know what the user is thinking to design properly, as Carey and Rusli (1995) argue, and (2) we have a larger conceptual space into which to place differing user interface paradigms such as intelligent agents and direct manipulation.

Of course, psychologists have studied attention and consciousness for a long time; this is not new to activity theory. Activity theory, however, embeds consciousness in a wider activity system and describes a dynamic by which changes in consciousness are directly related to the material and social conditions current in a person's situation (see Kaptelinin, chapters 3, 5; Nardi, chapter 4; Bødker; Raeithel and Velichkovsky, this volume). This extends the concept of consciousness past an idealistic, mentalistic construct in which only cognitive resources and attention "inside the head" are at issue, to a situated phenomenon in which one's material and social context are crucial.

An important perspective contributed by activity theory is its insistence on the asymmetry between people and things (see Kaptelinin, chapter 5; Nardi, chapter 4; Zinchenko, this volume). Activity theory, with its emphasis on the importance of motive and consciousness—which belong only to humans—sees people and things as fundamentally different. People are not reduced to "nodes" or "agents" in a system; "information processing" is not seen as something to be modeled in the same way for people and machines. In activity theory, artifacts are mediators of human thought and behavior; they do not occupy the same ontological space. This results in a more humane view of the relationship of people and artifacts, as well as squarely confronting the many real differences between people and things.

Cognitive science has been the dominant theoretical voice in HCI studies since the inception of our young field. We are beginning to feel a theoretical pinch, however—a sense that cognitive science is too restrictive a paradigm for finding out what we would like to know (Bannon and Bødker, 1991; Kuutti, this volume). Activity theory is not a rejection of cognitive science (see Kaptelinin, chapter 5, this volume) but rather a radical expansion of it. One reason we need this expansion is that a key aspect of HCI studies must be to understand *things*; technology—physical objects that mediate activity—and cognitive science have pretty much ignored the study of artifacts, insisting on mental representations as the proper locus of study. Thus we have produced reams of studies on mentalistic phenomena such as "plans" and "mental models" and "cognitive maps," with insufficient attention to the physical world of artifacts—their design and use in the world of real activity (Hutchins 1994). Norman (1988) has done much to alleviate this situation, turning our attention toward what Sylvia Plath called the "thinginess of things" (Plath 1982), but we still have a long way to go.

Activity theory proposes that activity cannot be understood without understanding the role of artifacts in everyday existence, especially the way artifacts are integrated into social practice (which thus contrasts with Gibson's notion of affordances). Cognitive science has concentrated on *information*, its representation and propagation; activity theory is concerned with *practice*, that is, *doing* and *activity*, which significantly involve "the mastery of ... external devices and tools of labor activity" (Zinchenko 1986). Kaptelinin (chapters 3, 5, this volume) and Zinchenko (this volume) describe the activity theory concept of "functional organ," a fundamental notion pinpointing the way the mind and body are profoundly extended and transformed by artifacts (see also Vygotsky 1929, Leont'ev 1981). There are echoes of Haraway's (1990) cyborg here but in a different (and much earlier) voice. The notion of the functional organ, rather than being a riveting poetic image like the cyborg, is a tenet of a larger system of theoretical thought and a tool for further scientific inquiry.

Some readers may be impatient with activity theory terminology. It can be inelegant in translation from the Russian and, worse, confusing. The notion of an "object," in particular, becomes a point of confusion as activity theorists use terms such as "object-oriented" in an entirely different way than they are used in the programming community. A degree of forbearance is helpful when first confronting activity theory terminology.

Activity theory challenges much that we have held useful and important in HCI research. But this book is not mounted as an attack on previous work; rather, it is an inquiry into satisfying ways to extend, and where necessary to reformulate, the basis for the study of problems in human-computer interaction. This inquiry is intended to be ecumenical and inclusive yet probing and questioning. There is a new kind of post-postmodern voice struggling to speak clearly here; it is polyvocal and dialogical, to be sure, but also committed to social and scientific engagement. This voice has little use for the peevish debate and posturing that mark much current (and past) discourse; instead the aim is to acknowledge, learn from, and yet go beyond existing theory, to reach for what Bertelsen (1994) calls a "radical pragmatic science of HCI." Many who have come to find activity theory useful for HCI acknowledge a debt to cognitive science, especially the pioneering work of Card, Moran, and Newell (1983), for the suggestion that HCI design can benefit from a rigorous scientific foundation, as well as a debt to participatory design work (Kyng 1991; Muller and Kuhn 1993), which urges a humane, socially responsible scientific practice. That activity theory fuses these two intellectual impulses into a unified approach perhaps explains why we are seeking its counsel at this particular time in the history of our field.

REFERENCES

Bakhurst, D. (1991). *Consciousness and Revolution in Soviet Philosophy*. Cambridge: Cambridge University Press.

Bannon, L., and Bødker, S. (1991). Beyond the interface: Encountering artifacts in use. In J. Carroll, ed., *Designing Interaction: Psychology at the Human Computer Interface*. Cambridge: Cambridge University Press.

Bertelsen, O. (1994). Fitts' law as a design artifact: A paradigm case of theory in software design. In *Proceedings East-West Human Computer Interaction Conference* (vol. 1, pp. 37–43). St. Petersburg, August 2–6.

Bobrow, D. (1972). Requirements for advanced programming systems for list processing. *Communications of the ACM* (July).

Brooks, R. (1991). Comparative task analysis: An alternative direction for human-computer interaction science. In J. Carroll, ed., *Designing Interaction: Psychology at the Human Computer Interface*. Cambridge: Cambridge University Press.

Card, S., Moran, T., and Newell, A. (1983). *The Psychology of Human-Computer Interaction*. Hillsdale, NJ: Lawrence Erlbaum Associates.

Carey, T., and Rusli, M. (1995). Usage representations for re-use of design insights: A case study of access to on-line books. In J. Carroll, ed., *Scenario-based Design for Human Computer Interaction.* New York: Wiley.

Draper, S. (1993). Critical notice: Activity theory: The new direction for HCI? *International Journal of Man-Machine Studies* 37(6):812–821.

Engeström, Y. (1993). Developmental studies of work as a testbench of activity theory. In S. Chaiklin, S. and J. Lave, eds., *Understanding Practice: Perspectives on Activity and Context* (pp. 64–103). Cambridge: Cambridge University Press.

Haraway, D. (1990). *Simians, Cyborgs and Women: The Reinvention of Nature.* London: Routledge.

Hutchins, E. (1994). *Cognition in the Wild.* Cambridge, MA: MIT Press.

Kyng, M. (1991). Designing for cooperation—cooperating in design. *Communications of the ACM* 34(12):64–73.

Leont'ev, A. (1974). The problem of activity in psychology. *Soviet Psychology* 13(2):4–33.

Leont'ev, A. (1981). *Problems of the Development of Mind.* Moscow: Progress.

Malone, T. (1983). How do people organize their desks? *ACM Transactions on Office Information Systems* 1, 99–112.

Muller, M., and Kuhn, S. (1993). Introduction to special issue on participatory design. *Communications of the ACM* 36:24–28.

Norman, D. (1988). *The Psychology of Everyday Things.* New York: Basic Books.

Plath, S. (1982). *The Journals of Sylvia Plath.* New York: Ballantine Books.

Vygotsky, L. S. (1925/1982). Consciousness as a problem in the psychology of behaviour. In *Collected Works: Questions of the Theory and History of Psychology.* Moscow: Pedagogika.

Vygotsky, L. S. (1929). The problem of the cultural development of the child. *Journal of Genetic Psychology* 36:415–432.

Zinchenko, V. P. (1986). Ergonomics and informatics. *Problems in Philosophy* 7:53–64.

2

Activity Theory as a Potential Framework for Human-Computer Interaction Research

Kari Kuutti

In recent years the mainstream framework for human-computer interaction research—information processing cognitive psychology—has come under increasing criticism because of serious problems in applying it in both research and practical design. In a debate within the HCI research community, the capability of information processing psychology has been questioned and new theoretical frameworks considered. This chapter presents an overview of the situation and discusses the potential of activity theory as an alternative framework for HCI research and design.

Human-computer interaction has existed for some time as a research domain and gained a reputation as one of the central elements in designing computer applications. Several international journals cover the domain, several international conferences have been held every year, and a huge number of books on the topic have been published. Many, if not most, curricula for software design professionals contain a course in HCI. Given this record, one would assume that there exists a well-established body of harmonious scientific knowledge covering the basic foundation of the discipline. At first sight this belief seems to be valid, because apparently HCI seems to be based on the application of the information processing branch of cognitive psychology: "The chapters in this volume provide an interim report on the project of establishing an applied science of human-computer interaction grounded in the framework of cognitive science" (Carroll 1987).

This harmony is, however, fallacious. Research is not ahead of practice—on the contrary. In fact, a considerable number of researchers have been studying successful solutions in order to understand why they are working. We can take "direct manipulation" here as, an example. This type of interaction was used in practice as early as the sixties and there were working commercial products during the seventies, but it was not before the eighties that researchers started to gain some grasp of the phenomenon (Hutchins, Hollan, and Norman 1986). Still, researchers are unable to provide grounded advice on how such interfaces should be developed. It is also quite difficult to speak about the accumulation of knowledge, a feature usually connected with "mature sciences," because the field consists of fragmented subareas that evince little coherence or connection.

There is a well-known gap between research results and practical design. Bellotti (1988) surveyed English software designers in leading software houses and found that they were not using any results, methods, or recommendations derived from HCI research. Many of these designers were even unaware of the existence of this research. The contents of HCI handbooks aimed at practical designers mostly support that result: although almost all books have a chapter or two about "theoretical background" (usually simple cognitive psychology), it is difficult to find any connection between this material and the "practical guidelines" offered in the balance of these books. Often the only proposal with some theoretical connection is a demand to take into account the limited abilities of the human brain as an information processor. The guidelines then are usually derived from practical experience, with no underlying theory. Thus they suffer from fragmentation, incoherence, and context sensitivity, which needs to be cured by adding guidelines. The largest sets of guidelines already contain of hundreds of recommendations, but with very little internal structure, and they are virtually impossible to use in practice.

Thus it is obvious that there exist many systems where interface has not been an object of explicit design but that nevertheless serve their users well enough to be in continuous use. On the other hand, some of the most remarkable new interfaces have been developed with almost no help from research into cognitive psychology: As Carroll (1991) notes, "Some of the most seminal and momentous user interface design work of the past 25 years made no explicit use of psychology at all."

RISING CRITICISM

This state of affairs is obviously not satisfying, and during the late eighties a debate against the use of information processing psychology as the foundation of HCI surfaced, criticizing even the very basic assumptions. (Examples of existing problems and corresponding criticism can be found in Bannon 1990, 1991a, 1991b; Bødker 1990; Ehn 1988; Suchman 1987; Thomas and Kellogg 1989; Whiteside and Wixon 1987; Winograd and Flores 1987.) Both the object and methods of mainstream research have been questioned. Critics would like to add to the research object the users and their actual work tasks. Methodologically the Cartesian ideal of cognitive science—continuing the use of experimental apparatus of laboratory-oriented classical psychology borrowed from natural sciences—has been seen as unable to penetrate the human side of the interface. So now, in the midnineties, we have both the established, cognitive science–based "orthodoxy" and the emerging although diverse "opposition." Although it is certainly too early to speak of a shift in paradigm, we are nevertheless witnessing some kind of crisis in HCI research. The development of the criticism can easily be studied by comparing two collections of HCI research articles, published only four years apart and both edited by John C. Carroll, a well-known and productive member of the HCI research community. The collections are *Interfacing Thought: Cognitive Aspects of Human-Computer Interaction* (1987) and *Designing Interaction: Psychology at the Human-Computer Interface* (1991).

How do these books differ from each other? In the earlier one, the possibilities and prospects of cognitive psychology are mostly seen in a rosy light: "[HCI] represents a rather unusual opportunity for cognitive science: the opportunity to change future technology by producing an understanding of contemporary technology and thereby perhaps to affect the future directly and constructively" (Carroll 1987, xiv). The only place where considerable criticism can be found is the polemic commentary by Whiteside and Wixon at the end of the book. They evaluate the benefits of the book from the viewpoint of practical design. Their view is much less optimistic than elsewhere in book, and they are somewhat disappointed with how little help research is giving to practice:

"What systems have already been affected by the work described here and similar work that led up to it? In what time frame will the profound influence on interface design be felt?" (Whiteside and Wixon 1987, 355). They also suggest future venues for research, as these subheads in their chapter show: "Could we study HCI in a richer context? Why not tackle real systems? Explore alternatives to studying people as objects to be modeled. Address the political realities of system design."

Four years later, the overall tone had changed considerably. The former critics now have the leading voice: all the authors are disatisfied with the state of affairs and all searching for ways to change it. The alleviation of the problems is sought either from expanding and enriching current cognitive psychology or by exploring totally new approaches. Carroll (1991) writes, "Currently, a reanalysis of HCI as a practical and scientific endeavor is underway. This reanalysis incorporates (at least) these three aspects: (1) reconceiving the relationship between psychological science and HCI design to be one of interaction, (2) integrating richer and more diverse areas of psychology into HCI, and (3) taking the process and products of design more seriously" (74). As part of this effort, several basic assumptions of current HCI research have to be reevaluated: "However, many of the chapters [of the book] advocate and develop more radical proposals. On one hand, they argue that we need to apply approaches to psychology beyond information processing psychology, and perhaps social and behavioral sciences beyond psychology. On the other hand, they argue that information processing psychology itself must be fundamentally enriched as a science base" (5).

What kind of problems and pressures are causing the criticism and movement away from mainstream information processing psychology?

THE NATURE OF PERCEIVED PROBLEMS AND THE DIRECTION OF CHANGE

Liam Bannon (1991b) presented a set of problematic issues in mainstream HCI research that should be remedied. One of the problems he recognized is expressed in this paper title: "From Human Factors to Human Actors." According to Bannon, one of the characteristic features of the ongoing change is a new vision of human beings as active actors and not only as collections of attributes of cognitive processors, a view not unusual in mainstream cognitive psychology:

> Within the HF (human factors) approach, the human is often reduced to being another system component with certain characteristics, such as limited attention span, faulty memory, etc., that need to be factored into the design equation for the overall human-machine system. This form of piecemeal analysis of the person as a set of components de-emphasizes important issues in work design. Individual motivation, membership in a community of workers, and the importance of the setting in determining human action are just a few of the issues that are neglected. By using the term *human actors* emphasis is placed on the person as an autonomous agent that has the capacity to regulate and coordinate his or her behavior, rather than being simply a passive element in a human-machine system. (Bannon 1991b, 27–29).

There are also other trends Bannon recognized in recent HCI research. One of them is connected with the problem of using predetermined fixed requirements for product design. The rigidity of the requirements has caused developers to recognize that to understand what is really needed in the situation, users must be consulted. This may be a long, cooperative process, not just an initial asking of some questions. Instead of considering only a single individual, it has been recognized that features of cooperation, communication, and coordination are often vital in the successful performance of tasks. Thus HCI research seeking practical relevance cannot restrict itself to the study of individual acts.

Another issue Bannon identified is the diminishing reliance on laboratory experiments. Restricted and artificial laboratory experiments have been in favor in much of the HCI research, but there is now a tendency to move closer to actual work practices and the demands they pose. "That is, starting with a focus on interface, the subject matter inevitably expands to encompass the complete working circumstances that occasion and motivate the human interaction with the machine" (Henderson 1991, 257).

A third issue for Bannon has been the growing recognition that the actual use of systems is a long-term process that cannot be adequately understood by studying just the initial steps of usage. A large part of HCI research has studied only inexperienced users and usually during a relatively short period. In real life, people develop their skills during longer periods, and this skill-achieving dynamics and its factors have received too little emphasis in research.

Bannon has also found evidence that an emphasis on design has been increasing. Frequently HCI research has concentrated on evaluating some features of existing designs and judging their appropriateness in the situation. Design however, required advice on how to design those features right in the first place, not when it is too late and users are struggling.

The willingness to involve users in the design process has been growing, and that has led to iterative design. When problems in system use seriously surfaced during the eighties, the term "user-centered" arose to denote that designers should study user populations much more carefully than had been the case. Studying users from the "outside" is not enough; users must be involved in the design process itself. Users drawn into the design process however do not usually fully understand all the possibilities offered by information technology. They need some food for thought in order to imagine what the future might be like. This process will lead toward iterative design.

Bannon summarized his findings under the following categories:

- "From Product to Process in Research and Design"
- "From Individuals to Groups"
- "From the Laboratory to the Workplace"
- "From Novices to Experts"
- "From Analysis to Design"
- "From User-Centered to User-Involved Design"
- "From User Requirements Specifications to Iterative Design"

If there is a common denominator for this list, it would perhaps be "better contextuality" because all of the directions discussed aim at taking some aspect of actual use situations into account better. Beside active actors and contextuality, the third major new direction Bannon recognized is the constructive relation between users and systems: "In fact, it is often still the case that computer users need to make some modifications to the system in various ways, tailoring the system before it is truly usable. So in a very real sense *users are designers* as well" (Bannon 1991b, 29).

What is behind this kind of change and development? Is there a larger pattern where it would fit?

ENLARGING THE RESEARCH OBJECT

Jonathan Grudin, who has written about the historical continuity of interface design (1990), found a continuing, phased development "outward" from the hardware: "there is a continuity to the outward movement of the computer's interface to its external environment, from hardware to software to increasingly higher-level cognitive capabilities and finally to social processes" (1). He notes that the phases or steps show the relative importance of the corresponding problems of design and research at any time: "When we have solved the most pressing problems at one level—or can handle them adequately—human and computer resources are available to work on the next level" (4). Grudin recognized five phases or levels in the development: the interface at the hardware, the interface at the programming task, the interface at the terminal, the interface at the interaction dialogue, and the interface at the work setting. Grudin's view of development is quite similar to that of A. Friedman in his influential book about the development history of computer systems (Friedman 1989). Both see that older problems are never totally solved but remain beside the newer, larger ones; only their relative importance diminishes gradually.

Grudin's paper can be criticized because of its implicit "computer centrism," but the idea of having interface defined at different, coexisting levels is very interesting, because it obviously can relieve some conceptual problems and confusions. Thus it is not surprising that the idea of looking at the interface from several perspectives or levels has been attractive to many researchers (Bentley et al. 1992) and is gaining in popularity (Booth 1989; Clarke 1986; Gaines and Shaw 1986; Kammersgaard 1988; Rasmussen 1986; Smithson and Hirschheim 1990; Stary 1990; Weir 1988). There are, however, some problems with these attempts. Although the use of different perspectives may help in clarifying different approaches to the interface, it does not necessarily help in relating them to each other because of the lack of any unifying background. Even when a hierarchical, layered model has been proposed (Clarke 1986; Bentley et al. 1992; Stary 1990), the result is ad hoc. Although Grudin does not attempt to develop a background framework in his classification paper, the connection of the levels to the historical development is certainly an important step in the right direction.

Bannon and I have continued this line of thinking by using the experience collected in information systems (IS) research as a basis for our own levels of classification (Kuutti and Bannon 1991). IS research has developed a certain consensus that three levels of description are necessary and sufficient to describe information systems, and because interfaces are part of information systems, it might be possible to deal with them using the same classification. We have recognized the following three levels: a technical level, a conceptual level and a work process level. Although the strong connection with the IS research tradition may give our classification some practical credibility, it still suffers from the same problem as the other ones: the lack of a unifying theoretical background. In the paper we connected the growing importance of the work process level in HCI with changes in work practices themselves—with the movement from predetermined work sequences of Tayloristically organized work toward flexibility and self-direction in "neo-Taylorized" work organization.

If we follow the IS tradition and accept the postulate of those three levels—the technical, the conceptual, and the work process—a hypothesis can be made that the problems and debates within HCI research discussed here are due to a change or enlargement of the research object of HCI from one level to another. The nature of this change is a movement between the conceptual and work process levels: conceptually oriented cognitive HCI research is criticized in the debate because it does not take work process aspects properly into account.

Thus we have three broad traditions in HCI research: the technical one, with its roots in "knob-and-dial" ergonomics, concentrating human perceptive abilities and motor skills and corresponding features of technical devices;[1] the conceptual one that has formed the information processing psychology-based mainstream of HCI research; and the emerging new one searching new frameworks and theories in order to deal with the complexity. What could the role of activity theory be in this situation?

ACTIVITY THEORY: SOME KEY IDEAS

Both parts of the term *activity theory*, referring to the Soviet-originated cultural-historical research tradition, are slightly misleading, because the tradition is neither interested in activities in general[2] nor is it a theory, that is, a fixed body of accurately defined statements.[3] Nevertheless, the term has become established in use, and so we have to cope with it.

Activity theory has long historical roots that are quite unfamiliar to most Anglo-American readers. The oldest background tradition—the eighteenth- and nineteenth-century classical German philosophy, from Kant to Hegel—has remained distant because it opposed the emerging (British) empiricism that later became the foundation of mainstream Anglo-American scientific thought. The classical German philosophy emphasized both developmental and historical ideas and the active and constructive role of humans. Another root—also unfamiliar to many—consists of the writings of Marx and Engels, who elaborated the concept of activity further.[4] The third source is the Soviet cultural-historical psychology, founded by Vygotsky, Leont'ev, and Luria.[5]

Although the background traditions of activity theory may be unfamiliar, some Anglo-American research traditions have followed similar avenues of thought. Thus it is possible to recognize parallels between activity theory and Dewey's pragmatism (Tolman and Piekkola 1989) and G. H. Mead's symbolic interactionism (Star, forthcoming).

Activity theory originated within Soviet psychology, but today there is an emerging multidisciplinary and international community of scientific thought united by the central category of activity—a community reaching far beyond the original background.[6] Broadly defined, activity theory is a philosophical and cross-disciplinary framework for studying different forms of human practices as development processes, with both individual and social levels interlinked at the same time. The following discussion highlights the key principles of activity theory.

Activities as Basic Units of Analysis

Many psychological theories use human action as the unit of analysis. This makes it relatively easy to design laboratory experiments, but the use of isolated actions in analyzing real-life situations outside a laboratory is much less fruitful. The reason is that actions are always situated into a context, and they are impossible to understand without that context (e. g., Suchman 1987). The solution offered by activity theory is that a minimal meaningful context for individual actions must be included in the basic unit of analysis. This unit is called an activity. Because the context is included in the unit of analysis, the object of our research is always essentially collective even if our main interest is in individual actions. An individual can and usually does participate in several activities simultaneously.

History and Development

Activities are not static or rigid entities; they are under continuous change and development. This development is not linear or straightforward but uneven and discontinuous. This means that each activity also has a history of its own. Parts of older phases of activities often stay embedded in them as they develop, and historical analysis of the development is often needed in order to understand the current situation.

Artifacts and Mediation

An activity always contains various artifacts (e.g., instruments, signs, procedures, machines, methods, laws, forms of work organization). An essential feature of these artifacts is that they have a mediating role. Relations between elements of an activity are not direct but mediated; for example, an instrument mediates between an actor and the object of doing; the object is seen and manipulated not "as such" but within the limitations set by the instrument (Engeström 1991b). Artifacts themselves have been created and transformed during the development of the activity itself and carry with them a particular culture—a historical residue of that development. Because of the nature of artifacts, they should be never treated as given. "The idea is that humans can control their own behavior—not 'from the inside', on the basis of biological urges, but 'from the outside', using and creating artifacts. This perspective is not only optimistic concerning human self-determination. It is an invitation to serious study of artifacts as integral and inseparable components of human functioning" (Engeström 1991a, 12).

The Structure of an Activity

An activity is a form of doing directed to an object, and activities are distinguished from each other according to their objects. Transforming the object into an outcome motivates the existence of an activity. An object can be a material thing, but it can also be less tangible (such as a plan) or totally intangible (such as a common idea) as long as it can be shared for manipulation and transformation by the participants of the activity. It is possible that the object and motive themselves will undergo changes during the process of an activity; the object and motive will reveal themselves only in the process of doing. Mediation is carried out by introducing a third, intermediate term, which carries with it the history of the relationship. Thus the (reciprocal) relationship between the subject and the object of activity is mediated by a tool, into which the historical development of the relationship between subject and object thus far is condensed. The tool is at the same time both enabling and limiting: it empowers the subject in the transformation process with the historically collected experience and skill "crystalized" to it, but it also restricts the interaction to be from the perspective of that particular tool or instrument only; other potential features of an object remain "invisible" to the subject (figure 2.1). This structure is too simple to fulfill the needs of a consideration of the systemic relations between an individual and his or her environment in an activity, however, and thus a third main component, community (those who share the same object), has to be added. Two new relationships are then formed: subject-community and community-object. Both of them are also mediated, and thus we have the structure shown in figure 2.2.

This systemic model, which is based on the conceptualization by Engeström (1987), contains three mutual relationships between subject, object, and community. (An activity is actually a systemic whole in the sense that all elements have a relationship to other elements, but all those connections have not been presented in figure 2.2 for the sake of clarity.) The relationship between subject and object is mediated by tools, the

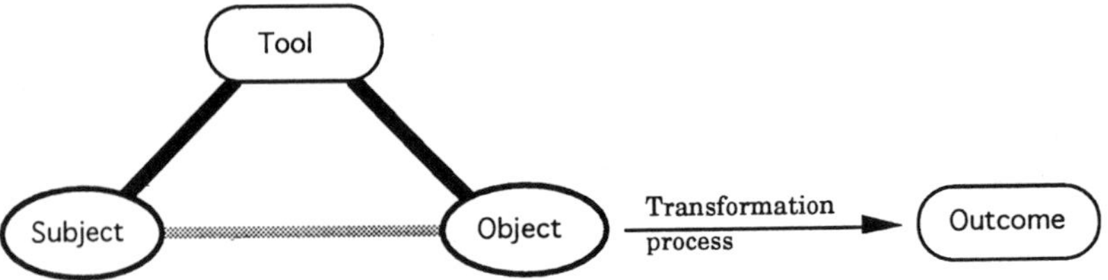

Figure 2.1
Mediated relationship at the individual level.

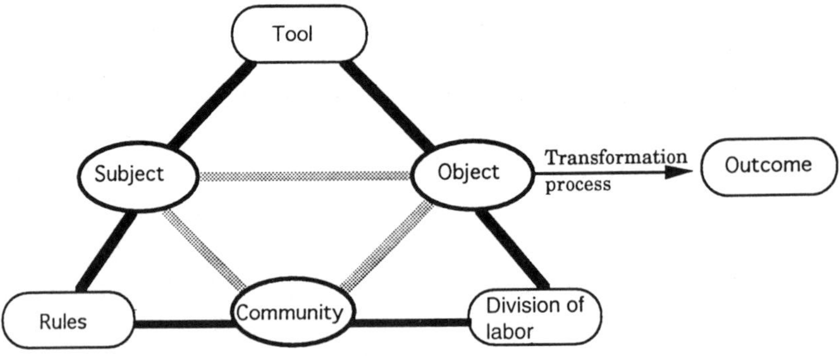

Figure 2.2
Basic structure of an activity.

relationship between subject and community is mediated by rules, and the relationship between object and community is mediated by the division of labor. These three classes should be understood broadly. A *tool* can be anything used in the transformation process, including both material tools and tools for thinking. *Rules* cover both explicit and implicit norms, conventions, and social relations within a community. *Division of labor* refers to the explicit and implicit organization of a community as related to the transformation process of the object into the outcome. Each of the mediating terms is historically formed and open to further development.

An activity is the minimal meaningful context for understanding individual actions. The famous example of Leont'ev (1978) concerns primitive hunters who, in order to catch game, separate into two groups: catchers and bush beaters. Bush beaters frighten the game toward the catchers. When compared with the goal of hunting—to catch the game, for food and clothing—the actions of the bush beaters in themselves are irrational; they can be understood only as part of the larger system of the hunting activity.

Let us take a more contemporary example of an activity: a software team programming a system for a client. The object is the not-yet-ready system, which should be transformed into a delivered, bug-free application. The team is the community sharing the object, perhaps joined by some representatives of the customer. There is a certain division of labor: between manager and subordinates, between software developers and user representatives, and between the team members. There is a set of rules covering what it means to be a member of this community. Some of these rules may be explicit—set by law, the parent organization, or the team manager—but many of them are most certainly implicit, either as a part of the general working culture or developed as the team works together. Some rules may be constructed for this particular project, for example, how the user representatives of this particular customer shall be treated. In each step of the transformation process, a different set of tools and instruments is used in the transformation process—for example, analysis methods, computers, programming tools, walk-throughs, or rules of thumb. The collection of these tools has a history; it is a result of a process of cumulation and rejection at both company and team level, and additions and deletions to it may occur during any project. Whatever the members of the team do during the project is shaped by the context of activity.

At the same time there is another activity; here the object is the financial status of the software company, and the community consists of team managers and their superiors. Every team manager has tools and tricks designed to keep the project within budget and profitable, and superiors have their own as well. There is a certain division of labor and a certain set of rules—most certainly different from that within a team.

We can imagine a third activity whereby some of the team managers compete against each other for an available position as a department manager. The object "field" is the relative weight of capabilities and assets, real or imagined, of each applicant in the eyes of the selection committee. These assets can be transformed by increasing one's own assets or diminishing those of others. Each participating team manager has the relevant tools—excellent financial results from the current project, for example. Again, there is also a division of labor, at least between applicants—those who do the selection and those who can affect the selection. And certainly there is a set of explicit and implicit rules of what constitutes correct behavior in the situation and what does not.

Thus real-life situations always involve an intertwined and connected web of activities that can be distinguished according to their objects. Participation in connected activities having very different objects can cause tensions and distortions (e.g., the position of the team manager in the example: bug-free delivery versus excellent financial results). Psychologically, activity theorists believe that participation in different activities is the major factor in creating consciousness and shaping personality.

Levels of an Activity

Activities are longer-term formations; their objects are transformed into outcomes not at once but through a process that typically consists of several steps or phases. There is also a need for shorter-term processes: activities consist of actions or chains of actions, which in turn consist of operations, forming the levels in figure 2.3.

Activities are realized as individual and cooperative actions, and chains and networks of such actions that are related to each other by the same overall object and motive. Participating in an activity is performing conscious actions that have an immediate, defined goal. The actions cannot be understood, however, without a frame of reference created by the corresponding activity. One activity may be realized using different actions, depending on the situation; for example, the software development activity as above consists of different actions depending on how much

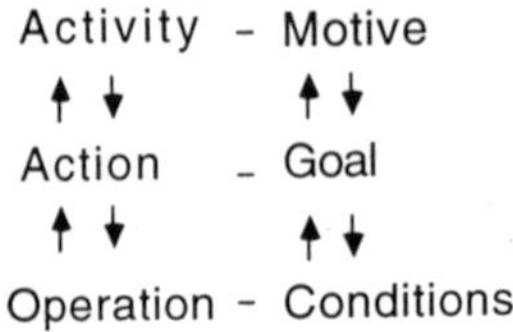

Figure 2.3
Hierarchical levels of an activity.

actual code has to be produced and how much old code can be used, whether parts of applications are purchased from outside, and so forth. On the other hand, one and the same action can belong to different activities, in which case the different motives of activities will cause the action to have a different personal sense for the subject in the context of each activity. For example, the action of reporting on the progress of a project will have a different connotation if it belongs to the activity of internal project management than if it belongs to the activity of competing for promotion—even if the action and its other ingredients are exactly the same.

Before an action is performed in the real world, it is typically planned in the consciousness using a model. The better the model the more successful the action. This phase is called *orientation.* Thus models and plans are not rigid and accurate descriptions of the execution steps but always incomplete and tentative—*resources,* in the sense of Suchman (1987). For their part, actions consist of chains of operations, which are well-defined habitual routines used as answers to conditions faced during the performing of the action. Initially each operation is a conscious action, consisting of both the orientation and execution phases, but when the corresponding model is good enough and the action has been practiced long enough, the orientation phase will fade and the action will be collapsed into an operation, which is much more fluent. At the same time a new action is created that will have broader scope and will contain the recently formed new operation as a subpart. On the other hand, when conditions change, an operation can again "unfold" and return to the level of conscious action (so that it is not a conditioned reflex).

This action-operation dynamics and the broadening scope of actions is a fundamentally typical feature of human development. For a person to become more skilled in something, operations must be developed so that one's scope of actions can become broader as the execution itself becomes more fluent. A good example of action-operation dynamics is learning to use a manual gearbox when driving a car. At the beginning, every step in the process (ease the gas pedal, push the clutch pedal, move the gear lever to a new position, release the clutch, give more gas again) is a conscious action that needs planning, sequencing, and decision; many times a hasty look at the gear lever is even necessary in order to move it.

But soon these conscious actions begin to transform into operations; the planning and decision making will fade away, resulting in a smooth gear-changing action, far from the clumsiness of the initial attempts. Eventually this gear-changing action will also become an operation in broader corner-turning, lane-changing, and distance-maintaining actions. It will fade from the consciousness.

The border between action and activity is also blurred, and movements are possible in both directions:

> Thus an activity can lose its motive and become an action, and an action can become an operation when the goal changes. The motive of some activity may become the goal of an activity, as a result of which the latter is transformed into some integral activity. . . . The mobility of the constituents of activity is also manifested in the fact that each of them may become a part of a unit or, conversely, come to embrace previously relatively independent units (for example, some acts may be broken down into a series of successive acts, and, correspondingly, a goal may be broken down into subgoals). (Davydov, Zinchenko, and Talyzina 1983, 36)

The flexibility of the basic concepts makes them useful in describing developmental processes. On the other hand, it also means that it is impossible to make a general classification of what an activity is, what an action is, and so forth because the definition is totally dependent on what the subject or object in a particular real situation is. The classification in figure 2.4 is by no means exhaustive, but it does provide a first grasp of how the levels of the hierarchy could be realized in hypothetical, individual-level activities. There are no firm borders; a software project may be an activity for the team members, but the executive manager of the software company may see each of the projects as actions within his or her real activity at the level of the firm.

One very important feature is that activities have a double nature; every activity has both an external and an internal side. The subject and the object of an activity are in a reciprocal relationship with each other: the subject is transforming the object, while the properties of the object penetrate into the subject and transform him or her. In this internalization, "processes are subjected to a specific transformation: they are generalized, verbalized, abbreviated, and, most importantly, become suscep-

Activity level ↓↑	Building a house	Completing a software project	Carrying out research into a topic
Action level ↓↑	Fixing the roofing Transporting bricks by truck	Programming a module Arranging a meeting	Searching for references Participating in a conference Writing a report
Operation level	Hammering Changing gears when driving	Using operating system commands Selecting appropriate programming language constructs	Using logical syllogisms Selecting appropriate wording

Figure 2.4
Examples of activities, actions, and operations.

tible of further development which exceeds the possibility of external activity" (Leont'ev 1974, 18).

Activity theory does not accept a dualistic conception of an isolated, independent "mind." The internal side of an activity cannot exist without the external one. A person's internal activity assimilates the experience of humanity in the form in which it manifests itself in the corresponding external activity. "Cognitive processes," says A. R. Luria, "are not independent and unchanging 'abilities' or 'functions of human consciousness;' they are processes occurring in concrete, practical activity and are formed within the limits of this activity" (cited by Stetsenko 1993, 43). And Leont'ev (1974) notes, "It means that a person's mental processes acquire a structure necessarily linked to sociohistorically formed means and modes, which are transmitted to him by other people through teamwork and social intercourse" (19).

Although the triangle model may seem somewhat rigid, it is only for the sake of representational simplicity and convenience. Remember that activity theory considers activities not as given or static but as dynamic. Activities are always changing and developing. Development is taking place at all levels; new operations are formed from previous actions as participants' skills increase; correspondingly, at the level of actions the scope of new actions is enlarging, and totally new actions are being invented, experimented with, and adapted as responses to new situations or possibilities encountered in the process of transforming the object. Finally, at the level of activity the object/motive itself (and the whole structure of activity related to it) is reflected, questioned, and perhaps adapted, reacting to larger changes and other activities.

Because activities are not isolated units but are more like nodes in crossing hierarchies and networks, they are influenced by other activities and other changes in their environment. External influences change some elements of activities, causing imbalances between them. Activity theory uses the term *contradiction* to indicate a misfit within elements, between them, between different activities, or between different developmental phases of a single activity. Contradictions manifest themselves as problems, ruptures, breakdowns, clashes. Activity theory sees contradictions as sources of development; activities are virtually always in the process of working through contradictions.

What, then, is the relationship between activities and information technology? The answer is not simple, because information technology can support and penetrate activities at all levels. First, a considerable share of all technology in use was developed to automate human operations. According to Leont'ev (1978), in principle all operations can be automated; for example, an automatic transmission automates human gear-changing operations. Information technology is no exception; the major driving force in the development of the first computers was the need to automate human calculating operations, and one of the forces behind the expansion of information technology has been the need to automate administrative data manipulation operations. By automating and substituting human operations, information technology can become part of an activity and vastly expand the scope of actions available to the participants. Automation is the oldest and perhaps best understood way to support activities, but it is not the only way. Information technology can also support actions, in various ways. Information technology can serve as a tool in manipulative and transformative actions directed to an object or to a part of it—as with different editors and other symbol-manipulation tools (spreadsheets, drawing, painting, etc.).

Information technology can also help in actions that are directed toward sense making. Zuboff (1988) uses the term *informate* in characterizing the situation whereby information technology provides a "window" to look at the object of work in order to understand it better. In a sense, managers have been "informated" from the first report ever produced by a system, but an enormous variety of other activities could be supported in this way as well. In Oulu, we have for example been studying how a novice can be helped to learn the ropes more easily by making some elements of a particular activity more visible through information technology (Favorin and Kuutti 1994; Kuutti 1993). Another class of potential actions to be supported are communicative actions between participants. These are directed not toward manipulating or transforming the object but making the activity "run": coordinating or negotiating the motive, or some other facet of the activity.

Finally, at the activity level, information technology can form the matrix of activities; it can be the principal enabler for an activity. At least two different possibilities can be identified. First, information technology may make an activity possible and feasible (e.g., by linking the participants by a network or system). Second, information technology may enable an activity to have an object that would otherwise have been impossible to grasp. In Kuutti and Virkkunen (1994) we discuss a case in which only a computerized "organization memory" enabled health inspectors to grasp and handle new, broader problems as the object of their work activity.

The support possibilities can be illustrated by using the classification in figure 2.5, where the internal side of activities is compressed under the "actor" heading. This classification does not aim to be a complete explication of the relationships between information technology and an activity, but it illustrates the wide scope and variety of these relations. The classification is somewhat artificial because activities are systemic wholes, and it is impossible to delineate accurately different types in practice. For example, the support types classified as action-level support in the tool area and in the object area overlap because tools are defined as the means of interaction between an actor and the object. Also "supporting sense-making" overlaps naturally with all instances of "making visible" in the same column.

The support given to work activities by traditional information systems seems to match nicely with the first column; practically any such system supports the full range of potential types. It indicates that in the

Operation-level support	Action-level support	Activity-level support
Tool, instrument		
Automating routines	Supporting transformative and manipulative actions Making tools and procedures visible and comprehensible	Enabling the automation of a new routine or construction of a new tool
Object		
Providing data about an object	Making an object manipulable	Enabling something to become a common object
Actor		
Triggering predetermined responses	Supporting sense-making actions within an activity	Supporting learning and reflection with respect to the whole object and activity
Rules		
Embedding and imposing a certain set of rules	Making the set of rules visible and comprehensible	Enabling the negotiation of new rules
Community		
Creating an implicit community by linking work tasks of several people together	Supporting communicative actions Making the network of actors visible	Enabling the formation of a new community
Division of labor		
Embedding and imposing a certain division of labor	Making the work organization visible and comprehensible	Enabling the reorganization of the division of labor

Figure 2.5
A classification of potential ways of supporting activities by information technology.

area of work automation, we have already reached a certain level of sophistication, and those types of support are not by any means less important to work activities than more "advanced" or complicated ones. But the further we go from left to right in the classification, the more sparse are the systems designed for giving a particular type of support and the bigger are the challenges of HCI design.

THE POSITION AND POSSIBILITIES OF ACTIVITY THEORY

The complexity of the field explains a great deal about why the study of HCI has met limited success. Three broad classes of complexity have been recognized: the levels of actions to be supported, dynamics inherent to all levels, and a wide variety of potential support types. Against this background, the "slice" covered by mainstream HCI research is narrow, covering most adequately the area of error-free execution of predetermined sequences of actions. Unfortunately, that is the area where HCI is not crucially needed; humans are so adaptive that eventually the error rate will fall to an acceptable level in most cases, whatever the interface may be. But when we move toward supporting work and sense-making in work, the situation is drastically different; a badly designed interface can paralyze all efforts. The broadening of scope in research and design is both important and difficult, as the parallel debates in different areas of design—HCI, CSCW, and in information systems—show.

What could be the role and contribution of activity theory in these discussions? In this overview I emphasize three perspectives: multilevelness, interaction context, and development.

Multilevelness

By using activity theory, it is in principle possible to discuss issues belonging to different levels within an integrated framework (figure 2.6). This is certainly a major task, and worth trying in order to overcome the fragmentation that now characterizes the field.

Interaction in Social Context

The question of context and sense-making in contexts has recently come to the fore of research. Activity theory and the concept of activity seem

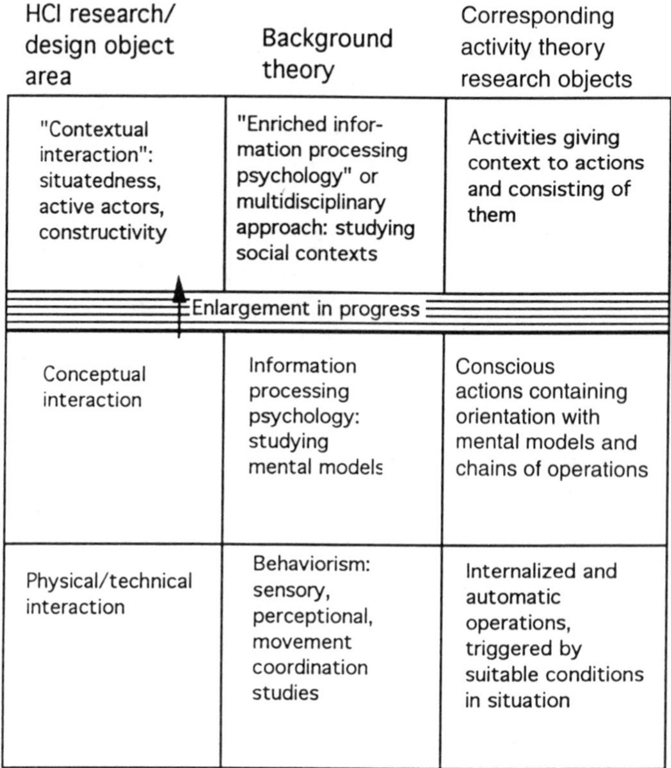

HCI research/ design object area
Background theory
Corresponding activity theory research objects
"Contextual interaction": situatedness, active actors, constructivity
"Enriched information processing psychology" or multidisciplinary approach: studying social contexts
Activities giving context to actions and consisting of them
Enlargement in progress
Conceptual interaction
Information processing psychology: studying mental models
Conscious actions containing orientation with mental models and chains of operations
Physical/technical interaction
Behaviorism: sensory, perceptional, movement coordination studies
Internalized and automatic operations, triggered by suitable conditions in situation

Figure 2.6
Activity theory areas corresponding to the defined levels of research objects.

to be particularly suited to being used as the starting point in studying contextually embedded interactions. Activity theory contains many features—the recognition of actors, mediation, historicity, constructivity, dynamics, and others—considered essential in recent discussions.

Dynamics and Development

In HCI, little has been learned about how the formation of new operations, sense-making and creation of new actions, or, ultimately, reconfiguring entire activities, could be supported by information technology. One reason has clearly been a lack of frameworks and theories capable of dealing with developmental and dynamic features of human practices. In this respect, activity theory offers a promising avenue of thought because the ideas of change and development are fundamental to it. It is not possible to cover the whole field of possibilities here, but I will highlight one area where benefits might be accrued rapidly: the potential for using action-operation dynamics in computer interfaces.

Despite the fundamental nature of action-operation dynamics in the development of all kinds of skilled practices, these dynamics have largely been neglected in interface research and development. This is emphasized by the fact that in principle computers are suitable for automating operations even more. In fact, it is quite difficult to find any examples where the dynamics have been properly supported and a "smooth" formation of operations from older actions and the broadening scope of new actions would have been achieved. Certainly many programs have different short-cuts for experienced users. But these do not qualify as a support for action-operation dynamics because usually they are totally different from the original command and thus form a new learning task for the user instead of a collapse of a former action into an operation. It is also true that after a certain level of competence is attained, the broadening scope of actions by combining old operations can be supported to some extent by a powerful operating system such as UNIX with its command files, pipes, and filters. But again, there is no natural path where an operation would develop almost automatically with increasing experience of use.

To support the dynamics properly, it is necessary that the orientation phase of an action be dropped, but that something from the old action remain as a feedback in order to trigger the next possible operation. Fortunately, there is a simple example apposite here: well-known "type-ahead" menus (Shneiderman 1992, 119–120). A type-ahead menu is a chain- or tree-organized menu with an input buffer into which a user can write a selection without having to wait for the menus themselves to appear. When the user knows beforehand all the selections he or she will make when going through the chain or tree of menus, they can be written together as one command at the beginning. Shneiderman provides the following example: "To users of a photo library search system that offered menus with type-ahead, a color slide portrait quickly become known as a CSP and a black and white print of a landscape became known as a BPL. These mnemonics come to be remembered and chunked as a single concept" (Shneiderman 1992, 120). In this example of action-operation dynamics, a whole chain of former actions with a full orientation phase (look at the menu and find the option to be selected) has been collapsed into a single action that has a considerably larger scope than the pieces had. And it is easy to return to the original actions, because they remain permanently as part of the background.

According to activity theory, formation of operations from actions is ubiquitous. This hints that the action-operation dynamics should be a common feature of all computer programs. This raises a series of interesting questions. Because supporting the dynamics is not impossible, why it is so rare? Can this be done in other programs as well? In what kind of use situations might this strategy prove successful? Can a similar effect be realized in a graphical interface? Could it be done over several successive levels, so that an action that has already been formed by collapsing several actions into operations could be collapsed again in the formation of an even more powerful action? The effort to find answers to such questions and to experiment might open a new path for HCI research and design—not an easy one but certainly worth pursuing.

When trying to cope with the interface design problem in all its complexity, it would be enormously helpful if there were a discipline studying, from a design perspective, the problem of how artifacts are utilized in individual and cooperative work in general. Many of the fundamental questions in HCI are common to a broad class of artifacts. Unfortunately, such a discipline does not exist, but if there is a shift in emphasis from automating work toward supporting it, the more general problem eventually will be dealt with. Perhaps it is a sort of accident, stemming from the "opaqueness" of computer systems and the need to formulate and formalize whatever is put into them, that HCI research and design have been the first to formulate and attack these problems. As pioneers in the field, we have met with somewhat limited success. There is no reason to be ashamed or depressed, however. Instead we should be proud of being in the forefront and move ahead. There is no risk of becoming too proud; the field will teach us all the humbleness we will ever need.

NOTES

1. It must be remembered that the publication of some journals actively publishing HCI research started well before the "cognitive turn" in psychology; ex-

ample are *Human Factors* and the *International Journal of Man-Machine Studies*.

2. The term *activity* does not carry the essential connotation "doing in order to transform something," as do the corresponding German or Russian terms (*Tätigkeit* and *dejatel'nost*, respectively).

3. The term can be used in two senses: referring to the original Soviet tradition Leont'ev 1978, 1981; Wertsch 1981) or referring to the international, multivoiced community applying the original ideas and developing them further (Engeström and Punamäki forthcoming). The chapter is based mainly on the "Finnish" interpretation of original ideas, worked out by Y. Engeström and his coworkers (Toikka 1985; Engeström 1987).

4. The origins of the concept of activity lie in German idealistic philosophy, in which Kant, Fichte, and Hegel emphasized the role of mental activity (*Tätigkeit*) in constituting the relationship between subject and object. This was nevertheless an idealistic-subjective interpretation. The concept of activity was brought into materialistic philosophy by Feuerbach, who emphasized the primary role of objective reality but only as an object of contemplation. The activity concept of Marx was developed as "practical-critical" activity, the central aspect in activity being the transforming of material objects (*gegenständliche Tätigkeit*) (Klaus and Buhr 1987, pp. 1203–1207).

5. The foundation of activity theory was laid by L. S. Vygotsky during the 1920s and early 1930s as a cultural-historical school of psychology. His work was continued by A. N. Leont'ev and A. R. Luria, who developed his ideas and started to use the term *activity*. A good historical review of the development can be found in Leont'ev (1989).

6. Activity theory is useful and flexible in other disciplines as well, such as education, the social sciences, cultural research, anthropology, and work science (Hildebrand-Nilshon and Rückriem 1988; Engeström and Punamäki forthcoming). The activity theory school is only getting organized, the First International Congress on Activity Theory having been held in Berlin 1986 and the Second Congress in Lahti, Finland, in 1990. From 1988 there has also been a journal, the *Multidisciplinary Newsletter for Activity Theory*.

REFERENCES

Bannon, L. J. (1990). A pilgrim's progress: From cognitive science to cooperative design. *AI and Society* 4:259–275.

Bannon, L. J. (1991). From human factors to human actors: The role of psychology and human-computer interaction studies in system design. In J. Greenbaum and M. Kyng, eds., *Design at Work: Cooperative Design of Computer Systems* (pp. 25–44). Hillsdale, NJ: Lawrence Erlbaum.

Bannon, L., and Bødker, S. (1991). Beyond the interface: Encountering artifacts in use. In J. M. Carroll, eds., *Designing Interaction: Psychology at the Human-Computer Interface*. Cambridge: Cambridge University Press.

Bellotti, V. (1988). Implications of current design practice for the use of HCI techniques. In D. M. J. and. R. Winder, eds., *People and Computers IV* (pp. 13–34). Cambridge: Cambridge University Press.

Bentley, R., Hughes, J. A., Randall, D., Rodden, T., Sawyer, P., Shapiro, D., and Sommerville, I. (1992). Ethnographically-informed systems design for air traffic control. *CSCW'92* (pp. 123–129). Toronto: ACM Press.

Bødker, S. (1990). *Through the Interface—A Human Activity Approach to User Interface Design*. Hillsdale, NJ: Lawrence Erlbaum.

Booth, P. (1989). *An Introduction to Human-Computer Interaction*. London: Lawrence Erlbaum.

Carroll, J. M. (ed.). (1987). *Interfacing Thought: Cognitive Aspects of Human-Computer Interaction*. Cambridge, MA: MIT Press.

Carroll, J. M. (ed.). (1991). *Designing Interaction; Psychology at the Human-Computer Interface*. Cambridge: Cambridge University Press.

Clarke, A. A. (1986). A three-level human-computer interface model. *International Journal of Man-Machine Studies* 24:503–517.

Davydov, V. V., Zinchenko, V. P., and Talyzina, N. F. (1983). The problem of activity in the works of A. N. Leont'ev. *Soviet Psychology* 21(4):31–42.

Ehn, P. (1988). *Work-Oriented Design of Computer Artifacts*. Stockholm: Arbetslivscentrum.

Engeström, Y. (1987). *Learning by Expanding*. Helsinki: Orienta-konsultit.

Engeström, Y. (1991a). Activity theory and individual and social transformation. *Multidisciplinary Newsletter for Activity Theory* (7/8):6–17.

Engeström, Y. (1991b). Developmental work research: Reconstructing expertise through expansive learning. In M. I. Nurminen and G. R. S. Weir, eds., *Human Jobs and Computer Interfaces*. Amsterdam: North-Holland.

Engeström, Y., and Punamäki, R.-L. (eds.). (forthcoming). *Perspectives on Activity Theory*. Cambridge: Cambridge University Press.

Favorin, M., and Kuutti, K. (1994). To support learning at work by making work visible through information technology: An activity theory approach. In *Interdisciplinary Workshop on Complex Learning in Computer Environments (CLCE'94): Technology in School, University, Work, and Life-Long Education*. Finland, University of Joensuu, May 16–19.

Friedman, A. (1989). *Computer Systems Development: History, Organization and Implementation*. Chichester: Wiley.

Gaines, B. R., and Shaw, M. L. (1986). Foundations of dialog engineering: the development of human-computer interaction. *International Journal of Man-Machine Studies*, 24:101–123.

Grudin, J. (1990). The computer reaches out: The historical continuity of user interface design. In *Proceedings of CHI '90, ACM SIGCHI Conference*. Seattle, WA: ACM.

Henderson, A. (1991). A development perspective on interface, design and theory. In J. M. Carroll, ed., *Designing Interaction: Psychology at the Human-Computer Interface*. (pp. 254–268). Cambridge: Cambridge University Press.

Hildebrand-Nilshon, M., and Rückriem, G. (ed.). (1988). *Proceeding of the 1st International Congress on Activity Theory* (vols. 1–4). Berlin: System Druck.

Hutchins, E., Hollan, J., and Norman, D. A. (1986). Direct manipulation interfaces. In D. A. Norman and. S. Draper, eds., *User Centered System Design: New Perspectives on Human-Computer Interaction*. Hillsdale, NJ: Lawrence Erlbaum.

Kammersgaard, J. (1988). Four different perspectives on human-computer interaction. *International Journal of Man-Machine Studies*, 28:343–362.

Klaus, G., and Buhr, M. eds., (1987). *Philosophises Wörterbuch, Band 1–2*. Berlin (West): Das Europäeische Buch.

Kuutti, K. (1993). Notes on systems supporting "organizational context"—an activity theory viewpoint. In L. Bannon and K. Schmidt, eds., *Issues of Supporting Organizational Context in CSCW Systems* (pp. 105–121). ESPRIT Basic Research Project 6225 COMIC. Lancaster: Lancaster University.

Kuutti, K., and Bannon, L. J. (1991). Some confusions at the interface: Re-conceptualizing the "interface" problem. In M. I. and. W. Nurminen G. R. S. Weir, eds., *Human Jobs and Computer Interfaces* (pp. 3–19). Amsterdam: North-Holland.

Kuutti, K., and Virkkunen, J. (1994). *Developing teamwork and Organizational Memory: The Case of Finnish Labor Protection Inspectors*, no. COMIC-OULU-1-3). Oulu: University of Oulu, Department of Information Processing Science.

Leont'ev, A. N. (1974). The problem of activity in psychology. *Soviet Psychology* 13(2):4–33.

Leont'ev, A. N. (1978). *Activity, Consciousness and Personality*. Englewood Cliffs, NJ: Prentice-Hall.

Leont'ev, A. N. (1981). *Problems of the Development of the Mind*. Moscow: Progress.

Leont'ev, A. N. (1989). The problem of activity in the history of Soviet psychology. *Soviet Psychology* 27(1):22–39.

Rasmussen, J. (1986). *Information Processing and Human-Machine Interaction. An Approach to Cognitive Engineering*. New York: North-Hollandh/Elsevier.

Shneiderman, B. (1992). *Designing the User Interface: Strategies for Effective Human-Computer Interaction* (2nd ed.). Reading, MA: Addison-Wesley.

Star, S. L. (forthcoming). Working together: Symbolic interactionism, activity theory and distributed artificial intelligence. In Y. Engeström and D. Middleton, eds., *Communication and Cognition at Work*. Cambridge: Cambridge University Press.

Stary, C. (1990). A knowledge representation scheme for conceptual interface design. In A. Finkelstein, M. J. Tauber, and R. Traunmuller, eds., *Human Factors in Information Systems Analysis and Design* (pp. 157–171). Amsterdam: North-Holland.

Stetsenko, A. P. (1993). Vygotsky: Reflections on the reception and further development of his thought. *MNAT*(13/14):38–45.

Suchman, L. (1987). *Plans and Situated Actions*. Cambridge: Cambridge University Press.

Thomas, J. C., and Kellogg, W. A. (1989). Minimizing ecological gaps in interface design. *IEEE Software* (January):78–86.

Toikka, K. and. E., Y and Norros, L. (1985). Entwickelnde Arbeitsforschung. Theoretische und methodologisce Elemente. *Forum Kritische Psychologie* 15:5–41.

Tolman, C. W., and Piekkola, B. (1989). Anticipations of activity theory in the critique of the reflex arc concept. *MNAT*(3/4):43–46.

Weir, G. R. S. (1988). *HCI Perspectives on Man-Machine Systems*, (Report No. AMU 3588/01S). Scottish HCI Centre, Strathclyde University.

Wertsch, J. W. (ed.). (1981). *The Concept of Activity in Soviet Psychology*. Armonk, NY: M. E. Sharpe.

Whiteside, J., and Wixon, D. (1987). Discussion: Improving human-computer interactionn—a quest for cognitive science. In J. Carroll, eds., *Interfacing Thought: Cognitive Aspects of Human-Computer Interaction* (pp. 353–365). Cambridge, MA: MIT Press.

Winograd, T., and Flores, F. (1987). *Understanding Computers and Cognition: A New Foundation for Design*. Norwood, NJ: Ablex.

Zuboff, S. (1988). *In the Age of the Smart Machine: The Future of Work and Power*. New York: Basic Books.

3

Computer-Mediated Activity: Functional Organs in Social and Developmental Contexts

Victor Kaptelinin

The field of human-computer interaction (HCI) presents an enormous theoretical challenge to researchers trying to establish it as an integrated field of studies. To become such a field, HCI should be based on a conceptual scheme powerful enough to incorporate both human beings and computer technology within a coherent theoretical framework. One possible solution is based on the cognitive approach, according to which both human beings and computers can be considered as information processing units.[1] If the basic mechanisms underlying human cognition and those underlying the functioning of computer systems are essentially the same, it is possible to use the same concepts and methods to analyze both entities and eventually to build a general theory that explains the functioning of higher-level systems composed of both human beings and computers.

Another broad approach, which is becoming more popular, is based on a radically different assumption. It assumes that what is needed to make HCI a conceptually integrated field is a theory that describes and explains the larger context of human interaction with computers. This second approach employs another feature human beings and computers have in common: both are involved in real-life activities of computer use. If we can provide an account of the general context of computer use and identify the place of human beings and computers within this overarching scheme, we can understand interaction between them without assuming that they are basically the same kinds of entities.

There are several versions of the contextual approach to HCI (see Nardi, chapter 4, this volume), which are almost unrelated to each other. What they have in common is their opposition to the currently dominant cognitive approach and related methodology and the more or less explicitly formulated idea that both human beings and computers develop in the process of cultural history and can be understood only within a social context.

Activity theory is one of the concrete versions of the contextual approach. The theory is becoming more talked about in the field of HCI, but is still "opaque" for most researchers (Brusilovsky, Burmistrov, and Kaptelinin 1993). This chapter discusses the potential advantages and limitations of activity theory as a conceptual framework for HCI. It is not intended to present the basic ideas and principles of activity theory in relation to HCI (for such an introduction, see Bødker 1989, 1991; Kaptelinin 1992, this volume; Kuutti 1992, this volume; Zinchenko 1992, this volume) but instead attempts to put the theory into the context of the problems that researchers in the field are currently encountering.

EXPANSION OF HUMAN-COMPUTER INTERACTION

One of the most important claims of activity theory is that the nature of any artifact can be understood only within the context of human activity—by identifying the ways people use this artifact, the needs it serves, and the history of its development. Activity theory itself is a special kind of artifact. That is why it is important to understand the motivation behind the actual and potential use of this theory as a conceptual tool in the field of HCI. It can be useful in developing realistic expectations about the scope and potential outcomes of the theory.

Considering activity theory as a special kind of tool implies that accepting this perspective does not exclude other approaches and does not reject the usefulness of other conceptual schemes (because no tool, no matter how powerful it is, can serve all needs and help to solve all problems). In particular, activity theory does not reject the value of cognitive studies. However, the general conceptual position of activity theory is radically different from that of the cognitive approach. Specifically, activity theory does not allow for an equal status of human beings and computer technology in a theoretical framework of HCI. The relations between agents and tools cannot be symmetrical, and this fundamental fact should be taken into account in developing a theory of HCI.

The history of studies in HCI clearly demonstrates the tendency of ever-extending units of analysis (Grudin 1990). While the early attempts to understand the factors influencing human-computer interaction concentrated on low-level input-output processes, the current focus is on long-term events and large-scale aspects of HCI, such as the software development life cycle, computer-supported cooperative work (CSCW), and the implementation of information technologies at the organizational level. The reasons behind this tendency are not only theoretical; they also include practical considerations. It has turned out that the quality of the user interface and of interactive systems in general depends on factors that are in no way limited to the sensorimotor level of interaction (although the latter is still important).

The challenge of increasing units of analysis is faced by any theory of HCI. The solution offered by both the cognitive approach and activity theory is to consider human interaction with computers as a multilevel hierarchical structure. According to both the cognitive approach and activity theory, the tendency to focus on the higher-level HCI events is related to taking into consideration the higher levels of the hierarchical structure of computer use. However, as we will see, the meaning of hierarchical organization is different within these two approaches. According to the cognitive approach, the major theoretical task is to develop a conceptual scheme that can give a coordinated description of multilevel information processing in both human beings and computers. According to activity theory, the hierarchical organization of human-computer interaction is determined by its embeddedness into the hierarchical structure of human activity that mediates the user's interaction with reality.

The current expansion of the subject matter of HCI can be described as a three-dimensional "explosion" of the traditional paradigm, with "levels of interaction" being only one of these dimensions. Other dimensions, difficult to account for within the cognitive approach, are set out in figure 3.1.

First, there is a shift of focus from interaction between the user and the computer to a larger context of interaction of human beings with their environment, that is, transcending the user interface to reality beyond the "human-computer system." Computer tools are used by people to

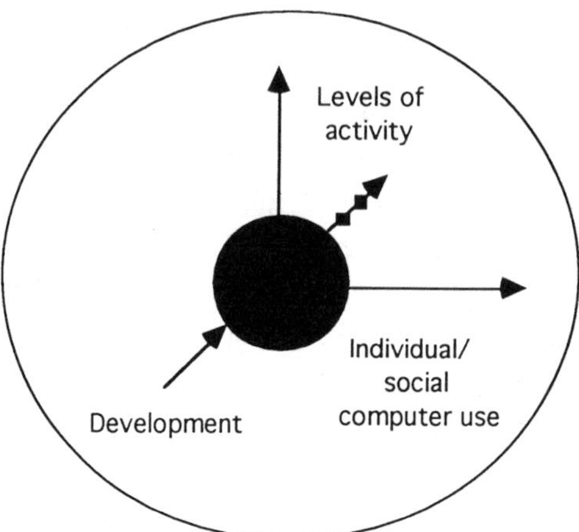

Figure 3.1
Expansion of the subject matter of HCI: three dimensions.

reach meaningful goals that usually exist beyond the situation of human-computer interaction, and, moreover, often serve as intermediate steps to higher-level goals that can be even more remotely related to the situation of computer use. This aspect was described in some ethnographic studies of the use of technology (Suchman 1993). It was shown that interactions with information technology are embedded into logically structured sequences of interaction with other objects and with people.

The next dimension is that of development. The components of human-computer interaction are not static. The user begins as a novice and often ends up an expert; assimilation of new artifacts can solve old problems, but changing the nature of the tasks performed by the user, it creates new problems that require still new artifacts to be used (Carroll, Kellogg, and Rosson 1991). An understanding of a particular case of computer use includes an analysis of its history and its potential developmental transformations.

Finally, there is the individual/social dimension. The current meaning of the word *user* now includes not only individuals but also groups and organizations.

The discovery of the rich, multifaceted, and multidimensional reality of human-computer interaction is probably one of the most salient features of the current situation in the HCI community (Bowers and Rodden 1993; Kuutti and Bannon 1993; Russell et al. 1993). The powerful expansion of the object of study opens important new horizons—and at the same time, creates a feeling of confusion. The field of HCI seems to be a collection of loosely related subfields; familiar concepts suddenly turn out not to be so simple anymore. (This feeling of confusion is evident in, for example, Bowers and Rodden 1993 and Monk et al. 1993.)

This situation in the HCI community constitutes the context that can explain the growing interest in activity theory. The new reality of human-computer interaction requires new theoretical tools to help overcome the "explosion" of the subject matter of HCI, to coordinate the efforts of the increasing number of researchers working in this interdisciplinary field, and to find a way to make the outcomes of the studies more relevant to practice. It is natural and logical to try various theoretical approaches that can potentially provide a consistent picture of the field, and activity theory seems to be one of the most promising candidate approaches. It is true that activity theory is not a ready-made universal solution to all the problems of human-computer interaction, but it is also true that the general vector of the current development in the field of HCI (Bannon 1991) is directly related to the very essence of this theoretical approach.

COMPUTER TOOLS AND FUNCTIONAL ORGANS

One of the most salient features that distinguishes activity theory from the cognitive approach is that activity theory considers computers as a special kind of tool mediating human interaction with the world. Meaningful, goal-directed activities constitute the context for both mental processes and external actions. Human beings usually use computers not because they want to interact with them but because they want to reach their goals beyond the situation of the "dialogue" with the computer. As formulated by Bødker (1991), users are acting "through the interface." Therefore, the subject matter of HCI should not be a closed system of "user-computer" but should include the meaningful context of the user's goals, environment, available tools, and interactions with other people.

The need to expand the object of analysis is dictated not only by general theoretical interests but also by specific design considerations. It is not possible to create a high-quality system while relying solely on abstract universal guidelines (such as logical consistency) and ignoring the larger context of human activity. As Grudin (1989) showed, designers sometimes deliberately violate the principle of logical consistency to make systems more usable. They do it to make systems more consistent with the general structure of the user's activities, and the logic of consistency in this sense can be different from the logic of internal consistency.

The tool mediation perspective has important theoretical implications for HCI. First, it questions the very name of the discipline. The emphasis on the interaction implied by this name seems to be a little misleading. The chronological sequence of terms used to cover the problems of HCI demonstrates the more and more sound accent on human activities rather than on computer systems ("human factors," "computer and human interaction," "human-computer interaction," "computer-supported cooperative work"). It would not be surprising to see a new term for the discipline, stressing the tool nature of computers (for example, "computer-mediated activity"), and even if the discipline retains its current name, it will probably be used just as a label that has little to do with its actual content, just as "computers" are no longer associated simply with calculating devices.

Second, if we accept the tool mediation perspective, we have to deal with two interfaces instead of one user interface, with two borders, separating (1) the user from the computer and (2) the user *and* the computer from the outside world (Bødker 1991; Grudin 1993; Norman 1991). This duality raises a problem that is almost identical to Bateson's (1972) blind man's stick dilemma: where is the boundary between the individual who uses a tool and the external world? Does it coincide with the individual-tool boundary or with the tool-world one?

The activity theory answer to this question is based on the concept of "functional organs" (Leont'ev 1981). Functional organs are functionally integrated, goal-oriented configurations of internal and external resources. External tools support and complement natural human abilities in building up a more efficient system that can lead to higher accomplishments. For example, scissors elevate the human hand to an efficient cutting organ, eyeglasses improve human vision, and notebooks enhance memory. The external tools integrated into functional organs are experienced as a property of the individual, while the same things not integrated into the structure of a functional organ (for example, during the early phases of learning how to use the tool) are conceived of as belonging to the outer world.

Computer tools share the common attribute of all tools: they are integrated into functional organs. From the point of view of activity theory, the nature of these functional organs is of special interest to HCI studies. Perhaps the central problem of HCI can be defined as that of optimal integration of computer tools into the structure of human activity (Kaptelinin 1992a). What are the needs that require the development of a new functional organ? What is the range of goals that are intended to be reached with the new tool? What is the structure of human activity before the assimilation of the tool, and what is the previous experience of computer users with the uncomputerized equivalent of this activity? All of these questions are no less relevant to the "transparency" of the user interface than an optimal width and depth of the menu system (Shneiderman 1987).

Certainly there are several kinds of functional organs based on the use of computer tools, because computer tools do not have one fixed function. One of the most important functions can be defined as an extension of the internal plane of actions (IPA; figure 3.2). The IPA is a concept developed within activity theory that refers to the human ability to perform manipulations with an internal representation of external objects before starting actions with these objects in reality. It is similar to the cognitive concepts of working memory and mental models, but it refers not to specific mental models but to the general ability to create and transform them.

The IPA appears at a certain stage of child development (the most critical period corresponds to the early school years, according to Ponomarev 1975) and constitutes a new kind of interaction between internal activities and external ones. Human activities include external and internal components at every developmental stage. Initially, however, the function of internal components is limited to the control of external activity; that is, the only way to get feedback to an action is to perform the action in reality. Over the process of internalization—the transformation

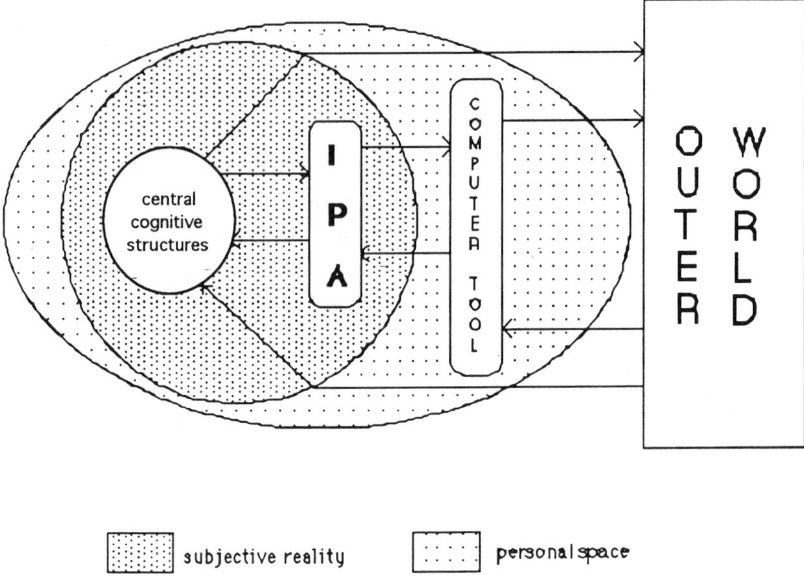

Figure 3.2
Computer tool as an extension of the internal plane of actions (IPA).

of external activities into internal ones—the child acquires an ability to perform some actions "in mind" and in this way avoids costly mistakes and becomes free from the immediate situation. A system of mental structures and abilities that makes it possible to perform actions "in mind"—the IPA—is the result of this development. The same control mechanisms that regulate external behavior can provide feedback on actions performed in the IPA (actually, these control mechanisms also develop, but this is a separate problem not directly related to this chapter). Oversimplifying, we can differentiate between two subsystems of human cognition: central cognitive structures and the IPA (see figure 3.2).

The potential of computer systems to create easily controllable models of target objects and to give the user the opportunity to evaluate them and to manipulate them explains why such applications as spreadsheets, word processors, and graphics editors became so popular.

Computers are not the only kind of tools used as an extension of the IPA, and this function is not the only function of computers (they are also used, for example, as communication tools), but an understanding of the mechanisms underlying the use of computer tools as extensions of the IPA is directly relevant to the development of useful and usable systems. Some recent systems have excellent representational facilities supporting experimentation with individual objects (such as the Print Preview window in Microsoft Word), but there is still much to be done to make computer tools more efficient extensions of the IPA. In particular, existing applications have rather limited potential to support comparison of multiple objects or to give a full picture of large objects. Of course, the screen size imposes severe limitations, but this problem can be partly solved by intelligent use of zooming and simulation of information integration during saccadic eye movements (after all, the focal vision of human beings is also very narrow). Another opportunity to make computer tools more adequate to their role as the IPA extension would be to support a backtracking search strategy, to provide the user with a representation of the search process history, to help the user in evaluating the results, to support coordination of the given task with other kinds of activities performed by the individual at the same time (for example, to give an estimation of the time needed to print out the specific document on the specific printer). In short, understanding the requirements to computer-based functional organs, as well as the mechanisms underlying the integration of computer tools into functional organs, can stimulate insights into the practical problems of HCI, problems related to the design of new kinds of interactive systems.

Finally, the tool mediation perspective in HCI brings to the field the issue of culture. Tool mediation is a way of transmitting of cultural knowledge. Tools and culturally developed ways of using tools shape the external activity of individuals and through the process of internalization influence the nature of mental processes (internal activity). The role of tools is not limited to transmission of operational aspects of human interaction with the world. As Latour (1993) emphasized, tools also shape the goals of the people who use the tools. There are implicit goals that usually are "built into" the tools by their developers. The goals achieved by people equipped with a tool are often influenced by the "tool's goal," and the final results differ from both goals, being a compromise between them. (According to Latour, the person who has a gun can be influenced by the implicit "goals" of the gun even if the gun is never used.) The same is applicable to computers and software. The values and goals intended by their developers can influence users who may not even be aware of these influences. This is obvious in the case of some computer games but might be true with respect to other kinds of applications, too; for example, the style of communication via e-mail can be influenced by the nature of this medium, or a database format can influence the way people differentiate between important and less important facts.

The tool perspective in HCI calls for a revision of many traditional concepts (e.g., the concept of "interface") and raises many problems, including the mechanisms underlying the integration of computer tools into the structure of human activity (functional organs) and the coordination of general cultural perspectives of the people involved in the development and use of computer tools.

DEVELOPMENT OF COMPUTER-MEDIATED ACTIVITY

Assimilation of computer tools, by either individual users or organizations, is a continuing process rather than a single act. The need for the constant change stems from several sources. The first is related to technological progress. New generations of hardware and software change standards and requirements for computer tools. To keep up with technological development, users have to adopt newer systems. Another source is related to the developing needs of users. The use of a particular tool changes the structure of activity and can result in new goals to be satisfied. This phenomenon, described by Carroll, Kellogg, and Rosson (1991) as the "task-artifact cycle," can be illustrated with numerous examples. Sometimes it is very difficult to predict the line of development, and in some cases it can hardly be characterized as progress toward more powerful tools. Several years ago the interface of an e-mail system I was using suddenly changed. The machine became so popular (it was one of the first e-mail servers in the former Soviet Union) that the system administrators had to provide most users with a very primitive interface that allowed them to save messages only as a file on the user's floppy disk and to send messages stored in a prespecified format as files on the floppy. This design was intended to limit the time the users spent working at this particular computer by preventing them from the use of advanced facilities of the system.

The changing requirements for computer tools raise a special problem of making it possible to meet these changing requirements efficiently. For this reason it is practical to be able to predict the changes or at least the general tendencies. Of course, it is important to make systems flexible, so that users can adapt them to their needs, but it would be a mistake to leave the problem of adaptation to users only. Many popular systems provide users with an opportunity to change the interface according to their wishes. However, a number of studies have shown that most users do not utilize these facilities at all, rather, they need help in implementing the necessary changes to the system.

The cognitive approach does not provide any substantial basis for solving this problem. Activity theory, which distinguishes between various levels of determination of the agent's (individual's or group's) behavior, can give some hints. The most general idea is that understanding the status of a process within the conceptual structure of activity can help to anticipate the direction of potential changes, as well as related costs and benefits. If a change is limited to the level of operations, the problems associated are technical ones (financial resources needed, time necessary for reautomatization of routines, etc.). If, however, it turns out that some goals are no longer meaningful, a careful analysis of motives impelling the individual and/or organizational activity, as well as alternative ways to reach this motive under the current circumstances, should be conducted. The most difficult problems arise if the changes reach the level of the whole activity. The changes of activity structure caused by the use of computer tools usually take place at different levels simultaneously.

It would be an exaggeration to say that the problem of development has not been studied within the cognitive approach. There are numerous studies of differences between novice and expert users (Allwood 1989) and many cognitive models explaining the mechanisms underlying skill acquisition (Anderson 1983). From my point of view, however, cognitive models cannot efficiently deal with qualitative changes of cognitive skill with practice.

Recently I (Kaptelinin 1993) investigated the phenomenon of poor recall of command names in pull-down menus by experienced system users, as discovered by Mayes et al. (1988). Subjects first practiced with a very simple menu-based system and were then exposed to two transformations of the initial interface: (1) all the command names were substituted with strings of dots but their order was the same, and (2) the items were scrambled within each menu during every new task. I found that after the initial loss of efficiency, subjects could quickly restore speed and accuracy level in the case of the "dotted" menus but not in the case of the scrambled ones. So while during the early phases of learning the menu selection was based on the command names, during a relatively short period of time of initial practice (about one and a half hours) the subjects seemed to switch from verbal clues to menu selection based on spatial locations of the items.

These data illustrate the complex nature of developmental skill transformations, which cannot be completely explained in terms of "chunking" or "knowledge compilation." They are also relevant to the concept of "affordances" as it was introduced to the field of HCI by Norman (1988). There is no doubt that affordances are very helpful if the situation is not familiar to the user (as during the exploratory learning of a system) or the goal is unambiguously determined by the situation, which does not allow for a wide range of possible actions (e.g., the goal is to open the door I want to go through), or both. However, the benefits of affordances beyond these limited conditions are not so obvious. The notion of affordances implies that the user is matching his or her goal against the set of opportunities offered by the environment, that he or she directly sees what can be done to reach the goal. In other words, the notion of affordances implies that the objects have some universal operational meanings (what can be done with these objects) that is directly communicated to the users. From the point of view of activity theory, human beings actively create the meaning of the objects in the process of interaction with the environment. This idea can be illustrated with the study of menu selection: the users ended up relying on spatial locations, which cannot be considered as affordances at the early phase of interaction with the system.

Besides, in most real-life situations there is no one-to-one correspondence between goals and ways to accomplish the goals. There are often many ways to achieve a goal. The use of affordances implies that the initiative, in a sense, is taken by the external situation. According to activity theory, the elementary components of activity—operations—are not just triggered by conditions, they are determined by the general structure of the action they are incorporated into. People learn to control their immediate impulses, and an important aspect of social norm acquisition by children seems to be learning to ignore some affordances.

GROUP AND ORGANIZATIONAL COMPUTER USE

Since the cultural-historical tradition represented by activity theory emphasizes the social nature of human beings and their activities, it appears natural to expect the most tangible benefits from activity theory in studies of social aspects of computer use, for example, in the field of CSCW. From my point of view, it would be too optimistic to think of activity theory as an approach that can provide ready-made answers to the problems related to group and organizational computer use. However, it appears that basic principles of activity theory can be elaborated on and operationalized to make the theory a useful tool for studying supraindividual levels of information technologies use. This section advances some arguments supporting this point of view.

Activity theory has been developed as a psychological approach, and it almost exclusively deals with individual human beings. Undoubtedly, social context plays an important role in activity theory, but it is mainly used to explain how individuals are influenced by social factors, not to give an account of activities of social units. However, the general notion of a developing active agent interacting with an environment in a social context is applicable not only to individuals but to groups and organizations as well.

Several attempts have sought to expand the concept of activity to supraindividual phenomena. One of them was made by Engeström (1987), who proposed a scheme of activity different from that by Leont'ev (1978, 1981); it contains three interacting entities—the individual, the object, and the community—instead of the two components—the individual and the object—in Leont'ev's original scheme. Engeström's version of activity theory has been adopted in some recent studies in the fields of HCI and CSCW (see Kuutti, this volume).

Another attempt to extend activity theory beyond the individual level was made by Soviet psychologists in the seventies and eighties (Petrovsky and Petrovsky 1983). The concept of collective subject (*kollektivnyj subjekt dejatelnosti*) was introduced to account for the processes of communication between individuals. According to this approach, communicative processes can be conceived as interactions between structural components of the collective subject, the interactions that are subordinated to the primary kind of interaction—the activity relating the subject to reality. The explanatory potential of the concept of collective subject is somewhat limited since there definitely are communication phenomena that do not fall into the category of interactions between members of a team pursuing a common goal. On the other hand, there no less definitely are phenomena of communication and cooperation that do fall into this category, and within its scope, the concept of collective subject can be useful.

Computer-supported activity of a group or organization can be analyzed along the general lines of activity theory: finding the motive, goals, and conditions of the activity; identifying structural components of the subject's interaction with reality (individual activities, actions, and operations) as well as tools mediating the activity; and tracing developmental changes of the activity. There are, however, some activity theory concepts whose meaning is not clear in the context of collective activity; it is not even clear whether they can be applied in this context.

One difference between individual and collective activities is rather obvious: a structural component of a collective subject can be a subject, too, with his or her own motives and goals. This difference is essential, yet it is still possible to address the problem of group activity decomposition from the standpoint of activity theory. According to Leont'ev (1978), actions are usually polymotivated; two or more activities can temporarily merge, motivating the same action, if the goal of one action is a prerequisite for reaching the motives of all of the activities simultaneously. This principle can also be applied to integrating individuals or groups within the structure of a higher-level collective subject; it is not necessary that all component subjects share the motive of the system they are incorporated into, but the goals of the subjects should permit polymotivation, that is, should satisfy motives of both the component subject

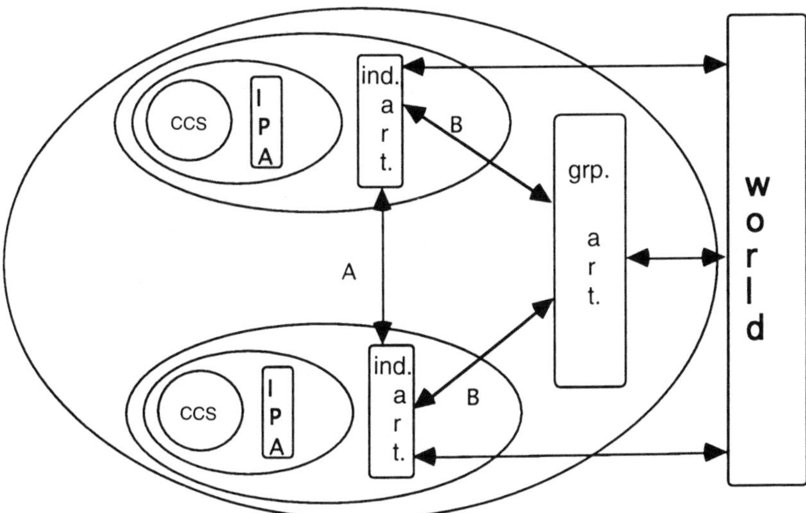

Figure 3.3
Computer-mediated group activity. ccs = central cognitive structures; IPA = internal plane of actions; ind. art. = individual artifact; grp. art. = group artifact.

and the system. A specific case of the polymotivation principle is "Grudin's law," as formulated by Norman (1993): "When those who benefit are not those who do the work, then the technology is likely to fail or, at least, be subverted."

The notion of computer tools as extensions of IPA can be applied to collective agents, too. In this case, the components of group activity can be presented as shown in figure 3.3. Shared virtual workspace is an extension of the group IPA, and the pattern of various links relating the components of the model represent the way computer-mediated communication, noncomputer communication, interpersonal communication mediated by references to a virtual common object, and individual human-computer interactions are integrated within the collective computer-mediated activity. Figure 3.3 is not intended to represent all aspects of the complex reality of computer-mediated group work, but it can help to relate individual and collective computer use and by this means contribute to bridging the gap between traditional HCI and CSCW (see, e.g., van der Veer 1994).

CONCLUSIONS

The difference between activity theory and the cognitive approach has been analyzed in relation to such aspects of human-computer interaction as affordances of the user interface and computer-mediated group activity. This concluding section will present two more examples of differences between the approaches and then, will focus on limitations of activity theory as a conceptual framework of human-computer interaction.

Both activity theory and the cognitive approach view human-computer interaction as a hierarchically organized process. However, there is an important difference between the cognitive approach to levels and the activity theory approach. The highest level the cognitive models are dealing with—the task level, according to Moran (1981)—is usually barely mentioned. The details of the dialogue structure can be ideally deduced from a higher-level specification of a system, but it is very difficult (if not impossible) to give a cognitive explanation of how this higher-level specification is being created by designers.

This point can also be illustrated with the GOMS model (Card, Moran, and Newell 1983), which is intended to be used in evaluating user interface designs. There are some striking similarities between activity theory and GOMS.[2] Both approaches are intended to give a description of goal-directed behavior. The use of the term "goal" in activity theory corresponds to the use of "goal" in GOMS. Other correspondences are between "operators" (GOMS) and "operations" (activity theory), "methods" (GOMS) and "actions" (activity theory). However, a closer look at these approaches reveals fundamental differences between them. First, according to activity theory, the relations between actions and operations are *dynamic*: actions become operations through automatization, and operations can transform into actions in cases of breakdown. The GOMS model, however, deliberately avoids considering nonroutine processes and does not even intend to describe the dynamics of the interaction structure. Second, activity theory describes both the subjective and the objective sides of interaction, and goals and conditions are understood as aspects of reality that direct and constrain the actions and operations of the individual. The GOMS model, on the other hand, is intended to represent individual behavior abstracted, as much as possible, from the environment. Third, and most important, activity theory puts goals and actions into the context of activities, while GOMS does not deal at all with the origins of goals (the model is just not intended for this purpose). Before applying the GOMS approach, one defines the goals. So, in the area of user interface evaluation, an application of cognitive models raises the same problem as in the area of the user interface design: how to identify the basic aspects of the system to be created, how to capture the everyday experience (actual and potential) into a description that can be used as a starting point for system development.

One potential solution would be to combine radically different approaches in proceeding through two major phases of creating system specifications. A contextual approach (for example, ethnography) can be applied at the first phase to analyze the everyday environment of the potential users, to understand their needs, and to take into account all possible factors that can influence the quality of the target system. The outcomes of this phase, a general specification of the system, can be passed to the second phase, where a version of the cognitive approach can be employed to specify the details of the system (this specification, in turn, can be used to start the whole process of iterative design).

Unfortunately, this ideal scheme has serious drawbacks. First, the mediating specification should be understandable for people working in different paradigms. It is not clear if this is possible at all (Monk et al. 1993). Second, the process of stepwise refinement of the system specification is not a strictly top-down one; important constraints are sometimes discovered at lower levels and make it necessary to come back to higher-level decisions and correct them so that it is possible to meet these constraints. Therefore, the coordination of various levels of specification could require continuous back-and-forth coordination of different perspectives and is a potential source of numerous problems. That is why it is desirable to rely on a single homogeneous conceptual scheme powerful enough to cover various levels of human-computer interactions. Activity theory integrates multilevel perspectives on human activities within a single conceptual framework, and this is probably the main reason it has attracted the attention of many researchers.

The difference between the cognitive approach and activity theory can also be illustrated by the interpretation of artifacts within the cognitive paradigm. Probably the most advanced attempt to introduce the idea of mediation into the cognitive approach was made by Norman. In his paper "Cognitive Artifacts," Norman (1991) points out the importance of analysis of a special kind of artifact that he defines as follows: "A cognitive artifact is an artifact designed to maintain, display, or operate upon information in order to serve representational function." The introduction of this concept leads Norman to differentiate between the personal view and the system view of human-computer interaction. These views correspond, respectively, to the border between the user and "the computer and the world" (the personal view), and the border between "the user and the computer" and the world (the system view). Norman concludes that the notion of empowering people with computer tools is true only from the system view, while from the personal view, the use of computers means just changing the nature of the task (which can become easier and require fewer capacities from the user).

These conclusions can be compared to the activity theory interpretation of the same phenomena. First, activity theory does not differentiate between the "personal view " and the "system view." Both views are considered personal; the functional organs employed in the two cases are, of course, different, but both are functional organs of the individual, and hence personal. Second, and more important, activity theory states that tools not only change the task but often empower the individual even if the external tool is no longer used. Numerous experiments have shown that activities mediated by symbolic tools often undergo three developmental stages: (1) the initial phase, when performance is the same with and without a tool because the tool is not mastered well enough to provide any benefits, (2) the intermediate stage, when aided performance is superior to unaided performance, and (3) a final stage, when performance is the same with and without the tool but now because the tool-mediated activity is internalized and the external tool (such as a checklist or a visualization of complex data) is no longer needed. Even if the tool does not seem symbolic at all, its external use can substantially influence the nature of internal activities. For example, a novice pool player has to hit a ball with the cue to see the results; an expert may not need the physical cue (with which to make the shot) to know the results of a planned shot.

The difference between Norman's view and that of activity theory illustrates that the principles underlying activity theory are closely interrelated. The concept of cognitive artifacts that Norman introduced is almost identical to the concept of psychological tools developed in the cultural-historical tradition (see, e.g., Engeström 1987), but the use of the concept out of the context of the other principles leads to conclusions opposite those of activity theory.

In this chapter, I have emphasized the potential advantages of activity theory rather than its disadvantages (since my point is to substantiate further attempts to apply activity theory to the problems of HCI, as well as to outline the most promising lines of such an application). But this emphasis does not imply that activity theory can provide solutions to all problems. Activity theory has very serious limitations too. Let us consider some of them.

First, activity theory was mainly developed as a psychological theory of individual activity. This is an important limitation, because the current meaning of the term "the user" includes not only individuals but also groups and organizations. Many researchers agree that activity theory can be applied to supraindividual units, such as groups and organizations; however, the specific conceptual system necessary for analysis of social systems is still under discussion. In the former Soviet Union, the opportunity to study social phenomena was limited for political reasons. Probably the only relevant idea developed by the Soviet proponents of activity theory was the notion of collective subject. This concept is less elaborated compared to the aspects of activity theory related to individual subjects, and it remains to be clarified to what extent the conceptual apparatus of activity theory is applicable to collective subjects. Important developments toward the extension of activity theory to the level of social processes have been made by Western researchers (Cole 1984; Engeström 1987; Raeithel 1992), but the problem is not solved yet.

Second, compared to the cultural-historical approach developed by Vygotsky (1978), activity theory adopted a narrower point of view of culture. Activity theory was oriented to practical needs of society, was greatly influenced by the example of natural science, and always tended to interpret reality in formal schemes (see Zinchenko 1992; this volume). While culture, values, motivation, emotions, human personality, and personal meaning are embraced by the conceptual system of activity theory, the theory does not aim at giving a comprehensive description of all these phenomena. It captures only some of their aspects: those related to rational understanding of human interaction with the world. This feature of activity theory can be considered a benefit because it is similar to the way many system developers think, but it might also be viewed as a disadvantage, because activity theory cannot completely substitute for an anthropology that defines and understands culture.

Third, the tool mediation perspective, which is considered the most important advantage of activity theory, can also impose some limitations on its potential application. In virtual realities, for example, the border between a tool and reality is rather unclear; information technology can provide the user not only with representations of objects of reality but also with a sort of reality as such, which does not obviously represent anything else and is intended to be just one more environment with which the individual interacts. Virtual realities present a problem to activity theory that probably cannot be solved without enriching activity theory's basic principles with new ideas from the cultural-historical tradition or other related approaches.

Finally, in the field of HCI, compared, for instance, to the field of education, activity theory is not yet operationalized enough. There are not enough methods and techniques that can be directly utilized to solve specific problems, so it would be unrealistic to expect immediate results from accepting activity theory as an approach guiding theoretical research or practical efforts.

The limitations of activity theory set out are not inevitable. It is a developing approach, and probably one of its strengths is its potential for integration with other conceptual systems.

ACKNOWLEDGMENTS

I am grateful to Rachel Bellamy, Susanne Bødker, and Bonnie Nardi for comments on prior drafts of this chapter.

NOTES

1. Usually cognitive scientists avoid explicit identification of the mind with the computer. It is stated that the basic concept underlying the cognitive approach is the concept of computability: "Theories of the mind should be modelled in a computer program" (Johnson-Laird 1988). It does not necessarily mean that the human mind is a computational device. However, concrete cognitive studies of the mind are based on the explicit or implicit assumption that the nature of the human mind is information processing, and it can be described in terms of architecture, procedures, flow of information, distributed processing, and so forth (Anderson 1983; Gardner 1987; Johnson-Laird 1988).

2. This chapter does not discuss the limitations of GOMS that can potentially be overcome within the cognitive approach, such as its inability to deal with parallel activities or its overreliance on the average times taken by elementary operations.

REFERENCES

Allwood, C. M. (1989). Computer usage by novices. In I. A. Kent and J. G. Williams, eds., *Encyclopedia of Microcomputers*. New York: Marcal Dekker.

Anderson, J. R. (1983). *The Architecture of Cognition*. Cambridge, MA: Harvard University Press.

Bannon, L. (1991). From human factors to human actors: The role of psychology and human computer interaction studies in system design. In J. Greenbaum and M. Kyng, eds., *Design at Work: Cooperative Design of Computer Systems*. Hillsdale, NJ: Lawrence Erlbaum.

Bateson, G. (1972). *Steps to an Ecology of Mind*. New York: Ballantine Books.

Bødker, S. (1989). A human activity approach to user interfaces. *Human Computer Interaction* 4(3):171–195.

Bødker, S. (1991). *Through the Interface: A Human Activity Approach to User Interface Design*. Hillsdale, NJ: Lawrence Erlbaum.

Bowers, J., and Rodden, T. (1993). Exploding the interface: Experiences of a CSCW network. In *Proceedings INTERCHI'93 Conference on Human Factors in Computing Systems* (pp. 255–262). Amsterdam, April 24–29.

Brusilovsky, P., Burmistrov, I., and Kaptelinin, V. (1993). Structuring the field of HCI: An empirical study of experts' representations. In *Proceedings East-West Human-Computer Interaction Conference* (vol. 3, pp. 18–28). Moscow, August 3–7.

Card, S., Moran, T., and Newell, A. (1983). *The Psychology of Human Computer Interaction*. Hillsdale, NJ: Lawrence Erlbaum.

Carroll, J. M., Kellogg, W. A., and Rosson M. B. (1991). The task-artifact cycle. In J. Carroll, ed., *Designing Interaction: Psychology at the Human-Computer Interface*. Cambridge: Cambridge University Press.

Cole, M. (1984). The zone of proximal development: Where culture and cognition create each other. In J. Wertsch, ed., *Culture, Communication, and Cognition: Vygotskian Perspectives*. Cambridge: Cambridge University Press.

Cypher A. (1986). The structure of users' activities. In D. Norman and S. Draper, eds., *User Centered System Design: New Perspectives on Human-Computer Interaction*. Hillsdale, NJ: Lawrence Erlbaum.

Engeström, Y. (1987). *Learning by Expanding: An Activity-Theoretical Approach to Developmental Research*. Helsinki: Orienta-Konsultit Oy.

Gardner, H. (1987). *The Mind's New Science: A History of the Cognitive Revolution*. New York: Basic Books.

Grudin, J. (1989). The case against user interface consistency. *Communications of the ACM* 32(10):1164–1173.

Grudin, J. (1990). The computer reaches out: The historical continuity of interface design. In *Proceedings CHI'90 Conference on Human Factors in Computing Systems* (pp. 261–268). Seattle, Washington, April 1–4.

Grudin, J. (1993). Interface: An evolving concept. *Communications of the ACM* 36(4):110–119.

Johnson-Laird, P. (1988). *The Computer and the Mind: An Introduction to Cognitive Science*. Cambridge, MA: Harvard University Press.

Kaptelinin, V. (1992a). Integration of computer tools into the structure of human activity: Implications for cognitive ergonomics. In *Proceedings Sixth European Conference on Cognitive Ergonomics* (pp. 285–294). Balatonfured, Hungary, September 6–11.

Kaptelinin, V. (1992b). Human computer interaction in context: The activity theory perspective. In *Proceedings East-West Human Computer Interaction Conference* (pp. 13–28). St. Petersburg, Russia, August 4–8.

Kaptelinin, V. (1993). Item recognition in menu selection: The effect of practice. In *Adjunct Proceedings, INTERCHI'93 Conference on Human Factors in Computing Systems* (pp. 183–184). Amsterdam, April 24–29.

Kuutti, K., and Bannon, L. (1993). Searching for unity among diversity: Exploring the interface concept. In *Proceedings INTERCHI'93 Conference on Human Factors in Computing Systems* (pp. 263–268). Amsterdam, April 24–29.

Latour, B. (1993). On technical mediation. Three talks prepared for "The Messenger Lectures on the Evolution of Civilization." Cornell University, April.

Leont'ev, A. N. (1978). *Activity. Consciousness. Personality*. Englewood Cliffs, NJ: Prentice-Hall.

Leont'ev, A. N. (1981). *Problems of the Development of Mind.* Moscow: Progress.

Mayes, J. T., Draper, S. W., McGregor, M. A., and Oatley, K. (1988). Information flow in a user interface: The effect of experience and context on the recall of MacWrite screens. In D. M. Jones and R. Winder, eds., *People and Computers IV.* Cambridge: Cambridge University Press.

Miller, G. A., Galanter, E., and Pribram, K. (1960). *Plans and the Structure of Behavior.* New York: Holt, Rinehart, and Winston.

Monk, A., Nardi, B., Gilbert, N., Mantei, M., and McCarthy, J. (1993). Mixing oil and water? Ethnography versus experimental psychology in the study of computer-mediated communication. In *Proceedings INTERCHI'93 Conference on Human Factors in Computing Systems* (pp. 3–6). Amsterdam, April 24–29.

Moran, T. (1981). The Command Language Grammar: A representation for the user interface of interactive computer systems. *International Journal of Man-Machine Studies* 15.

Munipov V. M. (1983). Leont'ev's contribution to engineering psychology and ergonomics [Vklad A. N. Leontjeva v razvitie inzhenernoj psikhologii i ergonomiki]. In A. V. Zaporozhets, V. P. Zinchenko, and O. V. Ovchinnikova, eds., *Leont'ev and Contemporary Psychology* [A. N. Leontjev i sovremennaja psikhologija]. Moscow: Izdatelstvo MGU. (in Russian)

Norman, D. (1988). *The Psychology of Everyday Things.* New York: Basic Books.

Norman, D. (1991). Cognitive artifacts. In J. Carroll, ed., *Designing Interaction: Psychology at the Human-Computer Interface.* Cambridge: Cambridge University Press.

Norman D. (1993). *Things That Make Us Smart: Defending Human Attributes in the Age of the Machine.* Reading, MA: Addison-Wesley.

Petrovsky, A. V., and Petrovsky, V. A. (1983). Active personality and Leont'ev's ideas [Lichnost i ee aktivnost v svete idej A. N. Leontjeva]. In A. V. Zaporozhets, V. P. Zinchenko, and O. V. Ovchinnikova, eds., *Leont'ev and Contemporary Psychology* [A. N. Leontjev i sovremennaja psikhologija]. Moscow: Izdatelstvo MGU. (in Russian)

Ponomarev Ja. A. (1975). *The Psychology of Creativity* [Psikhologija Tvorchestva]. Moscow: Nauka. (in Russian)

Raeithel, A. (1992). Activity theory as a foundation for design. In C. Floyd et al., eds., *Software Development and Reality Construction.* Berlin: Springer Verlag.

Russell, D. M., Stefik, M. J., Pirolli, P., and Card, S. (1993). The cost structure of sensemaking. In *Proceedings INTERCHI'93 Conference on Human Factors in Computing Systems* (pp. 269–276). Amsterdam, April 24–29.

Shneiderman, B. (1987). *Designing the User Interface: Strategies for Effective Human-Computer Interaction.* Reading, MA: Addison-Wesley.

Suchman L. (1993). Centers of coordination: A case and some themes. Presented at the NATO ARW on Discourse, Tools, and Reasoning, Lucca, Italy, November 2–7.

van der Veer, G. (1994). Groupware task analysis: Modeling complex reality. In *Proceedings Seventh European Conference on Cognitive Ergonomics* (pp. 341–352). Bonn, Germany, September 5–8.

Vygotsky, L. S. (1978). *Mind and Society.* Cambridge MA: Harvard University Press.

Zinchenko, V. P. (1992). Activity theory: Retrospect and prospect. In *Proceedings East-West Human Computer Interaction Conference* (pp. 1–5). St. Petersburg, Russia, August 4–8.

4

Studying Context: A Comparison of Activity Theory, Situated Action Models, and Distributed Cognition

Bonnie A. Nardi

It has been recognized that system design will benefit from explicit study of the context in which users work. The unaided individual divorced from a social group and from supporting artifacts is no longer the model user. But with this realization about the importance of context come many difficult questions. What exactly is context? If the individual is no longer central, what is the correct unit of analysis? What are the relations between artifacts, individuals, and the social groups to which they belong? This chapter compares three approaches to the study of context: activity theory, situated action models, and distributed cognition. I consider the basic concepts each approach promulgates and evaluate the usefulness of each for the design of technology.[1]

A broad range of work in psychology (Leont'ev 1978; Vygotsky 1978; Luria 1979; Scribner 1984; Newman, Griffin, and Cole 1989; Norman 1991; Salomon 1993), anthropology (Lave 1988; Suchman 1987; Flor and Hutchins 1991; Hutchins 1991a; Nardi and Miller 1990, 1991; Gantt and Nardi 1992; Chaiklin and Lave 1993), and computer science (Clement 1990; Mackay 1990; MacLean et al. 1990) has shown that it is not possible to fully understand how people learn or work if the unit of study is the unaided individual with no access to other people or to artifacts for accomplishing the task at hand. Thus we are motivated to study context to understand relations among individuals, artifacts, and social groups. But as human-computer interaction researchers, how can we conduct studies of context that will have value to designers who seek our expertise?

Brooks (1991) argues that HCI specialists will be most valuable to designers when we can provide (1) a broad background of comparative understanding over many domains, (2) high-level analyses useful for evaluating the impact of major design decisions, and (3) information that suggests actual designs rather than simply general design guidelines or metrics for evaluation. To be able to provide such expertise, we must develop an appropriate analytical abstraction that "discards irrelevant details while *isolating and emphasizing those properties of artifacts and situations that are most significant for design*" (Brooks, 1991, emphasis added). It is especially difficult to isolate and emphasize critical properties of artifacts and situations in studies that consider a full context because the scope of analysis has been widened to accommodate such holistic breadth. Taking context seriously means finding oneself in the thick of the complexities of particular situations at particular times with particular individuals. Finding commonalities across situations is difficult because studies may go off in so many different directions, making it problematic to provide the comparative understanding across domains that Brooks (1991) advocates. How can we confront the blooming, buzzing confusion that is "context" and still produce generalizable research results?

This chapter looks at three approaches to the study of context—activity theory, situated action models, and the distributed cognition approach—to see what tools each offers to help manage the study of context. In particular we look at the unit of analysis proposed by each approach, the categories offered to support a description of context, the extent to which each treats action as structured prior to or during activity, and the stance toward the conceptual equivalence of people and things.

Activity theory, situated action models, and distributed cognition are evolving frameworks and will change and grow as each is exercised with empirical study. In this chapter I ask where each approach seems to be headed and what its emphases and perspectives are. A brief overview of each approach to studying context will be given, followed by a discussion of some critical differences among the approaches. An argument is made for the advantages of activity theory as an overall framework while at the same time recognizing the value of situated action models and distributed cognition analyses.

SITUATED ACTION MODELS

Situated action models emphasize the emergent, contingent nature of human activity, the way activity grows directly out of the particularities of a given situation.[2] The focus of study is situated activity or practice, as opposed to the study of the formal or cognitive properties of artifacts, or structured social relations, or enduring cultural knowledge and values. Situated action analysts do not deny that artifacts or social relations or knowledge or values are important, but they argue that the true locus of inquiry should be the "everyday activity of persons acting in [a] setting" (Lave 1988).[3] That this inquiry is meant to take place at a very fine-grained level of minutely observed activities, inextricably embedded in a particular situation, is reflected in Suchman's (1987) statement that "the organization of situated action is an emergent property of moment-by-moment interactions between actors, and between actors and the environments of their action."

Lave (1988) identifies the basic unit of analysis for situated action as "the activity of persons-acting in setting." The unit of analysis is thus not the individual, not the environment, but a relation between the two. A *setting* is defined as "a relation between acting persons and the arenas in relation with which they act." An *arena* is a stable institutional framework. For example, a supermarket is an arena within which activity takes place. For the individual who shops in the supermarket, the supermarket is experienced as a setting because it is a "personally ordered, edited version" of the institution of the supermarket. In other words, each shopper shops only for certain items in certain aisles, depending on her needs and habits. She has thus "edited" the institution to match her personal preferences (Lave 1988).

An important aspect of the "activity of persons-acting in setting" as a unit of analysis is that it forces the analyst to pay attention to the flux of ongoing activity, to focus on the unfolding of real activity in a real setting. Situated action emphasizes responsiveness to the environment and the improvisatory nature of human activity (Lave 1988). By way of illustrating such improvisation, Lave's (1988) "cottage cheese" story has become something of a classic. A participant in the Weight Watchers program had the task of fixing a serving of cottage cheese that was to be three-quarters of the two-thirds cup of cottage cheese the program normally allotted.[4] To find the correct amount of cottage cheese, the dieter, after puzzling over the problem a bit, "filled a measuring cup two-thirds full of cheese, dumped it out on a cutting board, patted it into a circle, marked a cross on it, scooped away one quadrant, and served the rest" (Lave 1988).

In emphasizing improvisation and response to contingency, situated action deemphasizes study of more durable, stable phenomena that persist across situations. The cottage cheese story is telling: it is a one-time solution to a one-time problem, involving a personal improvisation that starts and stops with the dieter himself. It does not in any serious way involve the enduring social organization of Weight Watchers or an analysis of the design of an artifact such as the measuring cup. It is a highly particularistic accounting of a single episode that highlights an individual's creative response to a unique situation.

Empirical accounts in studies of situated action tend to have this flavor. Lave (1988) provides detailed descriptions of grocery store activity such as putting apples into bags, finding enchiladas in the frozen food section, and ascertaining whether packages of cheese are mispriced. Suchman (1987) gives a detailed description of experiments in which novices tried to figure out how to use the double-sided copy function of a copier. Suchman and Trigg (1991) describe the particulars of an incident of the use of a baggage- and passenger-handling form by airport personnel. These analyses offer intricately detailed observations of the temporal sequencing of a particular train of events rather than being descriptive of enduring patterns of behavior across situations.

A central tenet of the situated action approach is that the structuring of activity is not something that precedes it but can only grow directly out of the immediacy of the situation (Suchman 1987; Lave 1988). The insistence on the exigencies of particular situations and the emergent, contingent character of action is a reaction to years of influential work in artificial intelligence and cognitive science in which "problem solving" was seen as a "series of objective, rational pre-specified means to ends" (Lave 1988) and work that overemphasized the importance of plans in shaping behavior (Suchman 1987). Such work failed to recognize the opportunistic, flexible way that people engage in real activity. It failed to treat the environment as an important shaper of activity, concentrating almost exclusively on representations in the head—usually rigid, planful ones—as the object of study.

Situated action models provide a useful corrective to these restrictive notions that put research into something of a cognitive straitjacket. Once one looks at real behavior in real situations, it becomes clear that rigid mental representations such as formulaic plans or simplistically conceived "rational problem solving" cannot account for real human activity. Both Suchman (1987) and Lave (1988) provide excellent critiques of the shortcomings of the traditional cognitive science approach.

ACTIVITY THEORY

Of the approaches examined in this chapter, activity theory is the oldest and most developed, stretching back to work begun in the former Soviet Union in the 1920s. Activity theory is complex and I will highlight only certain aspects here. (For summaries see Leont'ev 1974; Bødker 1989; and Kuutti 1991; for more extensive treatment see Leont'ev 1978; Wertsch 1981; Davydov, Zinchenko, and Talyzina 1982; and Raeithel 1991.) This discussion will focus on a core set of concepts from activity theory that are fundamental for studies of technology.

In activity theory the unit of analysis is an activity. Leont'ev, one of the chief architects of activity theory, describes an activity as being composed of subject, object, actions, and operations (1974). A *subject* is a person or a group engaged in an activity. An *object* (in the sense of "objective") is held by the subject and motivates activity, giving it a specific direction. "Behind the object," he writes, "there always stands a need or a desire, to which [the activity] always answers." Christiansen (this volume) uses the term "objectified motive," which I find a congenial mnemonic for a word with as many meanings in English as "object." One might also think of the "object of the game" or an "object lesson."

Actions are goal-directed processes that must be undertaken to fulfill the object. They are conscious (because one holds a goal in mind), and different actions may be undertaken to meet the same goal. For example,

> a person may have the object of obtaining food, but to do so he must carry out actions not immediately directed at obtaining

> food.... His goal may be to make a hunting weapon. Does he subsequently use the weapon he made, or does he pass it on to someone else and receive a portion of the total catch? In both cases, that which energizes his activity and that to which his action is directed do not coincide (Leont'ev 1974).

Christiansen (this volume) provides a nice example of an object from her research on the design of the information systems used by Danish police: "[The detective] expressed as a vision for [the] design [of his software system] that it should be strong enough to handle a 'Palme case,' referring to the largest homicide investigation known in Scandinavia, when the Swedish prime minister Oluf Palme was shot down on a street in Stockholm in 1986!" This example illustrates Raeithel and Velichkovsky's depiction of objects as

> actively "held in the line of sight." ... the bull's eye of the archer's target, which is the original meaning of the German word *Zweck* ("purpose"), for example, is a symbol of any future state where a real arrow hits near it. Taking it into sight, as the desired "end" of the whole enterprise, literally causes this result by way of the archer's action-coupling to the physical processes that let the arrow fly and make it stop again (Raeithel and Velichkovsky, this volume).

Thus, a system that can handle a "Palme case" is a kind of bull's eye that channels and directs the detective's actions as he designs the sofware system that he envisions.

Objects can be transformed in the course of an activity; they are not immutable structures. As Kuutti (this volume) notes, "It is possible that an object itself will undergo changes during the process of an activity." Christiansen (this volume) and Engeström and Escalante (this volume) provide case studies of this process. Objects do not, however, change on a moment-by-moment basis. There is some stability over time, and changes in objects are not trivial; they can change the nature of an activity fundamentally (see, for example, Holland and Reeves, this volume).

Actions are similar to what are often referred to in the HCI literature as tasks (e.g., Norman 1991). Activities may overlap in that different subjects engaged together in a set of coordinated actions may have multiple or conflicting objects (Kuutti 1991).

Actions also have operational aspects, that is, the way the action is actually carried out. Operations become routinized and unconscious with practice. When learning to drive a car, the shifting of the gears is an action with an explicit goal that must be consciously attended to. Later, shifting gears becomes operational and "can no longer be picked out as a special goal-directed process: its goal is not picked out and discerned by the driver; and for the driver, gear shifting psychologically ceases to exist" (Leont'ev 1974). Operations depend on the conditions under which the action is being carried out. If a goal remains the same while the conditions under which it is to be carried out change, then "only the operational structure of the action will be changed" (Leont'ev 1974).

Activity theory holds that the constituents of activity are not fixed but can dynamically change as conditions change. All levels can move both up and down (Leont'ev 1974). As we saw with gear shifting, actions become operations as the driver habituates to them. An operation can become an action when "conditions impede an action's execution through previously formed operations" (Leont'ev 1974). For example, if one's mail program ceases to work, one continues to send mail by substituting another mailer, but it is now necessary to pay conscious attention to using an unfamiliar set of commands. Notice that here the object remains fixed, but goals, actions, and operations change as conditions change. As Bødker (1989) points out, the flexibility recognized by activity theory is an important distinction between activity theory and other frameworks such as GOMS. Activity theory "does not predict or describe each step in the activity of the user (as opposed to the approach of Card, Moran and Newell, 1983)" as Bødker (1989) says, because activity theory recognizes that changing conditions can realign the constituents of an activity.

A key idea in activity theory is the notion of *mediation* by artifacts (Kuutti 1991). Artifacts, broadly defined to include instruments, signs, language, and machines, mediate activity and are created by people to control their own behavior. Artifacts carry with them a particular culture and history (Kuutti 1991) and are persistent structures that stretch across activities through time and space. As Kaptelinin (chapter 3, this volume) points out, recognizing the central role of mediation in human thought and behavior may lead us to reframe the object of our work as "computer-mediated activity," in which the starring role goes to the activity itself rather than as "human-computer interaction" in which the relationship between the user and a machine is the focal point of interest.

Activity theory, then, proposes a very specific notion of context: the activity itself is the context. What takes place in an activity system composed of object, actions, and operation, *is* the context. Context is constituted through the enactment of an activity involving people and artifacts. Context is not an outer container or shell inside of which people behave in certain ways. People consciously and deliberately generate contexts (activities) in part through their own objects; hence context is not just "out there."

Context is both internal to people—involving specific objects and goals—and, at the same time, external to people, involving artifacts, other people, specific settings. The crucial point is that in activity theory, external and internal are fused, unified. In Zinchenko's discussion of functional organs (this volume) the unity of external and internal is explored (see also Kaptelinin, this volume, chapters 3 and 5). Zinchenko's example of the relationship between Rostropovich and his cello (they are inextricably implicated in one another) invalidates simplistic explanations that divide internal and external and schemes that see context as external to people. People transform themselves profoundly through the acquisition of functional organs; context cannot be conceived as simply a set of external "resources" lying about. One's ability—and choice—to marshall and use resources is, rather, the result of specific historical and developmental processes in which a person is changed. A context cannot be reduced to an enumeration of people and artifacts; rather the specific transformative relationship between people and artifacts, embodied in the activity theory notion of functional organ, is at the heart of any definition of context, or activity.

DISTRIBUTED COGNITION

The distributed cognition approach (which its practitioners refer to simply as distributed cognition, a convention I shall adopt here)

> is a new branch of cognitive science devoted to the study of: the representation of knowledge both inside the heads of individuals

> and in the world . . . ; the propagation of knowledge between different individuals and artifacts . . . ; and the transformations which external structures undergo when operated on by individuals and artifacts. . . . By studying cognitive phenomena in this fashion it is hoped that an understanding of how intelligence is manifested at the systems level, as opposed to the individual cognitive level, will be obtained. (Flor and Hutchins 1991)

Distributed cognition asserts as a unit of analysis a cognitive system composed of individuals and the artifacts they use (Flor and Hutchins 1991; Hutchins 1991a). The cognitive system is something like what activity theorists would call an activity; for example, Hutchins (1991a) describes the activity of flying a plane, focusing on "the cockpit system." Systems have goals; in the cockpit, for example, the goal is the "successful completion of a flight."[5] Because the system is not relative to an individual but to a distributed collection of interacting people and artifacts, we cannot understand how a system achieves its goal by understanding "the properties of individual agents alone, no matter how detailed the knowledge of the properties of those individuals might be" (Hutchins 1991a). The cockpit, with its pilots and instruments forming a single cognitive system, can be understood only when we understand, as a unity, the contributions of the individual agents in the system and the coordination necessary among the agents to enact the goal, that is, to achieve "the successful completion of a flight." (Hutchins 1994 studies shipboard navigation and makes similar points.)

Thus distributed cognition moves the unit of analysis to the system and finds its center of gravity in the functioning of the system, much as classic systems theory did (Weiner 1948; Ashby 1956; Bertalanffy 1968). While a distributed cognition analyst would probably, if pushed, locate system goals in the minds of the people who are part of the system, the intent is to redirect analysis to the systems level to reveal the functioning of the system itself rather than the individuals who are part of the system. Practitioners of distributed cognition sometimes refer to the "functional system" (instead of the "cognitive system") as their central unit of analysis (Hutchins 1994; Rogers and Ellis 1994), hinting at an even further distance from the notion of the individual that the term *cognitive* cannot help but suggest.

Distributed cognition is concerned with structure—representations inside and outside the head—and the transformations these structures undergo. This is very much in line with traditional cognitive science (Newell and Simon 1972) but with the difference that cooperating people and artifacts are the focus of interest, not just individual cognition "in the head." Because of the focus on representations—both internal to an individual and those created and displayed in artifacts—an important emphasis is on the study of such representations. Distributed cognition tends to provide finely detailed analyses of particular artifacts (Norman 1988; Norman and Hutchins 1988; Nardi and Miller 1990; Zhang 1990; Hutchins 1991a, Nardi et al. 1993) and to be concerned with finding stable design principles that are widely applicable across design problems (Norman 1988, 1991; Nardi and Zarmer 1993).

The other major emphasis of distributed cognition is on understanding the coordination among individuals and artifacts, that is, to understand how individual agents align and share within a distributed process (Flor and Hutchins 1991; Hutchins 1991a, 1991b; Nardi and Miller 1991). For example, Flor and Hutchins (1991) studied how two programmers performing a software maintenance task coordinated the task among themselves. Nardi and Miller (1991) studied the spreadsheet as a coordinating device facilitating the distribution and exchange of domain knowledge within an organization. In these analyses, shared goals and plans, and the particular characteristics of the artifacts in the system, are important determinants of the interactions and the quality of collaboration.

DIFFERENCES BETWEEN ACTIVITY THEORY, SITUATED ACTION MODELS, AND DISTRIBUTED COGNITION

All three frameworks for analyzing context that we have considered are valuable in underscoring the need to look at real activity in real situations and in squarely facing the conflux of multifaceted, shifting, intertwining processes that comprise human thought and behavior. The differences in the frameworks should also be considered as we try to find a set of concepts with which to confront the problem of context in HCI studies.

The Structuring of Activity

An important difference between activity theory and distributed cognition, on the one hand, and situated action, on the other hand, is the treatment of motive and goals. In activity theory, activity is shaped first and foremost by an object held by the subject; in fact, we are able to distinguish one activity from another only by virtue of their differing objects (Leont'ev 1974; Kozulin 1986; Kuutti 1991, this volume). Activity theory emphasizes motivation and purposefulness and is "optimistic concerning human self-determination" (Engeström 1990). A distributed cognition analysis begins with the positing of a *system goal*, which is similar to the activity theory notion of object, except that a system goal is an abstract systemic concept that does not involve individual consciousness.

Attention to the shaping force of goals in activity theory and distributed cogntion, be they conscious human motives or systemic goals, contrasts with the contingent, responsive, improvisatory emphasis of situated action. In situated action, one activity cannot be distinguished from another by reference to an object (motive); in fact Lave (1988) argues that "goals [are not] a condition for action.... An analytic focus on direct experience in the lived-in world leads to ... the proposition that goals are *constructed*, often in verbal interpretation" (emphasis in original). In other words, goals are our musings out loud about why we did something *after* we have done it; goals are "retrospective and reflexive" (Lave 1988).

In a similar vein, Suchman (1987), following Garfinkel (1967), asserts that "a statement of intent generally says very little about the action that follows." If we appear to have plans to carry out our intent, it is because plans are "an artifact of our *reasoning about* action, not ... the generative *mechanism* of action." (emphasis in original). Suchman (1987) says that plans are "retrospective reconstructions."[6] The position adopted by Lave (1988) and Suchman (1987) concerning goals and plans is that they are post hoc rationalizations for actions whose meaning can arise only within the immediacy of a given situation.

Lave (1988) asks the obvious question about this problematic view of intentionality: "If the meaning of activity is constructed in action ... from whence comes its intentional character, and indeed its meaningful basis?" Her answer, that "activity and its values are generated simultaneously," restates her position but does not explicate it. Winograd and Flores (1986) also subscribe to this radically situated view, using the colorful term "throwness" (after Heidegger) to argue that we are actively embedded, or "thrown into," in an ongoing situation that directs the flow of our actions much more than reflection or the use of durable mental representations.

In activity theory and distributed cognition, by contract, an object-goal is the beginning point of analysis. An object precedes and motivates activity. As Leont'ev (1974) states, "Performing operations that do not realize any kind of goal-directed action [and recursively, a motive] on the subject's part is like the operation of a machine that has escaped human control."

In activity theory and distributed cognition, an object is (partially) determinative of activity; in situated action, every activity is by definition uniquely constituted by the confluence of the particular factors that come together to form one "situation." In a sense, situated action models are confined to what activity theorists would call the action and operation levels (though lacking a notion of goal at the action level in the activity theory sense). Situated action concentrates, at these levels, on the way people orient to changing conditions. Suchman's (1987) notion of "embodied skills" is similar to the notion of operations, though less rich than the activity theory construct which grounds operations in consciousness and specifies that operations are dependent on certain conditions obtaining and that they may dynamically transform into actions when conditions change.

While in principle one could reasonably focus one's efforts on understanding the action and operation levels while acknowledging the importance of the object level, neither Lave (1988) nor Suchman (1987), as we have seen, does this. On the contrary, the very idea of an object's generating activity is rejected; objects (goals) and plans are "retrospective reconstructions," post hoc "artifacts of reasoning about action," after action has taken place. Why people would construct such explanations is an interesting question not addressed in these accounts. And why other people would demand or believe such retrospective reconstructions is another question to be addressed by this line of reasoning.

Situated action models have a slightly behavioristic undercurrent in that it is the subject's reaction to the environment (the "situation") that finally determines action. What the analyst observes is cast as a response (the subject's actions/operations) to a stimulus (the "situation"). The mediating influences of goals, plans, objects, and mental representations that would order the perception of a situation are absent in the situated view. There is no attempt to catalog and predict invariant reactions (as in classical behaviorism) as situations are said to vary unpredictably, but the relation between actor and environment is one of reaction in this logic.[7] People "orient to a situation" rather than proactively generating activity rich with meaning reflective of their interests, intentions, and prior knowledge.

Suchman and Trigg (1991) cataloged their research methods in describing how they conduct empirical studies. What is left out is as interesting as what is included. The authors report that they use (1) a stationary video camera to record behavior and conversation; (2) "shadowing" or following around an individual to study his or her movements; (3) tracing of artifacts and instrumenting of computers to audit usage, and (4) event-based analysis tracking individual tasks at different locations in a given setting. Absent from this catalog is the use of interviewing; interviews are treated as more or less unreliable accounts of idealized or rationalized behavior, such as subjectively reported goals as "verbal interpretation" (Lave 1988) and plans as "retrospective reconstructions" (Suchman 1987). Situated action analyses rely on recordable, observable behavior that is "logged" through analysis of a videotape or other record (Suchman and Trigg 1993; Jordan and Henderson 1994).[8] Accounts from study participants describing in their own words what they think are doing, and why, such as those in this book by Bellamy, Bødker, Christiansen, Engeström and Escalante, Holland and Reeves, and Nardi, are not a focal point of situated action analyses.

Activity theory has something interesting to tell us about the value of interview data. It has become a kind of received wisdom in the HCI community that people cannot articulate what they are doing (a notion sometimes used as a justification for observational studies and sometimes used to avoid talking to users at all). This generalization is true, however, primarily at the level of operations; it is certainly very difficult to say how you type, or how you see the winning pattern on the chessboard, or how you know when you have written a sentence that communicates well. But this generalization does not apply to the higher conscious levels of actions and objects; ask a secretary what the current problems are with the boss, or an effective executive what his goals are for the next quarter, and you will get an earful!

Skillful interviewing or the need to teach someone how to do something often bring operations to the subject's conscious awareness so that even operations can be talked about, at least to some degree. Dancers, for example, use imagery and other verbal techniques to teach dance skills that are extremely difficult to verbalize. The ability to bring operations to a conscious level, even if only partially, is an aspect of the dynamism of the levels of activity as posited by activity theory. When the subject is motivated (e.g., by wishing to cooperate with a researcher or by the desire to teach), at least some operational material can be retrieved (see Bødker, this volume). The conditions fostering such a dynamic move to the action level of awareness may include skillful probing by an interviewer.

In situated action, what constitutes a situation is defined by the researcher; there is no definitive concept such as object that marks a situation. The Leont'evian notion of object and goals remaining constant while actions and operations change because of changing conditions is not possible in the situated action framework that identifies the genesis of action as an indivisible conjunction of particularities giving rise to a unique situation. Thus we find a major difference between activity theory and situated action; in the former, the structuring of activity is determined in part, and in important ways, by human intentionality before the unfolding in a particular situation; in situated action, activity can be known only as it plays out in situ. In situated action, goals and plans cannot even be realized until after the activity has taken place, at which time they become constructed rationalizations for activity that is wholly created in the crucible of a particular situation. In terms of identifying activity, activity theory provides the more satisfying option of taking a definition of an activity directly from a subjectively defined object rather than imposing a definition from the researcher's view.

These divergent notions of the structuring of activity, and the conceptual tools that identify one activity distinctly from another, are important for comparative work in studies of human-computer interaction. A framework that provides a clear way to demarcate one activity from another provides more comparative power than one that does not. Analyses that are entirely self-contained, in the way that a truly situated description of activity is, provide little scope for comparison. The level of analysis of situated action models—at the moment-by-moment level—would seem to be too low for comparative work. Brooks (1991) criticizes human-factors task analysis as being too low level in that all components in an analysis must "be specified as at atomic a level as possible." This leads to an ad hoc set of tasks relevant only to a particular domain and makes cross-task comparison difficult (Brooks 1991). A similar criticism applies to situated action models in which a focus on moment-by-moment actions leads to detailed descriptions of highly particularistic activities (such as pricing cheeses in a bin or measuring out cottage cheese) that are not likely to be replicated across contexts. Most crucially, no tools for pulling out a higher-level description from a set of observations are offered, as they are in activity theory.

Persistent Structures

An important question for the study of context is the role that persistent structures such as artifacts, institutions, and cultural values play in shaping activity. To what extent should we expend effort analyzing the durable structures that stretch across situations and activities that cannot be properly described as simply an aspect of a particular situation?

For both activity theory and distributed cognition, persistent structures are a central focus. Activity theory is concerned with the historical development of activity and the mediating role of artifacts. Leont'ev (1974) (following work by Vygotsky) considered the use of tools to be crucial: "A tool mediates activity that connects a person not only with the world of objects, but also with other people. This means that a person's activity assimilates the experience of humanity." Distributed cognition offers a similar notion; for example, Hutchins (1987) discusses "collaborative manipulation," the process by which we take advantage of artifacts designed by others, sharing good ideas across time and space. Hutchins's example is a navigator using a map: the cartographer who created the map contributes, every time the navigator uses the map, to a remote collaboration in the navigator's task.

Situated action models less readily accommodate durable structures that persist over time and across different activities. To the extent that activity is truly seen as "situated," persistent, durable structures that span situations, and can thus be described and analyzed *independent of a particular situation*, will not be central. It is likely, however, that situated action models, especially those concerned with the design of technology, will allow some latitude in the degree of adherence to a purist view of situatedness, to allow for the study of cognitive and structural properties of artifacts and practices as they span situations. Indeed, in recent articles we find discussion of "routine practices" (Suchman and Trigg 1991) and "routine competencies" (Suchman 1993) to account for the observed regularities in the work settings studied. The studies continue to report detailed episodic events rich in minute particulars, but weave in descriptions of routine behavior as well.

Situated action accounts may then exhibit a tension between an emphasis on that which is *emergent*, *contingent*, *improvisatory* and that which is *routine* and *predictable*. It remains to be seen just how this tension resolves—whether an actual synthesis emerges (more than simple acknowledgment that both improvisations and routines can be found in human behavior) or whether the claims to true situatedness that form the basis of the critique of cognitive science cede some importance to representations "in the head." The appearance of routines in situated action models opens a chink in the situated armor with respect to mental representations; routines must be known and represented somehow. Routines still circumambulate notions of planful, intentional behavior; being canned bits of behavior, they obviate the need for active, conscious planning or the formulation of deliberate intentions or choices. Thus the positing of routines in situated action models departs from notions of emergent, contingent behavior but is consistent in staying clear of plans and motives.

Of the three frameworks, distributed cognition has taken most seriously the study of persistent structures, especially artifacts. The emphasis on representations and the transformations they undergo brings persistent structures to center stage. Distributed cognition studies provide in-depth analyses of artifacts such as nomograms (Norman and Hutchins 1988), navigational tools (Hutchins 1990), airplane cockpits (Hutchins 1991a), spreadsheets (Nardi and Miller 1990, 1991), computer-aided design (CAD) systems (Petre and Green 1992), and even everyday artifacts such as door handles (Norman 1988). In these analyses, the artifacts are studied as they are actually used in real situations, but the properties of the artifacts are seen as persisting across situations of use, and it is believed that artifacts can be designed or redesigned with respect to their intrinsic structure as well as with respect to specific situations of use. For example, a spreadsheet table is an intrinsically good design (from a perceptual standpoint) for a system in which a great deal of dense information must be displayed and manipulated in a small space (Nardi and Miller 1990). Hutchins's (1991a) analysis of cockpit devices considers the memory requirements they impose. Norman (1988) analyzes whether artifacts are designed to prevent users from doing unintended (and unwanted) things with them. Petre and Green (1992) establish requirements for graphical notations for computer-aided design (CAD) users based on users' cognitive capabilities. In these studies, an understanding of artifacts is animated by observations made in real situations of their use, but there is also important consideration given to the relatively stable cognitive and structural properties of the artifacts that are not bound to a particular situation of use.

Distributed cognition has also been productive of analyses of work practices that span specific situational contexts. For example, Seifert and Hutchins (1988) studied cooperative error correction on board large ships, finding that virtually all navigational errors were collaboratively "detected and corrected within the navigation team." Gantt and Nardi (1992) found that organizations that make intensive use of CAD software may create formal in-house support systems for CAD users composed of domain experts (such as drafters) who also enjoy working with computers. Rogers and Ellis (1994) studied computer-mediated work in engineering practice. Symon et al. (1993) analyzed the coordination of work in a radiology department in a large hospital. Nardi et al. (1993) studied the coordination of work during neurosurgery afforded by video located within the operating room and at remote locations in the hospital. A series of studies on end user computing have found a strong pattern of cooperative work among users of a variety of software systems in very different arenas, including users of word processing programs (Clement 1990), spreadsheets (Nardi and Miller 1990, 1991), UNIX (Mackay 1990), a scripting language (MacLean et al. 1990), and CAD systems (Gantt and Nardi 1992).

In these studies the work practices described are not best analyzed as a product of a specific situation but are important precisely because they span particular situations. These studies develop points at a high level of analysis; for example, simply discovering that application development is a collaborative process has profound implications for the design of computer systems (Mackay 1990; Nardi 1993). Moment-by-moment actions, which would make generalization across contexts difficult, are not the key focus of these studies, which look for broader patterns spanning individual situations.

People and Things: Symmetrical or Asymmetrical?

Kaptelinin (chapter 5, this volume) points out that activity theory differs fundamentally from cognitive science in rejecting the idea that computers and people are equivalent. In cognitive science, a tight information processing loop with inputs and outputs on both sides models cognition. It is not important whether the agents in the model are humans or things produced by humans (such as computers). (See also Bødker, this volume, on the tool perspective.)

Activity theory, with its emphasis on the importance of motive and consciousness—which belong only to humans—sees artifacts and people as different. Artifacts are mediators of human thought and behavior; people and things are not equivalent. Bødker (this volume) defines artifacts as instruments in the service of activities. In activity theory, people and things are unambiguously asymmetrical.

Distributed cognition, by contrast, views people and things as conceptually equivalent; people and artifacts are "agents" in a system. This is similar to traditional cognitive science, except that the scope of the system has been widened to include a collaborating set of artifacts and people rather than the narrow "man-machine" dyad of cognitive science.

While treating each node in a system as an "agent" has a certain elegance, it leads to a problematic view of cognition. We find in distributed cognition the somewhat illogical notion that artifacts are cognizing entities. Flor and Hutchins (1991) speak of "the propagation of knowledge between different individuals and artifacts." But an artifact cannot know anything; it serves as a medium of knowledge for a human. A human may act on a piece of knowledge in unpredictable, self-initiated ways, according to socially or personally defined motives. A machine's use of information is always programmatic. Thus a theory that posits equivalence between human and machine damps out sources of systemic variation and contradiction (in the activity theory sense; see Kuutti, this volume) that may have important ramifications for a system. The activity theory notion of artifacts as mediators of cognition seems a more reasoned way to discuss relations between artifacts and people.

Activity theory instructs us to treat people as sentient, moral beings (Tikhomirov 1972), a stance not required in relation to a machine and often treated as optional with respect to people when they are viewed simply as nodes in a system. The activity theory position would seem to hold greater potential for leading to a more responsible technology design in which people are viewed as active beings in control of their tools for creative purposes rather than as automatons whose operations are to be automated away, or nodes whose rights to privacy and dignity are not guaranteed. Engeström and Escalante (this volume) apply the activity theory approach of asymmetrical human-thing relations to their critique of actor-network theory.

In an analysis of the role of Fitts's law in HCI studies undertaken from an activity theory perspective, Bertelsen (1994) argues that Fitts's "law" is actually an effect, subject to contextual variations, and throws into question the whole notion of the person as merely a predictable mechanical "channel." Bertelsen notes that "no matter how much it is claimed that Fitts' Law is merely a useful metaphor, it will make us perceive the human being as a channel. The danger is that viewing the human being as a channel will make us treat her as a mechanical device.... Our implicit or explicit choice of world view is also a choice of the world we want to live in; disinterested sciences do not exist" (Bertelsen 1994). Seeing Fitts's findings as an effect, subject to contextual influence, helps us to avoid the depiction of the user as a mechanical part.

Activity theory says, in essence, that we are what we do. Bertelsen sees Fitts's law as a tool of a particular kind of science that "reduces the design of work environments, e.g., computer artifacts, to a matter of economical optimization." If we wish to design in such a manner, we will create a world of ruthless optimization and little else, but it is certainly not inevitable that we do so. However, no amount of evidence that people are capable of behaving opportunistically, contingently, and flexibly will inhibit the development and dispersal of oppressive technologies; Taylorization has made that clear. If we wish a different world, it is necessary to design humane and liberating technologies that create the world as we wish it to be.

There are never cut-and-dried answers, of course, when dealing with broad philosophical problems such as the definition of people and things, but activity theory at least engages the issue by maintaining that there is a difference and asking us to study its implications. Many years ago, Tikhomirov (1972) wrote, "How society formulates the problem of advancing the creative content of its citizens' labor is a necessary condition for the full use of the computer's possibilities."

Situated action models portray humans and things as qualitatively different. Suchman (1987) has been particularly eloquent on this point. But as I have noted, situated action models, perhaps inadvertently, may present people as reactive ciphers rather than fully cognizant human actors with self-generated agendas.

DECIDING AMONG THE THREE APPROACHES

All three approaches to the study of context have merit. The situated action perspective has provided a much-needed corrective to the rationalistic accounts of human behavior from traditional cognitive science. It exhorts us not to depend on rigidly conceived notions of inflexible plans and goals and invites us to take careful notice of what people are actually doing in the flux of real activity. Distributed cognition has shown how detailed analyses that combine the formal and cognitive properties of artifacts with observations on how artifacts are used can lead to understandings useful for design. Distributed cognition studies have also begun to generate a body of comparative data on patterns of work practices in varying arenas.

Activity theory and distributed cognition are very close in spirit, as we have seen, and it is my belief that the two approaches will mutually inform, and even merge, over time, though activity theory will continue to probe questions of consciousness outside the purview of distributed cognition as it is presently formulated. The main differences with which we should be concerned here are between activity theory and situated action. Activity theory seems to me to be considerably richer and deeper than the situated action perspective.[9] Although the critique of cognitive science offered by situated action analysts is cogent and has been extremely beneficial, the insistence on the "situation" as the primary determinant of activity is, in the long run, unsatisfying. What is a "situation"? How do we account for variable responses to the same environment or "situation" without recourse to notions of object and consciousness?

To take a very simple example, let us consider three individuals, each going on a nature walk. The first walker, a bird watcher, looks for birds. The second, an entomologist, studies insects as he walks, and the third, a meteorologist, gazes at clouds. The walker will carry out specific actions, such as using binoculars, or turning over leaves, or looking skyward, depending on his or her interest. The "situation" is the same in each case; what differs is the subject's object. While we might define a situation to include some notion of the subject's intentions, as we have seen, this approach is explicitly rejected by situated action analysts. (See also Lave 1993.)

To take the example a step further, we observe that the bird watcher and the meteorologist might in some cases take exactly the same action from a behavioral point of view, such as looking skyward. But the observable action actually involves two very different activities for the subjects themselves. One is studying cloud formations, the other watching migrating ducks. The action of each, as seen on a videotape, for example, would appear identical; what differs is the subject's intent, interest, and knowledge of what is being looked at.

If we do not consider the subject's object, we cannot account for simple things such as, in the case of the bird watcher, the presence of a field guide to birds and perhaps a "life list" that she marks up as she walks along.[10] A bird watcher may go to great lengths to spot a tiny flycatcher high in the top of a tree; another walker will be totally unaware of the presence of the bird. The conscious actions and attention of the walker thus derive from her object. The bird watcher may also have an even longer-term object in mind as she goes along: adding all the North American birds to her life list. This object, very important to her, is in no way knowable from "the situation" (and not observable from a videotape). Activity theory gives us a vocabulary for talking about the walker's activity in meaningful subjective terms and gives the necessary attention to what the subject brings to a situation.[11] In significant measure, the walker construes and creates the situation by virtue of prior interest and knowledge. She is constrained by the environment in important ways, but her actions are not determined by it. As Davydov, Zinchenko, and Talyzina (1982) put it, the subject actively "'meets' the object with partiality and selectivity," rather than being "totally subordinate to the effects of environmental factors ... the principle of reactivity is counterposed to the principle of the subject's activeness."

It is also important to remember that the walker has consciously chosen an object and taken the necessary actions for carrying it out; she did not just suddenly and unexpectedly end up in the woods. Can we really say, as Suchman (1987) does, that her actions are "ad hoc"? Situated action analyses often assume a "situation" that one somehow finds oneself in, without consideration of the fact that the very "situation" has already been created in part by the subject's desire to carry out some activity. For example, Suchman's famous canoeing example, intended to show that in the thick of things one abandons plans, is set up so that the "situation" is implicitly designated as "getting your canoe through the falls" (Suchman 1987). Surely the deck is stacked here. What about all the plotting and planning necessary to get away for the weekend, transport the canoe to the river, carry enough food, and so forth that must also be seen as definitive of the situation? It is only with the most mundane, plodding, and planful effort that one arrives "at the falls." To circumscribe the "situation" as the glamorous, unpredictable moment of running the rapids is to miss the proverbial boat, as it were. An activity theory analysis instructs us to begin with the subjectively defined object as the point of analytical departure and thus will lead not simply to crystalline moments of improvisatory drama (whether measuring cottage cheese or running rapids) but to a more global view that encompasses the totality of an activity construed and constructed, in part, prior to its undertaking, with conscious, planful intent.

Holland and Reeves (this volume) studied the differing paths taken by three groups of student programmers all enrolled in the same class and all beginning in the same "situation." The professor gave each group the same specific task to accomplish during the semester and the students' "performances were even monitored externally from an explicit and continually articulated position." The students were all supposed to be doing the same assignment; they heard the same lectures and had the same readings and resources. But as Holland and Reeves document, the projects took radically different courses and had extremely variable outcomes *because the students themselves redefined the object of the class.* Our understanding of what happened here must flow from an understanding of how each group of students construed, and reconstrued, the class situation. The "situation" by itself cannot account for the fact that one group of students produced a tool that was chosen for demonstration at a professional conference later in the year; one group produced a program with only twelve lines of code (and still got an A!); and the third group "became so enmeshed in [interpersonal struggles] that the relationships among its members frequently became the object of its work."

Bellamy (this volume) observes that to achieve practical results such as successfully introducing technology into the classroom, it is necessary to understand and affect the objects of educators: "to change the underlying educational philosophy of schools, designers must design technologies that support students' learning activities and design technologies that support the activities of educators and educational administrators. Only by understanding and designing for the complete situation of education

... will it be possible for technology to bring about pervasive educational reform."

Situated action models make it difficult to go beyond the particularities of the immediate situation for purposes of generalization and comparison. One immerses in the minutiae of a particular situation, and while the description may feel fresh, vivid, and "on-the-ground" as one reads it, when a larger task such as comparison is attempted, it is difficult to carry the material over. One finds oneself in a claustrophobic thicket of descriptive detail, lacking concepts with which to compare and generalize. The lack of conceptual vocabulary, the appeal to the "situation" itself in its moment-by-moment details, do not lend themselves to higher-order scientific tasks where some abstraction is necessary.

It is appropriate to problematize notions of comparison and generalization in order to sharpen comparisons and generalizations, but it is fruitless to dispense with these foundations of scientific thought. A pure and radically situated view would by definition render comparison and generalization as logically at odds with notions of emergence, contingency, improvisation, description based on in situ detail and point of view. (I am not saying any of the situated theorists cited here are this radical; I am playing out the logical conclusion of the ideas.) Difficult though it may be to compare and generalize when the subject matter is people, it is nonetheless important if we are to do more than simply write one self-contained descriptive account after another. The more precise, careful, and sensitive comparisons and generalizations are, the better. This is true not only from the point of view of science but also of technology design. Design, a practical activity, is going to proceed apace, and it is in our best interests to provide comparisons and generalizations based on nuanced and closely observed data, rather than rejecting the project of comparison and generalization altogether.

Holland and Reeves compare their study to Suchman's (1994) study, which centers on a detailed description of how operations room personnel at an airport coordinated action to solve the problems of a dysfunctional ramp. Holland and Reeves point out that they themselves might have focused on a similar minutely observed episode such as studying how the student programmers produced time logs. However, they argue that they would then have missed the bigger picture of what the students were up to if they had, for example, concentrated on "videotapes and transcriptions ... show[ing], the programmers' use of linguistic markers in concert with such items as physical copies of the time-log chart and the whiteboard xeroxes in order to orient joint attention, for example."

Holland and Reeves's analysis argues for a basic theoretical orientation that accommodates a longer time horizon than is typical of a "situation." They considered the entire three-month semester as the interesting frame of reference for their analysis, while Suchman looked at a much shorter episode, more easily describable as a "situation." (See also Suchman and Trigg 1993, where the analysis centers on an hour and a half of videotape.) Holland and Reeves's analysis relies heavily on long-term participant-observation and verbal transcription; Suchman focuses on the videotape of a particular episode of the operations room in crisis. In comparing these two studies, we see how analytical perspective leads to a sense of what is interesting and determines where research effort is expended. Situated action models assume the primacy of a situation in which moment-by-moment interactions and events are critical, which leads away from a longer time frame of analysis. Videotape is a natural medium for this kind of analysis, and the tapes are looked at with an eye to the details of a particular interaction sequence (Jordan and Henderson 1994). By contrast, an activity theory analysis has larger scope for the kind of longer-term analysis provided by Holland and Reeves (though videotapes may certainly provide material of great interest to a particular activity theory analysis as in Bødker, this volume, and Engeström and Escalante, this volume).

Of course the observation that theory and method are always entangled is not new; Hegel (1966) discussed this problem. Engeström (1993) summarized Hegel's key point: "Methods should be developed or 'derived' from the substance, as one enters and penetrates deeper into the object of study." And Vygotsky (1978) wrote, "The search for method becomes one of the most important problems of the entire enterprise of understanding the uniquely human forms of psychological activity. In this case, the method is simultaneously prerequisite and product, the tool and the result of the study."

Situated action models, then, have two key problems: (1) they do not account very well for observed regularities and durable, stable phenomena that span individual situations, and (2) they ignore the subjective. The first problem is partially addressed by situated action accounts that posit routines of one type or another (as discussed earlier). This brings situated action closer to activity theory in suggesting the importance of the historical continuity of artifacts and practice. It weakens true claims of "situatedness" which highlight the emergent, contingent aspects of action.

There has been a continuing aversion to incorporating the subjective in situated action models, which have held fast in downplaying consciousness, intentionality, plans, motives, and prior knowledge as critical components of human thought and behavior (Suchman 1983, 1987; Lave 1988, 1993; Suchman and Trigg 1991; Lave and Wenger 1991; Jordan and Henderson 1994). This aversion appears to spring from the felt need to continue to defend against the overly rationalistic models of traditional cognitive science (see *Cognitive Science* 17, 1993 for the continuing debate) and the desire to encourage people to look at action in situ. While these are laudable motivations, it is possible to take them too far. It is severely limiting to ignore motive and consciousness in human activity and constricting to confine analyses to observable moment-by-moment interactions. Aiming for a broader, deeper account of what people are up to as activity unfolds over time and reaching for a way to incorporate subjective accounts of why people do what they and how prior knowledge shapes the experience of a given situation is the more satisfying path in the long run. Kaptelinin (chapter 5, this volume) notes that a fundamental question dictated by an activity theory analysis of human-computer interaction is: "What are the objectives of computer use by the user and how are they related to the objectives of other people and the group/organization as a whole?" This simple question leads to a different method of study and a different kind of result from a focus on a situation defined in its moment-by-moment particulars.

METHODOLOGICAL IMPLICATIONS OF ACTIVITY THEORY

To summarize the practical methodological implications for HCI studies of what we have been discussing in this section, we see that activity theory implies:

1. *A research time frame long enough to understand users' objects*, including, where appropriate, changes in objects over time and their relation to the objects of others in the setting studied. Kuutti (this volume) observes that "activities are longer-term formations and their objects cannot be transformed into outcomes at once, but through a process consisting often of several steps or phases." Holland and Reeves (this volume) document changing objects in their study of student programmers. Engeström and Escalante (this volume) trace changes in the objects of the designers of the Postal Buddy. Christiansen (this volume) shows how actions can become objectified, again a process of change over time.
2. *Attention to broad patterns of activity* rather than narrow episodic fragments that fail to reveal the overall direction and import of an activity. The empirical studies in this book demonstrate the methods and tools useful for analyzing broad patterns of activity. Looking at smaller episodes can be useful, but not in isolation. Bødker (this volume) describes her video analysis of episodes of use of a computer artifact: "Our ethnographic fieldwork was crucial to understanding the sessions in particular with respect to contextualization."[12] Engeström and Escalante apply the same approach.
3. *The use of a varied set of data collection techniques* including interviews, observations, video, and historical materials, without undue reliance on any one method (such as video). Bødker, Christiansen, Engeström and Escalante, and Holland and Reeves (this volume) show the utility of historical data (see also McGrath 1990; Engeström 1993).
4. *A commitment to understanding things from users' points of view*, as in, for example, Holland and Reeves (this volume). Bellamy (this volume) underscores the practical need for getting the "natives'" point of view in her study of technology in the classroom.

For purposes of technology design, then, these four methodological considerations suggest a phased approach to design and evaluation. Laboratory-based experiments evaluating usability, the most commonly deployed HCI research technique at present, are a second phase in a longer process initiated by discovering the potential usefulness of technology through field research. Raeithel and Velichkovsky (this volume) describe an innovative technique of monitored communication for facilitating collaboration between designers and users. This technique sits somewhere between experimental and field methods and shows promise of providing a good way to encourage participatory design in a laboratory setting.

CONCLUSION

Activity theory seems the richest framework for studies of context in its comprehensiveness and engagement with difficult issues of consciousness, intentionality, and history. The empirical studies from all three frameworks are valuable and will undoubtedly mutually inform future work in the three areas.

Human-computer interaction studies are a long way from the ideal set out by Brooks (1991): a corpus of knowledge that identifies the properties of artifacts and situations that are most significant for design and which permits comparison over domains, generates high-level analyses, and suggests actual designs. However, with a concerted effort by researchers to apply a systematic conceptual framework encompassing the full context in which people and technology come together, much progress can be made. A creative synthesis of activity theory as a backbone for analysis, leavened by the focus on representations of distributed cognition, and the commitment to grappling with the perplexing flux of everyday activity of the situated action perspective, would seem a likely path to success.

ACKNOWLEDGMENTS

My grateful thanks to Rachel Bellamy, Lucy Berlin, Danielle Fafchamps, Vicki O'Day, and Jenny Watts for stimulating discussions of the problems of studying context. Kari Kuutti provided valuable commentary on an earlier draft of the chapter. Errors and omissions are my own.

NOTES

1. This chapter is an expanded version of the paper that appeared in *Proceedings East-West HCI Conference* (pp. 352–359), St. Petersburg, Russia. August 4–8, 1992, used with permission of the publisher.

2. I concentrate here on what Salomon (1993) calls the "radical" view of situatedness, to explore the most fundamental differences among the three perspectives.

3. Lave (1988) actually argues for the importance of institutions, but her analysis does not pay much attention to them, focusing instead on fine-grained descriptions of the particular activities of particular individuals in particular settings.

4. Weight Watchers is an organization that helps people lose weight. Dieters must weigh and measure their food to ensure that they will lose weight by carefully controlling their intake.

5. The word *goal* in everyday English usage is generally something like what activity theorists call an object in that it connotes a higher-level motive.

6. Suchman (1987) also says that plans may be "projective accounts" of action (as well as retrospective reconstructions), but it is not clear what the difference is between a conventional notion of plan and a "projective account."

7. Rhetorically, the behavioristic cast of situated action descriptions is reflected in the use of impersonal referents to name study participants when reporting discourse. For example, study participants are referred to as "Shopper" in conversational exchanges with the anthropologist in Lave (1988), or become ciphers, e.g., A, B (Suchman 1987), or initials denoting the work role of interest, such as "BP" for baggage planner (Suchman and Trigg 1991). The use of pseudonyms to suggest actual people would be more common in a typical ethnography.

8. A good overview of the use of video for "interaction analysis" in which moment-by-moment interactions are the focus of study is provided by Jordan and Henderson (1994). They posit that understanding what someone "might be thinking or intending" must rely on "*evidence* ... such as errors in verbal production or certain gestures and movements" (emphasis in original). The "evidence" is not a verbal report by the study participant; it must be something visible on the tape—an observable behavior such as a verbal mistake. Jordan and Henderson observe that intentions, motivations and so forth "can be talked about *only by reference to evidence on the tape*" (emphasis in original). The evidence, judging by all their examples, does not include the content of what someone might say on the tape but only "reactions," to use their word, actually seen on the tape.

This is indeed a radical view of research. Does it mean that all experimental and naturalistic study in which someone is said to think or intend that has heretofore been undertaken and for which there are no video records does not have any "evidence"? Does it mean that a researcher who has access only to the tapes has as good an idea of what study participants are up to as someone who has done lengthy participant-observation? The answers would appear to be yes since the "evidence" is, supposedly, encased in the tapes. In the laboratory where Jordan and Henderson work, the tapes are indeed analyzed by researchers who have not interacted personally with the study participants (Jordan and Henderson

1994). While certainly a great deal can be learned this way, it would also seem to limit the scope and richness of analysis. Much of interest happens outside the range of a video camera. The highly interpretive nature of video analysis has not been acknowledged by its supporters. The method is relatively new and in the first flush of enthusiastic embrace. Critiques will follow; they are being developed by various researchers taking a hard look at video.

Jordan and Henderson do invite study participants into the lab to view the tapes and comment on them. This seems like a very interesting and fruitful idea. However, their philosophy is to try to steer informats toward their own epistemology—that is, that what is on the video is reality—not some other subjective reality the study participants might live with. As Jordan and Henderson (1994) say, "elicitation" based on viewing tapes "has the advantage of staying much closer to the *actual events* [than conventional interviews]" (emphasis added).

9. Rogers and Ellis (1994) make this same argument but for distributed cognition. However they do not consider activity theory.

10. Many bird watchers keep "life lists" in which they write down every individual bird species they have ever seen. They may want to see all the North American birds, or all the birds of Europe, or some other group of interest to them.

11. I use the term *subjective* to mean "emanating from a subject" (in activity theory terms), not "lacking in objectivity" in the sense of detachment, especially scientific detachment (a common meaning in English).

12. While Jordan and Henderson state that participant-observation is part of their method in interaction analysis, they use participant-observation to "identify interactional 'hot spots'—sites of activity for which videotaping promises to be productive" (Jordan and Henderson 1994). Participant observation is used as a heuristic for getting at something very specific—interactions—and further, those particular interactions that will presumably be interesting on tape. In a sense, interaction analysis turns participant-observation on its head by selectively seeking events that will lend themselves to the use of a particular technology—video—rather than using video if and when a deeper understanding of some aspect of a culture is revealed in the process of getting to know the natives in their own terms, as in classic participant-observation. Note that Bødker (this volume) pairs ethnographic fieldwork with video to provide for contextualization; she thus uses ethnography to *add to* what can be seen on the tape, while Jordan and Henderson use it to *pare down* what will appear on the tape and thus what will be analyzed as "evidence."

REFERENCES

Ashby, W. R. (1956). *Introduction to Cybernetics*. London: Chapman and Hall.

Bertalanffy, L. (1968). *General System Theory*. New York: George Braziller.

Bertelsen, O. (1994). Fitts' law as a design artifact: A paradigm case of theory in software design. In *Proceedings East-West Human Computer Interaction Conference* (vol. 1, pp. 37–43). St. Petersburg, Russia, August 2–6.

Bødker, S. (1989). A human activity approach to user interfaces. *Human-Computer Interaction* 4:171–195.

Brooks, R. (1991). Comparative task analysis: An alternative direction for human-computer interaction science. In J. Carroll, ed., *Designing Interaction: Psychology at the Human Computer Interface*. Cambridge: Cambridge University Press.

Chaiklin, S., and Lave, J. (1993). *Understanding Practice: Perspectives on Activity and Context*. Cambridge: Cambridge University Press.

Clement, A. (1990). Cooperative support for computer work: A social perspective on the empowering of end users. In *Proceedings of CSCW'90* (pp. 223–236). Los Angeles, October 7–10.

Davydov, V., Zinchenko, V., and Talyzina, N. (1982). The problem of activity in the works of A. N. Leont'ev. *Soviet Psychology* 21:31–42.

Engeström, Y. (1990). Activity theory and individual and social transformation. Opening address at 2d International Congress for Research on Activity Theory, Lahti, Finland, May 21–25.

Engeström, Y. (1993). Developmental studies of work as a testbench of activity theory. In S. Chaiklin and J. Lave, *Understanding Practice: Perspectives on Activity and Context* (pp. 64–103). Cambridge: Cambridge University Press.

Fafchamps, D. (1991). Ethnographic workflow analysis. In H.-J. Bullinger, eds., *Human Aspects in Computing: Design and Use of Interactive Systems and Work with Terminals* (pp. 709–715). Amsterdam: Elsevier Science Publishers.

Flor, N., and Hutchins, E. (1991). Analyzing distributed cognition in software teams: A case study of team programming during perfective software maintenance. In J. Koenemann-Belliveau et al., eds., *Proceedings of the Fourth Annual Workshop on Empirical Studies of Programmers* (pp. 36–59). Norwood, N.J.: Ablex Publishing.

Gantt, M., and Nardi, B. (1992). Gardeners and gurus: Patterns of cooperation among CAD users. In *Proceedings CHI* '92 (pp. 107–118). Monterey, California, May 3–7.

Garfinkel, H. (1967). *Studies in Ethnomethodology*. Englewood Cliffs, NJ: Prentice-Hall.

Goodwin, C., and Goodwin, M. (1993). Seeing as situated activity: Formulating planes. In Y. Engeström and D. Middleton, eds., *Cognition and Communication at Work*. Cambridge: Cambridge University Press.

Hegel, G. (1966). *The Phenomenology of Mind*. London: George Allen & Unwin.

Hutchins, E. (1987). Metaphors for interface design. ICS Report 8703. La Jolla: University of California, San Diego.

Hutchins, E. (1990). The technology of team navigation. In J. Galegher, ed., *Intellectual Teamwork*. Hillsdale, NJ: Lawrence Erlbaum.

Hutchins, E. (1991a). How a cockpit remembers its speeds. Ms. La Jolla: University of California, Department of Cognitive Science.

Hutchins, E. (1991b). The social organization of distributed cognition. In L. Resnick, ed., *Perspectives on Socially Shared Cognition* (pp. 283–287). Washington, DC: American Psychological Association.

Hutchins, E. (1994). *Cognition in the Wild.* Cambridge, MA: MIT Press.

Kozulin, A. (1986). The concept of activity in Soviet psychology. *American Psychologist* 41(3):264–274.

Kuutti, K. (1991). Activity theory and its applications to information systems research and development. In H.-E. Nissen, ed., *Information Systems Research* (pp. 529–549). Amsterdam: Elsevier Science Publishers.

Jordan, B., and Henderson, A. (1994). Interaction analysis: Foundations and practice. IRL Technical Report. Palo Alto, IRL.

Lave, J. (1988). *Cognition in Practice.* Cambridge: Cambridge University Press.

Lave, J. (1993). The practice of learning. In S. Chaiklin and J. Lave, eds., *Understanding Practice: Perspectives on Activity and Context.* Cambridge: Cambridge University Press.

Lave, J., and Wenger, I. (1991). *Situated Learning: Legitimate Peripheral Participation.* Cambridge: Cambridge University Press.

Leont'ev, A. (1974). The problem of activity in psychology. *Soviet Psychology* 13(2):4–33.

Leont'ev, A. (1978). *Activity, Consciousness, and Personality.* Englewood Cliffs, NJ: Prentice-Hall.

Luria, A. R. (1979). *The Making of Mind: A Personal Account of Soviet Psychology.* Cambridge, MA: Harvard University Press.

McGrath, J. (1990). Time matters in groups. In J. Galeher, R. Kraut, and C. Egido, eds., *Intellectual Teamwork: Social and Technological Foundations of Cooperative Work* (pp. 23–61). Hillsdale, NJ: Lawrence Erlbaum.

Mackay, W. (1990). Patterns of sharing customizable software. In *Proceedings CSCW'90* (pp. 209–221). Los Angeles, October 7–10.

MacLean, A., Carter, K., Lovstrand, L., and Moran, T. (1990). User-tailorable systems: Pressing the issues with buttons. In *Proceedings, CHI'90* (pp. 175–182). Seattle, April 1–5.

Nardi, B. (1993). *A Small Matter of Programming: Perspectives on End User Computing.* Cambridge: MIT Press.

Nardi, B., and Miller, J. (1990). The spreadsheet interface: A basis for end user programming. In *Proceedings of Interact'90* (pp. 977–983). Cambridge, England, August 27–31.

Nardi, B., and Miller, J. (1991). Twinkling lights and nested loops: Distributed problem solving and spreadsheet development. *International Journal of Man-Machine Studies* 34:161–184.

Nardi, B., and Zarmer, C. (1993). Beyond models and metaphors: Visual formalisms in user interface design. *Journal of Visual Languages and Computing* 4:5–33.

Nardi, B., Schwarz, H., Kuchinsky, A., Leichner, R., Whittaker, S., and Sclabassi, R. (1993). Turning away from talking heads: The use of video-as-data in neurosurgery. In *Proceedings INTERCHI'93* (pp. 327–334). Amsterdam, April 24–28.

Newell, A., and Simon, H. (1972). *Human Problem Solving*. Englewood Cliffs, NJ: Prentice-Hall.

Newman, D., Griffin, P., and Cole, M. (1989). *The Construction Zone: Working for Cognitive Change in School*. Cambridge: Cambridge University Press.

Norman, D. (1988). *The Psychology of Everyday Things*. New York: Basic Books.

Norman, D. (1991). Cognitive artifacts. In J. Carroll, ed., *Designing Interaction: Psychology at the Human Computer Interface*. New York: Cambridge University Press.

Norman, D., and Hutchins, E. (1988). Computation via direct manipulation. Final Report to Office of Naval Research, Contract No. N00014-85-C-0133. La Jolla: University of California, San Diego.

Petre, M., and Green, T. R. G. (1992). Requirements of graphical notations for professional users: Electronics CAD systems as a case study. *Le Travail humain* 55:47–70.

Raeithel, A. (1991). Semiotic self-regulation and work: An activity theoretical foundation for design. In R. Floyd et al., eds., *Software Development and Reality Construction*. Berlin: Springer Verlag.

Rogers, Y., and Ellis, J. (1994). Distributed cognition: An alternative framework for analysing and explaining collaborative working. *Journal of Information Technology* 9:119–128.

Salomon, G. (1993). *Distributed Cognitions: Psychological and Educational Considerations*. Cambridge: Cambridge University Press.

Scribner, S. (1984). Studying working intelligence. In B. Rogoff and J. Lave, eds., *Everyday Cognition: Its Development in Social Context*. Cambridge, MA: Harvard University Press.

Seifert, C. and Hutchins, E. (1988). Learning from error. Education Report Number AD-A199. Washington, DC: American Society for Engineering.

Suchman, L. (1987). *Plans and Situated Actions.* Cambridge: Cambridge University Press.

Suchman, L. (1993). Response to Vera and Simon's situated action: A symbolic interpretation. *Cognitive Science* 1:71–76.

Suchman, L. (1994). Constituting shared workspaces. In Y. Engeström and D. Middleton, eds., *Cognition and Communication at Work.* Cambridge: Cambridge University Press.

Suchman, L., and Trigg, R. (1991). Understanding practice: Video as a medium for reflection and design. In J. Greenbaum and M. Kyng, eds., *Design at Work: Cooperative Design of Computer Systems.* Hillsdale, NJ: Lawrence Erlbaum.

Suchman L., and Trigg, R. (1993). Artificial intelligence as craftwork. In S. Chaiklin and J. Lave, eds., *Understanding Practice: Perspectives on Activity and Context.* Cambridge: Cambridge University Press.

Symon, G., Long, K., Ellis, J., and Hughes, S. (1993). Information sharing and communication in conducting radiological examinations. Technical report. Cardiff, UK: Psychology Department, Cardiff University.

Tikhomirov, O. (1972). The psychological consequences of computerization. In O. Tikhomirov, ed., *Man and Computer.* Moscow: Moscow University Press.

Vygotsky, L. S. (1978). *Mind in Society.* Cambridge, MA: Harvard University Press.

Wertsch, J. (ed.). (1981). *The Concept of Activity in Soviet Psychology.* Armonk, NY: M. E. Sharpe.

Wiener, N. (1948). *Cybernetics.* New York: Wiley.

Winograd, T. and Flores, F. (1986). *Understanding Computers and Cognition: A New Foundation for Design.* Norwood, NJ: Ablex.

Zhang, J. (1990). The interaction of internal and external information in a problem solving task. UCSD Technical Report 9005. La Jolla: University of California, Department of Cognitive Science.

5

Activity Theory: Implications for Human-Computer Interaction

Victor Kaptelinin

Recently interest has grown in applying activity theory, the leading theoretical approach in Russian psychology, to issues of human-computer interaction. This chapter analyzes why experts in the field are looking for an alternative to the currently dominant cognitive approach. The basic principles of activity theory are presented and their implications for human-computer interaction are discussed. The chapter concludes with an outline of the potential impact of activity theory on studies and design of computer use in real-life settings.

THE NEED FOR A THEORY OF HUMAN-COMPUTER INTERACTION

It is generally accepted that the lack of an adequate theory of human-computer interaction (HCI) is one of the most important reasons that progress in the field of HCI is relatively modest, compared with the rate of technological development. People coming to the field of HCI from different disciplines—psychology, computer science, graphics design, and others—have serious problems in coordinating and combining their efforts. For example, typical HCI curricula for undergraduate and graduate students present a mixture of knowledge from various disciplines rather than an integrated perspective.

Traditional conceptual approaches cannot provide an appropriate basis for addressing many important aspects of HCI, including computer-supported cooperative work (CSCW) and cross-cultural aspects of computer use. Consequently the impact of HCI studies on current design practice is limited, with user interface design being based mainly on intuition and expensive trial and error.

The form of a suitable HCI theory has been subjected to much debate recently (Carroll, Kellogg, and Rosson 1991). A major trend in the debate has been the growing dissatisfaction with the dominant cognitive approach (Bannon 1991; Wood 1992; Monk et al. 1993). In contrast to the general agreement that current attempts to apply cognitive psychology to HCI are not very successful, there is little agreement on the most promising theoretical alternatives. Proposals vary from an enrichment of the traditional cognitive scheme (Barnard 1991) to a radical shift in paradigms, for example, from scientific experimental studies to ethnographic methodology (see Monk et al. 1993).

In this period of theoretical uncertainty there has been a growing interest in activity theory, greatly stimulated by Bødker's works (1989, 1991). She was the first Western researcher who presented the basic ideas and potential benefits of activity theory to the HCI community. Recently, a number of papers discussing the activity theory approach to HCI have appeared in major international journals and conference proceedings (Bannon and Bødker 1991; Draper 1993; Kaptelinin 1992a; Kuutti 1992; Kuutti and Bannon 1993; Norman 1991; Raeithel 1992; Wood 1992; Nardi 1992).

The aim of the present chapter is to summarize current work in activity theory and its implications for the field of human computer-interaction. It examines the main differences between activity theory and cognitive psychology, reviews recent attempts to apply activity theory to HCI, and outlines some directions for further development.

FROM COGNITIVE PSYCHOLOGY TO CONTEXTUAL ANALYSIS OF HCI

According to cognitive psychology, the human mind is a specific type of an information processing unit. Various architectures of human cognition have been proposed, all differentiating among three basic modules or subsystems: (1) a sensory input subsystem, (2) a central information processing subsystem, and (3) a motor output subsystem. Another fundamental idea underlying most cognitive models is that of levels of processing. Essentially this is the dimension of concreteness-abstractness. Input and output represent low levels of human information processing since they deal with the "raw" data of external reality. Higher-level processing provides identification and classification of these data, as well as their assimilation into mental representations, understanding, analysis, decision making, and so forth. For a specific action to be made, abstract goals and strategies must be formulated in a concrete form. In other words, the information is processed in both directions: from reality to models and from models to reality.

The theoretical constructs of cognitive psychology have direct analogies in computer science, and the difference in terminology used in these two disciplines is minimal, which was a major factor contributing to the dominant role of cognitive psychology in HCI.

From the traditional cognitive point of view, the HCI system is composed of two information processing units, the human being and the computer, so that the output of one unit enters the other's input, and vice versa. In other words, human-computer interaction can be described as an information processing loop (figure 5.1). The advantages of this scheme are rather obvious. First, it provides a coherent description of the whole system of human-computer interaction within the information processing framework. Second, it structures the problem space of HCI in

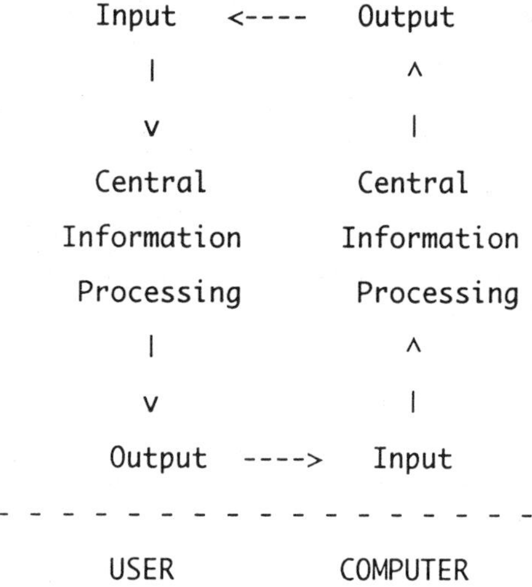

Figure 5.1
The information processing loop of human-computer interaction.

a useful way. Aspects of human-computer interaction, such as presentation of the information to the user, the user's perceptions, mental models, the user's control of the system, input devices, and user interface versus functionality of the system, can be easily located within this scheme.

The idea of levels of processing has also influenced studies of HCI. For instance, many researchers were influenced by the hierarchical structure of the human-computer interface proposed by Moran (1981). He identified five levels: the task level, the semantic level, the syntactic level, the level of interaction, and the level of physical devices. This structure is explicitly design oriented; it is supposed to support an analogy with top-down programming in user interface design.

It appears that cognitive psychology can be successfully applied to a number of HCI problems. However, this approach has some limitations. An important one is that the "ecological validity" of cognitive psychology is questionable (Neisser 1976).

The information processing loop is closed, so it is difficult to take into consideration the phenomena that exist outside it. It is obvious, however, that human-computer interaction can be understood only within a wider context. People use computers to create documents, to communicate with others, and for other purposes, but the main reason is that they seek to achieve some goals that are meaningful beyond actual computer use. Essentially, the "task level," according to the hierarchy proposed by Moran (1981), is supposed to put computer use into the right global context. Yet the relevant concepts and procedures were not articulated by Moran specifically enough, and HCI models based on his ideas (Nielsen 1986; Clarke 1986) are just models of the closed information processing loop (or a hierarchy of virtual loops).

There is an emerging consensus that the cognitive approach to HCI may be limited. It does not provide an appropriate conceptual basis for studies of computer use in its social, organizational, and cultural context, in relation to the goals, plans, and values of the user or in the context of development. In consequence, current studies of HCI that concentrate not only on the low-level events of computer use but on the higher-level events as well (Grudin 1990) require an appropriate theoretical framework in which to analyze the context of computer use.

Among the several candidate approaches, including situated action models and distributed cognition, activity theory (see Nardi, this volume, chapter 4) holds the best conceptual potential for studies of human-computer interaction.

BASIC PRINCIPLES OF ACTIVITY THEORY

The general philosophy of activity theory can be characterized as an attempt to integrate three perspectives: (1) the objective, (2) the ecological, and (3) the sociocultural. Like cognitive psychology, and unlike some other approaches in psychology, activity theory tends to be a "real," that is, a "natural sciencelike," theory. Like Piaget's (1950) and J. J. Gibson's (1979) approaches, and unlike traditional cognitive psychology, activity theory analyzes human beings in their natural environment. Moreover, activity theory takes into account cultural factors and developmental aspects of human mental life (Bødker 1991; Leont'ev 1978, 1981; Wertsch 1981).

The most fundamental principle of activity theory is that of the unity of consciousness and activity. "Consciousness" in this expression means the human mind as a whole, and "activity" means human interaction with the objective reality. This principle, therefore, states that the human mind emerges and exists as a special component of human interaction with the environment. Mind is a special "organ" that appears in the process of evolution to help organisms to survive. Thus, it can be analyzed and understood only within the context of activity.

The next principle is object-orientedness. This principle specifies the activity theory approach to the environment with which human beings are interacting. Unlike Piaget and Gibson, activity theorists consider social and cultural properties of the environment to be as objective as physical, chemical, or biological ones. These properties exist regardless of our feelings about them. "The object is a book" is no less an objective property of a thing than "the surface of the object mostly reflects the light of the red spectrum" (that is, that the object is "red").

So human beings live in an environment that is meaningful in itself. This environment consists of entities that combine all kinds of objective features, including the culturally determined ones, which, in turn, determine the way people act on these entities. The principle of object-orientedness is an obvious contrast to the assumption behind the cognitive approach that the human mind contacts reality only through low-level input-output processes.

The third basic principle of activity theory is the hierarchical structure of activity. Activity theory differentiates between processes at various levels (or, rather, groups of levels), taking into consideration the objects to which these processes are oriented. *Activities* are oriented to motives, that is, the objects that are impelling by themselves. Each motive is an object, material or ideal, that satisfies a need. *Actions* are the processes functionally subordinated to activities; they are directed at specific conscious goals. According to activity theory, the dissociation between objects that motivate human activity and the goals to which this activity is immediately directed is of fundamental significance. Actions are realized through *operations* that are determined by the actual conditions of activity.

The importance of these distinctions is determined by the ecological attitude of activity theory. In a real-life situation, it is often necessary to predict human behavior. For this purpose it is of critical importance to differentiate among motives, goals, and conditions. In particular, people behave differently in different situations of frustration. When operations are frustrated (that is, familiar conditions are changed), people often do not even notice and automatically adapt themselves to the new situation. When a goal is frustrated, it is necessary to realize what to do next and to set a new goal. This is often done without much effort and without any negative emotion. Also, it is possible to predict what the new goal will be, provided that the motive remains the same. But when a motive is frustrated, people are upset, and their behavior is most unpredictable.

In consequence, to understand and to predict the changes of people's behavior in different situations, it is necessary to take into account the status of the behavior in question: is it oriented to a motive, a goal, or actual conditions? This is why activity theory differentiates among activities, actions, and operations. The criteria for separating these processes are whether the object to which the given process is oriented is impelling in itself or is auxiliary (this criterion differentiates between activities and actions), and whether the given process is automatized (this criterion differentiates between actions and operations).

The fourth principle of activity theory, that of internalization-externalization (Vygotsky 1978), describes the mechanisms underlying the originating of mental processes. It states that mental processes are derived from external actions through the course of internalization.

The concept of internalization was also introduced by Piaget, but the meaning of this concept within activity theory is somewhat different. According to Vygotsky (1978), internalization is social by its very nature. The range of actions that can be performed by a person in cooperation with others comprises the so-called "zone of proximal development." In other words, the way human beings acquire new abilities can be characterized as "from *inter-subjective* mental actions to *intra-subjective* ones." The opposite process of internalization is externalization. Mental processes manifest themselves in external actions performed by a person, so they can be verified and corrected, if necessary.

The fifth principle is mediation. Human activity is mediated by a number of tools, both external (like a hammer or scissors) and internal (like concepts or heuristics). These tools specify their modes of operation, that is, those developed over the history of society. The use of these culture-specific tools shapes the way people act and, through the process of internalization, greatly influences the nature of mental development. Tools are thus the carriers of cultural knowledge and social experience. Tool mediation is no less an important source of socialization than formal education is.

The mechanism underlying tool mediation is the formation of "functional organs," the combination of natural human abilities with the capacities of external components—tools—to perform a new function or to perform an existing one more efficiently. For example, human eyes equipped with glasses compose a functional organ that provides better vision.

The last (but not least!) principle is the principle of development. According to activity theory, to understand a phenomenon means to know how it developed into its existing form. The principle of development gives an opportunity to conduct thorough, scientific analysis of complex phenomena while avoiding mechanistic oversimplifications.

These principles are not isolated ideas. They are closely interrelated; the nature of activity theory is manifested in this set of principles taken as an integrated whole.

ACTIVITY THEORY AND HUMAN-COMPUTER INTERACTION

According to activity theory, the computer is just another tool that mediates the interaction of human beings with their environment. The only way to come to an adequate understanding of human-computer interaction is to reconstruct the overall activity of computer use. As Kuutti (1992) argued, activity provides a "minimal meaningful context" for human-computer interaction. The questions that arise when computer use is considered from the point of view of activity theory are the following: What is the hierarchical level of human-computer interaction within the structure of activity? Does computer use correspond to the level of particular activities, to the level of actions, or to the level of operations? Which tools, other than computerized tools, are available to the user? What is the structure of social interactions surrounding computer use? What are the objectives of computer use by the user, and how are they related to the objectives of other people and the group or organization as a whole?

These questions may seem to be too global and loosely related to the practice of user interface evaluation and design. However, when these questions are ignored, undesirable consequences may follow; for example, there may be a low level of software usability (Grudin 1991a, 1991b) or software not suited to a specific culture (Borgman 1992).

Another general idea directly relevant to the field of human-computer interaction is that of development. The importance of analyzing computer use within a developmental context is relevant to both the individual level and the group or organizational level. An assimilation of new technologies causes new tasks to emerge (the so-called task-artifact cycle, according to Carroll, Kellogg, and Rosson 1991). A possible way to cope with unpredictable structural changes in a user's activity is to support users in customizing the system according to their current needs (Henderson and Kyng 1991). Yet this is not a universal solution because users often need substantial assistance even in formulating their own needs.

Thus, a conceptual analysis of the basic factors and regularities of organizational development is needed to predict this development and to provide an efficient use of information technologies.

The development of individual expertise is also an important factor that is not adequately addressed by the cognitive approach. Cognitive models of skill acquisition, based on ideas of procedural knowledge compilation or chunking, have trouble accounting for the qualitative changes that cognitive skills undergo in the process of development (Kaptelinin 1992b). Yet these very transformations can be studied and predicted from the standpoint of Bernshtein's (1967) theory, which is usually closely associated with activity theory.

The tool mediation perspective suggests a structure for human-computer interaction that is radically different from the information processing loop. The components of the structure should be not only the user and the computer but also the object the user is operating on through the computer application and the other people with whom the user is communicating (Bødker 1991).

The tool mediation perspective means that there are actually two interfaces that should be considered in any study of computer use: the human-computer interface and the computer-environment interface (figure 5.2).

Interface in the traditional sense is not only a border separating two entities but also a link that provides the integration of a computer tool into the structure of human activity. The mechanisms underlying this integration can be understood from the point of view of activity theory as the formation of a functional organ. It means therefore, that computer applications are the extensions of some precomputer human abilities. One of the most important functions of computer tools in the structure of

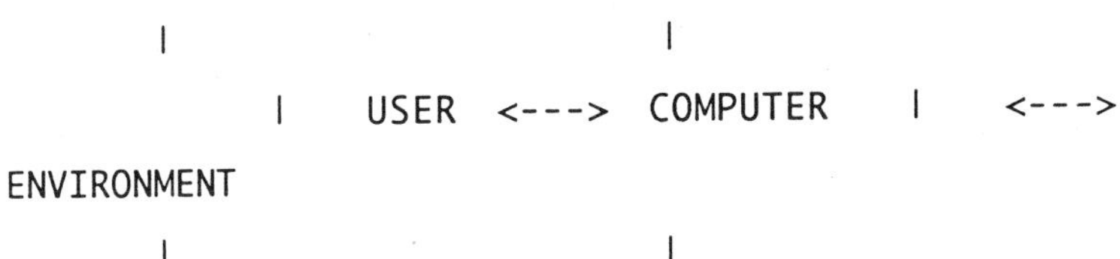

Figure 5.2
Two interfaces in human-computer interaction.

human activity seems to be the extension of the cognitive structure referred to within activity theory as the internal plane of actions (IPA). The equivalent of the IPA within the cognitive tradition is the mental space where mental models are located. Its function is to simulate potential outcomes of possible events before making actions in reality.

In sum, activity theory provides a wider theoretical basis for studies of human-computer interaction than does cognitive psychology. It can take account of social interactions and cultural factors, the developmental aspects, and higher-level goals and values. At the same time, this conceptual framework does not reject the experimental results and techniques accumulated within the cognitive tradition. According to Michael Cole, "U.S. standard cognitive psychology is a reduced subset of a cultural-historical activity approach—without realizing it" (Cole, personal communication, October 1992). Actually, if we compare the information processing loop (figure 5.1) and the tool mediation scheme (figure 5.2), we can see that the former can easily be placed in the context of the latter.

PROSPECTS FOR THE FUTURE

One fundamental difficulty related to building up a theory of human-computer interaction is the changing nature of the subject matter of the study. In contrast to physical laws, the laws of human-computer interaction are not necessarily invariant over time. When the current methods, styles, and standards are used, the results are inevitably obsolete soon after they are formulated. Activity theory puts HCI into the context of basic, invariant principles underlying human activity, so it provides a better chance for creating a theoretical framework that has a predictive potential.

Attempts to apply activity theory to the field of HCI have been made only recently. In my view, there are good reasons to expect more tangible results from activity theory in the coming years. First, I believe a new model of human-computer interaction will replace the information processing loop underlying the cognitive approach. This model will identify and present in a thorough way the most important aspects of computer use by individuals and by groups and organizations. This model will, I hope, provide various parties involved in the study and design of human-computer interaction with a framework that can make their mutual understanding and cooperation more efficient.

Activity theory can influence the methodology, analysis, and evaluation of human-computer interaction. Bødker's results (this volume) can be considered a first step toward the development of methods that provide the opportunity to organize appropriate field observations or laboratory studies and to obtain valid and reliable data relevant to real-life contexts.

Finally, activity theory can make an important impact on the development of design support tools. The design of a new interactive system involves the design of a new activity—individual or organizational. However, even the perfect design of an ideal activity does not guarantee the success of a system. The transformation of an activity from an initial to a target state can be difficult and even painful. Activity theory can be used to develop a representational framework that will help designers to capture current practice and build predictive models of activity dynamics. Such conceptual tools would enable designers to achieve appropriate design solutions, especially during the early phases of design.

ACKNOWLEDGMENTS

I would like to thank Mike Oaksford, Donald Day, and Kirsten Foot for valuable comments on an earlier draft of this chapter.

NOTE

This chapter is a revised version of a paper that appeared in *Proceedings of NATO Advanced Study Institute on Basics of Man-Machine Communication for the Design of Education Systems*, eds., M. Brouwer-Janse and T. Harrington (Amsterdam: Springer-Verlag, 1993). It is used with permission of the publisher.

REFERENCES

Bannon, L. (1991) From human factors to human actors: The role of psychology and human computer interaction studies in system design. In J. Greenbaum and

M. Kyng, eds., *Design at Work: Cooperative Design of Computer Systems*. Hillsdale, NJ: Lawrence Erlbaum.

Bannon, L., and Bødker, S. (1991). Beyond the interface: Encountering artifacts in use. In J. Carroll, ed., *Designing Interaction: Psychology at the Human-Computer Interface*. Cambridge: Cambridge University Press.

Barnard, P. (1991). Bridging between basic theories and the artifacts of human computer interaction. In J. Carroll, ed., *Designing Interaction: Psychology at the Human-Computer Interface*. Cambridge: Cambridge University Press..

Bernshtein, N. (1967). *The Co-ordination and Regulation of Movements*. Oxford: Pergamon Press.

Bødker, S. (1989). A human activity approach to user interfaces. *Human Computer Interaction* 4.

Bødker, S. (1991). *Through the Interface: A Human Activity Approach to User Interface Design*. Hillsdale, NJ: Lawrence Erlbaum.

Borgman, C. (1992). Cultural diversity in interface design. *SIGCHI Bulletin* (October).

Carroll, J., Kellogg, W., and Rosson, M. (1991). The task-artifact cycle. In J. Carroll, ed., *Designing Interaction: Psychology at the Human-Computer Interface*. Cambridge: Cambridge University Press.

Clarke, A. (1986). A three level human-computer interface model. *International Journal of Man-Machine Studies* 24.

Draper, S. (1993). Activity theory: The new direction for HCI? *International Journal of Man-Machine Studies* 37(6):812–821.

Gibson, J. J. (1979). *The Ecological Approach to Visual Perception*. Boston: Houghton Mifflin.

Grudin, J. (1990). The computer reaches out: The historical continuity of interface design. In *Proceedings of CHI'90*, Seattle, Washington.

Grudin, J. (1991a). Interactive systems: Bridging the gaps between developers and users. *Computer* (April).

Grudin, J. (1991b). Utility and usability: Research issues and development contexts. In *Proceedings of the 1st International Moscow HCI'91 Workshop*. Moscow: ICSTI.

Henderson, A., and Kyng, M. (1991). There's no place like home: Continuing design in use. In J. Greenbaum and M. Kyng, eds., *Design at Work: Cooperative Design of Computer Systems*. Hillsdale, NJ: Lawrence Erlbaum.

Kaptelinin, V. (1992a). Human computer interaction in context: The activity theory perspective. In J. Gornostaev, ed., *Proceedings of EWHCI'92 Conference*. Moscow: ICSTI.

Kaptelinin, V. (1992b). Can mental models be considered harmful? In *Proceedings of CHI'92*. Short talks and posters. Monterey, Calif.: CA: ACM.

Kuutti, K. (1992). HCI research debate and activity theory position. In J. Gornostaev (ed.), *Proceedings of the EWHCI'92 Conference*. Moscow: ICSTI.

Kuutti, K., and Bannon, L. (1993). Searching for unity among diversity. In *INTERCHI'93 Conference Proceedings*. Amsterdam: ACM.

Leont'ev, A. (1978). *Activity, Consciousness, and Personality*. Englewood Cliffs, NJ: Prentice-Hall.

Leont'ev, A. (1981). *Problems of the Development of Mind*. Moscow: Progress.

MacLean, A., Young, R., Belotti, V. and Moran, T. (1991). Questions, options, and criteria: Elements of design space analysis. *Human-Computer Interaction* 6.

Monk, A., Nardi, B., Gilbert, N., Mantei, M., and McCarthy, J. (1993). Mixing oil and water? Ethnography versus experimental psychology in the study of computer-mediated communication. In *INTERCHI'93 Conference Proceedings*. Amsterdam: ACM.

Moran, T. (1981). The command language grammar: A representation for the user interface of interactive computer systems. *International Journal of Man-Machine Studies* 15.

Nardi, B. (1992). Studying context: A comparison of activity theory, situated action models and distributed cognition. In *Proceedings East-West HCI Conference* (pp. 352–359). St. Petersburg, Russia, August 4–8.

Neisser, U. (1976). *Cognition and Reality*. San Francisco: W. H. Freeman and Company.

Nielsen, J. (1986). A virtual protocol model for computer-human interaction. *International Journal of Man-Machine Studies* 24.

Nielsen, J. (1990). International user interfaces: An exercise. *SIGCHI Bulletin* (April).

Norman, D. (1988). *The Psychology of Everyday Things*. New York: Basic Books.

Norman, D. (1991). Cognitive Artifacts. In J. Carroll ed., *Designing Interaction: Psychology at the Human-Computer Interface*. Cambridge: Cambridge University Press.

Piaget, J. (1950). *The Psychology of Intelligence*. London: Routledge.

Raeithel, A. (1992). Activity theory as a foundation for design. In C. Floyd, et al., eds., *Software Development and Reality Construction*. Berlin, Springer.

Shneiderman, B. (1992). Human values and the future of technology. *Journal of Psychology* (*Psikhologicheski Zhurnal*) 13(3). (in Russian)

Vygotsky, L. S. (1978). *Mind and Society*. Cambridge, MA: Harvard University Press.

Wertsch, J. (1981). The concept of activity in Soviet psychology: An introduction. In J. Wertsch, ed., *The Concept of Activity in Soviet Psychology*. Armonk, NY: M. E. Sharpe.

Wood, C. (1992). A cultural-cognitive approach to collaborative writing. In *Human Computer Interaction: Tasks and Organizations. ECCE 6 Conference Proceedings*. Balatonfured, Hungary: EACE.

II

Activity Theory in Practical Design

Introduction to Part II

The chapters in part II show practical ways to apply activity theory to technology design, including schematic tools for analysis that provide leverage and traction in the messy world of user data. The activity theory concepts pressed into service most often in these chapters are the levels of activity, distinguished by level of consciousness, and mediation. The use of history to understand activity is also important, especially in Bødker and Christiansen's chapters.

In chapter 6, Rachel Bellamy asks a fundamental question: why should technology change education? Drawing in particular on Vygotsky's work and the extensions to activity theory provided by Cole and Engeström (1991), she explores this question by examining educational artifacts she has participated in designing and evaluating. She highlights the need to design for the education community as a whole, not just learners, if we are to deploy technology in schools successfully. In two succinct tables, Bellamy shows how she structured her analysis using concepts from Vygotsky to provide a clear view of the design problems she faced.

Next, Susanne Bødker tackles the difficult subject of "tracing and characterizing the web of different activities that take place around a computer application." Kaptelinin (chapter 3) has already noted the confusion attending the "explosion" of our subject matter, and surely one of the most difficult problems to be faced is that any given activity is part of a larger web of activities. Bødker shows, through a careful analysis of focus shifts and breakdowns, how an individual's object or actions, or both, can move in specific situations of use. She offers tools for video analysis to track focus shifts and breakdowns as well as a "checklist for HCI analysis" to help confront the mass of real-world data resulting from a study.

Ellen Christiansen uses a traditional ethnographic approach in chapter 8, along with concepts from activity theory, to compare three instances of computer use by Danish detectives. She notes that activity theory concepts help to "overcome the analytical problem of interpreting the diversity of activities in a community of practice." Instead of relying solely on interviews and observations, as is standard in an ethnographic study, Christiansen studies activities, arguing, "You may observe and interview actors in a community of practice, but you will not come to understand why they use the artifacts the way they do until you have come to understand what kinds of activity are involved in that practice." Christiansen enriches her understandings with a consideration of the history of practice in the police units she studies. Her data nicely illustrate a key notion of activity theory, the dynamic nature of activity; in her analysis we see especially the way actions may become objectified.

Arne Raeithel and Boris Velichkovsky focus on mediating representations that facilitate the design process. Their examples in chapter 9 move from the operational to the action levels. They note that some operations are learned at a very low perceptual level (such as a double click) and may never pass through the action stage, as activity theory proposes. This has implications for technology design which they elaborate in "The Case of the Evaporated Outline." Raeithel and Velichkovsky propose a way to enable the co-construction of the task and goal structure of an activity between domain experts and designers. Using an activity theory framework, they summarize problems and methods appropriate to their solution, providing a coherent framework for researchers to consult when considering the design of a study.

In chapter 10, I reanalyze some data from a field study of slide makers, using activity theory concepts, and argue that the analysis would have proceeded more smoothly with an activity theory treatment the first time around.

After readers have finished parts I and II, it should be possible for conversations about technology design and evaluation to be articulated, at least in part, by consideration of the objects, actions, and operations of users of the technology, as well as relevant historical background of users and artifacts. The practical tools informed by activity theory presented in this part help structure the naturalistic study of technology use, avoiding an ad hoc approach.

REFERENCE

Cole, M., and Engeström, Y. (1991). A cultural-historical approach to distributed cognition. In G. Salomon, ed., *Distributed Cognition* (pp. 1–47). Cambridge: Cambridge University Press.

6

Designing Educational Technology: Computer-Mediated Change

R. K. E. Bellamy

It has been suggested that the introduction of technology into schools can be the catalyst for educational change (Papert 1980; David 1991; McClintock 1992; Dwyer 1994). McClintock argues that this relationship between technology and educational reform is evident when one takes a historical perspective on educational technology. For example, when books were rare resources, only a few people had access to the teachings written in them. With the arrival of the printing press, books became more widely available, and education also became available to a wider audience. Although these facts offer historical evidence for technology-driven educational change, they do not explicate why technology should be a catalyst for change, and if it is, what technology should be placed in schools. They do not even describe how a designer of educational technology should go about answering such a question.

This chapter describes the preliminary stages of work that seeks to answer these questions. It uses activity theory as a framework and vocabulary to understand the relationship between technology and educational change and to suggest future directions for work in education. Activity theory is an appropriate framework because it seeks to understand technological innovation as part of a general process of cultural evolution in which artifacts mediate human activity (Leont'ev 1981).

WHY TECHNOLOGY CAN LEAD TO CHANGE

Activity theory, which derives from the work of Vygotsky (1978, 1981) and was developed by Leont'ev (1981), posits that tools mediate thought. Vygotsky argued that the mind emerges through interaction with the environment. In particular, through a process of internalization of external activity, artifacts such as instruments, signs, procedures, machines, methods, laws, forms of work organization, and accepted practices affect the kinds of mental processes that develop. In turn, humans can control their own behavior by using and creating artifacts.

This process of mediation provides a basis for arguments suggesting that technology can lead to educational reform. Nevertheless, activity theory does not suggest that technology alone mediates behavior; any artifact, technological or otherwise, has the potential to change activity. In addition, the constellation of artifacts within a given activity will affect whether, and how, the introduction of a particular technology into a situation will change that situation.

Following Leont'ev, Cole and Engeström (1991) suggest that to understand an activity fully, one must understand how artifacts mediate the activity within the cultural context in which the activity is situated. Figure 6.1 illustrates Cole and Engeström's formulation of the complex relationships between elements in an activity. As in the activity analysis of Leont'ev, Cole and Engeström show that in an activity, artifacts such as tools and symbol systems mediate between the individual (the subject of the activity) and the individual's purpose (the object of the activity). In addition, they extend the analysis of activity to show that in an activity the individual is not isolated but is part of a community, and the activity

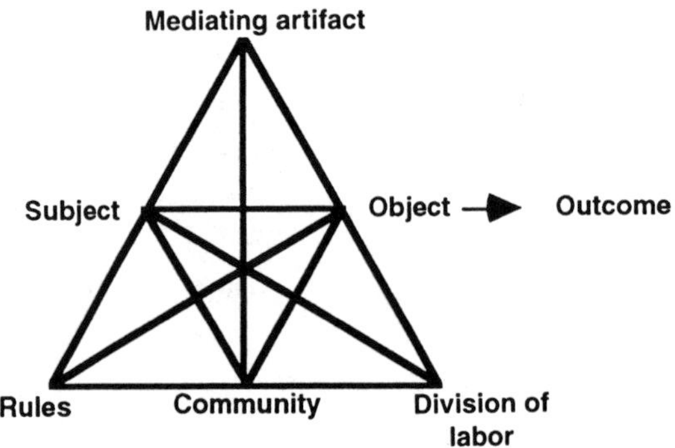

Figure 6.1
Cole and Engeström's analysis of activity and the mediating relationships among the individual, tools, or artifacts and organizations participating in the activity.

will be affected by the individual's participation within this community. Additionally, the subject's relationship to the community is mediated by rules and the community's full collection of tools. And, in turn, the community's relationship to the object of the activity is mediated by the division of labor–how the activity is distributed among the members of the community, that is, the role each individual in the community plays in the activity, the power each wields, and the tasks each is held responsible for. This last relationship occurs because in order for a community to achieve a common objective, the activities of the individuals in it must be organized, and the paths of communication coordinated, so that together they form the set of actions that will achieve the common objective.

Cole and Engeström illustrate very clearly that from the perspective of the individual participating in an activity, the individual's actions toward the object (objective) of the activity will be affected by three factors: the tools used (instruments, signs, language, etc.), the community he or she belongs to in terms of the rules of that community (the laws, accepted practices, etc.), and the division of labor in that community (the roles, communication procedures, etc.). In addition, given the bidirectional nature of mediation, the tools, rules of the community, and division of labor within the community will affect the mental processes that develop for the individual.

This discussion suggests that mediation can provide an explanation of why the introduction of new technology into education has the potential to reform the educational system. The introduction of new artifacts into an activity affects, from the perspective of the activity, the kinds of processes, social and individual, that develop. Similarly, the existing social processes of the community in which the activity takes place, and the mental processes of the individuals performing the activity, will affect how a new artifact will be used.

MEDIATION IN K–12 EDUCATION

Accepting the proposal of activity theorists that artifacts mediate human activity and accepting Cole and Engeström's extension of activity theory provides a framework within which to understand how new technologies

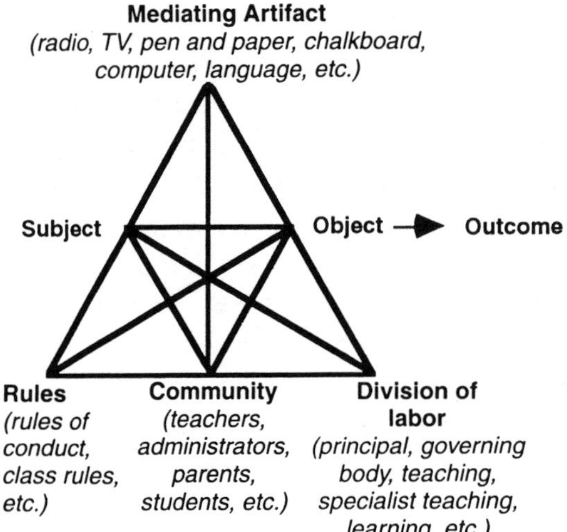

Figure 6.2
Application of Cole and Engeström's activity analysis to K–12 education.

can affect educational change. Cole and Engeström's analysis can be used as a framework for describing the activity of K–12 education (figure 6.2).[1] The activity of K–12 education involves a community consisting of teachers, parents, students, and administrators. This community lives by a set of rules, both explicit and implicit, that govern the individuals in it—for example, school rules concerning attendance, lesson times, appropriate dress, the behavior of teachers, corporal punishment, equity. The division of labor reflects the different roles individuals play within the education system: the school administrators who deal with school budget and other records, teachers in the classroom with the students, and others. It also reflects the responsibilities these individuals have toward other members of the community. The object of the education system is learning; some might say it is to educate children to be contributing members of society. This objective is mediated by multiple artifacts: books, pen and paper, and more recent technologies such as radio and television. The outcome of this activity is educated students.

Cole and Engeström's analysis suggests that when considering whether technology could be the catalyst for educational change, it is not enough to consider individual artifacts. Rather, any analysis must consider the whole complex of educational activity. The effect of a new technology on education will be as much determined by individuals' mediating their objectives through the technology as it will be determined by the existing tools and community structures.

The importance of such factors is confirmed by studies in which technology has been introduced into schools to effect educational reform. Ringstaff, Kelley, and Dwyer (1993) described four factors that influenced how much technology changed the educational process: psychological factors (teachers' being comfortable with the idea of using the technology and seeing it as an exciting opportunity rather than a threat), technical support, ease of access to technology, and collegial and institutional support. Technical support is important because if something goes wrong, teachers often do not have the time or the experience with the technology to solve the problem. Access is important because if there are not enough computers, then it is difficult to integrate them effectively into the students' activities and for the students to treat them as tools. Students waste time waiting around and get bored. Finally, collegial and institutional support are important because although individual teachers may be ready to adopt technology, obstacles are often put in place in schools where not everyone is in favor of the technology or when the administration feels that the technology is causing it to lose control.

Thus we can see, from an educational technology perspective, the importance of Cole and Engeström's introduction of community, division of labor, and rules into the analysis of an activity.

IMPLICATIONS OF ACTIVITY THEORY FOR THE DESIGN PROCESS

Activity theory can inform our thinking about the process of designing educational technology to effect educational reform. In particular, through emphasis on activity, it becomes clear that technology cannot be designed in isolation of considerations of the community, the rules, and the divisions of labor in which the technology will be placed. Multiple approaches to design have evolved that argue for taking into account the situation for which an artifact is being designed. One of these is participatory design (Ehn 1988). A second is situated action (Suchman 1987). The approach to design used for the work described in this chapter is based on the participatory design approach; the whole situation is taken into account when designing, and the end users for whom the technology is being designed are involved in the design process.

This approach to design is iterative. I seek to inform the design of technology by studying the use of initial prototypes in realistic situations. I discover what is good and bad about the prototype with respect to its initial design goals. This information is then used to inform the subsequent redesign of the technology, which itself is subjected to further study. I recognize that it is not just the technology that is important in determining its usability and usefulness. The context and participants are also important factors. Thus, my design process starts by involving researchers, teachers, students, collaborative partners, and others. Together we think about and design both the technology and the situation in which the technology will ultimately be studied.

In the designs described, this participatory design approach was used. During the technology development stage of the projects, my colleagues and I worked directly with teachers and students to confirm the validity of the design goals, iron out technical issues, and get feedback about the design. We worked with teachers to familiarize them with the technology and to give them an understanding of the technology from a learner's perspective, so that they could take ownership of the technology as learners before thinking about it from a teacher's perspective. This is usually hard for teachers to do, because they often do not have either the opportunity or the time to become familiar with technology. In addition to involving students and teachers in the design of the technology, we worked with them to develop the associated curriculum and auxiliary materials that were important to the use of the technology.

IMPLICATIONS OF ACTIVITY THEORY FOR EDUCATIONAL TECHNOLOGY

The description of activity theory offered to this point has focused on mediation as a process of cultural change. However, Vygotsky argued that mediation is a process underlying both phylogenetic development—

where culture is seen as the highest form of development—and also genetic development. Thus, more detailed examination of the concept of mediation within child development can provide a basis for the development of principles for the design of particular educational technologies.

Just as cultural evolution is a process of mediation between subject and object, Vygotsky believed that learning for individuals is mediated by the world. Human learning, he argued, proceeds from external action to internal mental activity. Children act in the world without understanding what they are doing; however, through the process of acting in the world, gradually they notice patterns in their behavior and come to understand their external activity. With this new understanding of their activity comes the internalization of that activity. Gradually children rely less on the external supports of people and objects in the world to cue their behavior as their behavior becomes directed by internal mental processes. However, because the process is one of internalization of external activity, a child's thought processes are inextricably tied to the structure of the external activity that initiated this learning. Once internalized, however, a child's thought processes can go beyond those permitted by the external activity. Vygotsky argues that this development occurs through the child's actively changing the external world to support new ways of thinking.

Activity theorists argue that human activity and the means that mediate it have arisen through social interaction. Given their belief that the same processes underlie both cultural and individual development, social interaction is also key to Vygotsky's theory of child development. One of the ways children interact with the world they do not understand is by mimicking adult activity. Similarly, adults can provide a secondary means of mediation or a social scaffold (Bruner 1960, 1975) between the child and the world. In other words, with the aid of an adult, children are often able to perform tasks that as individuals they would be incapable of. For example, a father asks his daughter where her toy is. She replies that she doesn't know. He then asks, "Is your toy in the bedroom?" to which she responds, "No." He next asks, "Is your toy in the bathroom?" to which she responds, "No." He then asks, "Is your toy in the car?" His daughter runs off and returns seconds later from the direction of the car, clutching her toy in her hand. Thus, the child has two levels of performance: the level that she can achieve alone and the level that she can achieve with the help of a more experienced individual. Vygotsky refers to this latter performance ability as the zone of proximal development.

Vygotsky's theory of human development has a number of implications for education. First, because thought is mediated by artifacts, the styles of thinking exhibited by a particular culture are based on the tools used within that culture. This suggests that if the aim of education is to provide children with the means to actively engage in the culture of which they are part, then they should have access to, and participate in, cultural activities similar to those of adults and should be using artifacts similar to those used by adults. Children cannot use the same artifacts as adults because they are at a different developmental level; however, artifacts modeled on adult artifacts and simplified in certain ways can mediate children's development of the skills necessary for use of the same artifacts and participation in the same activities as adults.

The idea of children's engaging in similar activities and using artifacts similar to those used by adults is related to the idea of authentic learning recently described in the educational literature (Lave 1991). Besides using artifacts in their culture, adults actively change culture through the invention and development of new artifacts. This suggests that children should be educated so that they can participate in this process. Education should enable children to design new artifacts and give children the experience of evolving their culture through their own designs entering the culture and being used by others. Such artifacts could take any form, but typical examples might be presentations, written documents, models, diagrams, pictures, and videos. The main point is that children should be constructing such artifacts and sharing them with their community.

Second, according to Vygotsky, thought is mediated not only by artifacts but also by social structures, conventions, and rules. This social nature of child development suggests that learning situations should feature collaboration among people with all levels of expertise, adults and children. In such a situation, those with more experience provide models of appropriate behavior and social scaffolding. This suggests, in addition, that if understanding is socially mediated, children should be engaging in discussion and debate with a community consisting of experts and fellow learners. In this situation, experts, teachers, and students all learn from one another, although the student may be the one most transformed. This is why recent educational literature stresses the need for collaborative learning.

Embedding learning within a community of people at different skill levels has recently been described in the educational literature as communities of practice (Lave 1991; Lave and Wenger 1991). In a community people at all skill levels work together to achieve the community's shared goals. Those with less skill work side by side with the experts, and over time the less skilled, through observation and directed participation, become experts. Thus, experts provide a social scaffold for novices. In such situations, beginners move from peripheral participation in an activity to central participation. On the periphery of the activity they are expected to do tasks that they may not yet have mastered, but only with the support of their more expert colleagues.

Three principles for the design of educational environments have been derived from Vygotsky's work:

- Authentic activities: Children should have access to, and participate in, similar cultural activities to those of adults and should be using age-appropriate tools and artifacts modeled on those used by adults,
- Construction: Children should be constructing artifacts and sharing them with their community,
- Collaboration: Educational environments should involve collaboration between experts and students and between individual learners and fellow learners.

Below I describe two examples of educational technology designed according to the principles derived from Vygotsky's view of child development.

EXAMPLES OF EDUCATIONAL TECHNOLOGY

Based on the theories of mediation and its basis in social interaction, I have, in collaboration with others, been engaged in the design and evaluation of educational technology that seeks to support learning in schools. In the two systems described, the process of design used was one in which the whole educational environment was designed. The technology was just one component.

Dinosaur Canyon

Dinosaur Canyon (Fenton and Bellamy 1994), designed for teaching earth sciences to middle school students, is a simulation of a canyon, a petrology and a paleontology lab. It was designed to allow students who could not study petrology and paleontology by visiting a real canyon and collecting fossils and rocks for later analysis in a real paleontology or petrology lab. Dinosaur Canyon provides a simulated context for students to engage in the activities of interpretation of rocks and fossils engaged in by expert petrologists and paleontologists. To date Dinosaur Canyon has been used in one school, for two middle school science classes, for one semester. Figure 6.3 shows typical screens from Dinosaur Canyon.

Students using Dinosaur Canyon work in small groups, each group studying a portion of a geological sequence through a canyon. They select a 10-meter by 10-meter square in their area and proceed to map features and to collect fossils and rock samples. They then take these samples to two simulated research laboratories. In the Petrology Lab, they can analyze the rocks, looking at them under a petrologic microscope, and obtain radiometric dates and trace element analyses. In the Paleontology Lab, they can view and measure fossils.

The program is highly visual and interactive. For example, at a location in the canyon, students drag hammer icons to the place they wish to sample; when the mouse is clicked, the hammer icon strikes the rock and hammering noises sound. A rock sample icon appears, which they drag to a backpack and can take to the lab. Once in the lab, which contains a bench and several instruments, the student drags the sample icon across the lab to the instrument that he or she wishes to use, and the relevant information appears. Students can store and retrieve samples and can move freely back and forth through the entire program.

Table 6.1 shows how Dinosaur Canyon relates to the three principles for educational environments and Vygotsky's theory of child development. In terms of support for authentic activities, Dinosaur Canyon was

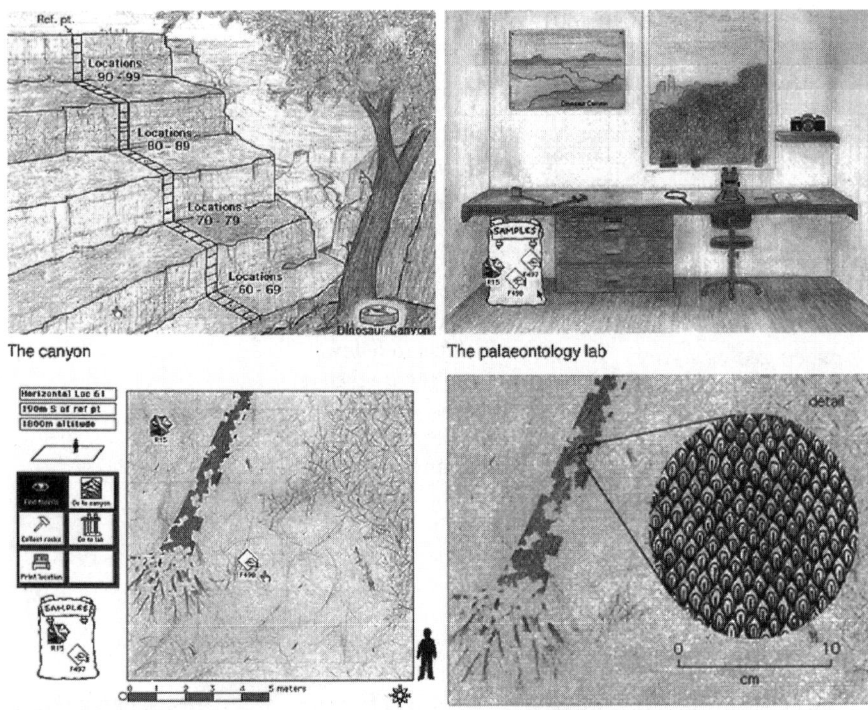

Figure 6.3
Typical screens from Dinosaur Canyon.

designed specifically to enable students to engage in the same activities of expert petrologists and paleontologists: the interpretation and analysis of rocks and fossils. To this end, during the classroom use of Dinosaur Canyon, the students were very much on their own in managing their work and finding the appropriate interpretations. To help them in their research, the students were provided with a list of references and a number of books were available in the classroom. The library staff were primed ahead of time so that they were ready to help students find additional appropriate materials.

Obviously a simulation has disadvantages in terms of providing for authentic activity; it can never be as tangible and immediate as reality or as inexhaustible a source for research. Additionally, it can contain little that is not at least partially known and understood, because its contents

Table 6.1
Dinosaur Canyon's support of Vygotsky's principles of educational technology

Collaboration	Construction	Authentic activities
Students work in small groups to study a set of locations. Groups must collaborate in order to reach a coherent interpretation of the canyon. Expert geologists are available to talk to students about their discoveries. Teachers throughout the school are designated as subject matter experts. Students become local experts.	Students must construct an interpretation of the canyon using their findings from the program and through research of the literature. Each student presents his or her findings to fellow learners and the teacher in the form of a presentation to the class and a report on any aspect of the canyon he or she chooses to study in detail.	Students engage in the same activities as expert geologists and paleontologists do.

spring from the experience of its creator. However, simulations also have some overwhelming advantages. Some of these are immediately apparent: the simulation is repeatedly, quickly, and inexpensively available to students; it is easily expandable (a brand-new laboratory or research site is available for the price of a few hours of designer and programmer time). Most vitally of all, the simulation can be designed so that its data are easily accessible to school-age children. For example, it is rare to find a fossil mammal skeleton in the field, and it is even rarer to find one that is not twisted, crushed, and missing several bones. The problems of identification, for a school-age student, would be insuperable. In a simulation, such a skeleton can be presented in an identifiable form. Similarly, few field sites contain the variety of rock types, fossils, structures, and geological problems that can be easily incorporated into a simulation. Although the canyon is a construct, it is important to note that every effort was made in the design to ensure the integrity of the geological information with respect to dates, paleoenvironments, and sequence. This integrity of information is vital if students are to feel that they are engaging in meaningful activity.

Construction is central to Dinosaur Canyon. The whole purpose of the program is to provide an environment that children explore in order to come to a coherent understanding of the history of the canyon. To help them in managing this task, students were provided with research notebooks containing templates for recording their research findings. There was also a shared schematic of the canyon placed on the classroom wall that students used to post findings and possible interpretations. These templates helped students manage their work and the process of interpreting the canyon, but they were not given any answers. The students had to construct their own answers and explanations based on all the information they had available. They were also required to write and present a report of an aspect of the canyon that they found particularly interesting.

Most students eagerly seized the opportunity to shape and carry out their own work. They were very inventive in their approaches, as in the case of one pair of students who sought to derive insights into the dinosaur footprints they had discovered by videotaping themselves running and by attempting various mathematical analyses. The conversations between such students and the teacher tended to be collegial in nature, with the students in near-total charge of their work. Students tended to take strong ownership of their work once their research became specialized, and they often wrote fine reports. Only three (of twenty-seven) students proved reluctant to propose questions or topics for research; two of these students eventually worked in a moderately independent manner, but one did not. She was eventually given a conventional book research topic, which she completed very well. All of these students had achieved well in previous units, and it may be that the degree of autonomy that Dinosaur Canyon demanded was threatening to them.

Support for collaboration is another important principle for educational environments derived from activity theory. Although collaboration is not a necessary part of interacting with the program, collaboration is a central part of Dinosaur Canyon as it is used in the classroom. Collaboration occurs on many levels: student-student, teacher-student, expert-student, and group-group, for example. When working with Dinosaur Canyon, students meet in small groups, with each group studying a set of five locations. The complete set of locations has been purposely designed to encourage between-group collaboration in that findings from any single location or even set of five locations can have a coherent interpretation, but that interpretation breaks down when those findings are seen in the context of the whole canyon. Only through understanding the particular locations in the context of the whole canyon can a coherent interpretation be reached. Thus, a coherent explanation of the canyon can be achieved only by talking to other groups and understanding their findings and interpretations.

Another example of collaboration was that between experts and students. To support this style of collaboration, we identified teachers throughout the school who had an area of expertise—physics, chemistry, or geology (the teacher of the class in which the program was used was an expert geologist)—that might be relevant to the program. Students could go to these experts with questions relevant to the expert's domain of expertise. Obviously, not all schools have teachers who are expert, and this is one of the problems faced in trying to generalize the use of Dinosaur Canyon to other schools. An additional form of student-expert collaboration occurred between students and student experts. Through the course of using Dinosaur Canyon, particular students in the class developed specialties. These students became local experts who could answer questions about their specialty.

Classroom use of Dinosaur Canyon entailed all three of the principles for an educational environment derived from activity theory. The simulated canyon allowed students to engage in authentic activities of expert paleontologists and petrologists without overwhelming the students with the complexity of an actual research situation. In this way, the simulation mediated the students' learning about how to conduct paleontologic and petrologic research. Students created an interpretation of the canyon, represented that interpretation, and presented it to their fellow students and teacher. Finally collaboration was pervasive throughout the classroom use of Dinosaur Canyon. Although the classroom use of Dinosaur Canyon did address all three principles, the principle of support for collaboration was addressed only at the level of the school and in some cases only at the level of the classroom. I have already discussed the problem of access to experts faced in generalizing the use of Dinosaur Canyon to other schools. The next example of educational technology directly addresses support for collaboration between distant locations. Such a tool could be used together with Dinosaur Canyon to link students researching Dinosaur Canyon with appropriate subject matter experts who may possibly be located at distant locations

Media Fusion

Media Fusion (Bellamy, Cooper, and Borovoy 1994), a program developed using model-based communication technology (Borovoy and Cooper 1993), allows students to construct digital video (or text) messages that can contain embedded pointers to a data analysis application. The data analysis tool is Tabletop, designed at the Technology and Research Center in Cambridge, Massachusetts. Tabletop is ideally suited for use with Media Fusion because it has been designed specifically for use by school students, with the design goal of enabling authentic inquiry with data.

Media Fusion focuses on allowing students to explore issues concerning global warming. It contains seed video and text messages created by experts on global warming and actual global warming data that the students can explore. An example screen is shown in figure 6.4. The top video message, "MacNeil/Lehrer Global Warming," contains two pointers that are positioned along its scroll bar. As the QuickTime™ digital video clip plays, the scroll box moves along the scroll bar. When the scroll box "hits" the first pointer, it launches a data analysis application, called Tabletop (Hancock, Kaput, and Goldsmith 1992), and configures a prespecified graph derived from a particular database. All of this information (the application, the file, and the various parameters that describe the scatter plot) was encoded into the pointer when the message was created.

Thus, Media Fusion seeks to support collaboration, one of the principles for the design of educational environments derived from activity theory (table 6.2). Using Media Fusion, students can create their own video messages (provided they have a video camera and a digitizing board), specify various analyses of the data (in Tabletop), and drag these analyses onto the QuickTime digital video. These pointers[2] can then be moved around or deleted. When the student is satisfied that the video

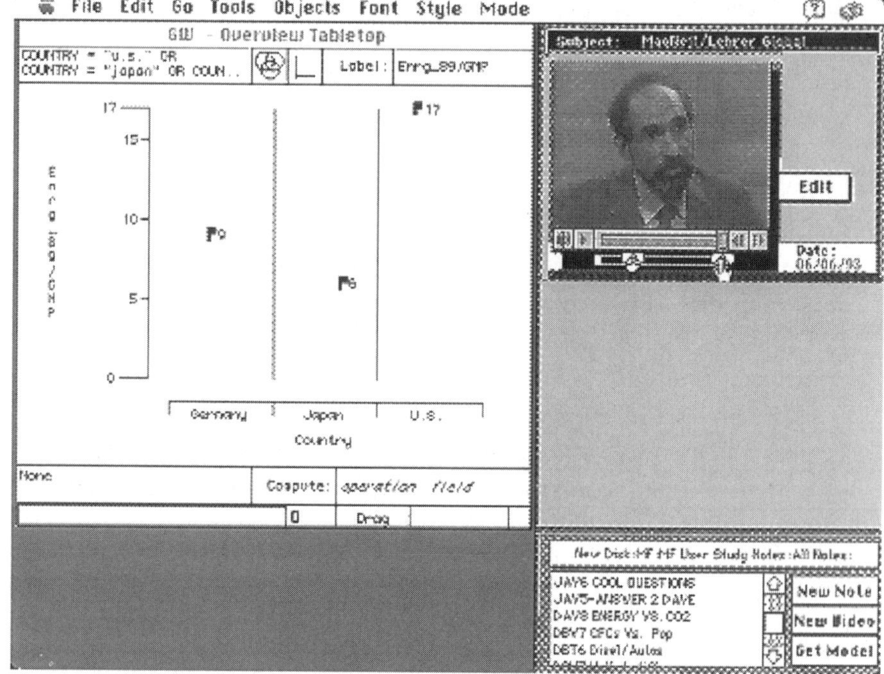

Figure 6.4
Screen from Media Fusion. The top right shows the MacNeil/Lehrer video clip. The bottom right shows a list of existing messages. On the left is the Tabletop data analysis tool.

message conveys the appropriate message, it can be saved. Later it is sent to other students at the same or other locations.

Construction is also central to the use of Media Fusion because the only way students can communicate is by constructing a message that represents their current understanding of some aspect of global warming. The technology underlying Media Fusion allows the user to create a narrative that explicates his or her path of reasoning. A single video message might have several pointers, all perhaps to the same application and the same database file, but each showing a different way of looking at the data. This might mean plotting different fields against each other, changing the scales of an axis, or simply highlighting certain data points in one view and others in subsequent views. Collectively these can be used as evidence to support the argument delivered in the message.

Table 6.2
Media Fusion's support of Vygotsky's principles of educational technology

Collaboration	Construction	Authentic activities
Students work in small groups. Students collaborate via electronic networks with students in another school across the country.	Students construct an interpretation of the domain through data analysis, sharing their analyses and discussing them with other students.	Students investigate issues that are of current importance to the world. Students use real-world data to understand current events. Students have access to the arguments presented to government and to current discussions between scientists.

The receiver of such a message can both inspect the graph embedded within a message and manipulate that graph. In this way users come to understand the data not only in terms of the graphical view constructed by the sender of the message but in their own terms. In turn, the receiver of a message can create a personal view of the data (through direct manipulation of the graph that they have received) and can embed the new view in his or her response. In this way, users can discuss issues shown in the video, use data to augment their reasoning about those issues, and share their understandings. The collection of messages developed in this manner serves as a history of the community's inquiry and understanding of the issues being discussed.

Media Fusion has been used by two schools over four days, for two hours per day. During that time, students worked at the machines in small groups of three, four, or five. The results of this preliminary study suggest that being able to collaborate with fellow learners by sending video and text messages helped the students come to a better understanding of the issues. As one student put it: "It helps you understand things better, to be able to make a graph and stuff like that and talk to people on the other side of the country about it." Much of the discussion centered around alternative interpretations of the data or discussion of whether the data supported the argument.

Having to negotiate an understanding may have been a factor in students' ability to reason about the data. In previous studies of Tabletop, it has been noted that students still held on to their own opinions even in the face of data that seemed to contradict them. This was not evident in the study. When a student stated something that was not shown in the graph, others would question the view, and the student typically would reevaluate what he or she had said.

All of the teachers emphasized the importance of the audience in motivating the students; one sad, "instead of 'let's explain this to the teacher because we have to,' it's 'we want to say something that's valid to these kids, we don't want to look really stupid, so we want to find some interesting information.'" Part of the power of collaboration appeared to be increased self-assessment of work because it was being subjected to peer assessment. Students want to say something sensible and to say it in a manner that sounds appropriate.

Media Fusion supported collaboration between students at different locations and between students in the same classroom, particularly those working together in a group around the computer. This within-group collaboration was particularly evident when students were composing messages. Students would continually discuss among themselves the issues, data, messages they had received, how the data related to different issues, and so forth as they decided what to say in a video message. The teachers noted that there was also a great deal of peer teaching within the groups. This peer tutoring helped the weaker students and more able students, who were able to learn through teaching.

Media Fusion was also designed to support expert-student collaboration. To this end, seed video and text messages linked to views of the database were created and added to the system before it was given to the students. Video messages of experts discussing global warming were created from footage taken from the "MacNeil/Lehrer News Hour." This particular video was used because the show presents authentic issues, treats them in depth, and represents each one from multiple perspectives—a format that invites response. Additional messages made by an expert in the field of study were also included.

Compared to an isolated individual learner, the community has access to a much more varied and rich pool of information, because all the members of the community can pool their knowledge and cognitive resources in order to understand an issue. In retrospect, however, the amount of knowledge available in this study was not as great as it might have been had experts been fully integrated into the learning community. In this study, the students were not able to communicate with the experts shown in the MacNeil-Lehrer video or the expert who made the seed messages.

Support for authentic activity is provided by Media Fusion in a number of ways. First, the topic chosen, global warming, is a current concern for governments and citizens throughout the world. Second, the content of the seed video and text message contained arguments about global warming made by experts. These are the same kinds of arguments being presented to governments and which are the basis for much discussion among scientists. Finally, the databases designed for use in the system consisted of actual data, making this unlike the storybook situations sometimes invented for textbooks. Here students have access to the same kinds of data used by policy analysts and policymakers.

By linking discovery tools (data analysis tools) and communication tools Media Fusion supports learning because it allows students to explore and manipulate the kinds of data that are being used to support opinions presented in messages they receive, formulate their own understanding, and express it in messages they send. Collaboration with fellow learners provides meaning to the students' inquiry and a direct way of sharing their understanding of issues, in this way influencing the development of the community's understanding of global warming. However, although communication and collaboration with other learners is important, the principles derived from activity theory also stress the need for communication and collaboration with experts at all levels. Future development and use of Media Fusion will involve not just students but also experts as part of the learning community. In this way, students will have access to experts' arguments and will be able to engage in discussion with experts.

EDUCATIONAL TECHNOLOGY AND EDUCATIONAL CHANGE?

The argument I have investigated is that technology can be a catalyst for educational change. I have described two examples of technology-based educational environment designed according to principles derived from Vygotsky's theories of child development. Our informal studies suggest that these tools do change educational activity. In the classrooms in which these tools were studied, students and teachers engaged in very different behaviors from those typically seen in a traditional classroom. For example, the teachers found themselves in the role of facilitator. One teacher in an interview following the Media Fusion study saw the role of teacher "not so much somebody who's telling the students exactly what to do and how to do it, but rather to guide them through a process." Another said, "I'm not the sole giver of information anymore. . . . I set sort of an academic playing field and kind of let them go for it." Furthermore, our informal studies suggest that these students are learning valuable lessons and important, lasting skills. However, it is not clear that these technologies will promote such changes in all educational situations.

Recognizing the importance of community in determining the mediating role of new artifacts within an activity we spend much time designing not only the technology, but the whole educational environment in which we test our technology. Following Ringstaff, Kelley, and Dwyer (1993) we pay special attention to psychological factors: teachers' being comfortable with the idea of using the technology and seeing it as an exciting opportunity rather than a threat, technical support, ease of access to technology, and collegial and institutional support. In all the studies described here, much time was spent preparing teachers and working with them to make them comfortable with the idea of using technology in their classrooms. We do not necessarily teach them to use the technology; rather, we try to make them comfortable with not always understanding how the technology works and with exploring the technology with the students. In our studies we are always present to deal with technical support issues, and we always provide sufficient technology. Finally, collegial and institutional support is an important factor. We spend much time ensuring that the school administration, parents, and support staff are comfortable with the use of technology. Thus the environment in which our user studies take place is not always representative of the situations that we are seeking to change.

Thus the question remains: Can technology be a catalyst to educational reform in schools that do not have ready solutions to issues of community support? The two examples discussed in this chapter address only a small portion of the total activity of an educational situation. These tools focus on the activity of the learner. However, teachers, administrators, parents, and others are also part of a learning situation. In order to effect change, systems of artifacts must be designed that address the needs of all the participants in the situation and help them all move toward roles and ways of thinking appropriate for an alternative approach to education.

Yocam, Wilmore, and Dwyer (1994) have been investigating how to support teachers in changing their educational practices with an approach that embodies the principles of authentic activities, construction, and collaboration described in this chapter. They have created a number of teacher development centers (TDCs) that teachers can attend. These TDCs are situated in schools that have already been infused with technology and where the classes are technology-based educational environments that model the principles of students engaging in authentic activities, construction, and collaboration. When teachers visit these centers, they are immersed in classrooms that model particular teaching practices—the practices that they want the teachers to adopt. Thus, the teachers engage in exactly those teaching activities that it is hoped they will take back and use in their own classrooms. Teachers work in collaboration with a coordinator and the teachers leading the model classroom to construct their own personal curriculum, which they can then use when they return to their own school. The intent is through this process to move teachers from their current educational approach to a new approach.

Yocam (personal communication) has discovered some problems with this approach, however, the largest being that of the community to which attending teachers belong. Teachers attending a TDC can within the environment of the TDC practice their new understanding; however, on returning to their own community, they are unable to practice their new skills because the structure, rules, and division of labor in their own school community does not readily allow for their new practices. Using the approaches described in this chapter, I am currently engaged in the design of tools and processes that seek to overcome these problems. By describing the complete situation of educational activity in detail, activity theory provides a powerful framework within which to start investigating possible tools or processes to effect pervasive educational reform.

CONCLUSIONS

This chapter started with a number of questions about how technology promotes educational change. The first question was why technology should be a catalyst for change. I have suggested that technology can promote change because, according to activity theory, artifacts mediate human activity. The second question posed was that if technology does promote change, what technology should be placed in schools. Activity theory and in particular Vygotsky's theories of child development were used to answer this question. Three principles for the design of educational environments were derived from these theories: educational technology should support collaboration between communities of learners, construction of artifacts, and authentic activities. However, I also suggest that to promote educational change, it is not enough to design technology that only supports student learning. Students are just one set of participants in the activity of education. Furthermore, it is necessary to address not just classroom activity but all aspects of the educational situation. Thus to change the underlying educational philosophy of schools, designers must design technologies that support students' learning activities and the activities of educators and educational administrators. Only by understanding and designing for the complete situation of education described in figure 6.2 will it be possible for technology to bring about pervasive educational reform.

NOTES

1. Although the arguments presented in this chapter are probably applicable throughout many Western education systems, because the particular organizational and political structures differ from country to country, I discuss education only within the United States. K–12 refers to kindergarten through twelfth grade, the complete school education system in the United States for children from the ages of three through eighteen.

2. It is important to point out that this type of embedding is significantly different from other seemingly similar types of linking. Some applications allow the user to

insert bitmap images of other applications, but these are static pictures that do not support exploration. Some applications allow the user to create a "hot link" to another file (possibly opened by another application), but these typically take the user to a fixed document (e.g., a text editor document or a HyperCard stack).

REFERENCES

Bellamy, R. K. E., Borovoy, R. and Cooper, E. B. W. (1994). Supporting collaborative learning through the use of electronic conversational props. In *Proceedings of East-West Conference on Human Computer Interaction*. St. Petersburg, Russia, August 2–6.

Borovoy R. and Cooper, E. (1993). Model-based communication. Apple patent pending.

Bruner, J. S. (1960). *The Process of Education*. Cambridge, MA: Harvard University Press.

Bruner, J. S. (1975). The ontogenesis of language. *Journal of Child Language* 2:1–19.

Cole, M., and Engeström, Y. (1991). A cultural-historical approach to distributed cognition. In G. Salomon, ed., *Distributed Cognition* (pp. 1–47). Cambridge: Cambridge University Press.

David, J. L. (1991). Partnerships for change. *Apple Classrooms of Tomorrow Report* 12.

Dwyer, D. (1994). Apple classrooms of tomorrow: What we've learned. *Educational Leadership* (April).

Ehn, P. (1988). *Work-Oriented Design of Computer Artifacts*. Stockholm: Swedish Center for Working Life.

Fenton, M., and Bellamy, R. K. E. (1994). Ecotype: A simulated geological research environment for the classroom. In *Proceedings of the International Conference on Technology in Education*. London, UK.

Hancock, C., Kaput, J. J., and Goldsmith, L. T. (1992). Authentic inquiry with data: Critical barriers to classroom implementation. *Educational Psychologist*.

Lave, J. (1991). *Cognition in Practice*. Cambridge: Cambridge University Press.

Lave, J., and Wenger, E. (1991). *Situated Learning: Legitimate Peripheral Participation*. Cambridge: Cambridge University Press.

Leont'ev, A. N. (1981). The problem of activity in psychology. In J. V. Wertsch, ed., *The Concept of Activity in Soviet Psychology*. Armonk, NY: M. E. Sharpe.

McClintock, R. (1992). *Power and Pedagogy: An Essay on Technology in Education*. Bloomington, Indiana: Phi Delta Kappa Educational Foundation.

Papert, S. (1980). *Mindstorms: Children, Computers, and Powerful Ideas*. New York: Basic Books.

Ringstaff, C., Kelley, L., and Dwyer, D. (1993). Breaking the mold of instruction with technology: Formative case studies of the unit of study process. *ACOT Report* (August).

Suchman, L. A. (1987). *Plans and Situated Action: The Problem of Human-Machine Communication*. Cambridge: Cambridge University Press.

Vygotsky, L. S. (1978). *Mind in Society: The Development of Higher Mental Processes*. Cambridge, MA: Harvard University Press.

Vygotsky, L. S. (1981). The instrumental method in psychology. In J. V. Wertsch, ed., *The Concept of Activity in Soviet Psychology*. Armonk, NY: M. E. Sharpe.

Yocam, K. Wilmore, F., and Dwyer, D. (1994). *Situated Teacher Development: ACOT's Two-Year Pilot Project*. Apple Classrooms of Tomorrow Report.

7

Applying Activity Theory to Video Analysis: How to Make Sense of Video Data in Human-Computer Interaction

Susanne Bødker

This chapter examines how activity theory can be applied to studing artifacts in use. Based on an analysis of the context of use, I outline a technique for the mapping of use situations that have been recorded on videotape and show how focus shifts and breakdowns are instrumental in analyzing human-computer interaction. The analysis uses examples from a project with the Danish National Labor Inspection, where the computer applications used by labor inspectors were studied in detail.

Activity theory helps to structure an analysis of hours of videotape without totally prescribing what to look for. An analysis of the context and history of the actions and operations prevents looking at the interaction in isolation.

In 1991, Liam Bannon and I (Bannon and Bødker 1991) discussed the potential role of a human-computer interaction (HCI) theory based on activity theory. Our focus was the limited view of the use of computer applications put forth by most cognitive science–inspired HCI research. We were further concerned with the lack of breakthrough attempts to reframe HCI research from within the field despite the growing awareness of the limitations of cognitive science. In our paper, we emphasized that a better understanding of use was important to the continuing development of methods and theories in HCI, argued that design must be based on use, and noted the importance of including on the design team those using the technology. We emphasized that activity theory seems to provide an interesting alternative framework for developing a more comprehensive unit of analysis for our studies.

More recently I have sought to develop ways of working with HCI questions based on activity theory (Bødker 1989, 1991, 1993). In various ways, this work has aimed at developing techniques for analyzing computer applications in use in empirical settings, and the analyses have gone hand in hand with various other analyses of the work settings and with design work in these settings (Bødker 1992; Bødker and Grønbæk 1991, 1993; Bødker et al. 1993; Trigg and Bødker 1994). Activity theory challenges us to make analyses on several levels, although not all at the same time. Certainly we need different approaches depending on the focus of analysis.

Engeström's (1987, 1990, 1993; Engeström, Engeström, and Saarelma 1988) approach to work development research emphasizes the development of work of specific groups of people in specific communities of practice. He shows how practice is continuously evolving and notes the role that instruments of work play in this evolution: a change of instruments changes practice, and changes in practice reshape the instruments (in use). His view—that we cannot bring the world to a standstill while we do our analysis, and neither do we leave the world around us unchanged by our analysis—is important to HCI research (see also Ehn 1988; Mogensen, 1994).

These approaches constitute the basis for this chapter, which explores various ways of doing analyses of human-computer interaction based on activity theory. The analyses will be presented and discussed through examples taken from a project with the Danish National Labor Inspection Service (Bødker 1992; Bødker et al. 1993; Markussen 1994). (A more thorough analysis of the examples may be found in Bødker 1993.)

THE GENERAL ROLE OF COMPUTER-BASED ARTIFACTS IN USE

Activity theory lets us study the relationship between the development of the individual and the society in which the person exists. Human activities are driven by certain needs where people wish to achieve a certain purpose. Activity is usually mediated by one or more instruments and is directed toward a certain object.

This mediation is essential to the ways in which we can understand artifacts, leading Kaptelinin (chapter 5, this volume) to suggest that we talk about computer-mediated activity instead of human-computer interaction. Artifacts are there for us when we are introduced to a certain activity, but they are also a product of our activity and as such are constantly changed through the activity. Artifacts thus have a double character: they are objects in the world around us that we can reflect on, and they mediate our interaction with the world, in which case they are not themselves objects of our activity in use.

Although *collective*, each activity is conducted through the *actions* of individuals, directed toward an object or another subject. Activity gives meaning to our actions, though actions have their own focus, and the same actions can appear in different activities. Each action is implemented through a series of *operations*. Each operation is connected to the concrete physical or social conditions for conducting the action and is triggered by the specific conditions present at the time. Operations allow us to act without thinking consciously about each discrete step. They are *transformed actions*, which were consciously conducted in the beginning. Through learning we transform them into operations; but on encountering changed conditions, we may have to change our focus again, and thus former operations once more become conscious actions.

Activities never take place in isolation; they are interwoven with other activities that deal with the same or connected objects, or produce the instruments used in the activity in question. In the course of a specific activity, the object change may be viewed as a change of activity or as a change in the purposeful actions or *clusters* of actions. We can analytically separate the categories of activity, action, and operation by asking why something takes place, what takes place, and how it is carried out (Bærentsen 1989). With this perspective, artifacts need to be studied in use, with a focus on their role as mediators. And even more so, since we may be dealing with artifacts as instruments of a web of activities, we are dealing with artifacts-in-use-in-a-certain-practice. Many computer applications are generic, and their use may be shaped very differently by different communities of practice (Nardi 1993).

An artifact works well in our activity if it allows us to focus our attention on the real object and badly if it does not. Breakdowns (Winograd and Flores 1986) and focus shifts are useful for studying artifacts-in-use. Breakdowns are openings for learning, and in our unhampered daily activity, we can see some breakdowns causing a focus shift by which a use situation becomes the object of our learning activity (Engeström 1987; Bisgaard et al. 1989). Learning can take place in deliberate learning actions as well, as when one actor teaches another actor about his or her work practice.

Breakdowns related to the use process occur when work is interrupted by something; perhaps the tool behaves differently than was anticipated, thus causing the triggering of inappropriate operations or not triggering any at all. In these situations the tool as such, or part of it, becomes the object of our actions. Breakdowns can occur for other reasons as well. What is important for this analysis are breakdowns somehow caused by the computer application.

A *focus shift* is a change of focus or object of the actions or activity that is more deliberate than those caused by breakdowns. For example, a focus shift can occur when a user teaches a researcher about the technology; here a focus shift occurs not because of a breakdown caused by the artifact, but because the user is trying to articulate the "otherwise unarticulated." Now the operations that she normally does become actions to her. In the following analysis, we investigate focus shifts to determine whether they are breakdowns caused by the computer application and whether breakdowns are caused by poor design.

To learn something about the present shape and use of an artifact, a historical analysis of the artifacts as well as of practice is important (Engeström 1987). That artifacts are historical devices also means that artifacts-in-use are under more or less continuous reconstruction. Replacing one generation of technology with the next is perhaps the most dramatic example of such a change, but use changes also through the influence of other artifacts and through learning—that is, through the development of and breakdowns in the actions and operations in which the computer application is used, as well as the opposite movement (Engeström 1990). In Engeström's model of work development (figure 7.1), he sees contradictions in what he calls the activity system as the major driving force of such change; he bases his analysis on *contradictions* within the activity and between the activity and surrounding activities, since they constitute the basis for learning and change. He looks at contradictions in how tools, objects, and subjects are seen and

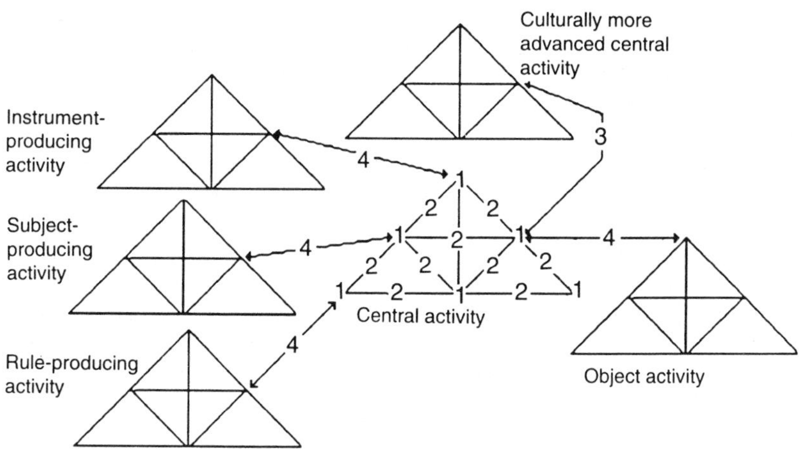

Figure 7.1
Engeström's model (Engeström's 1987, 89, from Kuutti).

suggests studying contradictions between, for example, the tools currently used and the object created, or the norms that are part of practice and the division of work, showing how such an analysis may facilitate a change-oriented perspective on work. Here we are particularly interested in changes that occur when computer-based artifacts are involved. (These contradictions are dealt with chapter 2 by Kuutti.) Looking from the point of view of the artifact, which is shaped and used in several different activities, makes it very difficult to identify and delimit the activity system that is of interest for the analysis. This would potentially include all use activities, all teaching and artifact production activities, as well as ideals for changes in the use activities. Despite this, an awareness of contradictions is an important component in our analysis.

Computer applications cause and support focuses and focus shifts through various means. If we want to know more about how this happens, we may distinguish different aspects of the computer application based on characterization of the different focuses in the use activity—for example (Bødker 1991):

- The *physical aspects*—support for operations toward the computer application as a physical object. The physical aspects are the

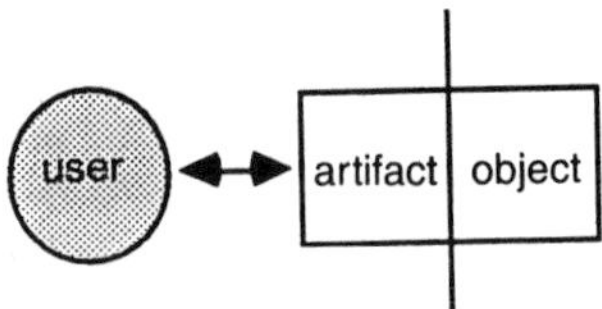

Figure 7.2
The object is present only in the artifact.

conditions for the physical handling of the artifact. The human adapts to the forms and shapes of the artifact. A maladaptation might prevent the forming of certain operations.

• The *handling aspects*—support for operations toward the computer application. A breakdown in these operations will make the user focus on the artifact. The handling aspects are the conditions for the transparency of the artifact that allow the user to focus on the "real" objects and subjects of the activity. This type of operation can be conceptualized (for instance, in breakdown situations), as the user being forced to conduct actions toward the artifact as an object.

• The *subject/object-directed aspects*—the conditions for operations directed toward objects or subjects that we deal with "in" the artifact or through the artifact. Different subject/object-directed aspects relate to different subjects or objects, but it is also part of these aspects to support the shift between subjects/objects. This means that although it is possible to talk generically about subject/object-directed aspects, in a specific analysis it will make sense to identify such aspects for each relevant subject or object.

A user may be handling an object through the computer-based artifact in different types of situations. First, the object may be present only in the artifact (figure 7.2). An example is a spreadsheet, which has no direct relation to objects outside the artifact (a printout of a spreadsheet does not have the same capabilities as the spreadsheet). Second, the object exists as a physical object too but is present in the use activity only as the representation in the computer application (figure 7.3). An example is a word processor; the object is a letter that is present only in the use activity as what can be seen and manipulated "on the screen." Finally, the object is present physically outside the artifact (figure 7.4). Exam-

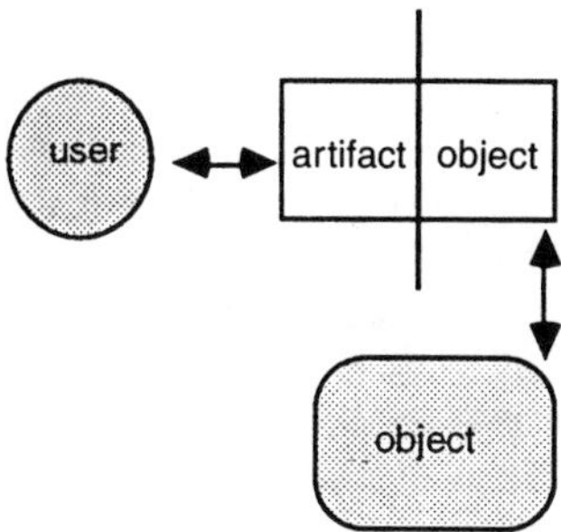

Figure 7.3
The object exists as a physical object but is only present in the use activity as the representation in the computer application.

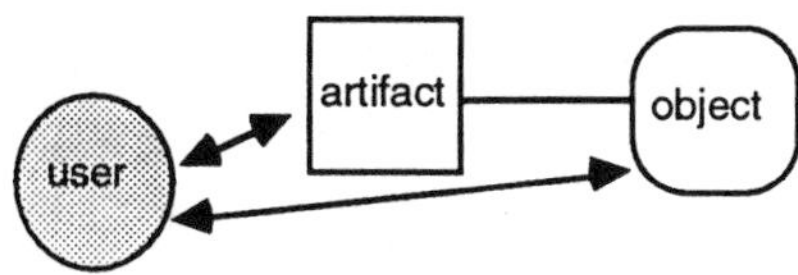

Figure 7.4
The object is physically co-present outside the artifact.

ples are different kinds of control panels; the object is handled through the artifact but is also physically accessible for inspection. The second and third situations similarly apply to relations between human beings as well.

I have used the terms *system*, *tool*, and *medium* to refer to important ways of mediating between users and their surroundings (Bødker 1993). The systems perspective is the bird's-eye control perspective, which views the human user and the computer component as functioning rather equally in exchanging data. The subject is lost in the systems perspective or removed from the level of those who are conducting actions and operations. A system mediates between the individual contributors of actions and operations and their object. At the same time the system is the instrument of the acting subject, who is not directly contributing to the production of the outcome.

The tool perspective emphasizes the human engagement with materials through the computer application. A tool mediates the relation between

	System	Tool	Medium
Why	Planning/control	Material production	Communication
What	Data entry plus extraction	Shaping material	Creating and interpreting signs
How	"Low-risk" data entry	Transparency: good access to material	Transparency: undisturbed interpretation

Figure 7.5
Characteristics of the system, tool, and media perspectives.

the subject and the material object being worked on. The tool perspective emphasizes the production of outcome and the direct learning taking place by the material "speaking back" to its user. And in a similar way, the media perspective emphasizes the human engagement with other human beings through the computer application. Thus, a medium mediates the relation between the acting subject and the community of practice surrounding the subject and the activity. It is the perspective emphasizing communication, and learning through conceptualization and negotiation. (Figure 7.5 summarizes these perspectives.)

Almost no real-life computer application can be understood in terms of only one of these perspectives. Analytically they are applied by tracing and characterizing the web of different activities that takes place around a computer application and in particular, contradictions among the different uses.

We see an artifact as supporting several interwoven activities that deal with the same or connected objects. In the course of a specific activity, various focus shifts and breakdowns occur, by which the object changes. In some cases, this change may be viewed as a change of activity; in others, the overall activity remains the same, but the purposeful actions change. Being involved with different objects and subjects through or in the artifact is partly determined by the purpose of the activity, and partly by the "intrusion" in breakdown situations. The analysis in this chapter suggests that one analyze relevant objects and subjects of the web of activities at two levels: a contextual level, where the purpose is to situate the artifact in the web of activities, and the level of analyzing and tracing the actual focus shifts in specific use situations. Certainly mapping of the contextual level objects could be useful in a general attempt to understand the relationships between work activities and artifacts, but this chapter examines the mapping of specific use situations.

The inquiry into specific focus shifts uses figure 7.6 as an illustration. The secretary initially focuses on the report to be produced. The report generator is mediating her relationship with the material—some information about companies that are put together into a report, the outcome of the work process. For some reason, she changes her focus to part of the report generator—specifying search criteria—and uses the text editor to put together search criteria. Initially she works through the report generator on the report; the focus shift to the search criteria occurs because the report generator does not handle well, that is, because of a breakdown in the handling aspects. The new focus is on an object that is totally in the computer: the mathematical formula and criteria. Further breakdowns may occur because the computer does not support the report writing very well. Here the physical aspects of the computer may play a role because the keyboard does not lend itself to typing formulas. Recovery from this situation requires getting back to a focus on the report as an object—a focus shift that is not a breakdown but nevertheless should be supported by the handling aspects.

The overall contextualization of the computer application in use takes place along several dimensions, considering development and contradictions along and between these dimensions: situating the work and computer application historically, situating the computer application in a web of activities where it is used, and characterizing the use according to system, tool, and medium.

Through the meeting with the artifact, the materials, and other aspects in use, the practice of use is shaped and reshaped, for the individual as well as the group. This process shapes the computer application-in-use, the primary interest of this analysis.

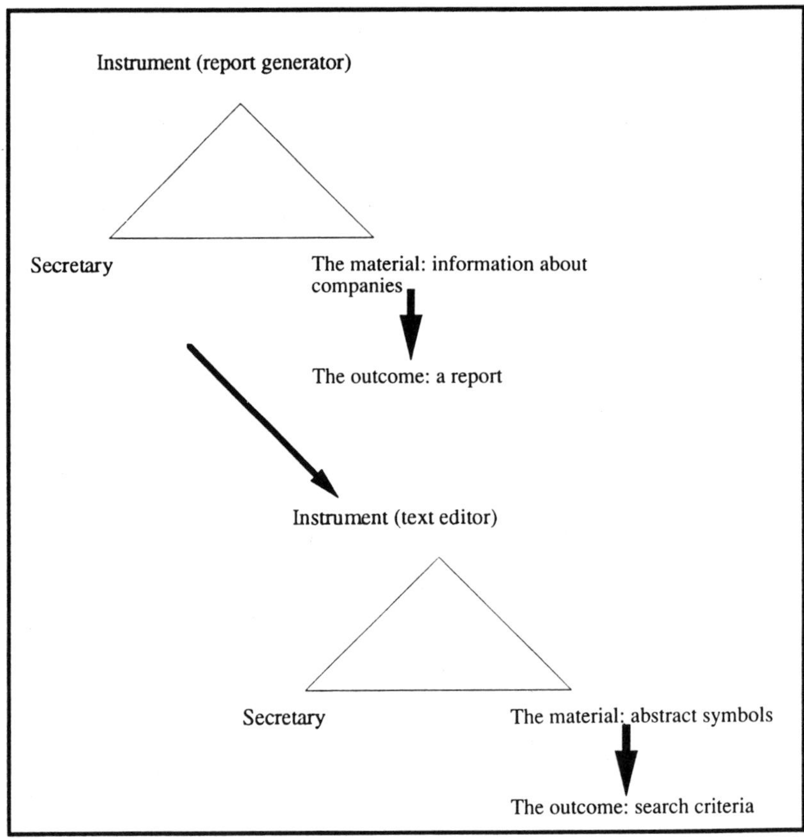

Figure 7.6
A breakdown using a report generator.

WORKING WITH HCI IN CONTEXT

The AT project and the Aarhus branch of the Danish National Labor Inspection Service (NLIS) worked together to design a number of computer applications for the branch and to develop a long-term strategy for decentralized development and maintenance.[1] At the same time, a major organizational restructuring was taking place in the branch, with new technology, new management, and new forms of work organization.

The AT project explored the potentials for reshaping the technology in use, partly through redesigning existing computer applications and uses and partly through new computer applications. In the following I shall describe some of the methodological questions applied in analyzing the use of new or existing computer technology and its relation to actual work/use activity.

NLIS uses Word Perfect/Windows, running on portable PCs, and a centralized system (VIRK) to record its interaction with companies. VIRK is a menu-based system, originally running on terminals, that connects to a central company database. VIRK runs in a window on the PCs.

Understanding VIRK in Use: The Empirical Foundation

In our initial interviews we found that employees used VIRK in many ways. Some people used the full capabilities of the system, but only a few knew what these full capabilities were. It was our impression that VIRK could provide many of the functions that people asked for, but they did not know how to access them. As part of our project, we sought to find out how we could help NLIS's secretaries and inspectors make better use of the system that they had available already. We therefore spent hours interviewing the NLIS employees, observed in their offices, presented seminars, and trained them to use VIRK. We also videotaped three activities: a session with two secretaries discussing their typical daily activities, in particular with respect to documentation and information retrieval in VIRK; a session in which a secretary demonstrated VIRK to us; and a session with a secretary who was the "super-user" (that is, used it the best) of VIRK. In total more than four hours of videotape of the use of the system were recorded.

Coming to Grips with the Analysis

An analysis of four hours of videotape is a complex matter, and activity theory is useful in identifying what to look for. The basis of the investigation was a combination of Markussen's (1994) historical account of the work practice of labor inspection with investigations of the various materials and artifacts used in this work; VIRK was situated with respect to the web of activities in which it served. We then viewed the videotape and selected interesting sequences for closer inspection (for further detail see Suchman and Trigg 1991; Trigg, Bødker, and Grønbaek 1991). Finally we mapped out interesting situations and analyzed them according to focus shifts and breakdowns.

Situating Artifacts Historically and in the Web of Activities

VIRK was created to help various groups of people, primarily managers, get an overview of the many cases and documents that came into play when the organization grew and diversified and to ensure that all incoming requests were handled according to the law. In the past, VIRK substituted a number of paper-based lists, which were kept to maintain an overview of files with material about companies and inspections. But as the organization grew, these lists had become inadequate. The files are still used, but VIRK has made retrieval easier, and some overview facilities for statistics have been added.

In order to identify the different activities in which VIRK is applied, the following questions were asked to identify the role that VIRK plays in use:

- Who are the users?
- What are the objects?
- Which are the activities in which VIRK is used (why is a certain activity taking place)?
- Can the mediation be characterized as tool, medium, or system?

We found many different use activities going on simultaneously, and VIRK has several roles in this web of activities (for detail, see Bødker 1993). It is, for example, a system of management for NLIS designed to ensure that the people who contact NLIS are answered in due time. Management at this point is not in any direct contact with VIRK. The why, what, and how map out as follows:

why (management) people get answered in due time

what (secretaries) enter registration of documents
distribute documents
follow up on deadlines

how (using VIRK) key in document data
extract inspectors' deadlines

VIRK is also a system for following up on the work of the inspectors and the whole branch office. Statistics are the important output; management uses them to control and plan work activity. Data entry is done by inspectors.

why (management) following up inspectors and branch office

what (management) statistics

how (using VIRK) (inspectors and secretaries) key in production data

VIRK is used as well when distributing cases to inspectors. Secretaries and inspectors complain that they lack access to appropriate statistics to see the work distributed to the individual inspectors and to plan work. VIRK should act as a medium with respect to this purpose, but it does not.

why distributing cases

what statistics

how (using VIRK) (mainly secretaries) look up who has case/area, how many cases, etc.

Furthermore, individual inspectors and secretaries use VIRK to handle specific cases. For this purpose VIRK is both a tool and a medium. The inspectors and secretaries would like more support in this area. In particular the kinds of information that can be written down regarding a visit or a case are very limited and in most cases quantitative.

why (inspector) handle case

what (inspector) "takes the travel card," makes notes, looks for correspondence, etc.

how (using VIRK) browse for relevant data, use search facilities

Finally, secretaries use VIRK every time a document is registered in the system (tool).

why (secretary) register document

what (secretary) register document

how (using VIRK) key in data using the correspondence form

This analysis brings into focus that VIRK is designed as a planning and control system, and it works rather well: Management gets what it wants, with respect to both the delegation of cases and monitoring the activity of individual inspectors and branch offices. Data entry works rather well too. But when inspectors and secretaries try to use VIRK to work on individual cases, both when registering information about the case and when retrieving information to get an overview of a case, VIRK is less helpful.

Inspectors are much more than bureaucrats, and they do not conceive of themselves as easily controlled. Their work is not easily planned; accidents happen, and what they have to do at a certain visit is not easily predicted. Furthermore the work is not easily reported on and measured. Thus, management seeks to make labor inspection more predictable and better planned. Secretaries and inspectors seek to coordinate cases, derive overviews of their own cases, and register more informal and qualitative data about the cases.

The historical development of the work of labor inspection is characterized by at least three generations of labor inspection activity. Until the mid-1970s, the inspection of the physical work environment in factories was carried out by engineers, each responsible for selecting and inspecting factories. Under new law in 1975, inspection was expanded to cover nonfactory work, the work environment, and the organization of work; now therapists and psychologists were employed for this work, and prevention of stress and injury became a topic. The late 1980s saw further decentralization, a client orientation, quality assurance, accounting "upward," and more structured activities. Only the oldest one of these is actually supported by VIRK, though VIRK was designed rather late in this historical development (Bødker 1993).

Now we see that many of Engeström's contradictions come into play. A primary contradiction concerns VIRK, the instrument: on the one hand, what is needed is an efficient means of registration and accounting, but on the other hand, what is needed is a means for cooperation and coordination of the effort. An important secondary contradiction (primarily seen from the activity of actual labor inspection) is between VIRK, the instrument for upward accounting, and the inspector as a skilled professional who is concerned primarily with the work environment in the inspected companies. The analysis has pointed to and made use of these contradictions, though not in a systematic way in this presentation.

Generally the objects that one can work on, in, or through VIRK have to do with recording the state of the overall activity. Descriptions and lists of documents, lists of cases, deadlines, and various statistics are the objects *in* VIRK. The contents of the cases—the objects dealt with by inspectors and secretaries when handling a case—are almost absent in the system. There are also some objects of normal daily activity present in VIRK, including travel cards that the inspectors take and various lists and overviews, and we shall focus on them next. They are hard to retrieve in VIRK because they can be reached only through the programming of a report generator. (See figure 7.7 for an overview of VIRK.)

Summary: A Checklist for Situation of Computer Applications in Use

The following analyses were carried out in the first part of the project.

- Situating work and computer application historically.
- Situating the computer application in a web of activities where it is used.
- Characterizing the use according to systems, tools, and media.
- Considering the support needed for the various activities going on around the computer application and the historical circumstances of the computer application.
- Identifying the objects worked on, in, or through the computer application.
- Considering Engeström's four kinds of contradictions with respect to activities for which the computer is used.

These analyses were not done in lockstep fashion. Rather, they took place in interaction and iteration.

MAPPING THE SITUATION

We combined ethnography and interaction analysis in working with the video analysis (Suchman and Trigg 1991). The ethnographic fieldwork was especially crucial to our understanding of the sessions particularly with respect to contextualization. Interaction analysis, as described by Suchman and Trigg (1991), involves the "detailed investigation of the interaction of people with each other and with the material environment. . . .

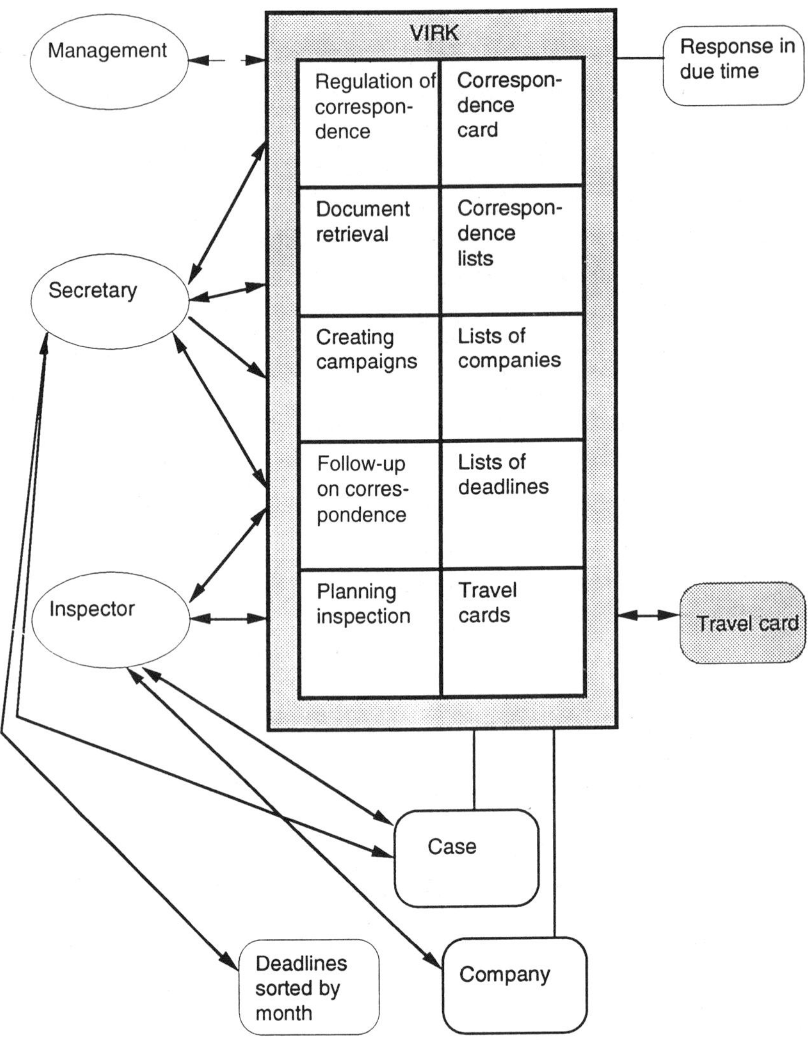

Figure 7.7
An overview of VIRK, its users, and the objects surrounding it. The syntax is introduced in figures 7.2 through 7.4.

In work settings..., [the] analyses focus on the joint definition and accomplishment of the work at hand, through the organization of interaction and the use of supporting technologies and artifacts" (Suchman and Trigg 1991).

I will not claim, however, that this study is a representative instance of interaction analysis. Rather, the goal was to apply certain practical techniques from interaction analysis to work better with situated human-computer interaction. For example, an event log of the video record provided a description and chronological index of observed events. The analysis then proceeded with an identification and careful transcription of sequences of activity of particular interest. Partly in opposition to Suchman and Trigg, I suggest the use of the theoretical concepts of focus shifts and breakdown as focus points in gathering collections of instances.

From the four hours of videotape, we selected four interesting situations of a few minutes' length for detailed analysis, and then mapped out the action. The mapping consisted of listing in one dimension the objects that the user focused on during the session and in the other the narrative of the situation, supplemented with annotations of the user's physical acting. The focus shifts appear as lines running from one "set of coordinates" to another. The objects can be categorized according to whether they have to do with the objects worked on (the subject/object directed-aspects) or what should have been the handling of the artifact. Furthermore, the focus shifts can be categorized along the same lines. Are they breakdowns caused by the work content, the handling of the artifact, or physical problems with the artifact? In the following example in figure 7.8 we can see what this means and where the analysis might take us.

What makes an interesting situation? It may be that one does not understand it, or that it remains intriguing or surprising even after many times of viewing. Situations in which users appear to be fundamentally uncertain, or certain but then a moment later uncertain, have been intriguing. These situations tell something about when the user feels in charge of or masters the use situation and when she does not. It is interesting to see when everyday routine situations turn into nonroutine ones and which everyday situations are nonroutine ones, and in the end to see what role VIRK has in this.

Understanding breakdowns and focus shifts in VIRK

Document	Screen image	Report generator	Field	Report	Dialog
	(1) •				A: I am going to enter the **next screen.** There it comes ...where we can make this...
					S: There are some elevator programs there
			(3) •	(2) •	A: **This is something** we have made. **This is what I want** sorted by registration number, this and that...
	(5) •	(4) •			..let me show you **how we do that.** That is a second search. Every time I need it I must go back. You have to enter a **subscreen**.
				(6) •	S: Then it is much more **about how to compare**
(9) •		(7) •	(8) •		A: [typing search criteria] Look here, what the hell! Here it is. No, **that is not it;** I am not, I don't have any good material about this. It needs **some more looking around**
					S: That is how it often goes.
			(10) •	(11) •	A: And then I need, and **then an x,** then it should work. **There it is,** that's how it looks.

Figure 7.8
Generating a report.
The · indicates the object focused on; boldface type is used to indicate a focus shift. Numbers in parentheses index the objects focused on for reference in the discussion. A is the secretary, S the interviewer.

The focus is initially on the screen image (1), but as soon as A makes her choice, she is working on the report (2). The handling aspects of the artifact support this focus as well as the focus shift. We have reason to assume that her focus was only on the screen image in the first place, because she was explaining VIRK to the researchers. She needs to specify which fields she wants. She has her focus on this; it is not done as an operation (3). This could be because she is explaining, but the way she talks to herself indicates that she is uncertain; she is conscious of the field because of a real breakdown. Dealing with the fields through operations is not possible; it is a matter for the subject/object-directed aspects.

At the end of the session we see more breakdowns with respect to the handling aspects (6–9); she is rapidly moving between focuses on the report, the report generator, the field (in particular, how criteria for this field are specified), and the written documentation and examples that she has available about the program. It is the handling of the search criteria that causes trouble: VIRK gives her no help in specifying syntax or contents. At the end, she finds some help in some examples, which allows her to focus back on the search criteria for the field, and over again at the report, and how the result looks on the screen. In other words, the handling aspects of VIRK cause the various breakdowns encountered here, and it does not give any help for shifting (10–11) the focus back to the real object of work.

In the example we see how the focus shifts back and forth and how only the objects "field" and "report" (figure 7.9) have to do with contents or purpose of the activity. When the secretary is trying to generate the report, the application is in no way transparent to her, which is seen by the breakdowns with respect to the handling aspects—the times when "screen image" and "report generator" (5 and 7) come into focus. Here A is concentrating hard on doing the task because it is so difficult; the latter part of the example is a series of breakdowns with respect to the artifact. There is very little attention left for her to explain to us what she is actually doing.

Extending Maps to Windows

As part of our research and design process, we applied the mapping technique to some sessions where pairs of inspectors were using Word-

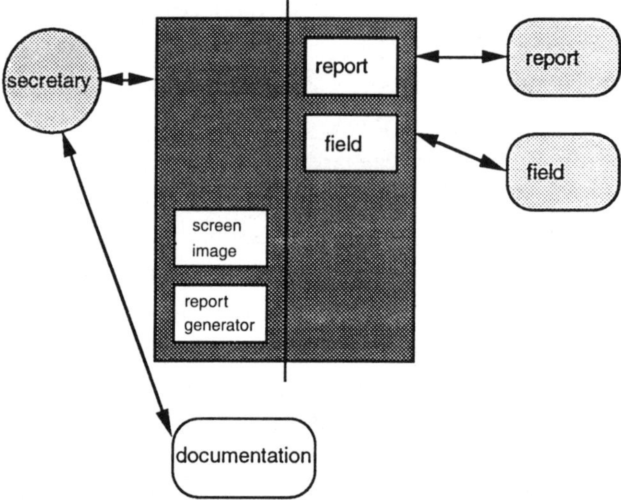

Figure 7.9
The objects and focuses involved in report generation. The syntax is described in figures 7.2 through 7.4.

Perfect to solve some exercises set up by the researchers. The mapping technique had to be modified to encompass the larger complexity of the screen images and the increased numbers of objects on the screen (anything from scroll bars and menu items to words in the documents) and the physical actions when using the program (dragging, pointing, etc.). Since we were dealing with several users in interaction, there was the possibility we would see that their focuses were different at times. Such differences may be important indicators of situations to examine more closely.

The exercises were meant to explore the "corners" of the inspectors' understanding of WordPerfect. In the example that follows, the inspectors were asked to number the pages in a document, excluding the first page and giving the second page number 1. In the following analysis, two inspectors have just looked at Help, where they are asked to put the cursor where the page number is to be placed. After placing the cursor at the top left corner of the page (the first possible character position in the document), they move on to the menu form to add the page numbers (figures 7.10 and 7.11).

This example illustrates that WordPerfect has an underspecified interpretation of what it means to place the cursor where one wants the page

Screen Action	Narrative	Page	Cursor	Scroll-bar	"Slots" on page
1	M: now let's place the cursor	•			
M tries to place cursor in the bottom right corner, but selects the whole line	Y: Oh, there it is (.......) where the hell did it go??		•		
M presses the space bar	M: We'll just move it				
Y points at the scroll bar	Y: Why don't you use that			Y: •	
	(mumble)		M: •		
	Y: Can't we move it with the other one?				
(M has meanwhile "spaced" his way to the bottom right corner)					
	M: No there is a NewLine up there, that's why - Let's just put it there.				•
M moves the cursor to the top left	(talks about the top line on the page)				

Figure 7.10
Using the **page numbering** form to insert page number. The • indicates the object focused on.

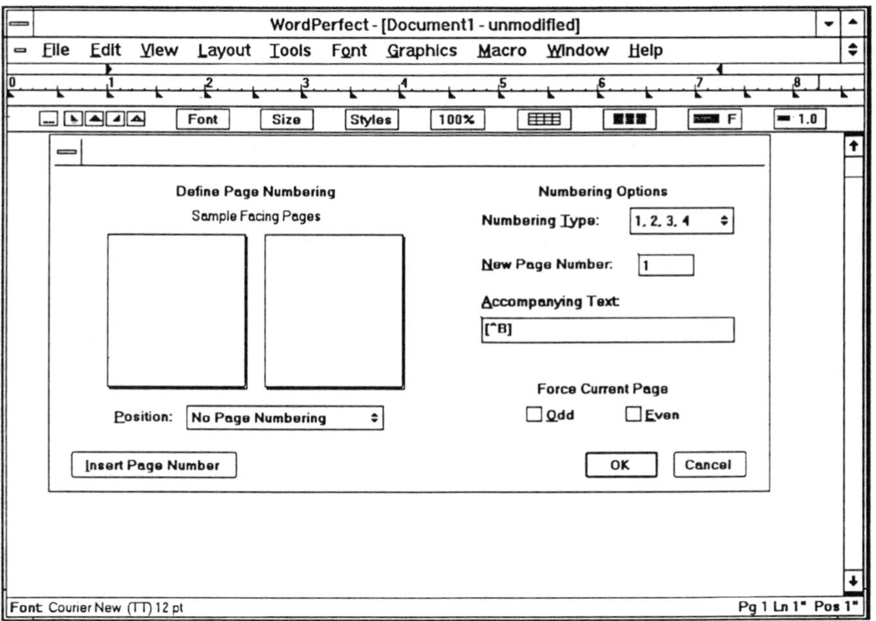

Figure 7.11
Screen.

number. If the user is using the **Insert Page Number** button, the number is placed at the location of the cursor. If the user is using the rest of the form to place the number in either corner of the paper, it matters only what page one works on.

Looking at the focus shifts in this example, we see that the two inspectors are exploring the menu form (figure 7.11); they are in a breakdown situation with respect to the use of WordPerfect for adding page numbers. From the rest of the exercise (not transcribed here), it became clear that they had never used this form before, yet they knew what to look for and how to explore the menus.

The form menu includes an example of how the page looks given the selection of page numbering. This example consists initially of two blank rectangles. After the selection in **Insert Page Number**, a number pops up in the bottom right corner of each rectangle, but the inspectors do not notice that; they do not get the intended feedback because they are so busy figuring out what else they need to do to finish the form. Obviously it is also not clear to them that **Insert Page Number** is an alternative way out of the menu to pressing OK/Cancel buttons (OK activates the page numbering done through the rest of the form). It is worth noticing, though, that **Insert Page Number** actually activates both kinds of page numbering; thus one gets dual page numbers. Though all breakdowns mentioned here have to do with the handling of the artifacts, they are not equally severe. The menu form is actually meant to be looked at, to explain itself in a breakdown situation, and it does not presume a frequent and everyday use. Though attempting to give a window onto the actual object of the work, the pages with numbers, it fails to do so, because of the confusion over the two alternative ways of numbering pages. This confusion could be avoided.

Summary: A Checklist for HCI Analysis through Focus Shifts and Breakdowns

For each specific focus, ask:

- What is the purpose of the activity/actions for the user?
- Which object is focused on by the user? Where is this object located (in, through, or outside the computer application)?

- What is the instrument? Where is it located (in, through, or outside the computer application)?

When two or more users are cooperating, ask:

- Are the purposes, objects, and instruments in accordance or conflicting (between the individuals, as well between the group and individuals)?

For each focus shift, ask:

- From what focus/object to what?
- Is it a breakdown or a deliberate shift?
- What causes the shift: the physical, handling, or subject/object-directed aspects of the computer application?

The mapping technique described above is one way of putting together an overview of the answers to these questions.

THE RESHAPING OF COMPUTER APPLICATIONS IN USE: PUTTING THE ANALYSIS INTO WORK

My perspective on HCI analyses suggests that we must always be concerned with understanding computer applications in use. Although we change the world while we investigate it, the purpose of doing the analysis is to understand how to change computer applications in use. We will look briefly at how the work analysis was situated in the technical and organizational change processes at NLIS.

Although VIRK was developed rather late in the historical development of work at NLIS, it was not designed to reflect this development (Bødker 1993). In many ways VIRK works to support a traditional quantitative perspective, coupled to management planning and control. The more qualitative perspective underlying the work of contemporary labor inspection is not supported with respect to information and activities regarding a company or with respect to how the work of the inspectors is viewed. These lacks are typically related to individual and group case handling, an area that was not given much attention historically or with respect to the design of the system. The needs and wishes of secretaries and inspectors go in the direction of integration, case coordination, case overviews, and registering more informal and qualitative data on the cases. There seems to be no easy way to extend VIRK to fill these needs even though the data are available in the database.

Based on the examples, though, we can identify various venues for change in VIRK-in-use: First, the labor inspectors who participated in our project found that the analysis constituted an important input to a major redesign of VIRK. Second, the analysis was important in our attempt to educate VIRK users. It pointed to areas where it was possible to do more with VIRK if the users were trained, and it pointed to the real obstacles built into VIRK. Third, it was easy to suggest some improvements in the interface to VIRK that could be implemented through integration of VIRK with WP/Windows. Some of these have happened, though with some difficulty (Trigg and Bødker, 1994).

Regarding WordPerfect, both the placement of the example in the form menu and the double functionality of the menu are inconsistent with how menus work otherwise in WordPerfect, causing confusion among the inspectors. For those inspectors who use the facility regularly, better teaching is a possibility. For less frequent users, training probably would not be worthwhile. This is an important indication that when it comes to complicated applications such as WordPerfect, education must be ongoing, inspectors must regularly be reminded of the available facilities, and they must concentrate on the facilities that they find useful. NLIS has chosen to offer frequent WordPerfect courses to users to help them brush-up and expand their use of the program.

The reshaping of computer applications such as VIRK and WordPerfect is a continuous process that may be influenced in various ways based on analysis of the computer application-in-use. Fundamental redesign of computer applications, customization, and training are among the possibilities that should be considered in interaction with the analysis.

A SECOND LOOK AT ASPECTS OF THE USER INTERFACE

The studies at NLIS show that there are different kinds of handling aspects. For example, the page number prompt is directed toward a rather natural breakdown situation: since many users do not do specific page numbering often, it is natural for them to stop and read the prompt.

(Whether this prompt disrupts the fluent conduct of a frequent user is a different matter and is not examined here. The phenomenon is discussed more generally in Bødker 1991.) The prompt should help the user get back to normal conduct, working on the now-numbered page instead of falling prey to more breakdowns. Thus, it is unfortunate that the user cannot identify the two alternative ways of ending the endeavor and that the view of the page with the numbers does not attract the attention of the user. The same is true for the report generator of VIRK. Thus it is possible to distinguish ordinary "everyday fluent conduct" from more exotic breakdowns; handling aspects must be designed to support these in different ways. For example, a prompt used when saving a document is encountered frequently by most users and will disrupt work if not easily dispatched. A prompt for advanced page numbering can count on attention from a larger user community, though not as frequently, and thus it must be designed for this aspect. These conclusions are not very different from those I made in 1991 (Bødker, 1991): "Although the physical and handling aspects should not call for actions from the user, it is also important that they support the user if a breakdown occurs. How this is done relates directly to the competence and education of the user, but it is important that *error situations be handled within the domain of use practice*. It is important that *the user be able to retract or undo* her operations, if this is important in the handling of the objects or subjects. Proper facilities can prevent breakdowns toward the artifact."

VIRK users have problems using the report generator, because what one does to specify a report is so unlike the actual report. This brings us to the realm of *subject/object-directed aspects*, though at the same time we are dealing with some very fundamental handling aspects, namely, the specification and selection of fields. There are some strong dependencies between the three aspects, and one should not be designed without the other; for example, it does not do the user much good to provide nice handling features for specifying fields if she does not understand what a report is.

Focus shifts, coupled with the three aspects of the user interface, or computer application-in-use, have been useful in spotting various kinds of problematic situations in the human use of a computer application. Furthermore, the examples pointed to the strong design dependencies among these aspects. These aspects help us to identify how to remedy problematic situations, among them training, better help facilities, and more prompts.

CONCLUSIONS

Activity theory allow us to be instrumental without being reductionist in our studies of human-computer interaction. It helps structure analysis without totally prescribing what to look for. It also means that we are constantly reminded in our analysis of the context and history of the actions and operations that we are looking at, thus preventing us from viewing the interaction in isolation.

Breakdowns and focus shifts provide good pointers for understanding how an application mediates (or does not mediate) work activity. They are useful in identifying problems of mediation and in designing an application as well as understanding it when it is brought into use.

ACKNOWLEDGMENTS

Soudabeh Goudarzi and Pia Lund provided the material for the WordPerfect study. I worked with Randy Trigg, Ellen Christiansen, and Liam Bannon on specific aspects of the research described in this chapter. I thank the AT project secretaries and inspectors for putting up with us, and showing an interest in our research; and the AT project group, which provided important pieces of the work presented here. Ellen Christiansen, Olav Bertelsen, Jakob Bardram, Erik Futtrup, Michael Thomsen, and Bonnie Nardi provided useful comments on drafts of this chapter.

NOTES

1. The project was conducted by Susanne Bødker, Ellen Christiansen, Pelle Ehn, Randi Markussen, Preben Mogensen, and Randy Trigg. For a description see (Bødker et al. 1993).

REFERENCES

Bærentsen, K. (1989). Mennesker og maskiner [People and machines]. In M. Hedegaard et al., eds., *Et Virksomt Liv* (An active life) (pp. 142–187). Aarhus: Aarhus Universitets Forlag.

Bannon, L., and S. Bødker (1991). Beyond the interface: Encountering artifacts. In J. Carroll, ed., *Designing Interaction: Psychology at the Human Computer Interface* (pp. 227–253). New York: Cambridge University Press.

Bisgaard, O., Mogensen, M., Nørby, M., and Thomsen, P. (1989). Systemudvikling som lærevirksomhed, konflikter som basis for organisationel udvikling (DAIMI IR-88). Åarhus: Aarhus University.

Bødker, S. (1989). A human activity approach to user interfaces, *Human Computer Interaction* 4(3).

Bødker, S. (1991). *Through the Interface—A Human Activity Approach to User Interface Design*. Hillsdale, NJ: Lawrence Erlbaum.

Bødker, S. (1992). *Technology as a Vehicle for Organizational Learning and Change*. First Socio-Cultural Research Conference, Madrid (DAIMI PB-425).

Bødker, S. (1993). Historical analysis and conflicting perspectives—contextualizing HCI. In L. Bass, J. Gornostaev, and C. Unger, *Proceedings of EWHCI '93* (vol. 1, pp. 132–142).

Bødker, S., Christiansen, E., Ehn, P., Markussen, R., Mogensen, P., and Trigg, R. (1993). *The AT project*. DAIMI PB-454. Aarhus: Aarhus University.

Bødker, S., and Grønbæk, K. (1991). Cooperative prototyping: Users and designers in mutual activity. *International Journal of Man-Machine Studies* 34 (Special Issue on CSCW).

Bødker, S., and K. Grønbæk (1993). Users and designers in mutual activity—an analysis of cooperative activities in systems design. In Y. Engeström and D. Middleton, eds., *Cognition and Communication at Work. Cambridge:* Cambridge University Press.

Ehn, P. (1988). *Work-Oriented Design of Computer Artifacts*. Falköping: Arbetslivscentrum/Almqvist and Wiksell International. Hillsdale, NJ: Lawrence Erlbaum.

Engeström, Y. (1987). *Learning by Expanding*. Helsinki: Orienta-Konsultit, 1987.

Engeström, Y. (1990). *Learning, Working and Imagining: Twelve Studies in Activity Theory*. Helsinki: Orienta-Konsultit.

Engeström, Y. (1993). *Interactive Expertise*. Helsinki: University of Helsinki.

Engeström, Y., Engeström, R., and Saarelma, O. (1988). Computerized medical records, production pressure and compartmentalization in the work activity of health center physicians. In *Proceedings of Conference on CSCW, Portland, Oregon, September* (pp. 65–84). New York: ACM.

Markussen, R. (1994). A historical perspective on work practices and technology. In P. Bøgh, B. Andersen, B. Holmqvist, and J. Jensen, eds., *The Computer as a Medium*. Cambridge: Cambridge University Press.

Mogensen, P. (1994). Cooperative analysis. Ph.D. thesis, University of Aarhus.

Mogensen, P., and Trigg, R. (1992). Artifacts as triggers for participatory analysis. In S. Kuhn, M. Muller, and M. Meskill, eds., *Proceedings from the PDC'92*. Cambridge, MA.

Nardi, B. (1993). *A Small Matter of Programming: Perspectives on End User Computing*. Cambridge, MA: MIT Press.

Suchman, L., and R. Trigg (1991). Understanding practice: Video as a medium for reflection and design. In J. Greenbaum and M. Kyng, eds. *Design at Work: Cooperative Design of Computer Systems* (pp. 65–90). Hillsdale, NJ. Lawrence Erlbaum.

Trigg, R., and Bødker, S. (1994). *From implementation to design: Tailoring and the emergence of systematization*. In *Proceedings CSCW '94*. Chapel Hill, NC.

Trigg, R., Bødker, S., and Grønbæk, K. (1991). Open-ended interaction in cooperative prototyping: A video-based analysis. *Scandinavian Journal of Information Systems* 3:63–86.

Winograd, T., and Flores C. (1986). *Understanding Computers and Cognition: A New Foundation for Design*. Norwood, NJ: Ablex.

8

Tamed by a Rose: Computers as Tools in Human Activity

Ellen Christiansen

> *It is the time you have wasted on your rose that makes it so precious*
> —The fox to the little prince

Saint-Exupéry in *The Little Prince* lets the fox explain to the prince what makes his rose so special to him: the rose has tamed him! The prince has cultivated and nursed and talked to the rose. He has cared for it and taken it to his heart. These efforts have caused him to fall in love.

That is exactly, I will claim, what any designer hopes for when delivering an artifact: that those who are going to use it will care for it, nurse, and cultivate it.

Today, when it comes to computer artifacts,[1] it is like the roses in the garden the prince enters on earth: there are so many, looking almost the same, that the designer must ask: "What could make *my* artifact-design precious to anyone?"

Or maybe I am wrong. Maybe it is not at all on the designer's mind whether his rose is taming anyone. But those who are going to use it, then? They are living out there in the workplaces where bunches of roses are bought and planted, and they are told to live with these flowers/computer artifacts because it will make life easier and better. So the managers say. And the artifacts are there, offering themselves to use, to be nursed and taken care of.

But how do we come to care for a computer artifact? In this chapter I am going to use the term *tool* to designate a computer artifact that has tamed someone so that she has come to care. *Tool* as a term for an artifact of this faculty to me covers functional as well as aesthetic and ethical dimensions of quality.

Of course, an artifact cannot have feelings. It is the relationship between artifact and user that creates a feeling inside the user, which in turn is projected to the artifact. The tool relationship becomes a kind of filter through which the user experiences the artifact. This conceptualization of tool matches the conceptualization of activity as Leont'ev has defined it:

> The activity is a molar, not additive, unit in the bodily, material life of a subject. In a narrower sense, which is at the psychological level, the activity is a unit in life, communicated by psychological reflection, the fundamental function of which is to orient the subject in the objective world. The activity is, in other words, not a reaction and not a collection of reactions, but a system with a structure, with inner transitions and transformations and a development of its own. (Leont'ev 1983, 86, my translation).

And Leont'ev stresses as most important that "the very conditions given by society carry the motives and goals for the activity together with its tools and methods" (Leont'ev 1983, 87, my translation).

In a way the activity as culture offers itself to the actor as a possibility but does not become real before the actor actively establishes a relationship between herself and her practice. Understood in this way, the term *activity* addresses the relationship between the actor and her objectified motive. The activity is the way the subjects see the practice. And they do not see it in a private way: "In all its richness the activity of the human individual forms a system embedded in the system of societal relationships. Outside these relationships there is no such thing as a human activity" (Leont'ev 1983, 86–87, my translation).

Tasks in a practice present themselves to the subject as something given by society (or the boss or someone else) as an entry into the activity system, provided they match a need felt by the subject because "only within the human activity system are the objects able to exist as incentive, goal or tool; outside this system they lose their existence as incentive, goal or tool" (Leont'ev 1983, 114, my translation).

From an analytical point of view it is quite complicated to handle this. Engeström (1987) has suggested a triangular structure: subject-mediating artifacts-object extended in different ways to incorporate the societal dimensions, a conceptualization I understand as a theoretical tool for thinking. For the purpose of analyzing a specific practice in order to understand behavior, I find it more suitable, however, to take *activity* as the term for the process through which a person creates meaning in her practice, a process we can neither see or fully recall but a process that is ongoing as part of the participation in a community of practice. Activity is a process that we can approach by unfolding the task as stated[2] within the community of practice and the objectified motive of the activity as stated by the actor, through historical inquiry, observation, and interviews.

Since an axiom of activity theory is that the activity (the relationship between subject and objectified motive) is always mediated and since the major concern of this chapter is to understand tools as artifacts integrated into and interpreted within an activity, the other (other than unfolding activities in a practice) part of an empirical investigation will be an attempt to understand the artifacts as mediators of different actors' activity. The assumption here is that an artifact attains its qualities of function, aesthetics, and ethics as it is integrated into an actual activity; only in actual practice does it become a tool. In other words, to become a tool is to become part of someone's activity.

You may observe and interview actors in a community of practice, but you will not come to understand why they use the artifacts the way they do until you have come to understand what kinds of activity are involved in their practice. This is the strong claim of activity theory, the usefulness of which for understanding human-computer interaction I seek to demonstrate in this chapter.

Methodologically, Vygotsky (1978) and Scribner (1985) have argued that the ideal data for an application of activity theory consist of longitudinal ethnographic observation, interviews, and discussion in real-life settings, supplemented by experiments (see also Engeström 1990 and Bødker, this volume). Compared to these requirements, the data presented here are less than ideal since I have spent days instead of weeks or months observing, interviewing, and collecting information about the historical development of the organization. However, for the sake of the argument that conceptualizing practice in activity theoretical terms provides the designer—often on a woefully tight schedule—with useful insight, it may well suffice.

The theory of activity as both culturally given and socially formed by the individual in a community of practice and the role of tool mediation are not easy to grasp and handle in empirical research. First, the activity is not immediately accessible consciously, so you cannot interview people about their activity directly through rote questions but must interpret their actions and opinions after some careful reflection. Second, the doublesidedness of creating, and at the same time being created by, a cultural frame makes analysis difficult.

To overcome the problem of getting relevant data for interpretation, I have, when reading documents, observing, and interviewing, focused on aspects of quality related to the performance of actions as well as to the outcome. Questions about good and bad, right or wrong, what makes one feel comfortable and in control, have been my way in.

To overcome the analytical problem of interpreting the diversity of activities in a community of practice I have worked with the idea of an activity typology based on the data from observation and interviews. The typology serves as a tool when interpreting the data and may also help to identify potential conflicts in views among actors.

To overcome the problem of identifying which artifacts are tools in which activities, I have used the typology, asking what kind of artifact would mediate which activity, and then I have analyzed the data I have on current use of a current artifact by using this frame.

To unfold the activities and tools as culturally given by tracing their history, I have interviewed and observed users of the artifacts in their current practice, and from that I try to establish an argument—hypothetically, of course—about what are the activities and why, or why not, artifacts are integrated as mediating tools in the settings observed. This specific study I try to generalize so as to formulate a hypothesis about what seem to be key factors for an artifact to move into an activity as a tool. This effort can be seen as an attempt to explore the argument of Kaptelinin (chapter 3, this volume) that activity theory provides a useful guideline for evaluating human-computer interaction in a field setting.

The data presented stem from a field study of a department of the Danish National Police called the Flying Squad. I investigated human-computer interaction within three investigation teams from various sections (homicide, theft, fraud) between May 1990 and January 1991.

TRACES OF ACTIVITIES AND TOOLS

The Flying Squad has existed as a unit within the National Police force since 1927. It numbers around 100 detectives[3] divided into five sections (homicide, fraud, theft, drugs, and environment). The Flying Squad works all over the country in cases that require more expertise than exists within the local police force. Since homicide is the major category of crime dealt with by the Squad, and the one that gets the most public attention, the Homicide Section is the largest in the squad and the one that every squad man has to work in during his apprenticeship. On the whole, the squad man's education is long and comprehensive. A typical curriculum starts with ordinary training as a police officer, partly at the police school, then two years of duty within the uniformed police, and then, on special recommendation or request, recruitment to the Flying Squad, where he will be an apprentice for years before he can call himself an all-around squad man. All the men I saw working were experienced and used to reflecting upon their current practice.

Objects and Objectified Motives

A way in to understand police investigation is to investigate the social organization of the paperwork, to see how documents as social constructions are part of the working division of labor (Hughes and King 1992) and the ongoing structure (Giddens 1984) of the work. In police investigation the paperwork is organized by cases.

A case begins with a notice, information about a situation that somebody suspects to be illegal. Based on the notice information, a case is framed in terms of category of potential crime, the form of investigation to be applied, and the amount and quality of skills required and available. Next, an investigation team is formed; it takes an overview of the existing information, chooses an initial investigation strategy, and devises an information system in terms of a list of headings under which the incoming information will be cataloged. Later, when the investigation is on track, the headings may be rearranged, indexes of various kinds may be created, and lists of effects made. When the case is closed, usually because the puzzle is solved and it is to be handed over to the court, a summary of the investigation is written, telling the reader what steps were taken to illuminate the initial suspicion given in the notice and what was found, with attached evidence.

The investigation may be divided into subtasks, a division reflected in the categories in which the case material is indexed and in the division of labor (formation of subteams and sequencing of tasks). In a larger case, say a homicide investigation, the investigation team would be divided into two-person subgroups, with team A investigating the notice, team B the technical evidence, team C the medical evidence, team D the victim, team E the interrogation in the area, team F the special items, and team G the suspects. The evidence collected and described in reports, as well as the archiving and the final summary, will follow and reflect this order. Because this order (with some variation) is essentially the same from case to case, it forms the backbone of the investigator's knowledge about how to carry out an investigation. The case material and narrative scheme form a structure through which every event (finding, interrogation, verification) is reflected. When a police officer interrogates a witness or a suspect, the questioning is always in terms of actors, time, location, ways, and means: who was present, where, at what time, and what did he or she do to whom by which means? When the investigator writes up a report he organizes his information according to this structure.

Taken as paperwork, the object of police investigation could be seen as the report material piling up until the final summary is presented in court. From society's point of view, however, represented, say, by Parliament and government, the outcome of police investigation may be justice, preservation of private property, or crime prevention. For the person on the street, it may be apprehending criminals, thereby creating a feeling of security. Since neither the minister of justice nor the person on the street participates in detective work, such conceptualization has only the quality of contributing to building the activity as a cultural frame, offering itself to the police officers entering the profession.

The police detectives working in the field take—depending on personal history and capacity—something from this cultural frame and something from the local culture within the team they are working with. They merge this with their personal experience, and from all this their activity/objectified motive emerges. They may not be very explicit about it, but it is reflected in their professional attitude, their priorities, and their choice of tools.

In my study, I found three major types of objectified motives: that of solving a puzzle, that of catching a criminal, and that of keeping track of all the documentation so as to reinvestigate it systematically and thoroughly. Most of the detectives I talked to related to all three but would give priority to one, and in fact it works quite well for a team to have each priority represented as a first priority for someone on the team. There are intellectual detectives and those who see themselves as hunters, and since investigation can be seen as a matter of clever hunting, this is a good mix. Because the overall development in the jurisdiction means that the amount of information to account for is often astronomic, the problems of keeping track of information for some detectives become an objectified motive in itself, a "paperwork" objectification of the motive that can be useful for a team. I have also met police detectives who apply the societal view on police investigation, typically among those in charge of management, but in general I found no significant difference with respect to location in the vertical hierarchy. And of course there are a variety of individual priorities, aggressive as well as therapeutic, and the priorities will vary over time and cases.

Since police investigation is not the only activity in which detectives engage and since physical conditioning is important for most of them, I asked additionally about engagement in sports and found indication of correspondence between those engaged in soccer and those expressing hunting as objectified motive, but the sample was too small to give more than a hint for further investigation. Besides the interplay with other activities, the formation of the objectified motive by an investigator will in general depend on the person's level of expertise (a freshman does not see the object of a case in as wide a perspective as does an expert, and when they are working together a third interpretation may emerge); the political and power relations within the team, in the headquarters, or in Parliament; the division of labor within the team and the section; the specific conditions of the actual case; and the objectification due to personal preferences.

You might expect the perpetrator to play the role as an object at some level. However, as far as I have observed, few detectives from a team ever get in personal contact with the suspects, and the role of the perpetrator or suspect is marginal.

Artifacts and Tools

When asking the squad men about their tools, they mentioned the telephone, their car, and the typewriter, and no doubt these artifacts are an integrated part of the police investigation. My hypothesis was that those expressing themselves as "the hunting type" would also express strong feelings for their car, while those in favor of solving a puzzle would tend to emphasize the equipment for technical investigations, and those focusing on the paperwork would be fascinated by new information systems. My sample is too small for drawing conclusions, but I definitely found support for this idea.

My observations of the squad men's work revealed also what I would call artifacts for thinking, which the detectives themselves referred to only as, "Well, that's just the right way to do it": schemes for categorizing the steps in an investigation, the narrative scheme for reporting an event, or the form to fill in when making descriptions of persons or cars, for example.

The relatively high degree of formalization of work procedures is partly inherited from the investigation tradition in general and partly adopted as part of the squad men's professional tool kit because of the specific history of the squad. Since the head police officer is situated in Copenhagen while the men are "flying" around the country, explications of how to do the job developed quite early, together with the habit of ongoing reflection upon the state of the case and successes and failures. And since in Denmark there has been a strong animosity against any kind of state police in general, and not least among local police authorities, the legitimacy and reputation of the squad rely on this ongoing "quality assurance" in terms of well-documented casework, brought about by discipline, by sticking to the schemes.

The primary reason that I consider the formalization of work procedures to be tools, despite the fact that they were not mentioned as tools by any of the investigators themselves, was the role they play in formal and informal discussions about right and wrong, good and bad moves in an investigation. I found that the schemes and forms created order in the information, provided a professional language of categories in which to discuss the case, and, when planning next steps, were reminders of what was still missing. Hence, they fulfill Ehn's (1988) requirement specification for a tool: it should serve the double purpose of "doing something for you and reminding you of something you can do." And the forms and schemes were very much part of the argument when people were justifying current action, be it a paperworker, puzzle solver, or even a hunter, which gave me the impression that the schemes and forms were imbued with ethical value as well.

When I visited the three sites where attempts had been made to use computers "as new tools in the investigation" (those were the words of the head and assistant head of the squad) I brought with me the hypothesis that a computer artifact, in order to turn into a tool, should match Ehn's requirements. When I realized the diversity as to how the artifacts fitted into the community of practice of my informants, even though none of them were novices in learning new technical devices and all of them were expert detectives, I understood that there was more to it, and this "more" I so far have come to understand as the diversity of activities and the corresponding diversity in which artifacts become tools and how that happens.

THE CASES

The homicide section was the first one in the squad to implement computer support for case handling and had started a year before my investigation. At the time of my investigation, a team from the theft section, assigned to a special mission, had computer support too, and a team of fraud investigators had as an initiative of their own asked for computer support and had procured some spare (and outdated) equipment. I observed, interviewed, and discussed with these three teams their use of computers, supplemented by rounds of interviews with the head and assistant head of the squad and inquiries into the written history of the squad and of police work in general.

Case 1: Computer Use in Homicide Investigation

The team consisted of seven squad members from the homicide section and seven local police detectives investigating a murder in a provincial town with about 70,000 inhabitants. The team was located at the local police station, Criminal Investigation Division, occupying the conference room (meetings, social gathering and office for the head and his partner, and two terminals), the registration unit next door (staff, files, and two terminals), and some of the offices down the corridor (a local detective sharing with a squad man). The coffee machine was in the corridor outside the conference room. In the conference room one terminal was put up for the detectives to search information and one for the head of the investigation.

The outcome materialized in many reports, physical items, and lists, located either in the registration unit or in the conference room. Summaries were made daily.

The main source of getting an overview of the case was the morning briefing, which everybody had to attend. It was chaired by the head, who opened by asking each subteam (A for the notice, B for technical evidence, C for medical, etc.) if it had something of general interest to report. If so, the information would be commented on and discussed before moving on to the next team. After this round, the head would give a summary of what was known so far and the most urgent steps to take. He would eventually praise or criticize, and mention messages from headquarters, or make announcements, such as that the team would be taken out to dinner.

When the briefing was over, the men would leave for their telephones, cars, and desks and not see each other again before the afternoon coffee break, which most of them attended before finishing off the day's reports. The summary given by the head would be based on report material given to him in typewritten form the previous evening, his attendance at talks at the coffee machine and during breaks, his cross-examinations of the material already in the database, and his previous experience put up against the hypotheses formed thus far.

My general impression was that case management was working smoothly, proceeding unquestioned by the head of the team. When asked about his management principles, the head of the team said without hesitation: "Being in control before the sun is down." By this he meant that he was to know what was known by the entire team and to know for sure that what was known was documented correctly.

Everybody would agree that documentation is crucial. A team has only as much on the case as can be documented, that is, written down, physically located, or proved by documented tests. The rest, no matter how fancy a hypothesis it may lead to, contributes nothing to the case. Therefore, almost everything is written down. Within a few days, a team like this produces about a thousand written reports. To make this material available puts heavy demands on the registration and retrieval system.

As in most other homicide cases, a special registration unit was formed, here consisting of a squad detective and two clerks from the National Police registration. They used the newly created computer-based information system as their prime artifact. Because it was only the fourth case in which the system was used, the designer was present most of the time, giving advice, doing a little tailoring, and nursing the use of "his" system.

The computerized information system in the homicide section had been developed in quite a large software development environment, a product called BRS.[4] The designer had twenty years of experience as a squad man, and already as an apprentice, he told me, a chief in command had said that he seemed to be talented with computers. To introduce computer support into the squad became a vital part of his professional ambition. After several attempts to get permission, he talked the head of the National Police into investing in BRS, and he sat down and learned the development environment inside out. Based on his personal experience as a squad man within the homicide section, he alone formulated the specifications and did the programming and tailoring.

When I asked about user—in this case, peer—involvement, he said: "I would not start the development process with another. Now I could do it, because now I can manage the program, but at that time, when I did not, it was of no use that they would ask me to teach a guy something I was not able to do myself. It would not do. At some point [the other guy] would get annoyed because I was not good at it."

The squad man was capable of learning on his own, because—in my interpretation—developing a computer tool matched with his conception of the investigation activity. He felt that his primary competence was on the systematic side and found a way to develop this capability. He deliberately chose the computer as a tool for enhancement of his competence, trying to make the professional investigation depend more heavily on systematic and computational skills. He expressed as a vision for his design that it should be strong enough to handle a "Palme case," referring to the largest homicide investigation known in Scandinavia, when the Swedish prime minister Oluf Palme was shot down on a street in Stockholm in 1986! The squad man saw information handling as the major challenge in police investigation. For him to unfold the potential in the use of a computer for this purpose satisfied his ultimate need of information control. The artifact was designed to handle all information in a case of homicide investigation from the notice to the final report to court.

The time I saw the system running, it was set up with four terminals running via a modem on a mainframe at the National Police computing center. The information retrieval was designed to support an overview, to provide specific information, and to ease the burden of summarizing the information when closing the case. It offered information about persons, vehicles, and other items and events. The user could get an overview by pushing a button called the "Little Inspector," a function key programmed with a specific automatic query procedure to produce a "state of the state" of the case in terms of what was known about circumstances of the crime: where was the victim, with whom, and so forth. The system also could produce an overview via several query procedures available through function keys and—for those familiar with SQL—it offered access to all the information in the database.

Before the age of the computer-based information system, the overview, as well as the overall responsibility for case management, were in the hands and head of the head of the team. Now everyone could in principle—by pressing the Little Inspector—share the head's level of information. He was, however, still the one to define the state of the case and to decide what to do next. The actual investigation—the interrogation, the collecting of evidence, the arrest—was performed by the subteams. The documentation, the paperwork, was done by the teams and the registration unit. The head himself did not feel a strong need for the computer system; he had no computer competence and did not intend to acquire much, since he felt on top of the investigation activity, including team management. He used only two or three query formats and did not plan to learn SQL, perhaps because his position in the hierarchy prevented him from engaging in peer interaction in order to learn. But in one respect the head found that he could benefit from using the computer in what to him was a real burden: relationships with the press. He got the designer to create a specific "press view" with facts he could get out on the screen the moment there was a journalist on the telephone.

When I observed the interaction with and around the computer in the conference room and interviewed and listened to conversations, I noticed some reluctance and uncertainty among the detectives who were frequent users. Although the computer clearly offered them benefits in terms of making overviews and saved time in making queries and in the final report writing, they seemed to prefer the old ways. They complained that the introduction of the computer application had put further constraints on the report format, for instance, a demand for a front-page summary, which they felt as a severe burden although acknowledging its potential usefulness (an excellent example of what Grudin 1988 describes as some —here the designer and the registration unit—having the benefit, while others—the detectives—do the additional work).

But there were differences among the detectives; I observed a tendency for teams B and C (technical and medical evidence) to be more enthusiastic than teams D and E (interrogation about the victim and in the area). And when I interviewed teams B and C, they expressed more of the "solving puzzle–approach," while the team D and E people talked more like "hunters."

The registration unit learned to use the system in detail. The detective used the system for the fourth case and was quite happy about it, primarily because it eased his burden of summing up in the end and because specific and time-consuming queries now could be handled within minutes. The clerks were using the artifact for the first time, but after a fortnight they felt able to suggest corrections and expansions. They got good support from the designer and the detective, they used the system all day long, and they became skilled in its use.

Using the computer put certain demands on the formulations. The clerks had to go and talk to the detectives to clear up misunderstandings. They began to catch errors because they now had an overview. They were consulted about how to make queries. This increased their social interaction and their self-confidence; they were surprised at how much they got out of the use of the system compared to the effort they had put into learning it. By virtue of having the cumbersome paperwork done, their work changed to that of expert information handling. Their competence as information handlers and computer users from the National Police Registration helped them to this transformation.

In my final interview with the designer, we talked about the introduction of new users to the artifact. The introduction was very brief each time the system was set up for a new case, but he was planning, he said, given some "peace time" (that is, time without cases with heavy time constraints and press coverage), to give a more systematic introduction to all members of the homicide section. I mentioned that the clerks seemed to become deeply involved with the facilities of the system and to take it very seriously and also to enjoy it, and he answered:

> The more you work with it and the closer you are to management, the deeper you get into it, because then you are swept into it. If it was made something crucial to each and every case handler, then he would do it, but so we are, at least in the police, and you see it everywhere, that if you are not forced, you do not go really deep into it, then you are satisfied with, say, using two buttons . . . and if they get hit, and get something they can use that way, then they are hooked and then they hang on to learn more.

Case 2: Computer Use in Theft Notice Monitoring

Two men from the theft section were located in a small town at the west coast of Jutland working on a pilot project. By going through notices about summer house burglaries along the coast and across several police districts, they were supposed to find patterns in the ways in which the burglaries were carried out and thereby find new leads to investigate. To support them, the National Police computing center put up an interface to the central database on theft notices. From the moment they started, they took over from the National Police registration the task of entering the notices from the local districts, written on paper forms.

The team was located in a pavilion outside the town hall, which also housed the local police force. Having passed the passport office and the motor vehicles office one arrived at a small room with a double desk covered by phones, ashtrays, typewriters, notebooks, and piles of paper in all sizes. Toward the back wall a table held two terminals, a portable, and a printer. The passage to the computer equipment was made difficult because of a chair next to each desk. I was puzzled as to why the detectives did not remove the chairs, since the chairs almost blocked the passage to the computers and since the project as they described it was not supposed to involve much interrogation. I did not ask but made the silent conclusion that in order to "feel at home" they had arranged the furniture as it normally is when working with theft investigation and spending a lot of time interrogating people.

Prevention is probably always a very open-ended endeavor, and this was certainly no exception. The head, the assistant head of the squad, and the members of the team had a rather vague problem formulation for the project. At the time of my visit the detectives had no clues as to what the final report would contain. And they were certainly not able to rely on tacit, well-known routines, as were their colleagues in the homicide section. According to the National Commissioner of the Danish Police, the project was part of a "general crime prevention endeavor." This formulation was echoed by the chief constables of the districts in the local newspapers. The idea was that working across districts would leave the thieves with the impression that the police are everywhere and know everything.

The detectives in their daily work, however, experienced the task as a row of cases, like pearls on a string. They operated with situations, suspects, and evidence just as in ordinary theft cases. Asked in more general terms about their reason for working as police detectives, they talked about the hunting as the most fascinating aspect but did also mention the pedagogic challenge in cases with young criminals. They found it hard to relate to the more abstract purpose of crime prevention. But since they were not to investigate concrete cases, they gradually took on a role as consultants for their colleagues in the districts, a role that was new to them but which gave them the feeling of being productive. They tried to cheer up their colleagues and give them the impression that investigation of ordinary theft notices was of importance not only for the sake of insurance. By this argument they also to some degree cheered up themselves about their mission.

In this way, the overview, rather than being an instrument for judging the next step in an investigation, became a purpose of its own, but a rather vague one. They could quantify the number of notices searched, the number of queries performed, and cases solved, but reading notices for days without finding a pattern is hard to define as an outcome of any sort, especially for detectives describing themselves as hunters. They were not after overview as much as they were after prey/burglars. However, day in and day out they tried to elicit hints from the computer screen. And they talked a lot. As they described it: "Together we walk the main road, that is, the line given from above, and then now and then, one of us may sidetrack a little, and come back with a report. Even though it may be without immediate results, such sidetracking may be useful later, and anyway, it supports a richer conceptualization of 'the main road'."

The documentation was used more than produced, and this made the detectives focus on the quality of the documentation. When they received a notice that was filled in poorly, they contacted the district and talked to the author. This effort had, so they said, already improved the quality of the notices.

They managed the projects jointly by articulating ideas and discussing priorities about which patterns to pay the most attention to. Most of the time they let the number of occurrences of specific patterns indicate priority, but often they suspended even this principle.

The detectives appeared self-confident about theft investigation and saw themselves as "technical minded," so they were ready to accept a computer as a prime tool. But although the computerized database of notices was their prime instrument at the time of my visit, and had been for three months, the detectives still expressed major reservations about the usability of the interface given to them from the Computing Center. It stemmed from a library system, and they kept getting information about internal states of the application when making queries. These messages were using library-specific terms the detectives did not understand. They had no influence on the query possibilities, which they found did not match their needs. For instance, they needed direct access to insurance companies, which they were offered only through complicated queries. Because they had online access to the central database, they were to re-arrange data in ad hoc databases when they wanted to make certain comparisons, and when they tried, they were confused about whether a query was supposed to be performed in the arranged data or in the entire database.

We discussed what could be done to remedy the situation. They saw no other way than a better interface and did not mention the possibility of having a consultant help them get deeper into the existing one.

Case 3: Computer Use in Fraud Investigation

At a medieval monastery north of Copenhagen, three men from the fraud section investigated economic crimes. Visiting them involved passing several heavy doors and chilly arcades. This office most of all reminded me of interiors from movies from the fifties: yellow walls, old green chairs and a triple desk in the middle, a refrigerator, and, the sole modern touch, a table with the PC and a printer. All walls hung with shelves of binders.

These detectives were truly a team. The oldest was a very experienced fraud investigator; he was not very enthusiastic about technology. The second detective had some years of experience and was taking theoretical courses to obtain a higher charge. He was able to read documents for a very long time (an outstanding quality in a fraud man). Both had been in the fraud section for years. The youngest, though still an apprentice, was highly respected, and, coming from the drug police, he was experienced in many kinds of technical equipment. The three together had investigated several cases before they got the idea to use computer support for their registration. All in all they felt confident about their competence. They were capable at reformulating their cases—"cutting" them, as they said—and they approached technological possibilities in the same way. They wanted to expand, in the sense of accumulating and digesting experience and becoming smarter. They felt sure that the smarter they became, the bigger fish they could catch. And they saw the computer as a symbol of this successful endeavor, useful perhaps in many more ways than they could imagine right now, they said.

Policemen investigating fraud spend most of their time going through enormous quantities of vouchers and related documents, and for months rather than weeks. The material outcome of a fraud case, as in homicide, is the summary with attached material. In fraud, the documentation is given high priority because detectives are used to seeing suspects escape trial because of "circumstances concerning the evidence." Since the cases are normally extremely complex and the court is busy, the way the summary is formulated is of utmost importance as to whether a case is dismissed or taken. Clearly the formulation of hypotheses and arguments is a priority matter of discussion throughout the case. These three fraud detectives worked in a joint effort, going over drafts again and again, to make the case hold up in court. By telling about this, they expressed a strong feeling that fraud detection was useful to society. They boasted of the many millions they earned for the state each year. They did not go for "small fish"; they went for justice at the societal level.

The overview was established and maintained in discussion. "The whole day is a briefing," they said, and the talkative atmosphere supported this expression. And they negotiated the case management all along: people chose to do what they felt like doing, what they were best at, or what they had to learn in order to become better. As a general rule, they tried to take turns to ease the burden of reading documents.

Documentation forms the building blocks of a fraud case. While in a homicide case investigation on location and interrogation result in documentation, in a fraud case it is going through the documentation that results in investigation on location and interrogation. Categorization of the material was subject to discussion throughout the investigation, and it was constantly modified as conditions and hypotheses changed.

When they got the idea of using a computer, the fraud men got a spare old and slow PC from the National Police Computing Center, an outdated dot matrix printer, and simple and easy-to-learn word processing and database software. Since it was their own idea, they were assigned no further support. They themselves had to figure out how the computer and the software worked.

The team described to me how, when taking up a new case, they used the necessary process of making up a list of headings under which to store the information, as an instrument to systematically walk through and overview the problems of the case. As the case took a new direction, they rearranged the setup so that the menu and key words always reflected their current overall conceptualization of the case. Since they had started to use the computer for all information storage, they found it useful to supplement the indexical structure reflected in the setup of the menu with a paper version pinned to the wall. They felt that they got from the computer what they hoped for: an easy way to see an overview and sum up the information in a case. It made them feel much more confident that everything would be in the final report. Besides this advantage, which they expected at the outset, they experienced an unexpected pleasure of clarification when using the computer while structuring and restructuring the case material.

HOW DO WE COME TO CARE FOR A COMPUTER ARTIFACT? OR, HOW TO MOVE AN ARTIFACT INTO THE ACTIVITY AS A TOOL

At the start of this chapter, I raised the question, How do we come to care for a computer artifact? And I took the liberty of letting the little prince give the initial answer: it is a matter of giving it of one's time! Later, I introduced a designer who really cares for his product and who wants potential users to care, and I quoted him for an answer in a similar vein, emphasizing that the more you work with the tool, the closer you are to management, the deeper you get into it, the more you will like to work with it and explore its potentials. To the time parameter he added the parameter of being in control, mentioning distance to management, and further on he touched on another parameter or necessary condition: "If you are not forced, you do not go really deeply into it." He continued, emphasizing as a reward: "and if they get hit, and get something they can use that way, then they are hooked and then they hang on to learn more."

These two answers—that of the prince and that of the designer—are both commonsense recommendations at an empirical level; in the case of the designer, a touch of behaviorism is added.

Activity theory (not to be mistaken as a behavioristic stand) is a theoretical line of thought, a hypothesis, a saying something about why it is that if you spend much time with the artifact, it helps you to relieve a feeling of pressure (most well known in working life these days probably as "produce higher quality—spend fewer resources"). If you feel—to paraphrase Grudin—that making the effort makes you also share the benefit, then it is because the artifact has moved into your activity, has become part of you, so that you see it with not only functional but also aesthetic and ethical qualities. and because of the double nature of the activity, objective and subjective at the same time, it is also so that when you take a new artifact into your activity as a mediating tool, then the entire activity changes as well.

This approach should be acknowledged as different from simply understanding artifact integration as being part of the actors' least effort (Scribner 1986) or whatever strategies we might invoke at the action level. If you are a hunter and then take a computer in as tool, you will unavoidably see your activity also as a matter of good paperwork. You will come to care for the paperwork along with coming to care for the computer that gets you a hit of information you could have had no other way, and then you are suddenly hooked on the paperwork too, at least to some degree.

I understand the concept of activity as a prism through which our interaction with the world is reflected in inner and outer processes. If our practice, our behavior, is not reflected through this prism, it is without the scope of our consciousness and does not take part in building our personality. Normally in participating in a community of practice, several prisms are in use at the same time; they interact, conflict, or support each other in multiple ways.

Applying activity theory to the empirical observation that an artifact apparently has tamed its user enriches understanding human-computer interaction but it also enables us to understand what it might take to reach that point.

Activity is, according to the theory, not simply a prism; it is a prism that moves and changes all the time as a consequence of the process of learning—not to be mistaken as development (Vygotsky 1978). Development is the result of the learning that has taken place because parts of the world moved into the scope of the prism and were reflected in and by the prism. And according to activity theory's principle of tool mediation, not only are the skills obtained through the incorporation of the tools inseparable from the tools themselves, the tools become an integrated part of the prism. As stated by Kaptelinin (chapter 5, this volume), entering a new, computer-mediated activity usually implies the combination of precomputer human abilities with capacities of external components into a more efficient or a new functionality. In this process the external components become functional organs, or tools. According to Vygotsky (1978), learning is firmly anchored in the person's accumulated skills and knowledge and always happens in the zone of proximal development: "Learning awakens a variety of internal developmental processes that are able to operate only when the child is interacting with people in his environment and in cooperation with his peers. Once these processes are internalized, they become part of the child's independent developmental achievement" (1978).

Adults have, besides the potential for learning from more capable peers, a potential for learning on their own, insofar as they have "learned to learn." "Stand-alone learning," of, for example, the use of a new computer tool, is dependent on a clear perception of the goals the learner is targeting with the tool, as was the case for the designer from the homicide section and for the detectives from the fraud section. And the potential of learning among peers was illustrated in the fraud case, while the fear of bothering others before being an expert himself prevented the designer from the homicide team from getting his colleagues involved from the beginning, and thereby from taking advantage of their insights from the very beginning. The theft people were learning together, but not with a more capable peer to support them, and their objectified motives did not match the task at hand, at least not immediately.

These conclusions inform the planning of design processes. Engeström, in his report of a project on reluctance among doctors at a municipal health center toward computerized medical records and possible ways to overcome it, concludes: "Communicatively meaningful use of computerized medical records can be effectively enhanced only through developmental interventions in the activity system as a whole" (1990). What Engeström has in mind is an expansion of the actors' conceptualization of the activity and a design that ensures that not only the new, expanded, objectified motive but also the subsumed actions and operations are mediated, an endeavor demanding that those engaged in change work explicitly with uncovering the structure of activities and social interaction during the design processes. This theme is also echoed in Bellamy's work (Bellamy, this volume).

But doesn't it matter what kind of rose it is? So far I have viewed the prince-rose relationship from the point of view of the prince. What about the rose, that is, the technical design? Does it mean anything in itself? As far as prince-rose relationships are concerned, the answer is probably no. But this answer should not be construed as meaning that new, wonderful technical designs do not matter. They clearly do. If BRS had not been relatively accessible for a novice programmer, the homicide system would not have come into being, and if the system used by the theft team had not caused so many breakdowns in the immediate interaction, it might very well have supported an emerging picture of the whole endeavor.

Technical design is oriented toward a way of living we do not know of yet, while it has to pay its debts to a way of living we know almost too well. It is about realistic visions and, by definition, a practical endeavor. What happens is that somebody gets a good idea, wants to try it out, experiments a little or maybe more, and comes up with something that is ready for systematic reflection, criticism, test, revision, and evaluation.

We should not try to take the unplanned and unforeseeable out of design because it is its very nerve, but we can try to make sure that what comes out of the unpredictable process of generating ideas is reflected on thoroughly and that the user's learning is made part of a careful—and ideally cooperative—process of reflection, as suggested by Engeström (1990), Bødker (1991), and Greenbaum and Kyng (1992). And if designers, as too often happens, have time for nothing and therefore produce a bad fit to the hierarchical structure of users' activity, the activity theory framework offers itself to users or analysts who may be interested in finding out why the damned thing does not work as intended.

ACKNOWLEDGMENTS

First and foremost I owe much to the Danish National Police, who allowed me in, and to the members of the Flying Squad who gave me of their time, shared their experience, and participated enthusiastically in discussion about computers and their work.

Thanks to Susanne Bødker, Tove Klausen, Kari Kuutti, Bonnie Nardi, and John Thøgersen for critical and inspiring comments on earlier versions, and to Bonnie Nardi for being a very inspiring editor.

NOTES

1. I have chosen the term "computer artifact" here to start out from something relatively open and anonymous; it may be a program; it may be program, computer, and printer; it may be program, computer, printer, network facilities, and multimedia extensions.

2. I take "stated" as "stated in the behavior," verbally and in all other ways.

3. There are no women in the Flying Squad and no plans to take women in, so I am going to refer to the detectives as men throughout the chapter.

4. The product BRS/SEARCH is sold by Dataware Technologies of the United Kingdom.

REFERENCES

Bødker, S. (1991). *Through the Interface: A Human Activity Approach to User Interface Design.* Hillsdale, NJ: Lawrence Erlbaum.

Ehn, P. (1988). *Work-Oriented Design of Computer Artifacts.* Stockholm: Arbetslivscentrum.

Engeström, Y. (1987). *Learning by Expanding.* Helsinki: Orienta-Konsultit Oy.

Engeström, Y. (1990). *Learning, Working, Imagining.* Helsinki: Orienta-Konsultit Oy.

Giddens, A. (1984). *The Constitution of Society.* Cambridge: Polity Press.

Greenbaum, J., and Kyng, M. (1992). *Design at Work.* Hillsdale, NJ: Lawrence Erlbaum.

Grudin, J. (1988). Why CSCW applications fail. In *Proceedings CSCW'88.*

Hughes, J., and King, V. Paperwork. (1992). COMIC Working Paper COMIC-LANCS-4-1. Lancaster, England: Lancaster University.

Kierkegaard, S. (1843). *Frygt og Bæven* (Fear and trembling). Copenhagen: Reizel.

Leont'ev, A. (1983). *Virksombed, bevidstbed, personligbed* (Activity, consciousness, personality). Moscow: Progress.

Saint-Exupéry, A. (1986). *Den lille prins* (The little prince). Viborg: Lindhardt and Ringhof (first published 1943).

Scribner, S. (1985). Vygotsky's uses of history. In J. Wertsch, ed., *Culture, Communication and Cognition: Vygotskian Perspectives.* New York: Cambridge University Press.

Scribner, S. (1986). Thinking in action: Some characteristics of practical thought. In R. Sternberg and R. Wagner, eds., *Practical Intelligence.* Cambridge: Cambridge University Press.

Star, S., and Griesemer, J. (1989). Institutional ecology, "translations" and boundary objects: Amateurs and professionals in Berkeley's Museum of Vertebrate Zoology, 1907–1939. *Social Studies of Science* 19:387–420.

Vygotsky, L. (1978). *Mind in Society.* Cambridge: Harvard University Press.

9

Joint Attention and Co-Construction: New Ways to Foster User-Designer Collaboration

Arne Raeithel and Boris M. Velichkovsky

This chapter explores some perplexing questions for designers and researchers in the field of human-computer interaction. We first give a concrete example for a problem situated on the level of operations. This is drawn from our personal and institutional experience and cast into a lively story about an anonymous user. In telling this story, we use the language of designers in order to discuss the "correct" research goal suitable for the case at hand. We then introduce a new research technique, "managing joint attention," and explain why it is singularly suitable for optimizing the operational means of the actors. In the second half of the chapter we focus on action and conscious goal formation when actors are confronted with a more complex task. Here we advocate another new technique: "eliciting common views of a domain." In closing, we present a table that sets out a possible optimal match between evaluation method and concrete research goal, dependent on the "focused level" of the actual design problem.

THE CASE OF THE EVAPORATED OUTLINE DOCUMENT

Scientific writing comes in bouts for most university people. For long stretches, they use their machines only for e-mail, course preparation, slides, database access to student files, numerical data analysis, and so forth. Then the need suddenly arises to write that abstract for the next important congress. Professor X starts up his favorite word processor by choosing its alias entry in the Apple menu of the Macintosh. He writes the sketch, using the outlining features as usual, and, also as usual, somebody calls at his door and demands immediate attention. Professor

X hits Command-S (shortcut for "Save File") the first time with this new document, types "Toronto," and hits Return without looking much at the screen, just waiting to see the FileDialog coming up with the new file name highlighted, as it should be.

Colleague Professor Y, who is the intruder, not unexpectedly tells X that the grants committee has once again turned down his latest proposal, this time the one that could have made things very much easier for the Toronto congress. Let us draw the curtain before the following scene, which will later be recalled as: "The day when X *shouted* at Y for the first time. *You shouldn't think that he could do it at all!*" Cooling down with some effort, after a long pause and two cups of strong coffee, the professor reluctantly goes back to his work on the abstract. The outline document is not on the desktop, so Professor X looks into the native folder of the word processor. It is not there either.

Feeling very lost, X doubts his memory. Did he save it at all? Once before, he had clicked the wrong button on the FileNotSaved Alarm when quitting with a "dirty" file open. Could it be that he did that again? In his mounting frustration, he does not recall the Find ... option in the FileMenu or the fact that his word processor keeps a list of most recently touched files. Normally, he knows exactly where his documents are, so he never uses those tools anyway. Frantically, he now opens several possible target folders, concocts wild hypotheses about colleague Y's throwing the outline into the trash while he was away getting coffee, and finally gives up. He opens another new document via AppleMenu, writes the piece all over again, then prints and mails the product.

Much later, in a discussion with the local expert, Professor X remembered that his newly acquired system extension changes the behavior of the FileDialog so that every application opens with the same default directory—the one used in the previous session. Before the incident of the evaporated outline, X found this behavior very helpful in coordinating work with the statistics, the graphical, and the database programs. But as X had changed contexts, from data analysis to writing the abstract, he had "naturally" assumed that his Macintosh would now offer him the "right" default directory for a new task, the one that the word processor was in. Now the case was clear: the first version of the outline must be still in the directory used for his latest data analysis. A quick check confirmed this to be indeed the case.

THE DILEMMA OF USER-CENTERED DESIGN: FREEDOM AND UNCERTAINTY OF COURSE

If we now declare this incident to be the typical case that calls for a new design of the FileDialog behavior, there will surely be some readers who challenge this with arguments like: "No design could prevent users from not looking at the available information." It is true that Professor X could have seen where the outline went. The file dialog shows the destination directory in its usual place at the top of the dialog window. For designers, this information sits squarely there for the pickup, yet some users, like X, choose not to grab it. For psychologists, it is unclear whether users see it at all or under which conditions this piece of information gains in salience. Even expert users, when asked, cannot report reliably about such cases of breakdown of their expectations, because they happen in the subconscious middle phase of an action (Schwarz 1933; Wehner 1984; see also Baars 1988). Details of this phase are very hard to remember, exactly because the action is realized through well-mastered operations.

In her chapter to this book, Bødker writes about operations that they "allow us to act without thinking consciously about each little step.... They are *transformed actions*, which were consciously conducted in the beginning." This statement is overgeneralized from the point of view of psychology, because we may distinguish several forms of awareness and consciousness (Velichkovsky 1990). Many common operations, like a double click for opening a virtual container or scrolling through documents, are learned imitatively as a barely ever conscious habit. With them, there is nearly no use of precise discursive rules that are necessary for consciousness in the sense of reflexive self-regulation. In the early phases of the emergence of such an operation, there certainly is an acute perceptual awareness of some details of the artifact and of the necessary hand and finger motions to handle it according to the present aims of the user. In many cases, the pattern of the operation self-organizes well before the person feels any need to put into self-instructional terms what she is learning or doing right now.

It follows, then, for the Case of the Evaporated Outline, that it is not even clear whether the majority of users knows about the availability of the target folder information at all. It is so easy for novices to start working with the graphical interface, opening folders and double-clicking documents, that a sizable proportion might never notice the target folder's name at the top of the FileDialog.

Our case, however, is only a mild example of a well-known and widely discussed fact: an average user—not only an average professor!—never approaches using even a fraction of the power built into modern computing systems by their designers (see Shneiderman 1992). Nobody will deny the tremendous progress made in human-computer interface design in the past two decades. All contemporary systems present users a colorful and spatially and figuratively articulated landscape of possibilities for action. This is undoubtedly a very much advanced stage of compatibility with human cognitive mechanisms in comparison with the initial, preergonomic phase of the computer revolution when to become a user one had first to learn by heart a long "spaghetti" of otherwise meaningless combinations of symbols (Velichkovsky 1982). The efforts in improving the interface design currently cost up to 40 percent of total expenses for a commercial software system's development.

But still, despite all these efforts, users are too often lost in the virtual landscape. They have to find their way on a trial-and-error basis, which certainly is not the best way to expertise even for behaviorists. What is more important, from a practical design point of view, is that designers can never be sure about the individual learning path each user has taken into the system. We call this the Dilemma of User-Centered Design: the more you design for freely choosable, trustworthy possibilities for users, the less you will be able to foresee the possible breakdowns of expectations that users may experience with your new design features.

Many symptoms of this dilemma are already well known. The "featuritis" of most general-purpose programs is a case in point, having led to the countermovement of providing minimalist programs, or plug-in modules, with clearly constrained but also clearly useful possibilities. The recent public presentation of the OpenDoc framework (Reinhardt 1994) showed that this may well be a viable path to better software. Another case of the dilemma is the Help functions of the various platforms. Despite the best intentions of their designers, they again show the unconstrained, abstract freedom of choice that a disconcerted and nervous user just does not want, at least not at the moment when he needs help most urgently. We will come back to this special form of the dilemma in a subsequent section.

Our main focus overall, however, is the methodology of research and evaluation. We aim to answer, in a principled way, these questions: How should we try to ascertain or dismiss hypotheses like the one that states that "users just don't see the information" about the target folder when using the FileDialog? What is a good method to use in such cases of automatic behavior? Should we make extensive user testing with variants of the FileDialog, sporting different ways to indicate the target folder? Should we interview novices and experts about their way of handling folders and the file system hierarchy? Or conduct ethnographic field research, closely watching users at their natural tasks, waiting patiently for the next use of the FileDialog? Or should we perhaps take a totally different tack and aim at creating "software agents" that monitor the action patterns of any one user, duly noticing that a context switch, a jump from one activity to a different one has occurred, and that "silently" adapt the dialog's defaults to the form that the user predictably expects, in the new context?

There are unexplored methodological and conceptual resources in evaluating the human dimension of modern information technologies. The heuristic trick is to a look first at the evolution, the history, and the individual development of humans. Then we immediately discover that the trend to visualization, characteristic for the past decade of interface design, is in line with the dominance of vision, typical not only for humans but also for all higher primates (Deacon 1992). The recent wave of interest in computer support for cooperative work (CSCW) appears as a quite natural move for a goods-sharing, talkative, and society-building species like ours. It is clear that the initiation for all of these changes in human beings can be possible only through the social and cultural forms of learning.

When we look at the current evaluation methods in the HCI field (Monk et al. 1993; Preece et al. 1994), however, we find a split between natural science and cultural science paradigms. On the one hand, users may be "subjected to experimental conditions" as if no collaboration of experimenters with their subjects exists, and on the other hand, social and cultural context is recognized as the most important factor influencing the use of computer systems, demanding ethnographic and interpretive research. Thus it seems that the interdisciplinary nature of HCI is not yet complete. We have cognitive science and experimental general psychology on the one hand, and anthropology and sociology of work on the other. They still leave the field of human learning and development between them. The rich experimental tradition in developmental and educational psychology offers a setup that always includes interaction between persons: parents and children, teachers and students, novices and experts. We now turn to one example of such a method, suitable for research into individual and collaborative learning paths in the virtual landscape presented by a graphical user interface.

MANAGING JOINT ATTENTION: RESULTS ON EXPERT-NOVICE COLLABORATION

What is special about human growth of expertise? First, growth processes are social and cultural by their very nature (see Tomasello, Kruger, and Ratner 1993 for a recent review). In particular, the notion of zone of proximal development (Vygotsky 1935; see also Rogoff and Wertsch 1984) is applicable to the situation of computer literacy growth. Second, there are several forms of cultural learning that usually coexist: sheer imitative learning complements systematic instructional efforts that occasionally can be amplified by multilateral collaboration with other people. Despite the emphasis on social and cultural learning, nobody—least of all the activity theory community—will deny that the paths to mastery are always very individual. There are also firm empirical data demonstrating that the art of collaboration management consists of a nonimperative recentering of the activities of participants (Raeithel 1992, 1994a).

On the part of the novice, learning leads to changes at many levels of cognitive organization involving very different psychophysiological mechanisms (Velichkovsky 1990, 1994). This fact is well illustrated by the results of comparative studies of peculiarities in cognitive facilities of experts and novices that were performed in dozens of domains of expertise, from juggling to computer programming. Violating expectancies based on the ideas that were first built into, and then borrowed from, modern expert systems (Dreyfus and Dreyfus 1985), these studies showed that experts do not just know more, although this is almost always the case. There are important changes well above and below the level of conceptual structures, that is, semantic knowledge about the relevant domain of reality. Experts demonstrate a higher awareness of the goals of their activity and different metacognitive attitudes to the task, as well as—moving down the cognitive hierarchy to relatively low-level processes—much more efficient perceptual and sensorimotor skills.

Often expertise involves significant nonverbal ability, as, for instance, in the cases of chess masters or medical doctors. This is why expertise in practical doing is very difficult to explicate for both researcher and expert (Norman, Brooks, and Babcock 1992; Velichkovsky 1994). Experts can literally see the situation in a different way from novices, being more sensitive to its relevant aspects. The problem for a scientific grasp of these crucial processes is that every scene potentially supports many different, and sometimes very subjective, interpretations. A good artistic metaphor for this is the painting of the Italian artist Giuseppe Arcimboldo who worked in the sixteenth century at the Prague imperial court (figure 9.1). In the history of art, this picture was one of the first in a long row of purposefully multistable and ambiguous artistic creations, a tradition exemplified in our times by the works of Escher and Dali. The Arcimboldo painting shows two completely different themes—various animals or a man's profile—depending on previous experience, current interests, and other difficult-to-enumerate individual factors.

Even more complex forms of expertise, however, are easily transmitted from adults to children in countless cases of individual development. Let us therefore look at the very early stages of appropriation of any cultural symbol system. The role of direct reference to objects, or "deixis" (see,

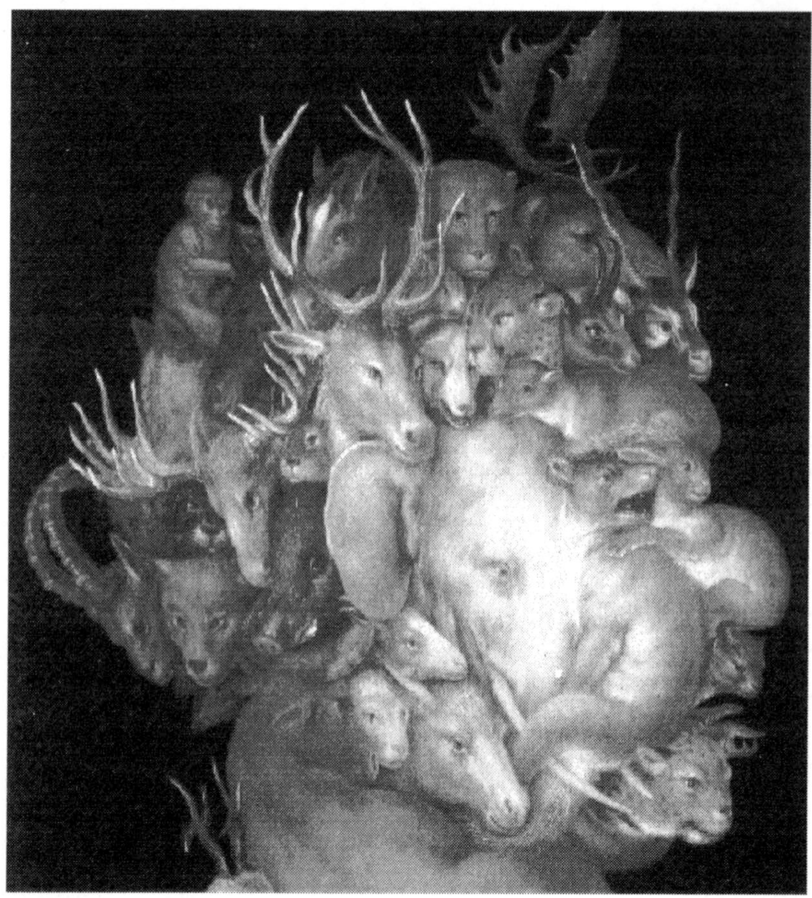

Figure 9.1
A fragment of *Earth* by Guiseppe Arcimboldo (1527–1593).

e.g., Clark 1991), in the early development of natural language cannot be overstated. Deixis is manifested in gesticulation and particularly in gaze direction, which is the most reliable (albeit not ideal) public index of focus of attention. Mother and child have to coordinate the distribution of their attentional resources in space and time. Indeed, the socialization of the child's attention is the major requirement for the cultural symbol systems to become appropriated. This was stressed by Vygotsky (1935/1962). In the United States, Bruner (1981) coined the term *joint attention* for this psychological requirement. Although several earlier studies of

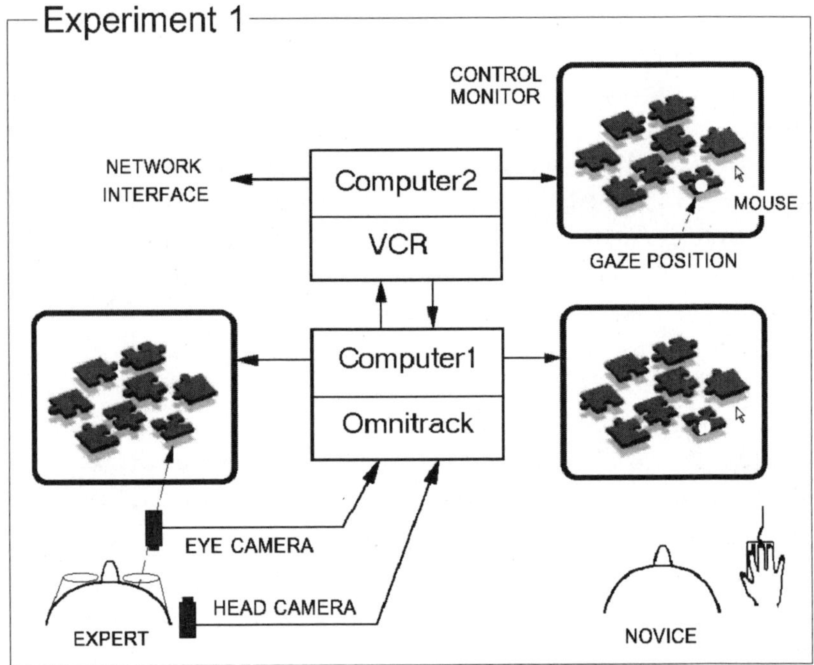

Figure 9.2
General design of the joint attention study (experiment 1).

cooperative problem solving had shown a benefit of face-to-face interaction in comparison to other modalities of communication (Chapanis et al. 1977), there was up to now no single analysis of the role of gaze direction in cooperative learning and problem solving.

Based on these theoretical considerations and on the use of an advanced, imaging eye-tracking method (see Pomplun, Velichkovsky, and Ritter 1994) we recently investigated computer-supported cooperative problem solving. The general arrangement of the first of our experiments is shown in figure 9.2. The tasks to be done were all of the puzzle type: a meaningful picture, such as a sunflower with a bee, was presented on a computer monitor as a random combination of twenty-five pieces that had to be rearranged with the mouse to reach the meaningful goal state. Two cooperating partners shared the same visual environment (both had identical information, replicated on each of the two screens), but their knowledge about the situation and ability to change it on the way to a solution were distributed between them. One of the partners—the "expert"—knew the solution in detail but had no means to act on the situation. Another partner—the "novice"—could act and had to achieve the goal without knowing more about the solution than what could be gained from a few seconds of looking at the assembled puzzle. The partners were free to communicate verbally. In one-third of the trials of the first experiment, in addition to verbal communication, the eye fixations of the expert were projected into the working space on the screen of the novice. In another condition the expert could use his mouse to show the novice the relevant parts of the task configuration.

Both ways of facilitating the joint attention state of the partners improved the performance. The absolute gain in performance in the case of gaze position transfer was close to 40 percent, approximately the same gain as obtained with mouse pointing. The nature of the dialogs as well as the parameters of the eye movements were different.

Of special interest are the results of our second experiment. Its general design is shown in figure 9.3. Here the direction of the gaze-position transfer was reversed, from the novice to the expert. As a consequence we had only two different conditions of communication: verbal communication only, and verbal communication with additional transfer of information about the gaze position of the novice to the visual field of the expert. In this second experiment we also found a significant gain in the efficiency of the distributed problem solving. Apparently experts could easily see the type of barriers that novices confront in their activity and therefore thought of more appropriate advice (Tomasello and Farrar 1986). This second case of facilitation of joint attention state is even more interesting than the first because it demonstrates that the gaze position transfer will be useful in situations where manual deixis is impossible; the novices could not use the mouse for pointing because they needed it to manipulate the puzzle pieces.

In further developments of this approach, we see a real possibility for arriving at more fundamental, and also more practical, results. Earlier in this chapter we exhibited a painting of Arcimboldo as a metaphor of the notoriously idiosyncratic and ambiguous nature of subjective perception.

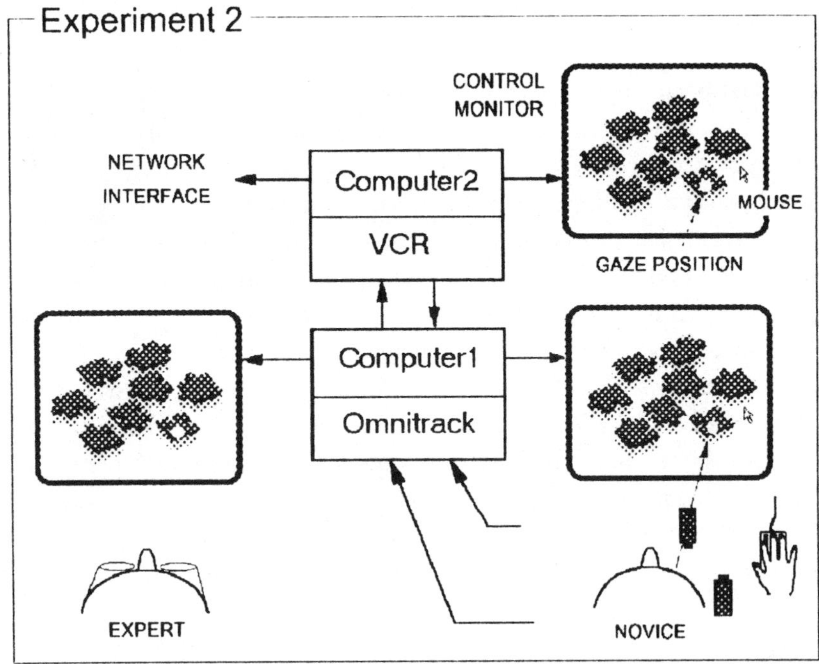

Figure 9.3
General design of the joint attention study (experiment 2).

How could designers and beginning users ever reliably collaborate if one is "the" expert, the other is "the" novice, and both see the same real or virtual landscape in widely different ways? The answer is that seeing for doing is an object-related activity too. We are always "grabbing" things with our gaze, putting something "mentally" elsewhere, grouping objects into separate imagined regions, and so on. Gal'perin's distinction of three planes of action—physical (external), perceptual, and mental (internal)—assigns to visual perception a clear and important mediating position in the developmental course of cognitive and metacognitive skills (Gal'perin 1992; see also Arievitch and van der Veer 1995). In the United States, Gibson and in particular Neisser stressed the mutual interdependency of perception and activity (e.g., the notion of the perception-action cycle; Neisser 1976). This means that one should—in line with the general spirit of activity theory—pay attention to the activity of the observer that accompanies some specific perceptual interpretation of a scene.

In figure 9.4 we show some results of a recent investigation (Velichkovsky together with Pomplun and Ritter) that clearly demonstrate that personal perceptions, although considered as essentially private and inaccessible, may be reconstructed to an essential degree on the basis of an analysis of a subject's activity. Thus we can externally reconstruct personal perceptions for public inspection and communication. We recorded the individual eye-movement paths of active exploration of the visual scene and used these data about "attentional landscapes" for the image processing of the original physical scene. There are hundreds of variants of technical realization of such an image processing from the perspective of an observer's activity. One can, for example, diminish the resolution and contrast in the valley regions of an attentional landscape and enhance them in "mountains." This is a completely unexplored field of future investigations. For the time being, we can testify that even the simplest approach to such a task conveys an unambiguous and lively impression of the scene perceived. The approach may also be used to yield an automatic reconstruction of the phases of the microgenesis of visual experience of the person—first seeing the details, then discovering the big picture, and vice versa (see figure 9.4).

This exploration opens the gate to a quantum leap in the field. Already on the level of sensorimotor and orienting operations for mastering a complex graphical interface one would overcome what can be called the "one-way-mirror paradigm" in the designer-user relationship. A much more symmetric interpersonal relation would be possible (see figures 9.2 and 9.3), something conceivable today only in the case of ethnographic studies: user interviewing, field research, and several styles of video lab studies (for a discussion see Nardi et al. 1993). The reason for a dominance of this one-way-mirror paradigm is quite clear. Currently the success of new software is dependent on extensive user testing more than on any other design principle, and it is a rule that designers will be highly surprised when they see newcomers begin to use their products. Often they cannot keep themselves from interfering, grabbing the mouse or the keyboard to show the user "how I would do it." The novices, however, will not be able to pick up the rapid sequence of operations even when designers slow down as much as they can. Therefore, many usability labs use video recording or one-way mirrors to separate designers and users. In contrast, our paradigm is one of exchanging personal views and intentions between designers and users. It would give public access to their different orienting strategies and thus would hopefully lead to a more productive collaboration at any stage of the software products' engineering and evaluation.

But it is not only collaboration in the usual sense that may be fostered by techniques like the one we have just sketched. Obviously any mirror can be used in two ways: to reflect observed others and to reflect the observer. And the reverse also holds: any collaborative technique may also be used as a means for self-reflection and self-regulation, much as a window to the other may be made a mirror by turning the light off behind it. Imagine Professor X having access to a reconstruction of his perceptual operations while handling the file dialog. A future system might keep his record of attentional switches in the very compact form of eye fixation data: time code, duration, spatial location, and pupil size as indicator of cognitive load. A replay, based on a search for the past moment of crisis, would let him discover his own tunnel vision at that moment of disruption. He might then insert a deliberate check for the target folder into his habitual file saving operation.

This utopian and slightly comical image of a bearded professor, wearing a fancy helmet with cameras, letting his machine record his orienting operations, just to be on the safe side for eventual breakdowns, is not meant as a serious proposition, of course. Yet it may serve to point out the necessity of public records of one's own course of action for self-reflective work. We all are blind to the details of our own expertise, the more so the more intuitive, free flowing, and masterful our accomplishments are. In a short methodological interlude, we shall now generalize this observation somewhat, emphasizing the inevitable shift in focus when we look at actions instead of operations or activities.

CHANGE OF FOCUS AND CHOICE OF METHODS

In today's Russian psychology, the textbook distinction of three levels of human social conduct is not looked at as a profound and indubitable fact

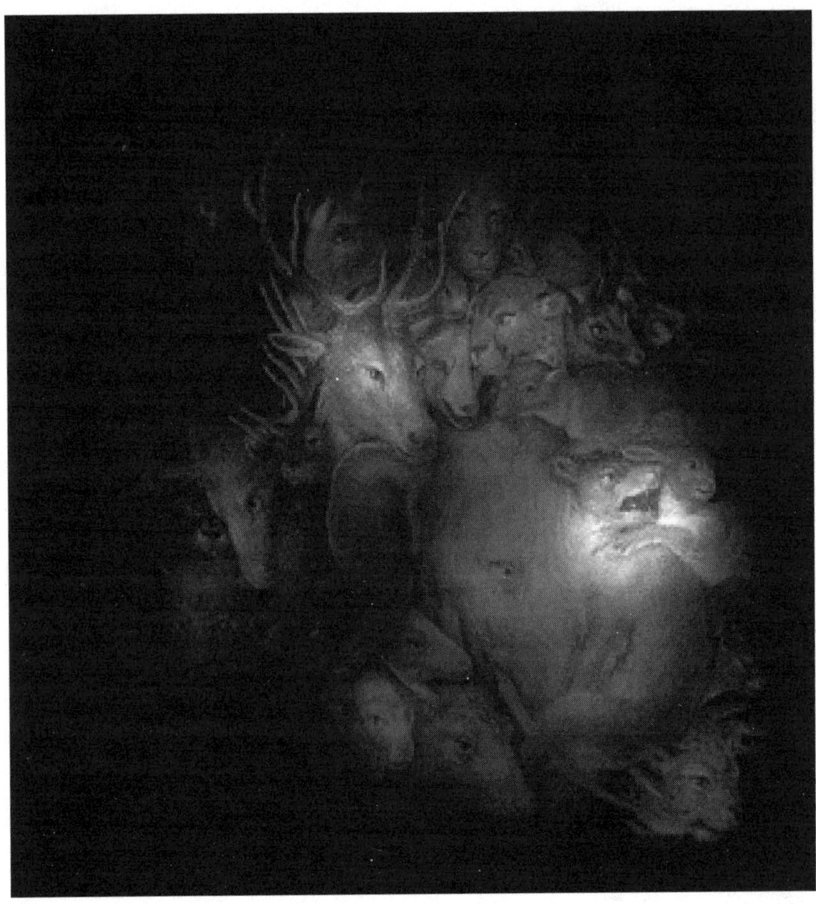

Figure 9.4
Two consecutive personal views of Arcimboldo's painting as reconstructed on the basis of gaze-dependent processing of the initial picture. See figure 9.1.

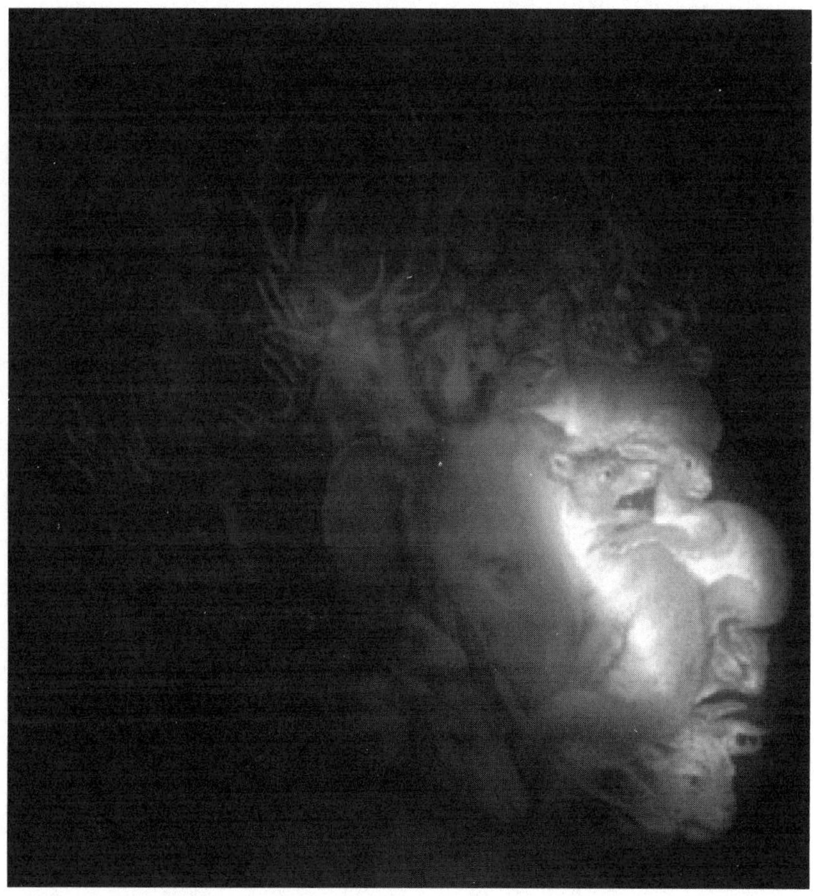

Figure 9.4 (cont.)

of psychology; rather it is taken as a rough first approximation to a more detailed and neurologically informed theory of the architecture of human organic self-regulation (Velichkovsky 1994). There is, however, one important sense of the simple distinction that is predominantly methodological, and we want to make this clearer by introducing the metaphor of "three levels of a river."

Consider geological processes, forming and changing the landscape wherein a river flows, as the first and highest process level, comparable to object-related joint activity. The river flowing in its bed, taking bends and turns, is the middle level (comparable to actions); this central process is at the same time constrained and made possible by the way in which the landscape evolves. Finally, we have the water currents inside and outside the river proper; with their own laws of motion and order of development. They are what makes the river real, constituting the third and lowest level (comparable to operations).

For any geologist this description must sound naive, because those experts would want to distinguish many more different kinds of subprocesses, both lower and higher ones. Perhaps there would be debate on how many different spatial or temporal scales are involved. On the other hand, most geologists and geographers would agree that there are indeed several widely different time scales and also very different ways to investigate the respective processes. While the "elementary" water currents are treated in the mathematical terms of fluid dynamics and may be investigated in the laboratory using scaled-down physical models, the "contextual" processes in geological time must be reconstructed from geological field data, using formal models of plate tectonics, erosion, and sedimentation. The middle level, describing and explaining the actual life and death of a single river, again needs a different set of data. Historical accounts of the meteorological events, and of the human, animal, or plant usage of the river through the ages, would have to be combined with knowledge from the other levels to explain a certain phenomenon, like a river finding a new path to a different ocean or the very rare case of a forking river (other than at a delta or swamp) that made Alexander von Humboldt decide to start on his famous research trip to South America.

We propose that the three-level distinction in activity theory is neither better nor worse than this sketch of a "science of rivers." We regard the three-level idea mainly as an orienting device to handle the necessary focus changes in the course of ongoing research. From the central process, which is human action, situated and steered by shared or private goals, we may shift focus to the context and look at historical records of the evolving activity systems, or make long-term observations of the changing patterns of joint activity, or of the internal differentiation in the community of practice, and so on. Usually such an upward shift seems sheer luxury for designers of tools and workplaces, although a good argument can be made that it will be always helpful—for example, as the first step of Engeström's expansive cycle of developmental work research (1987). Much more common is the downward shift: looking at more elementary processes than whole actions, observing and explaining how the actors handle their instruments, how they orient themselves in their surroundings, and with their partners, peers, or supervisors.

In both types of shift, however, the centrality of the conscious actions of the persons is preserved: as the point of origin of the problem and as the point to which one aims to return, with the design ready or the problem solved. In our introductory story we dramatized the downward shift to operations and back, starting from the concrete action goal of producing a conference abstract and returning to a safe condition for all future actions with a similar goal. We emphasized that the nature of operations as parts of the "living knowledge," the know-how of the person, makes it inevitable to engage observers or produce physical recordings, because operations are not accessible to the conscious self-reflection of the actor without such mediation.

In traditional research strategies, like the one-way-mirror paradigm, this usually means that researchers must be neutral observers, not participants. However, we have presented the joint attention study as an example to show that the strengths of both roles, participant and observer, may be combined with the help of a new technique that enables all actors to switch from one role to the other. We now want to show that keeping the focus on the action level naturally demands such a symmetric relation between researcher and informant, designer and user. Again, we use a knotty design problem as an introduction: providing online help for users of complex software. This is "metadesign" in a sense, one level above the program design proper, because helpful information must be provided that "is about," that is, explains, the available tools and options, and guides one in its use.

SOME OBSERVATIONS ABOUT USELESS HELP

Being helpless in front of the machine is a frequent state for today's users of sophisticated software. They are suddenly confronted with an obstacle, they cannot think of a way to achieve their aims and cannot ask somebody else. Here we have a dramatic difference in efficiency of even accidental observations of other persons who are well acquainted with the system, in comparison with the dull irrelevancy of seemingly always ready-to-support Help functions. Amazingly, the standard design of the Help typical for a platform makes the user, who needs concrete advice on how to overcome orientation difficulties, even more hopeless about her or his eventual success because it looks always the same, regardless of the current situation.

The problems of a newcomer to a graphical interface are of the constructive type; they concern the localization of the right objects and manipulating them so as to get on with the task at hand. But the usual written Help confronts our spatially disoriented user with long lists of verbal pointers to tersely formulated definitions or to prescriptions that use known words in unfamiliar patterns. What is a "scroll bar"? A long counter to inspect biblical texts on papyrus? This dramatic discrepancy, obvious to any cognitive psychologist, cannot be overcome by context sensitivity of the Help function alone. For instance, Macintosh System 7 offers "Balloon Help" that is context sensitive to the extreme. Like a hyper intelligent child it is constantly making wise remarks, and with every mouse move there is a new strange description, housed in a balloon, attached to some object on the screen. This surely is a nice way for a curious novice to learn about the abstract possibilities of the software when there is no pressing task to do, but it takes too much self-control in times of crisis to ignore all the irrelevant balloons that only add to the optical and conceptual clutter, until she or he finally finds the important piece.

Formal contexts, like the static array of interface elements at any one moment, remain very remote from the contexts of user actions, as well as from the designer's intentions. The way out, for some recent providers of

Help functions (Sellen and Nicol 1990), is at least to organize the text pointers according to the likely tasks that the users may be trying to accomplish at the time of their call of Help. Instead of lists of abstract, elementary, operational options (e.g., "Setting tab stops on the ruler"), there are now lists of more global and more concrete results that the user might intend to bring about (e.g., "How do I arrange numbers in columns?"). Still, it is hard for people to search for their task at hand in a list of items compiled by somebody else, especially when real help is desperately needed, because oversight and connection to the task have been lost.

Let us contrast this lonely user scenario of relying on abstract Help with the social support web of a typical PC-pool of today's universities or of a business department with many other users to ask for human help. The turn to another is a sane move, providing for some guidance in the solution to the knotty problem. The need to explain what the problem is all about may lead to a potential solution, with no other help from the partner other than curious listening. Furthermore, and more important, the others are familiar with the task in question, and they will not divert attention by enumerating other abstractly possible goals. Instead they will point out possible new directions. Last, but not least, the special combination of software at each site is something that the ready-made Help could never contain, except for the very rare locally edited Help systems. The bulk of the human help, however, consists of locally useful tricks and tips circulated from user to user.

CO-CONSTRUCTION OF THE TASK STRUCTURE OF AN ACTION DOMAIN

When people become new members of a community of practice, they have to appropriate a distributed and situated knowledge of the why, what, and how of the typical actions. Depending on the type of organization, there is a more or less rigid and explicit hierarchy of tasks and subtasks that acts as a coordinating force between the persons who normally plan and execute their actions individually while trying to fulfill their duties (Engeström 1992). Many organizations have a definite learning path for new members: handing out written rules and instructions, assigning older members as mentors, prescribing a series of steps that lead from the periphery of the action domain into its center, and gradually confronting the newcomers with all the objects and instruments of their new work (Rogoff 1990; Lave and Wenger 1991).

For the design of new software intended to fit into an existing organization, it is essential that designers understand the overall task structure, in both its present form and the possible future shape to be presented by the virtual objects and tools of the new software. Designers have developed several strategies to learn about task structure, and these are surely very helpful if the work to be computerized already has a definite organizational shape. For instance, one may collect descriptions of the material—paperwork forms, special types of binders and folders, filing systems, and so on—and then write scenarios in which the operations with these materials are recorded in enough detail to inform the design of virtual tools (Bødker 1990; Budde and Züllighoven 1992; Carroll and Rosson 1992).

However, the scenario method does not seem to be of use for the overall design of general-purpose software for desktop publishing, drawing illustrations, authoring hypertext media, and other uses because there is not just one traditional task structure to copy from. Rather there are so many of them that listing, analyzing, and reproducing all those styles of using materials and tools seems a hopeless and never-ending endeavor. Designers of such applications cannot really know the multitude of objects beforehand that will be built with their new tools and with the materials they provide for. Lacking good understanding of the tasks that the collection of tools will be put to, however, also means that the designers cannot provide task-oriented help in the concrete sense that users expect. This is a vicious circle leading to the explosion of features with accompanying icon strips and endless Help lists so typical of today's mammoth applications.

Again, we have a problem of how to do research and evaluation, now in the case of task structures, on the central level of self-regulation. It would not help much to use the joint attention technique here because the problem is not with handling the virtual tools or understanding the views, lists, and graphics presented on the screen. Rather, we need to know about the goals and subgoals of the "typical" user and how they interrelate to form different task structures. Additionally, we need to know whether there are several different types of users. Because the actions are carried out with deliberation and conscious effort to achieve the desired results, the main strategy for research is simply to ask the persons to tell us about their action plans and goals. A more distanced attitude of objective observation and analysis is not adequate here except as a behavioral or ethnographic check on the stories told.

Before we present one of the many existing interview techniques, we want to address a current controversy briefly. There are those who doubt the general usefulness of the concept of goal directedness and "internal" planning (Suchman 1987), and others who still stress the central tenet of cognitive science of the past twenty years: the existence of internal symbolic representations and the intentionality of the cognitive processes operating with or on them (Fodor 1983). From a cultural-historical viewpoint, both positions are one-sided and omit essential mediating structures or processes (see Nardi, chapter 4, this volume). Playing out "external" situational factors against "internal" cognitive processes is a mere prolongation of the Cartesian fallacy of positing a mindless physical world and an individual consciousness not located firmly in the world of living things (Leont'ev 1978).

Our position is this: actions in the sense given above, that people are able to explain what they aim for, make up a sizable portion of each working day, corresponding to a variety of verbal or otherwise symbolic prescriptions called tasks. Tasks and goals are understood here as intrinsically bound up with each other and with their verbal or otherwise symbolic presentation. As the historical roots of the words *aim*, or the German *Zweck*, reveal, many goals are external symbolic devices whose function is to channel the action. Such goals must be actively "held in the line of sight" by the actor to become effective in a semiotic sense (C. S. Peirce; Houser and Kloesel 1992). The bull's eye of the archer's target, which is the original meaning of both the German word *Zweck* ("purpose") and the Russian *tzel* ("goal"), for example, is a symbol of any future state where a real arrow hits near it. Taking it into sight, as the desired "end" of the whole enterprise, literally causes this result by way of the archer's action-coupling to the physical processes that let the arrow fly and make it stop again. In this description, we have concentrated on visual signs of the end exclusively. Yet goals pursued by individuals are often verbal or conceptual signs of the result and thus are equivalent to self-instruction. Their effectiveness then hinges on their being "held" in the ongoing dialogue of inner speech, replacing the index term in sentences like: "Now I will do *this*."

We thus recognize goal directedness as a specifically human type of intentional, object-related, joint activity. This also means that goals and tasks are as much a social and cultural phenomenon as they are a characteristic of individual persons, and their style and pattern of actions. Consequently, we again advocate a collaborative strategy of research and evaluation. With this context, it is possible to focus exclusively on the action regulation of the individual who has taken over a certain portion of an organization's tasks, without losing sight of the essentially social character of human activity.

COMMON VIEWS AS AN EXAMPLE FOR RULE-GUIDED CO-CONSTRUCTION

In the following, we present the new strategy of "eliciting common views of a domain," which uses the well-tried Repertory Grid Technique (Kelly 1955; Fransella and Bannister 1977; see also Gaines and Shaw 1993, for applications in knowledge engineering). We believe that the strategy explained in the following paragraphs is well suited to play the role of a *mediating descriptive resource* in the collaboration of designers and users. Yet, as in the joint attention study, we present no more than a preliminary example of what may be possible when the application of activity theory to software design is more complete than it is today.

In its very literal sense, a Repertory Grid (RepGrid) is a grid or matrix of symbols describing many judgments on a set of objects, made by an individual. It is the protocol of a quite ritualized interviewing technique, called the "elicitation of personal constructs." A personal construct, in the sense of Kelly's "personal construct psychology" (1955), is some important distinction that the person makes between the objects (also called "elements"), regarding some of them as similar to each other while the rest are *different*, in a contrast tightly coupled to the sense of the similarity. The exact content of the distinction, the verbal description of both

Repertory Grid of Respondent 1

elicited personal constructs

(1) emergent pole (0) contrast pole (–1)

bulletin board (BBS)	discussion list (List)	personal e-mail (PM)	telephone call (Tel)	talk over dinner (Dinner)	formal occasion (Formal)	sending facsimile (Fax)	official letter (offic.Letr)	private letter (priv.Letr)	visiting party (Party)	reading non-fiction (tech.Lit)	reading novel (Novel)	watching t.v. (TV)	reading newspaper (News)	emergent pole	contrast pole
-1	1	1	1	1	-1	1	-1	1	1	-1	-1	-1	-1	self-determined course	course not negotiable
-1	-1	1	1	1	0	-1	-1	1	0	-1	-1	-1	-1	personality is relevant	personality not relevant
1	-1	1	1	1	1	-1	-1	1	1	-1	-1	-1	-1	response expected	no response expected
1	1	0	-1	-1	-1	0	1	0	-1	1	0	1	1	search for information	contents emerge
-1	-1	1	1	1	0	-1	-1	1	1	-1	1	0	-1	pleasure seeking	serving a purpose
-1	1	1	1	1	-1	1	1	1	1	1	1	0	0	chosen partner	partner not chosen
-1	1	1	1	1	0	-1	-1	1	0	-1	-1	-1	-1	known partner	unknown partner
-1	1	0	1	1	-1	-1	-1	1	1	0	1	0	0	relaxed	tense
-1	1	1	1	1	-1	-1	-1	1	0	0	0	0	0	may speak my mind	must watch my words
1	1	1	1	1	-1	1	-1	1	0	0	1	1	1	voluntary	conventional
-1	-1	1	-1	0	-1	-1	-1	1	-1	0	1	0	1	leisure	quick and hasty
1	1	-1	-1	1	1	-1	-1	-1	1	0	0	0	0	adressing group	adressing person
-1	-1	1	1	1	0	-1	-1	1	1	-1	1	0	0	personal	technical
-1	-1	-1	1	1	1	-1	-1	-1	1	-1	-1	1	-1	synchronous	asynchronous
1	1	1	-1	-1	-1	1	1	1	-1	1	1	1	1	unilateral	interactive
-1	-1	-1	1	1	1	-1	-1	-1	1	-1	-1	1	-1	also nonverbal	nonverbal impossible
0	0	-1	1	1	-1	-1	-1	1	1	1	1	1	1	ideal	better not this

Figure 9.5
Sample protocol of the Repertory Grid technique.

"construct poles," comes from the informant. This is in contrast to most psychological assessments where the content of questionnaires or rating scales is fixed beforehand by the researchers.

In the case depicted in figure 9.5 the elements to be compared by the respondent were various types of communication (fourteen in all): three variants of e-mailing (personal mail, discussion lists, and bulletin boards), telephone calls, talks over dinner, writing formal letters, watching television, several types of reading, and so on. The first row of the RepGrid says that the first important distinction for this person was between a self-determined course of dialog, and other situations where the direction of the exchange is not negotiable. Taken together, the rows of the RepGrid constitute the repertory of this person's way to name and handle the differences and similarities of communicative actions or situations.

In itself, the initial product of the RepGrid interview (figure 9.5) is of limited use. You, our readers, may test this by trying to understand from reading the construct poles how the informant, a young woman who is a clerk in Hamburg, looked at her communicative tasks and activities. It helps if you compare the patterns of symbols in pairs of columns of the grid, because then you will find which elements are similar overall for this person. This takes a lot of "eyeballing," as British practitioners of the technique have come to call the skill (Button 1985); it is comparable to trying to read the idiosyncratic view of the Arcimboldo painting out of a simple plot of all recorded eye movements, crisscrossing the scene to the point of nearly hiding the original image, as in the early publications of students of eye movements (Yarbus 1969; Zaporozhets and Zinchenko 1974) where these were shown at their sensory work for the first time.

Just as figures 9.3 and 9.4 are reconstructions of a personal view of Arcimboldo's portrait in two consecutive stages of exploration, generated by a computer algorithm using the data input as constraints of the model, figures 9.6 and 9.7 are (re-)constructions of common views of two groups of respondents about the similarities and differences of communication types. The algorithm used in the second case is a mathematical procedure called Eigen-Structure-Analysis (ESA) of a single RepGrid matrix, combined with a general congruence rotation of all matrices to the best fit achievable between the element structures (Raeithel 1991). Additionally, the software uses the principles of exploratory data analysis (EDA; Tukey 1977) and of cartographical design and graphical data analysis (Bertin 1983) to produce a diagram suitable for lay readers with a minimum of reading rules and necessary practice. Finally, the human analyst also adds his or her skill to the diagram, because algorithms for a readable *and* automatic labeling of such diagrams are very hard to come by.

The spontaneous way to read such a diagram is also the correct way: elements pointing to (roughly) the same directions as do a bundle of constructs have the properties told by the construct pole names, in the collective construction of the group of respondents. Elements that lie diametrically opposite with regard to the center zero have contrasting characteristics.[1] The similarities between elements may be read off the diagrams in figures 9.6 and 9.7 as the spatial distances between the black squares, labeled to say which communication type is depicted. The zero point of the diagrams is significant—a totally neutral element without

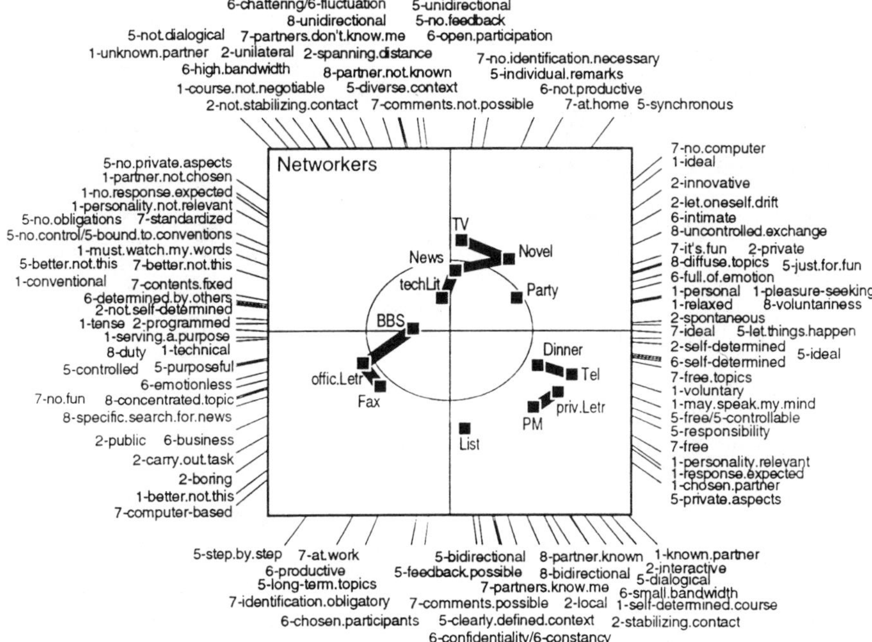

Figure 9.6
Common view of networkers (N = 6).

any namable property would come to lie at the center zero. The longer the distance of an element from this center, the clearer and more salient is its meaning for the persons whose common view is exhibited. In addition, the spatial direction similarity, measurable as an angle between the center-based vectors directed at the points, is significant too. It corresponds to the familiar correlation similarity (acute angles equal high positive correlations). At the outside of the diagram, the various personal constructs, assembled from the whole group of persons, are presented as directions labeled with the construct pole names. The number identifies the individual whose construct it is.

In figure 9.6 we see the common view of six Networkers who, mostly in their spare time, are communicating via bulletin boards, discussion lists, and e-mail with others in the ecology movement. Their elements form several tight clusters in the three-dimensional solution space, indicated by gray lines between the most similar elements. In the view of

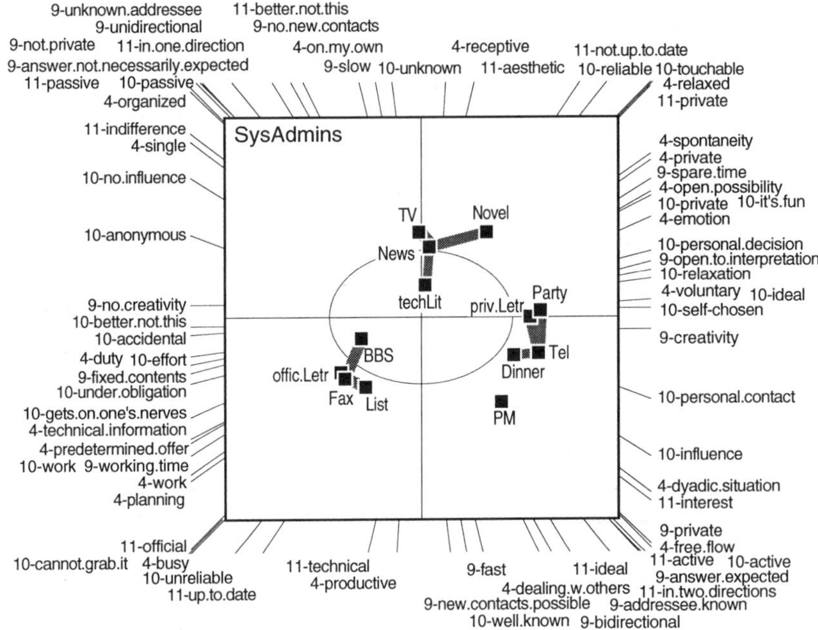

Figure 9.7
Common view of system administrators (N = 4).

Networkers, personal e-mail is very much like writing private letters; bulletin boards are seen quite differently as more impersonal, controlled, and worklike, kin to faxes and official letters. The discussion lists have an intermediate place and are still clearly partner related, with defined longer-term topics and stable relations. In contrast, we can gather that the common view of four system administrators ("SysAdmins," figure 9.7) has a more clear-cut clustering in three spheres: social events on the right, task-oriented work at the left, and recreational reading and TV on the top. Both bulletin boards and discussion lists are seen as work related and similar to each other. The SysAdmins do not see such a close similarity between personal e-mail and private letters, certainly because a large part of their dyadic e-mailing has to do with user support. The main part of the original study (Clases 1994) consisted of thematic interviews (the RepGrids were an addition); a third group, academic researchers, was included whose pattern is somewhat in between the two shown in figures 9.6 and 9.7. In both diagrams, only the second and third dimensions of the solutions are plotted. The first dimension, containing a contrast between the "formal occasion" and all other elements, has been left out, as well as this situation itself.

Apart from the fascination that these diagrams usually have, especially when presented in three dimensions by rotating them on a computer screen (for this very useful feature, see Donoho, Donoho, and Gasko 1988), what is the use of such a technique for the design of more accessible software? We think that RepGrid studies are suitable and expedient for identifying different task clusters between groups of users or in organizations. In common views, the prevailing polarities, and their meanings in the language of the informants, are exhibited. Researchers and designers get a global picture of the internal differentiation of the different action domains. This serves to pick out the target fields for more detailed task analysis, to be done with other techniques, in a way that maximizes the structural contrast between the users and thereby enables designers to compromise wisely between the task-specific and generic extremes (see Nardi and Johnson 1994) for different types of users.

CONCLUSION

Although the results of our small study of e-mail should be taken as preliminary, we think that the study presents a good example of a general methodological scheme that we call "cooperative modeling" (figure 9.8)—in contrast to psychometric or sociometric methodologies that aim for an objective measurement of attitudes or opinions. The core is cooperative production of a model (S in figure 9.8) that remains open for interpretation by two partners: the professional evaluator/analyst (Pro) and the respondent who is the expert (Exp) for the problem field in question. In the case of the RepGrids, the division of labor between them is that Pro regulates the comparison procedure and analyzes the results, using a computational system (C), while Exp furnishes the concepts and contents (the personal constructs) from her or his experience of the problem field (P) and also has the last word about the correctness of the resulting diagram—in a closing phase called "consensual validation" of the model (see Scheele and Groeben 1988). There are three levels of communication between the partners, corresponding roughly to the

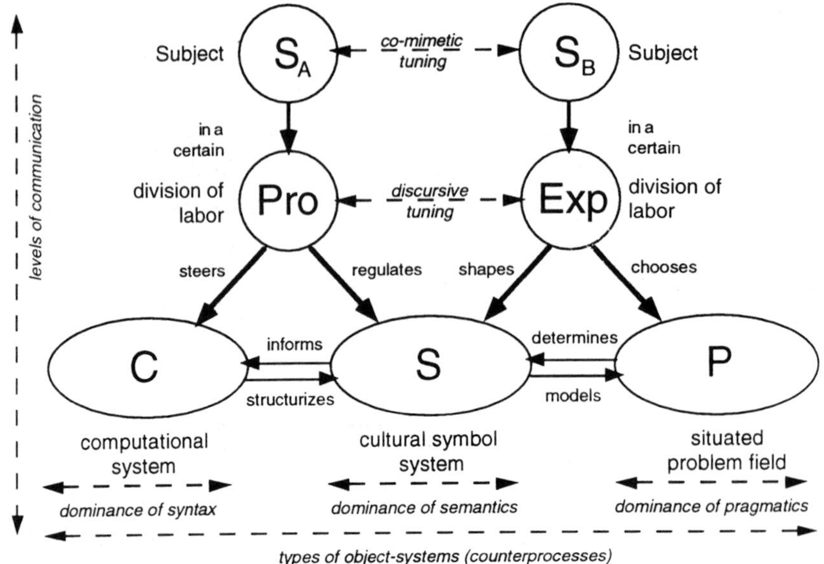

Figure 9.8
Diagram of cooperative modeling.

activities-actions-operations distinction. On the most encompassing and global level, the two persons (S_A and S_B) are tuned to each other by the unfolding interactional context of their meeting, expressed in body language, gestures, genre, and style of talking ("mimetic tuning"; see Raeithel 1994b). Their more immediate and differential tasks (Pro versus Exp) are co-regulated by requests and answers, hints, opinions, and so on (discursive tuning) on the central level. Finally, the accumulating symbolic results (in the operational domain S) on the basic level are also a form of communication, and this yields the aimed-for result of the whole effort.

The structure in the diagram of cooperative modeling is very much simplified compared with the ongoing interaction; it shows the minimally necessary structure for co-construction as a professional and expert collaboration. Because of this, the general scheme may also be used to analyze and regulate other interviewing techniques, for example, the scenario method mentioned earlier, or a recent innovation from German psychology called *Strukturlegetechnik* (laying out structures with concept cards and relation cards; Scheele and Groeben 1988). The latter has already been modified for the design and evaluation of task structures (Mangold-Allwin et al. 1993), using different card types for materials, tools and resources, and transformations, comparable to some elements of the widely used SADT diagrams (structured analysis and design technique; Marca and McGowan, 1988). In these cases, the most salient difference from the RepGrid technique concerns the lack of a computational system, strictly understood, on the side of the evaluator/analyst. Instead of computer programs, there are weak rules and a conceptual system imported from the scientific discipline (e.g., work psychology) that structure the resulting symbolic model. This is not to say that the RepGrid method is superior to these other methods because of the algorithmic analysis. It is clear that the constraints making this possible at the same time limit what may be said by the respondents. There is real superiority in the RepGrid technique only in the ease and speed of analysis and aggregation over a sample of observations or evaluations, and with the respondent's constructions (not only responses to the constructs of the researchers) still visible.

The important commonality between these methods suitable for co-construction of the task and goal structure of a domain is the mediating and semiotic nature of the model resulting from the cooperation. It has to be built so that both partners can understand it with a minimum of training, because otherwise the model could not be evaluated by the expert respondents themselves, and this would take us back to the objectification procedures suitable for measuring objects. The common element in both of our research examples is that a mediating external presentation, a model made out of the building blocks offered by a certain cultural symbol system, is constructed. This also means that the collaboration between persons with different roles in the process should be a deliberate facet of the design, either as the object of the research, as in the joint attention study, or as the contractual framework when the collaboration is between professional analysts and users, understood as experts for their own activities and action domains.

Table 9.1 sets out the distinction among the three process levels of human social conduct being used as a classification of types of development and of proper methods to foster and evaluate such development. It

Table 9.1
Matching methodology to process level

		Examples of adequate methodology for:	
Process level	Type of development	Observation and experiment	Design and evaluation
Activity	Historical	Ethnographic field research	Evolutionary
	Sociocultural	Naturalistic observation	Object oriented
	Microsocial	Field experiment	Participative
Action	Ontogenetic	Formative experiment	Stage genetical
	Deliberate	Aims and results assessment	Task oriented
	Habitual	Co-construction of views	Metaphors and prototypes
Operation	Microgenetic	Joint attention experiment	Tool oriented
	Self-organizing	Video analysis	Convivial tools, soft machines
	Conditioned	Factorial experiment	Ergonomic

should be understood as a kind of an agenda for the further development of HCI methodology rather than as a recipe for picking a suitable method. As we have shown with two examples, activity theory provides a historical and developmental approach. Furthermore, the activity of the researchers and designers was described and analyzed with the same concepts that are used for the activity of the users. Thus, the fundamental symmetry of human collaboration appears also as a characteristic of the relation of researchers and informants, of designers and users. We are convinced that it is possible and fruitful on all process levels to look for special methods and mediating devices suitable to make this ideal more real and to contribute to more trustworthy and usable software at the same time.

ACKNOWLEDGMENTS

Investigations described in this chapter were partially supported by a grant from German Science Foundation (DFG SFB/360) to the second author. We appreciate the participation of Marc Pomplun, Eyal Reingold, Helge Ritter, and Dave Stampe in the development of methods for communicating attention and gaze-contingent processing of graphical information. We also thank Christoph Clases for critical assistance with writing this chapter and translating his RepGrid data into English.

NOTES

1. In many cases, these diagrams are akin to circular schemes from various cultures. The cycle of the seasons also places similar plants, animals, weather, and so on in roughly the same direction, while the opposite beings come to lie on the other side of the circle. Also, astrological and many other types of Asian scholars' diagrams exhibit this abstract kind of order and are quite well known around the globe. This "similarity horizon" (Raeithel 1991) is an interesting instrument for thought, thinking understood here as the conceptual ordering of a personal world on a pretheoretic plane (see Vygotsky 1935/1962, chapter on concept formation). The RepGrid technique was modeled after the sorting tasks that Vygotsky used in his research on concept formation, as Kelly himself has noted in the foreword to the paperback edition of the first three chapters of his major work (Kelly 1955). Vygotsky himself borrowed the comparison ritual from the work of an early German school of cognitive psychology (Würzburger Denkpsychologie; see Ach 1921; Hanfmann and Kasanin 1937; Hovland 1952). The German source book for this thread of history that we used is C. F. Graumann's *Denken* (1965).

REFERENCES

Ach, N. (1921). *Über die Begriffsbildung.* (On concept formation). Bamberg: C. C. Buchners Verlag.

Arievitch, I., and v.d. Veer, R. (1995). Furthering the internalization debate: Gal'perin's contribution. *Human Development* 2.

Baars, B. J. (1988). *A Cognitive Theory of Consciousness.* London: Cambridge University Press.

Bertin, J. (1983). *Semiology of Graphics.* Madison, WI: University of Wisconsin Press.

Bødker, S. (1990). *Through the Interface—A Human Activity Approach to User Interface Design.* Hillsdale, NJ: Lawrence Erlbaum Associates.

Bruner, J. (1981). The pragmatics of acquisition. In K. Deutsch, ed., *The Child's Construction of Language.* New York: Academic Press.

Budde, R., and Züllighoven, H. (1992). Software tools in a programming workshop. In C. Floyd, H. Züllighoven, R. Budde, and R. Keil-Slawik, eds., *Software Development and Reality Construction* (pp. 252–268). Berlin: Springer.

Button, E., ed. (1985). *Personal Construct Theory and Mental Health. Theory, Research, and Practice.* Cambridge, MA: Brookline Books.

Carroll, J. M., and Rosson, M. B. (1992). Getting around the task-artifact cycle: How to make claims and design by scenario. *ACM Transactions on Information Systems* 10:181–212.

Chapanis, A., Parrish, R. N., Ochsman, R. B., and Weeks, G. D. (1977). Studies in interactive communication (2). The effect of four communication modes on the linguistic performance of a team during cooperative problem solving. *Human Factors* 19:101–125.

Clark, H. H. (1991). *Arenas of Language Use.* Chicago: University of Chicago Press.

Clases, C. (1994). Kommunikation in computervermittelten Tätigkeitszusammenhängen. Bilanzierung der Ergebnisse einer qualitativen Studie zur Nutzung und Bewertung elektronischer Postsysteme ("e-mail") (Communication in computer-mediated activity systems. Précis of the results of a qualitative study on the usage and valuation of electronic mail systems). *Harburger Beiträge zur Psychologie und Soziologie der Arbeit*, 8, May 199. Technical University of Hamburg-Harburg.

Deacon, T. W. (1992). Brain-language co-evolution. In D. A. Hawkins and M. Gell-Mann, eds., *The Evolution of Human Languages.* Redwood City, CA: Addison-Wesley.

Donoho, A. W., Donoho, D. L., and Gasko, M. (1988). MACSPIN: Dynamic graphics on a desktop computer. In W. S. Cleveland and M. E. McGill, eds., *Dynamic Graphics for Statistics* (pp. 331–352). Belmont, CA: Wadsworth and Brooks/Cole 1988.

Dreyfus, H. L., and Dreyfus, S. E. (1985). *Mind over Machine. The Power of Human Intuition and Expertise in the Era of the Computer.* New York: Free Press.

Engeström, Y. (1987). *Learning by Expanding. An Activity-theoretical Approach to Developmental Research.* Helsinki: Orienta-Konsultit Oy.

Engeström, Y. (1992): Interactive expertise. Studies in distributed working intelligence. Department of Education Research Bulletin 83. Helsinki: University Press.

Fodor, J. (1983). *The Modularity of Mind.* Cambridge, MA: MIT Press.

Fransella, F., and Bannister, D. (1977). *A Manual for Repertory Grid Technique.* London: Academic Press.

Gaines, B. R., and Shaw, M. L. G. (1993) Knowledge acquisition tools based on personal construct psychology. *Knowledge Engineering Review* 8(1):49–85.

Gal'perin, P. Ya. (1992). The problem of activity in Soviet psychology. Stage-by-stage-formation as a method of psychological investigation. *Journal of Russian and East European Psychology* 30(4):37–80.

Graumann, C. F. (1965 ed.). *Denken.* (Thinking). Neue Wissenschaftliche Bibliothek 3. Cologne: Kiepenheuer and Witsch.

Hanfmann, E., and Kasanin, J. (1937). A method for the study of concept formation. *Journal of Psychology* 3:521–540.

Houser, N., and Kloesel C. (1992). *The Essential Peirce.* Selected Philosophical Writings. Vol. 1, *1867–1893.* Bloomington: Indiana University Press.

Hovland, C. I. (1952). A "communication analysis" of concept learning. *Psychological Review* 59:461–472.

Kelly, G. H. (1955). *The Psychology of Personal Constructs.* 2 vols. New York: Norton.

Lave, J., and Wenger, E. (1991). *Situated Learning: Legitimate Peripheral Participation.* New York: Cambridge University Press.

Leont'ev, A. N. (1978). *Activity, Consciousness, and Personality.* Englewood Cliffs, NJ: Prentice-Hall.

Mangold-Allwin, R., et al. (1993). DEI: Ein wissensdiagnostisches Verfahren zur Erhebung von Aufgabenmodellen (DEI: A knowledge diagnostics technique for the assessment of task models). In *Proceedings of Workshop "Psychologie des Software-Entwurfs".* St. Augustin: GMD.

Marca, D. A., and McGowan, C. L. (1988). *SADT: Structured Analysis and Design Technique.* New York: McGraw-Hill.

Monk, A., Nardi, B. A., Gilbert, N., Mantei, M., and McCarthy, J. (1993). Mixing oil and water? Ethnography versus experimental psychology in the study of computer mediated communication. In *Proceedings of INTERCHI '93.* Amsterdam, April 24–29.

Nardi, B. A., and Johnson, J. A. (1994). User preferences for task-specific vs. generic application software. In *Proceedings of CHI'94.* Boston, April 24–28.

Nardi, B. A., Schwartz, H., Kuchinsky, A., Leichner, R., Whittaker, S., and Sclabassi, R. (1993). Turning away from talking heads: The use of video-as-data in neurosurgery. In *Proceedings of INTERCHI '93*, Amsterdam, April 24–29.

Neisser, U., (1976). *Cognition and Reality.* San Francisco: Freeman.

Norman, G., Brooks, L., and Babcock, C. J. (1992). Expertise in visual diagnostics. *Academic Medicine Rime Supplement* 67:78–83.

Pomplun, M., Velichkovsky, B. M., and Ritter, H. (1994). An artificial neural network for high precision eye movement tracking. In *Lecture Notes in Computer Science: AI-94 Proceedings.* Berlin/Heidelberg/New York: Springer.

Preece, J., Rogers, Y., Sharp, H., Benyon, D., and Carey, T. (1994). *Human-computer Interaction.* Wokingham, UK: Addison-Wesley.

Raeithel, A. (1991). Arbeiten zur Methodologie der Psychologie und zur Kelly-Matrizen-Methodik (Contributions to psychological methodology and to the

Repertory-Grid technique). Manuscript. Hamburg, Germany: University of Hamburg, Department of Psychology.

Raeithel, A. (1992). Activity theory as a foundation for design. In C. Floyd, H. Züllighoven, R. Budde, and R. Keil-Slawik, eds., *Software Development and Reality Construction* (pp. 391–415). Berlin: Springer.

Raeithel, A. (1994a). On the ethnography of cooperative work. In Y. Engeström and D. Middleton, eds., *Communication and Cognition at Work*. New York: Cambridge University Press.

Raeithel, A. (1994b). Symbolic production of social coherence: The look back into history prolongs the stretches of travel still lying before us. *Mind, Culture, and Activity* 1:69–101.

Reinhardt, A. (1994). Managing the new document. *Byte* 19 (August): 90–100.

Rogoff, B. (1990). *Apprenticeship in Thinking: Cognitive Development in Social Context*. New York: Oxford University Press.

Rogoff, B., and Wertsch, J. V., eds. (1984). *Children's Learning in the "Zone of Proximal Development."* San Francisco: Jossey-Bass.

Scheele, B., and Groeben, N. (1988). *Dialog-Konsens-Methoden zur Rekonstruktion subjektiver Theorien*. (Dialog-consensus-methods for the reconstruction of subjective theories). Tübingen: Franke.

Schwarz, G. (1933). Über Rückfälligkeit bei Umgewöhnung II (On relapses after readaptation). *Psychologische Forschung* 18:143–190.

Sellen, A., and Nicol, A. (1990). Building user-centred on-line help. In B. Laurel, ed., *The Art of Human Computer Interface Design*. Reading, MA: Addison-Wesley.

Shneiderman, B. (1992). *Designing the User Interface: Strategies for Effective Human-Computer Interaction*. Reading, MA: Addison-Wesley.

Suchman, L. (1987). *Plans and Situated Actions. The Problem of Human-Machine Communication*. Cambridge: Cambridge University Press.

Tomasello, M., and Farrar, M. J. (1986). Joint attention and early language. *Child Development* 57:1454–1463.

Tomasello, M., Kruger, A. C., and Ratner, H. H. (1993). Cultural learning. *Behavioral and Brain Sciences* 16:495–552.

Tukey, J. (1977). *Exploratory Data Analysis*: Reading, MA: Addison-Wesley.

Velichkovsky, B. M. (1982). Visual cognition and its spatial-temporal context. In F. Klix, E. v. d. Meer, and J. Hoffmann, eds., *Cognitive Research in Psychology*. Amsterdam: North-Holland.

Velichkovsky, B. M. (1990). The vertical dimension of mental functioning. *Psychological Research* 52:282–293.

Velichkovsky, B. M. (1994). The levels endeavor in psychology and cognitive science. In P. Bertelson, P. Eelen, and G. d'Ydewalle, eds., *International Perspectives on Psychological Science*. vol. 1: *Leading Themes*. Hove, UK: Lawrence Erlbaum Associates.

Velichkovsky, B. M. (1995). Communicating attention: Gaze position transfer in computer supported cooperative problem solving. *Pragmatics and Cognition* 3(2).

Vygotsky, L. S. (1935/1962). *Thought and Language*. Cambridge, MA: MIT Press.

Wehner, T. (1984). Im Schatten des Handlungsfehlers. Ein Erkenntnisraum motorischen Geschehens (In the shadow of the action slip. An epistemology of motor events). *Bremer Beiträge zur Psychologie*, Nr. 34. Bremen: Universität, Studiengang Psychologie.

Yarbus, A. (1969). *Eye Movements and Vision*. New York: Plenum Press. (1st Russian edition 1967)

Zaporozhets, A. V., and Zinchenko, V. P. (1974). Wahrnehmung als Handlung (Perception as action). In T. Kussmann, ed., *Sowjetische Psychologie. Auf der Suche nach der Methode* (pp. 100–122). Bern: Huber.

10

Some Reflections on the Application of Activity Theory

Bonnie A. Nardi

This chapter recounts an analysis of task specificity in software design that would have benefited from an activity theory treatment. The study of task specificity in slide-making software proceeded slowly and painfully in the absence of a strong conceptual framework. When the study was finally completed, it was seen that the application of some basic concepts from activity theory would have made immediate sense of the data.[1]

There have been a number of recent acknowledgments that we must study problems of human-computer interaction in the social matrix in which they occur (Winograd and Flores 1986; Suchman 1987; Bannon 1991). This is easier said than done; existing analytical frameworks such as GOMS analysis (Card, Moran and Newell 1983) or traditional ethnographic description (Glaser and Strauss 1967) either do not take account of the social (GOMS) or provide little in the way of conceptual underpinning (ethnography). In this chapter I present a simple example of a study that my colleague Jeff Johnson and I recently conducted that would have benefited from an activity theory treatment. I describe how the application of some of activity theory's basic concepts could have made the work easier and more fruitful.

The problem we were trying to understand was whether end users prefer "task-specific" or "generic" application software. It has been argued that a solution to the problems end users have with conventional software is to provide highly task-specific applications that leverage users' familiar domain knowledge and narrow the gap between what they know and what the computer demands (Hutchins, Hollan, and

Norman 1986; Vlissides and Linton 1990; Casner 1991; Gould, Boies, and Lewis 1991; Johnson et al. 1993).

To evaluate whether task specificity is important for end user application software, we studied users of presentation slide-making software (Nardi and Johnson 1994). We chose this domain because of the wide spectrum of software used to create slides, ranging from very generic (e.g., word processing, drawing programs) to very task specific (dedicated slide-making programs such as PowerPoint, Persuasion, and Charisma).[2] We wanted to understand what motivated users' choices so that we could better design end user programming systems (Johnson et al. 1993; Nardi 1993). As I will describe in this chapter, the analysis of our data became confused and convoluted, largely because we lacked a vocabulary in which to cast our thoughts and a conceptual framework to structure our analysis. After we finally came to grips with the data, I realized that the levels of activity formulated in activity theory were the analytic concepts we had needed all along.

Before going into the problems we encountered in analyzing our slide data and describing how activity theory could have helped, I will briefly sketch the problem we were studying, the methods used in the study, and our results.

TASK SPECIFICITY

What exactly do we mean by "task specific"? Consider the average kitchen. Most kitchens contain a large variety of tools. Some tools are used in many different tasks, among them, knives, bowls, spoons, stoves, and pots. Others are used for a relatively small set of tasks, for example, blenders, peelers, tongs, basters, graters, cutting boards, and butter knives. Still others are used for one task only: fish scalers, cheese slicers, nutmeg grinders, apple corers, cookie cutters, and coffee makers.

For many tasks in which computers are used, a similarly large variety of software tools is in use, ranging from extremely generic to extremely specific. Some people use calculators for preparing income tax returns, some use spreadsheets, and some use income tax programs designed for a particular year. Some companies do their accounting on calculators, some use spreadsheets, some use general accounting packages, some use accounting packages designed for a particular type of business (e.g., restaurants), and some use custom accounting software developed exclusively for them. For preparing organization charts, some people use painting programs, some use structured drawing programs, some use general tree-graph editors, and some use organization chart editors.

Slide preparation is a task for which a wide variety of computer-based tools is used. People prepare slides using text editors, desktop publishing systems, painting programs, drawing programs, spreadsheets, statistical analysis programs, business graphics programs, animation programs, and, recently, presentation-making programs. Charisma, Persuasion, and PowerPoint are highly task-specific programs intended only for slide making. Slides comprising a presentation are contained in one file. The format and common content of slides are specified once for the presentation rather than separately for each slide. Typical slide editing actions such as removing or adding a level of detail are explicitly supported.

Despite the existence of these programs, many people use structured drawing programs such as MacDraw for making presentation slides. With drawing programs, users place manipulable graphical objects on a canvas. Text and graphics, once placed, can be edited, moved, or copied. However, drawing programs' degree of support for slide making is limited. They offer, for example, no notion of a presentation set of slides. Users can compensate by putting slides into separate files and grouping them in folders or directories, or by placing all the drawings of a presentation together on one canvas, but such workarounds are inconvenient and inefficient. Drawing programs provide no support for consistency of format, font, and layout in a presentation. For example, to have the same margins on every slide, users must painstakingly arrange things that way, separately for each slide. If the formatting requirements change, users must change every slide. Standard slide content, such as logos, headers, and footers, must be explicitly placed on every slide, and changes require editing every slide. Drawing programs provide little help in changing the structure of a presentation's content; for example, splitting one slide into two requires much explicit copying, moving, and deleting of graphic objects. Drawing programs have no provision for task-specific actions such as attaching speakers' notes to a slide, as is possible with task-specific slide-making software.

In short, drawing programs lack the concepts of slides, relations between slides, and a set of slides comprising a presentation. Most of the other types of software used for preparing slides also lack support for the process of creating and editing presentation slides. Nonetheless, these programs are commonly used for slide making.

METHOD

To understand the reasons for the wide range of software programs used to create slides, we conducted an ethnographic study to examine how people create presentation slides. The informants in our study were sixteen people whose jobs involved creating, editing, and maintaining slide presentations.[3] All were college educated with several years of experience making slides. They worked for a variety of companies, ranging from single-person independent consultantships to large multinational corporations in the San Francisco Bay Area (most outside Silicon Valley). Six of the sixteen informants worked in research or marketing and made slides for their own use in presentations, with slide making being only one of many of their job responsibilities. The other ten can be considered professional slide makers; they had as a significant (for some, dominant) part of their job the creation of presentation slides for others, in a variety of business areas: legal, advertising, research, and general business.

We developed a set of questions that we asked each informant. Interesting conversational threads were opportunistically pursued as they arose. The interviews were audiotaped at the informant's workplace, often with a computer slide-making system ready-at-hand so that we could see the user's work online.

During the interviews, we began by explaining that the purpose of the study was to learn what is involved in making slide presentations, what sorts of software people use for the task, and what people's reasons are for using or not using various software tools. We asked each informant to describe the entire slide-making process, from start to finish. We allowed the conversation to flow naturally rather than strictly following the list of questions but made sure that answers to each of the predetermined questions were captured on tape. We did not explain the distinction between task-specific and generic software. Interviews ranged from one to three hours per informant.

FINDINGS

In a nutshell, we found that some users prefer generic software for making slides, and some prefer task-specific software. Users who infrequently make slides for their own use tend to choose generic software, such as whatever word processor they typically use. In terms of learning and installation time, and software purchase price, it just does not pay these users to bother with task-specific slide-making programs.

However, professional slide makers sometimes use generic software and sometimes use task-specific software. This was our most intriguing finding, and we wanted to understand what motivated the differing choices among professional slide makers. What we learned is that the choice of software program depends primarily on desired presentation quality. Is the slide maker doing a set of "quick-and-dirty" slides where there is a short turnaround time and the presentation does not require fancy text or graphics, or an elaborate presentation in which the best possible impression must be made for clients? If the presentation is simple and fast, professional slide makers typically choose task-specific software, such as Persuasion. But if the presentation is a fancy one, they choose generic drawing and/or text programs.

Why is this? For simple presentations, task-specific programs are preferred because they offer ease in containing and managing a set of slides, as described above. But for fancy presentations it is necessary to use generic drawing and/or text programs to get the elaborate graphics or text required. The task-specific programs are very limited in their ability to produce fancy text and graphics. They do only an adequate job, which is fine for many presentations but not when a really exciting set of slides must be produced.

DISCUSSION

These findings are quite straightforward and simple. Where is the confusion in our analysis that I alluded to at the start of the chapter? The trouble came as we attempted to generalize these findings, to get above the level of the simple ethnographic description I have given, in the most specific narrative terms. We wanted to say something about the nature of task specificity in general—something that might apply to domains other than slide making. We believed we had found two distinct kinds of task specificity in our study. The following quotation from one of our early drafts gives a flavor of the path we were heading down:

> It is now clear that there are at least two distinct kinds of task-specificity:
>
> • **Subtask specificity:** specialization for a specific subtask that occurs in a variety of higher-level tasks.
>
> • **End-to-end task-specificity:** specialization of a particular top-level task, i.e., supporting all subtasks in the process, from start to finish. (Johnson and Nardi, n.d.)

Here we introduced the clumsy concepts of subtask, subtask specificity, higher-level task, and end-to-end task specificity. Because our vocabulary was so unstable we created the redundant synonymous phrases "top-level task" and "higher-level task" without defining what we meant.

In activity theory terms, what we meant by *end-to-end task specificity* was simply a set of actions that comprise an activity. However, we had no notion of object to anchor the analysis; instead we posited a "top-level task," slide making. But our very data belied the reality of slide making as a task. As we saw, users constructed their activities according to whether they were making ordinary or fancy presentations;[4] slide making per se was not "the task." Thus, what at first appeared to be "a task" proved not to be a conceptually clean cut at the problem. It was necessary to understand users' objects and then to consider the actions needed to fulfill those objects. The actions involved in slide making varied crucially depending on the type of presentation desired, that is, on the users' object. An important presentation might entail an action such as constructing a beautiful graph requiring the use of a drawing package, while an ordinary presentation would make do with a simple graph that could be constructed in a task-specific program. Casting our analysis in terms of objects and actions is far cleaner and clearer than using the unwieldy terminology we made up as we went along. Had we used activity theory from the outset, our analysis would have proceeded faster, and there would have been no need to manufacture terminology.

The notion of "subtask-specificity" is also better specified in activity theory. Any object may involve the execution of specific actions that are common to many objects. For example, an action such as outlining may be needed in creating a slide presentation, or brainstorming a book, or creating a course syllabus. An outlining tool would be useful in all of these cases to support this action. As Kuutti and Bannon (1993) point out, "one and the same action can belong to different activities," which is exactly what we were trying to say with our notion of subtask specificity (see also Kuutti, this volume). Here again, activity theory provides a unified structure useful for describing what we were seeing; the conceptual vocabulary is already in place and is part of a larger, richer analytic framework than we could create with our notions of subtask and end-to-end task specificity.

The concept of task has further problems. The fact that we had to speak of tasks and subtasks is muddled to begin with, as there is no principled difference between the two (a situation that seems pervasive in HCI studies and cognitive science studies generally). And without the activity theory notion of a goal-action relation, we had no way to describe the conscious intent of a goal that is formulated to represent the action necessary for the fulfillment of the object. And yet it was obvious in our informants' statements that they structured their work according to such conscious intent, making deliberate choices that affected their work. For example, one informant described his choice of the MacDraw program versus Persuasion because of his need for good graphics:

> I think the main point about why we use MacDraw is because, yeah ... Persuasion would be better for a lot of word slides.... But nobody's willing to simplify their graphs that much. You know? It's like they would have to ... work at such a simple level to make a presentation, that ... the [clients] can't cut down on the complexity of their slides, to be able to fit in with the limitations of a program like that.

The concept of a "task" is suggestive of something atomic, neat, pure, when in fact people bring messy problems and variable points of view to their work (see Holland and Reeves, this volume). In this study it would have been far better to start from users' own points of view, with their own descriptions of their objects, rather than trying to carve out what seemed to us "a task," and which led us to the addled jargon apparent in the quote from our draft above. In fact it was only when we really came to grips with users' objects that any of our data made sense. How much easier it would have been if that had been our first step!

There was yet another problem with our analysis in the slide-making study. We learned that current task-specific software programs typically do not support teamwork very well, though teamwork is often important in the slide-making process and affects users' choice of software. This was something we should have looked for at the outset, and had we started with the activity theory notion of subject as an individual or a group, we would have. Instead, we unconsciously allowed a cognitive science bias to shape our thinking, focusing on the individual and his or her relationship to slide making. Understanding the importance of teamwork turned out to be critical to our thinking about the meaning of the slide-making study for software design, as is discussed in the next section.

I do not think it adequate to say that we could have substituted the concept of "task" for "object" and "subtask" for "goal/action" in our analysis or that we could do that now. By itself the notion of task does not suggest motive or directive force, as the activity theory concept of object clearly does (Leont'ev 1974). "Task" does not suggest a possibly collective motive as the notion of object does. The concept of subtask does not suggest the relation of goals and actions as delineated in activity theory, which allows us to make sense of users' accounts of what they are doing, as in the above quote from our informant. "Subtask" does not pick apart the crucial difference between the representation of the action and the action itself as constituted in the second level of activity. The activity theory vocabulary is much more precise, careful, and theoretically elaborated than our stock usage of the terms "task" and "subtask."

Kaptelinin (chapter 5, this volume) writes:

> The questions that arise when computer use is considered from the point of view of activity theory are: What is the hierarchical level of human-computer interaction within the structure of activity? Does computer use correspond to the level of particular activities, to the

> level of actions, or to the level of operations? Which tools, other than computerized tools, are available to the user? What is the structure of social interactions surrounding computer use? What are the objectives of computer use by the user, and how are they related to the objectives of other people and the group or organization as a whole?

These are precisely the questions that we should have asked as we set about analyzing our data. With the exception of the question about noncomputer tools, this is a veritable cookbook of questions that would have helped us to structure our analysis. Each of the issues inherent in the questions was expressly relevant to our analysis, and we ended up tackling these questions, but without benefit of the systematic framework provided by activity theory.

PRACTICAL IMPLICATIONS OF THE SLIDE STUDY

In the paper that finally emerged from our study, we recommended that the needs of end users will be best served by software architectures designed to provide modular collections of small, interoperable services (Nardi and Johnson 1994). This insight came after our labored analysis but falls out of an activity theory analysis almost "for free" in the sense that it becomes readily apparent that users' objects vary a great deal, even within "domains" such as "slide making," and that many variable actions, each of which needs a software service or set of services to support it, are needed to fulfill users' objects. This point has been made by Bødker (1991, this volume) who advocates a "tools" approach.

In our study we found that the limitations of generic and task-specific software systems were overcome by some of the professional slide makers who used both generic and task-specific software interoperably. In essence, they created their own sets of modular interoperable services out of existing software packages, using import-export mechanisms. When creating fancy presentations these slide makers might, for example, create illustrations with drawing tools and then export the files to a slide-making program such as Persuasion, which would be used to contain and organize the slides. (Slide-making programs that do not easily accept text and graphics files from other programs are, needless to say, not popular with these slide makers.) One user observed,

> Persuasion and PowerPoint are sort of integrated programs, and they're good for someone who isn't a power word processor, who isn't a power graphic artist, where they basically want to type in their own headers and dot points, and it's great for that.... But if you have to go beyond that—where you're ... doing real serious word processing or doing some real elaborate graphics—it just doesn't cut it either way.... *There hasn't been any software that does everything well.* (emphasis added)

We found further support for the idea of interoperable services in the need for teamwork among some of the professional slide makers who work collaboratively on presentations. One user explained,

> "But the way we work is that ... there are dozens of people out there thinking up things, and we integrate presentations for all of them. And so for us to be able *to distribute that work amongst enough people to get it done, we need to break it down into smaller units* ... For each job here, if we used Persuasion, each job ... would have its own ... file with all of its slides in it. But slides get used from one job to another ... And so I think because of that, [Persuasion] wouldn't work. The outlining ... you know, is wonderful. But [Persuasion is] really designed for a different type of work atmosphere. It's designed for the guy who's sitting down and going to do his own presentation. (emphasis added)

An architecture supporting the interplay of small modular services to be applied to the slides for varied purposes by different users would enable collaborative development distributed across a set of cooperating users.

CONCLUSION

I have tried to give a flavor of our efforts to analyze the slide data in a conceptual vacuum. While our insights were good, our conceptual vocabulary was not, and it cost us unnecessary time and effort. We struggled to find a means of expressing and explaining what was emerging in the slide data, when all along the data would have made immediate sense if we had applied the notions of subject, object, action, and goal from activity theory.

The lack of a shared vocabulary of concepts among HCI researchers costs us all time, effort, and insight as both thought and communication are hindered. Without a shared analytical frame of reference we fail to move beyond narrow interests and perspectives, to advance a practical science of HCI. Research findings are not cumulative in the way that scientific findings should be; we work autistically in our particularistic interests and promiscuous vocabularies. While activity theory is not a panacea for these problems, it has a well-articulated conceptual apparatus and a core set of concepts that are useful for empirical analyses of HCI problems. The example of the slide study shows that the basic concepts of activity theory can provide a solid framework with which to approach the analysis of data in problems of human-computer interaction.

ACKNOWLEDGMENTS

My warmest thanks to Vicki O'Day for her comments on an earlier draft of this chapter and to Jeff Johnson who insisted that we empirically test our ideas on task specificity.

NOTES

1. This chapter is a revised version of a paper published in *Proceedings East-West HCI Conference*, St. Petersburg, Russia, August 2–6, 1994, used with permission of the publisher.

2. Trademarks: Charisma, MicroGrafx; Persuasion, Aldus Corporation; PowerPoint, Microsoft.

3. In an ethnographic study, participants are called *informants*; their role is to inform the investigator. This is in contrast to the use of the term *subjects* for experimental studies, in which participants are subjected to experimental conditions and observed.

4. As well as some other factors that I do not have space to describe here, but there is a paper in preparation: Johnson and Nardi (n.d.).

REFERENCES

Bannon, L. (1991). From human factors to human actors: The role of psychology and human computer interaction studies in system design. In J. Greenbaum and M. Kyng, eds., *Design at Work*. Hillsdale, NJ: Lawrence Erlbaum Associates.

Bannon, L., and Bødker, S. (1991). Beyond the interface: Encountering artifacts. In J. M. Carroll, ed., *Designing Interaction: Psychology at the Human-Computer Interface* (pp. 227–253). New York: Cambridge University Press.

Bødker, S. (1991). *Through the Interface—A Human Activity Approach to User Interface Design.* Hillsdale, NJ: Lawrence Erlbaum Associates.

Card, S., Moran, T., and Newell, A. (1983). *The Psychology of Human Computer Interaction.* Hillsdale, NJ: Lawrence Erlbaum Associates.

Casner, S. (1991). A task-analytic approach to the automated design of graphic presentations. *ACM Transactions on Graphics* 10:111–151.

Glaser, B., and Strauss, A. (1967). *The Discovery of Grounded Theory.* New York: Aldine Publishing.

Gould, J., Boies, S., and Lewis, C. (1991). Making usable, useful, productivity-enhancing computer applications. *CACM* 34:75–85.

Hutchins, E., Hollan, J., and Norman, D. (1986). Direct manipulation interfaces. In D. Norman and S. Draper, eds., *User Centered System Design.* Hillsdale, NJ: Lawrence Erlbaum Associates.

Johnson, J., and Nardi, B. (n.d.). Creating presentation slides: A study of task-specific vs. generic application software. In preparation.

Johnson, J., Nardi, B., Zarmer, C., and Miller, J. (1993). ACE: Building interactive graphical applications. *CACM* 36:40–55.

Kuutti, K., and Bannon, L. (1993). Searching for unity among diversity: Exploring the "interface" concept. In *Proceedings InterCHI'93* (pp. 263–268). Amsterdam, April 24–29.

Leont'ev, A. (1974). The problem of activity in psychology. *Soviet Psychology* 13(2)4–33.

Nardi, B. (1993). *A Small Matter of Programming: Perspectives on End User Computing.* Cambridge, MA: MIT Press.

Nardi, B., and Johnson, J. (1994). User preferences for task-specific vs. generic application software. In *Proceedings CHI'94* (pp. 392–398). Boston, April 24–28.

Suchman, L. (1987). *Plans and Situated Actions.* Cambridge: Cambridge University Press.

Winograd, T., and Flores, F. (1987). *Understanding Computers and Cognition: A New Foundition for Design.* NJ: Ablex.

Vlissides, J., and Linton, M. (1990). Unidraw: A framework for building domain-specific graphical editors. *ACM Transactions on Information Systems* 8:237–268.

III

Activity Theory: Theoretical Development

Introduction to Part III

In the first chapter of part III, which explores theoretical extensions to activity theory, Dorothy Holland and James Reeves address the need for a concept of perspective. In a study of student programmers, they show how perspectives derive not just from institutions (in this case, the university) but from more personal objects developed and held by individuals or groups (the programming teams). There are institutional influences, but "the perspectives escaped total determination and so were diverse because they were also constructed by the teams contingently, from cultural discourses and symbols specific to their experience." Holland and Reeves show that perspectives may be fundamentally social (without arguing that perspectives cannot also be attributed to individuals). In their study, group perspectives emerged in a seamless, spontaneous way with very little interaction on the part of group members. Like Raeithel and Velichkovsky (this volume), they are concerned with the joint construction of a social reality based on collective activities in public arenas.

Vladimir Zinchenko's essay explores in depth two basic notions of activity theory—functional organs and the relation of internal and external forms. Zinchenko proposes a new spiritual dimension to activity, drawing on a wide variety of poetic, artistic, philosophical, and scientific sources, in the manner of scholars of the "Silver Age" of Russian culture. (The Silver Age lasted from roughly the beginning of the twentieth century to the early thirties when government persecution drove important scholars underground or to gulags, where many languished and some died, among them Bakhtin, Losev, Florensky, Spet, and Mandel'shtam, all of whom we encounter in Zinchenko's paper [Zinchenko 1995, personal communication].) While drawing on classical, intellectual sources and coming out of a completely different tradition, this approach to thinking about things by casting a wide net seems to be very much in the spirit of human-computer interaction design, which takes inspiration from many far-flung sources, among them film, theater, industrial design, graphic design, fine arts, dance, and games.

Zinchenko confronts the knotty problem of articulating the unity of the internal and external, which, despite our disavowals of Cartesian dualism, is extremely difficult to actually do. He explores this topic by proposing "convertible" internal and external forms, linked through "living motion," in which the boundary between internal and external is so fluid that it becomes impossible not to see them as a unity. Examples from poetry, art, and music are offered; for example, an arresting image of Rostropovich and his cello, delivered in the words of Rostropovich himself, wonderfully conveys the sense of the unity of internal and external that Zinchenko argues for.

Zinchenko's concern with the spiritual derives from his belief that society does not fully determine activity and experience; there is an unpredictable, ungovernable, and creative impulse in people, or at least those people who have attained a kind of spiritual ascendancy that he posits (see figures 12.4–12.7). This impulse resists even the most violent repression and reacts to culture by changing it. The word "spiritual" here does not refer to a belief in the supernatural (though it could) but is rather a property of human consciousness that exhibits the means to resist and to create. Following Foucault, Zinchenko identifies practical activity as an aspect of the spiritual; it is in doing that we transcend culture. Holland and Reeves (this volume) get at something like this in their study of student programmers (though in a benign form, not involving violent repressions!). Zinchenko proposes a scheme of development that might depict, if not fully explain, the students' insistence on doing things their own way, on finding their own path.

Zinchenko's concerns with the spiritual are timely. A trend in Western science (and pseudoscience) is a move to reductionistic schemes in which genes, or gender, or neurons, or regions of the brain, or other reductionist constructs are said to determine thought and behavior. These schemes are appealing because they seem to offer such clear, understandable explanations for the confusions of our times. They provide a moment of relief in the perplexing business of getting through a day of postmodern muddles.

But reductionist schemes rely on the simplifying fallacy of the Cartesian envelope, locating a deus ex machina carted around inside the individual: the gene, the gender, the neuron, the region of the brain. The seductions of reduction are hard to resist; they simplify the enormity of explaining thought and behavior by containing and confining the object of study "beneath the skin." Vygotsky's original brilliant project of providing a truly social theory of consciousness (see Bakhurst 1991), to which the chapters in this book are heir, as is the work of many other researchers both Eastern and Western, has proved an extremely difficult one. However, it is all the more important in today's social climate. The racist, sexist, and elitist implications of some reductionist views run very deep. If they were not so potentially pernicious they would be comical soundbite updates of the "devil made me do it" genre of explanation. But even the liberal press (in the United States) is taken with the easy explanations, despite their implications. Book reviewers write positive or "neutral" accounts of reductionist works, impoverishing debate and promoting socially degenerate discourse.[1]

To tie these concerns back to technology, we see that a view of human experience in which mediation is central clearly places key influences on thought and behavior outside the bodily shell in which neurons or genes or regions of the brain are the primary forces. To understand how profoundly technology changes a person, and how a person can profoundly change technology, is to place oneself outside a system of thought in which something like genes can be simplistically conceived as providing the fundamental answers. To go even further, as Zinchenko has, in talking about transcendent functional organs and a spiritual ascendancy made possible by culture, by experience, and by the something more that is the impulse to create and to resist, is to provide an alternative to reductionist accounts.

Zinchenko offers a startling view of culture as a complex vacuum in which people navigate around and through cultural boundaries in unpredictable ways. It is not easy to grasp such a concept; metaphorically, I imagine it as something like being very proficient in the use of a particular virtual reality system: you know the system well and navigate in it comfortably, even happily, and at the same time you are aware, perhaps dimly, that it is but one reality, a reality that you may give up or modify or challenge at some point in the future. Or you may become even more deeply immersed in it and wedded to it.

Zinchenko's essay certainly will not tell us how wide to make the scroll bars, but as a backdrop against which to think broadly about mediation, technology as functional organs, and the way we use mediators to create, and sometimes resist, culture, his essay is provocative and penetrating.

Finally, Yrjo Engeström and Virginia Escalante explore the history of the "Postal Buddy," a failed U.S. Post Office kiosk. They trace in detail the design influences of the many parties involved with the Postal Buddy, including Frog Design of Macintosh and NEXT fame.

Engeström and Escalante probe actor-network theory for possible enhancements to activity theory; in particular, they look for a means of dealing with "interactions between multiple activity systems." They find that while there are some useful concepts in actor-network theory, the abstractions yielding elegant network representations damp out an important source of energy and trouble in the system: "the inner dynamics and contradictions of the activities of the various actors in the network." (As mentioned in chapter 4, this is also likely to be a problem in distributed cognition analyses, which tend to focus on function at the system level.) The reasons for the failure of the Postal Buddy could not be located within actor-network theory because the theory lacks a way to talk about the actual experiences of end users, which turned out to be critical to the demise of the Postal Buddy. Actor-network theory is preoccupied with power, authority, the establishment and maintenance of large networks and institutions. End users do not figure prominently in this theoretical world; as Engeström and Escalante say, "Somehow the networks don't reach that far."

While an actor-network analysis is animated by the Machiavellian machinations of powerful actors, as Engeström and Escalante explain, activity theory considers an entire activity system, including and extending all the way to the activity system of the users of the technology. I find this an example of the essential humaneness of activity theory; activity theory does not forget the end user, the ordinary person of no particular power who is expected to use the technology created by others. This insistence on studying the total activity system also recalls Bellamy's study (this volume) in which she found she could not simply study learners but had to consider educators, parents, and other players in the educational system to design and deploy the technology correctly.

But isn't a "total activity system" what anthropologists have tried to study as "a culture," arguing axiomatically that "holism" is necessary to any understanding of culture? While there is a common thread between activity theory and anthropology in looking at the entire unit and not just selected pieces of it, an activity system is not the same as a culture. A culture is presumably bound by a common language, belief system, polity, and so forth (though even this is in dispute). An activity system, on the other hand, is organized around an activity, identified by both subject and researcher by an object, and activity entails a practice in which members of many cultures might participate. While it is not always easy to pinpoint an activity analytically, as Christiansen (this volume) points out, it is much easier than identifying a culture. An activity is less grand and less abstract than a culture; because it materially involves practice, you can see it and talk about it more readily. Looking at practice provides a focus that the concept of culture does not have; often culture is depicted in an entirely ideal-mental manner. At the same time, investigating an activity is not merely logging "behavior"; consciousness is at the forefront of the activity theorist's concerns.

Engeström and Escalante propose an alternative to actor-network theory in which the history of the Postal Buddy is analyzed with tools from the Scandinavian model of activity. This model adds some key concepts to activity theory: rules, community, and division of labor (see also Kuutti; Bellamy; Holland and Reeves, this volume, on the Scandinavian model). This is a dangerous move in one way, for it opens up the scope of analysis to potentially everything, as does anthropology. But by retaining the anchor of the activity system, which is much more precisely located than "a culture," the Scandinavian model enlarges the scope of analysis in a controlled fashion. Still, it remains to be seen how further extensions to this model are added. The concepts of "rules," "communities," and "division of labor" have been studied extensively by anthropologists, along with a multitude of other interesting aspects of culture, such as kinship, worldview, religion, magic, cosmology, polity, child-rearing practices, linguistic behavior, and cognitive skills, to name a few, and not to mention the current concerns with the influences of gender, race, ethnicity, nationality, and social class on human life. As soon as abstractions such as "rules" and "communities" are cracked open, they yield a plethora (or Pandora's box) of fresh, compelling topics of inquiry. This is another facet of the "explosion" of which Kaptelinin (chapter 3, this volume) writes and remains a challenge of future research.

Engeström and Escalante found that the design of the Postal Buddy failed because of the designers' misidentification of users' objects, the designers' conflation of objects and tools, and the transmogrification of designers' own objects played out in a "love affair" in which love proved, as it so often does, to be blind. The subtle analysis here would have been extremely difficult without the tools of activity theory. Engeström and Escalante demonstrate this artfully not only by using actor-network theory as a foil but by scrutinizing the explanations for the Postal Buddy's fate given by the Post Office and the Postal Buddy's creators. While they do not reject these explanations, they broaden and deepen them, delivering their analysis in a cogent, precise way, scaffolded by activity theory. While HCI specialists will not be at all surprised to learn that an unsatisfactory user experience was the Achilles' heel of the Postal Buddy, the coherence and depth of Engeström and Escalante's analysis get us beyond simply making assertions about the user experience and allow us to talk with economy and precision about just what went wrong with that user experience.

As a final remark on part III, I observe that Zinchenko ends his paper with some reflections on writing it and notes that his intention was to go beyond activity theory while "keeping safe at the same time all the valuable achievements accumulated" in activity theory. This sensible recipe seems like a good one to follow with respect to our own traditions as we explore new theoretical foundations for understanding and designing technology.

NOTE

1. Thus you can find out in the Sunday papers why you and your spouse sometimes do not understand each other (one is male, the other female); why men crave women and women crave babies (genes); why the underclass will never stop being the underclass (genes via IQ points); why "the races" differ (genes via se-

lection by climate); why you are an aware, responsive actor in the world (neurons); and so forth.

REFERENCES

Bakhurst, D. (1991). *Consciousness and Revolution in Soviet Philosophy.* Cambridge: Cambridge University Press.

Zinchenko, V. P. (1995). Cultural-historical psychology and the psychological theory of activity: Retrospect and prospect. In J. V. Wertsch, P. del Rio, and A. Alvarez, eds., *Sociocultural Studies of Mind.* Cambridge: Cambridge University Press.

11

Activity Theory and the View from Somewhere: Team Perspectives on the Intellectual Work of Programming

Dorothy Holland and James R. Reeves

The study we describe here, an ethnographic investigation of the cognitive work of three programming teams, led us to emphasize an aspect of activity that is relatively unexplored: the developing perspective of intellectual workers on their contexts of action.[1] *We followed teams of students in a department of computer science as they were being taught "software engineering." Despite their subordinate position as students, we found that the institution was not totally successful in dictating their work; we could not assume a similarity of work activity across teams. Instead, the teams' perspectives on their projects were collectively developed over the course of the project, and they diverged. Consequently, the teams differed in their construal of the objects of their intellectual work, the significance and time they devoted to the components of their work, and the ways in which they carried out the project. In this chapter we recount these differences and relate them ultimately to ongoing tensions and contradictions within and outside the university. "Perspective," we argue, usefully extends the applicability of theories of situated cognition, especially activity theory, to the type of diversity we encountered.*[2]

We began our ethnographic study of student programming teams with the assumption that intellectual work is embedded in socially organized activities. In *Cognition in Practice*, Lave (1988) recounts case studies of people solving math problems in different settings. She argues persuasively that "math" is situated in collectively created physical and social environments and in collectively organized activities. Because it is situated, problem solving with numbers is not constant across activities. Math in the grocery store, for example, turns out to be different from math in school. In our case we wanted to see how the cognitive tasks of designing programs and writing code were embedded in broader activities. We were also especially interested in each team's use and reuse of the intellectual resources they produced (e.g., whiteboard drawings, scheduling charts, minutes of meetings) with various supporting technologies. We saw our task as explicating the intellectual work of programming as it is situated within a set of historically emergent activities and technologies.

As is often the case with ethnographic studies, we were surprised by what we observed. One of our surprises had to do with the marked differences in the priorities that teams assigned to their tasks, including the programming itself. The three teams we followed from their projects' start to finish differed greatly in where and how they planned and carried out tasks such as designing the program, writing code, attending to relations with the boss and client, and preparing user and implementation manuals. These were student teams, whose projects were part of a class on software engineering. The class was designed to prepare them for future work on large-scale programming projects in either commercial firms or agencies. Yet despite constant lessons on the rational and business-oriented conduct of programming projects (including demands that the division of labor follow that of commercial software teams) and despite frequent supervision by the teacher (called "boss" for the purpose of the projects), all of the teams managed to organize their activities in ways that to a greater or lesser extent circumvented class lessons. Team A saw its project as an opportunity to develop an elegant, efficient program; Team B focused on satisfying institutional demands in exchange for institutional rewards (a good grade); and Team C became so enmeshed in internal and external struggles that the relationships among its members frequently became the object of its work.[3]

These deviations from class-dictated objects of work, procedures, and practices were not surprising from the vantage point of experience. Given our own histories as students in schools and workers in companies and government agencies, neither of us was too amazed that the university was unable to dictate the ways in which the teams would organize their programming activities. But the views offered by the preponderance of research on programming teams did not equip us to address the diversity.

As we argue elsewhere (Holland, Reeves, and Larme 1992), research on programming teams frequently begins with the implicit assumption that teams work from a rational, goal-oriented perspective on their projects. The program is assumed to be the object of the work, and efficient and orderly progress toward building the program the ideal to be approximated.[4] Coincident with these assumptions, which we referred to as the "ideological model of work," is a restricted methodology. Intellectual work by programming teams is typically studied as it is carried out in one or two events, such as a design meeting. Critically reflecting on this common approach, McGrath (1990) concludes that researchers have mainly studied groups carrying out tasks assigned by experimenters or management, not groups carrying out projects.[5] Such studies are, in effect, bound to a slice-of-time strategy, with the unfortunate result that historical processes particular to the project, including the development of what we discuss below as "perspective," usually go unobserved (McGrath 1990).[6] Grudin, in 1988 and again in 1994,[7] points to these shortcomings and their significance. From his analyses of failed computer-supported cooperative work (CSCW) applications, he concludes that "we need to have a better understanding of how groups and organizations function and evolve than is reflected in most of the systems that have been developed" (Grudin 1988). Otherwise, we would add in further interpretation of these failed applications, studies will continue to miss historical processes of power, politics, and control in the workplace that make programming projects more complex than is imagined by the ideological model of work.[8]

We also found theories of situated cognition to be of limited help in addressing the diversity among the teams. Here were teams formed in similar ways and supposedly participating in very similar activities. Their performances were even monitored externally from an explicit and continually articulated position. Yet the teams construed their work in different ways and in the process created different intellectual tasks for themselves. When explicating activity theory's emphasis on the contextualization of cognition in socially organized, historically derived activities, writers often use hunting as an example. They describe the individual's thought and action in procuring food as constituted within the collective activity of hunting (Axel 1992; Kuutti 1991; Leont'ev 1978). In these explications a constancy of the collective organization of hunting across teams is often implied. But in our case, any assumption of consistency was impossible to maintain. What we found is comparable to learning that, over time, the hunting groups develop different "takes" or "views" of hunting, so that the activity ends up differing from team to team. Perhaps one team focuses on hunting as a masculine competition, to the point that the hunters relentlessly pursue the prey that best symbolizes virility, disdaining all others. Perhaps another elaborates a second opportunity offered by hunting, namely, an escape from other domestic duties. This team begins to pursue whatever prey takes them farthest away for the longest time. It is the development of team "perspectives" on projects that we address in this chapter.

THEORIES OF SITUATED COGNITION AND PERSPECTIVE

Perspective has, of course, been previously addressed in cognitive studies of work. In their study of an airport, Goodwin and Goodwin (1994), for example, point out that airport personnel have different perspectives on their work. They "see" their work objects—in this case, planes—from a variety of perspectives. Baggage handlers look at planes in terms of destination; maintenance personnel in terms of histories of inspections and repair; operations room personnel in terms of their progress through landing, unloading, reloading, and takeoff. These ways of looking, Goodwin and Goodwin incisively argue, are integral to the work that gets done.[9]

Our question, asking how programming teams come to "see" the object of their intellectual labor, is somewhat similar to the problem Goodwin and Goodwin addressed. In the case they describe, however, the workers' perspectives are given by their place, or as current social theorists might say, their "subject-position," in the work activity and by the tools through which they are required to see the planes. Workers of the same type have little leeway to create different perspectives on the planes. Baggage handlers cannot get caught up in the repair histories of particular planes, forget about the planes' destinations, and still keep their jobs. At present the formation of perspective among programming teams is less successfully constrained. They are less organizationally circumscribed and disciplined in their work than these airport personnel appear to be (Holland and Reeves 1992; see also Carroll et al. 1992).[10] As we learned, they can and do conceive their projects in different ways, and their perspectives affect the ways in which they constitute their cognitive tasks. The example we examine, following additional background on the study and the institutional matrix of the teams, shows the effects of perspective on a particular task.

CLASS, TEAMS, AND TIME LOGS

We sat in on the software engineering class in the spring of 1991, hearing the same lectures that the students did. They were mostly about techniques and principles for the conduct of collaborative programming projects. During the same period we followed three of the seven teams that were formed from the class as they completed the major requirement of the class: a complex program for a client.

The class was a popular source of programming labor for members of the university community. Professors from various departments had programs written in exchange for serving as a client. Their project descriptions were placed by the instructor on a menu. The students indicated their choice of projects and were then divided into teams. Projects had to be completed by the end of the semester (roughly three months), and their size and complexity was such that they demanded collaboration, a central focus of the course. Team organization was closely specified, and team progress closely monitored, by the instructor in weekly meetings and by the client in other meetings. In addition, interim documents, such as the user manual, were created, criticized by a team of reviewers, revised, and submitted over the course of the project.

Despite all the instruction, critique, and supervision, the teams approached their projects in ways that were not totally determined by class direction. Consider Team A's work on its "time logs" on February 24, 1991.

TIME LOGS AND OTHER TASKS IN PERSPECTIVE

February 24 was the day before the first time logs were due. Supposedly the logs had been filled in as the work had progressed over the past month. The forms required that the work be sorted into a variety of tasks and that the hours worked on each task be recorded. When the instructor passed out the time log forms at the beginning of the four-week period, he had carefully detailed their rationale: keeping detailed time records sharpens one's ability to estimate the time one needs to do different programming tasks. This sense of time is important for managing work in a rational manner.

Fifteen minutes before the end of a meeting that had been otherwise devoted to design, team members pulled out the forms and began to work out what to put in the various slots. A few of their methods for reconstructing time records are exemplified in the following segments of the meeting's transcript:[11]

> *Tully:* So, that is, that is this week. Umm, well, in that case, I probably spent a couple hours, I [could do a, like, WC],[12] and find out how many lines that is.
>
> *Peter:* Oh ...
>
> *David:* These time logs are due in this next meeting [of the class]?
>
> *Peter:* Yeah, tomorrow.
>
> *David:* Tomorrow, oh.
>
> *Tully:* Are, are they due in class or are they due ...
>
> *Peter:* Uh, they're due tomorrow sometime....
>
> *Tully:* What's, what's the difference between "Design, Analysis, Documentation" and "Requirements, Analysis, Documentation"?
>
> *Peter:* I thought the design is like the [unintelligible], I mean, documentation stuff is like the implementation document.
>
> *Tully:* Yeah, that sounds right to me.
>
> *David:* [We] haven't really done a lot on that.
>
> *Tully:* Yeah, I mean, I did a little ...
>
> *Peter:* Okay, so ...
>
> *Tully:* ... for that thing I made up.
>
> *Peter:* Okay, I should put zero for the first week there. [Probably] zero the second. Umm, okay, "Action Meetings" for the second week.... I actually [we] have whiteboards, and that should give us a hint.
>
> *Tully:* [The anthropologist's] scribbling madly. She must be vastly amused by the fact that we're figuring this out now....

Peter: Okay, there was ... okay in the second week ... [Is it] ... ? Ending on 2/3 ... I don't think we were meeting tons then. I, I have a very early whiteboard from 1/29, so we must have met for at least an hour there, but I ...

Tully: Well ...

Peter: ... I bet we met for a couple that week.

Tully: ... we must of met for several because the, umm, the project definition document was due on ... the review was due on the fifth. And the, the document was due on the seventh of February.

Peter: Oh, jeesh. Yeah we worked a lot.

Tully: ... so, so, we, that would have been the week we were ...

Peter: Yeah, we probably met ... three or four times then?

Tully: Yeah, I suspect that the requirements ...

Peter: Well for, but for those action meetings that's probably three or four hours. Would y'all say that?

Tully: Yeah, we ... we [met] several times.

Peter: [simultaneously with Tully] Are we going for three, or four? ... Let's say four.

This segment of group work could be analyzed in several ways. It could be treated as an episode of joint remembering, of the type described by Middleton (1987), where a Morris troupe recollected a dance it was to perform. Individual members of the programming team, like the individual members of the dance troupe, rotated through the various tasks that contributed to the reconstruction of the time logs. The strategies and artifacts (e.g., whiteboard photocopies as reminders of past meetings) used by Team A to reconstruct the time logs would easily lend themselves to such an analysis. Another avenue is suggested by Suchman (1994), who describes an episode (at the same airport studied by Goodwin and Goodwin) in which several workers in the operations room tried to direct the replacement of a dysfunctional ramp. Suchman skillfully elucidates the kinesic and linguistic means by which the team members constituted the joint activity, handling the problem so that the passengers could disembark from the plane. A similar analysis could be performed on Team A's interactions while filling in their time logs. Videotapes and transcriptions would show the programmers' use of linguistic markers in concert with such items as physical copies of the time log chart and the whiteboard photocopies in order to orient joint attention, for example.

But for our purposes here, there is an even more striking aspect of the time log episode. Remembering a Morris dance seems, at least on the face of it, to be something that a dance troupe would be likely to do, and handling the problem of a dysfunctional ramp something that workers in the operations room of an airport would expect to perform. The fabrication of time logs by a programming team is not so obvious an undertaking.

In class, the professor had instructed the students to treat the time log as a tool for developing themselves as programmers. The goal of their action was supposed to be honing their skills at estimating the amount of time needed to carry out various programming tasks. But instead of treating the time logs as a tool, the team treated completion of the forms as the goal. They did not reflect on the amounts of time it had taken them to do the various tasks; they did not try to use the time logs to refine their sense of their work as measured by time. Rather they moved quickly on, completing the required form, submitting it by the due date, and having a laugh that an anthropologist was watching them do what they were not supposed to be doing.[13]

We are brought up short. Not only was the task carried out in a way that defied the goal set out by the instructor, it also was carried out with little discussion of any substitute goal. As far as the observer could tell, the reconstruction of the time logs at the end of the meeting was spontaneous. It had not been planned. Nonetheless, no one was surprised when his fellow programmers set about the task in the impromptu way that they did. No one voiced any difficulties with his participation. No one objected that the group was doing the task incorrectly and no one had kept full records of their time, as the professor had instructed. How could the group so easily constitute actions that were not only unwarranted by the professor but in fact, as evidenced by their laughter, somewhat clandestine? Although the collective definition of the actions at hand and the encompassing activities that informed them seem a matter of course in the case of the operations room and in that of the dance troupe, they are not so transparent in the students' case. In both the Middleton and the Suchman studies, the problem for analysis was (in the terms defined by Leont'ev) more clearly at the level of operations. The encompassing activities in which the groups' actions were embedded were not problematic. There was apparently no need, given the aims of the studies and the characteristics of the teams studied, to look in depth at the teams' perspectives, their points of view on their contexts of action. The dance troupe was doing what we expect dance troupes to do; the operations room people were doing what operations room people do. The programming team was not doing what we expect student programmers to do.

Team A's treatment of the time logs may not have made sense in relation to class lessons, but it made good sense in relation to its perspective on the project. Clues to its view of the class and the project had been present from the very start. At the beginning of Team A's first meeting after the class began, the newly elected producer (a leadership role the teams were instructed to fill)[14] turned to the anthropologist and gave a speech about the team. He explained that the team was "prewired." The members had gotten together several months before the semester started and decided what sort of project they wanted to do. Then they recruited a client who would submit their project to the class instructor. They "signed up" for the project even before the semester officially began; and the description of the project did not even appear on the menu of projects and did not figure as a choice for other students in the class. The rest of the class (except for several others who were also in special arrangements) dutifully signed up for projects that were on the menu. Most did not know whether they would get their first, second, or third choice of project nor, in many cases, which other students would be on their team.

Team A's perspective was also evident in the ways that its members talked about, and treated their relations with, the boss and the client. Whereas Team B directed much of its effort to maintaining good relations with boss and client, Team A considered the two supervisors somewhat superfluous. When asked about the client in a postproject interview, one of the members confused the persons who had served as boss and client. When he was reminded, he said about the client: "Umm ... he, he really didn't, didn't, Umm [pause] ... 'interfere' probably isn't the right word." Another member of the team gave a similar impression:

> *Anthropologist:* You think he [the client] had a really clear idea of what he wanted?

> *Peter:* No, it wasn't really clear, because it was really my, it was really our idea. We came up with it the previous semester; he [the client] just sort of said, yeah, I like that too, I'll be your client. So it was kind of a different situation than most people.

Team A conceived the project, in the words of one of the programmers, in terms of "wanting to make something neat." He went on to say:

> We've got such cool equipment at [this university], and some of it I have always felt, like, it's not being used to its fullest extent. You could do so much neat [stuff] with it and I've had ideas for other machines, too. I don't even know if I came up with the [idea we used]. It may have been me, it may have been one of the other guys, but the idea sounded great.... So we wanted a neat tool to use and I knew I had to take the class, so instead of making something boring and stupid that I'd never use again, why not make something that was neat and that people would say, wow, you made something really neat and something useful, too.

Team B, in contrast, was more oriented to grades. Its members worked assiduously on their relations with boss and client and polished their interim documents. A sense of their persistent focus can be gained from a segment of the transcript from the second week of February. They spent the project meeting discussing the next-to-final draft of the project definition, a document soon due to the boss, client, and reviewers:

> *Kyle*: So all we need to do is check my grammar and all that jazz and.... Yeah, you just made the corrections, didn't you?
>
> *Paula*: Did you think that the sentence on the second page, at the beginning of the paragraph where I wrote that question mark, do you think it's ...
>
> *Kyle*: The second sentence?
>
> *Paula*: Yeah. To me it was just hard to understand; it sounded funny.
>
> *Kyle*: You know why, don't you, Paula? Because you're retarded.
>
> *Paula*: Does that sound funny?
>
> *Leah*: It does a little, yes.
>
> *Paula*: And I didn't know ...
>
> *Kyle*: All right. All right.
>
> *Paula*: ... I didn't know if it needed a comma, "front end," comma, "generating the request." But then the comma didn't make sense when you say, "and the database." ... Okay, what if you ...

Leah: What if you put a semicolon after "request" and cross out "and." How about that?

Paula: Yeah, or you could say . . . "is the front." . . . Okay, okay. I was thinking about . . . Leave out "and," put a semicolon after . . .

Kyle: Uh huh.

Paula: Or actually we could make that a separate sentence.

Kyle: Uh huh.

Paula: The database executes the request [unintelligible]. Just make it a completely separate sentence. Because they're not really related enough to have a semicolon. Okay . . .

Team A's meetings, in contrast, were mostly devoted to the conceptual design of the program. Team A spent little energy on the required documents and at least once threw one together in record speed, upon suddenly remembering that it was due within a matter of hours. Time logs were irrelevant to Team A's central object, producing a "neat" program. Its members turned in required documents because they also wanted a good grade, but they did them in an expedient fashion. Team A ended up achieving its objective: creating a successful program the team members valued. A measure of the program's quality can be gained from its having been chosen for demonstration at a professional conference later in the year. Team B met its apparent objective, and its members were happy as well. They ended up with a high grade, an impressive achievement given that their program consisted of just twelve lines of code![15]

PERSPECTIVE AS JOINT CONSTRUCTION DEVELOPING OVER THE COURSE OF THE PROJECT

Suchman begins the article cited above by summarizing the episode of the missing ramp. Because her introductory description omits the way in which the episode was experienced, in time and from the particular perspectives of the different workers (e.g., the baggage person versus the mechanic), she dubs her initial overview description "the view from nowhere."[16] What we have seen in the case of the programming teams is that teams construct a point of view on their project, a view from somewhere. Here we highlight two aspects of "perspective" suggested by a preliminary analysis of our data. We propose that these team perspectives, these views from somewhere, were (1) contingent and historical (2) collective and (3) developed over the course of the project.

Perspectives as Contingent and Historical

Activity theory draws attention to changes in perspective that come with expertise. Although Leont'ev's (1974/1975) well-known example of the neophyte driver is often used to exemplify changes in the focus of attention and consciousness, one could also note the widening horizons that come with developing expertise. In the early phases of learning to drive, moving the car in the desired direction is the object of the activity, shifting gears one of the actions being consciously mastered. Eventually shifting gears moves to the level of out-of-awareness operations, and driving becomes an action in the service of a more encompassing activity, such as getting from home to a new vacation spot. The driver's perspective shifts from shifting gears as a focus of attention to getting from A to B. Holland (1992) provides a very different case, that of young women developing expertise in the culturally constructed world of romance. Neophytes had rulelike ideas about relatively circumscribed behaviors, such as going to talk to interesting guys at a party. Women with more experience, in contrast, talked about more involved and long-term strategies such as "getting the upper hand." They had a better understanding of what was possible and what to watch out for. With their growing expertise, their vantage point, their perspective, on romance had changed. (See also H. Dreyfus 1984 and H. Dreyfus and S. Dreyfus 1987 for related commentary on the widening of perspective as an aspect of the development of expertise in chess players.)

Perhaps some of the differences in perspective that we observed derived from differences in expertise among the teams. After all, Teams A and C, in contrast to Team B, consisted preponderantly of graduate students. But the teams' development of perspective also involved an element of contingency. Leont'ev's account of driving a car could be read as implying a logical or natural and necessary progression of horizons, but others have alluded to the possibility of a more fortuitous formation of motives as well. For instance, in the service of explaining concepts from activity theory, Axel (1992) discusses the following hypothetical example. A member of a hunting team whose task is to flush prey by beating the bushes gets caught up in the action of beating bushes. Over time he "elevates" it from an action to an activity. Axel's example implies that actors may elaborate and redirect activities in ways that go outside the bounds of traditional expertise. Our case bears out the contingent development of perspective.

The perspectives of our teams were not ones that we would have predicted simply from sitting through class lectures or even the teams' meetings with the boss. The teams' perspectives were not wholly determined by the institution that hosted their activities but rather were modified by the team members. As we discuss in more detail below, these perspectives were not novel or created de nouveau; they bear resemblance to themes to which the team members had been exposed in other work and school situations. Team B's concern for making good grades, for example, was scarcely odd given the focus on grades in much of student discourse. Team A's rejection of the procedures taught in class that were meant to organize their work according to the tenets of "software engineering" resonated with discourses of resistance to rationalization and deskilling in the profession in general (Holland and Reeves 1992). The points to be stressed at this juncture are that the teams, despite the constant homogenizing influence of the class and its demands, did not all arrive at the same perspective, nor were their differences easily attributable to different points of development of the sort described by Holland in the example of learning romance.

Perspectives as Collective Productions that Develop over the Course of the Project

Arguing that perspectives are collectively emergent stances is more difficult than arguing that they are not simply dictated by the institution. Within activity theory, perspective, as can be seen in most of the work cited above, is treated as a property of the individual (for an exception to the usual focus on the individual over groups, see Engeström, 1986). Even those who radically question Western concepts of the individual attribute subject positions (and so perspective) to individuals (Kondo 1990). In our case as well, it is tempting to treat perspective as a phenomenon of the individual. Why not simply assume that Team A treated the time logs irreverently because the members all, independently and fortuitously, had the same view on the irrelevance of time logs to the production of computer programs? Why not assume that the teams developed joint perspectives that were simply the sum of their individual members' perspectives?

Our argument is not that individual perspectives are unimportant in teamwork but that jointly composed perspectives develop as well. In the Middleton study, the troupe members took different perspectives for the task of reconstructing the dance and together produced the dance. In our own study, again drawing on Team A for an example, David contributed significantly to the final design by consistently bringing up problems and concerns from the perspective of the prospective user. Other members drew the group's attention to issues arising from other ways of viewing the emerging product. Individual perspectives were important for the resulting computer programs. Yet we would argue that in this case, and in general, the perspectives of the individual members do not exhaust the team's perspective. Rather they relate to its production in a complicated manner. Projects are situated temporally and spatially in institutions; their histories and fates are emergent. Although individual members separately bring understandings and experiences to a project, team responses to project events are collective.

For one, teams symbolize themselves and the project. To a degree they discursively construct, with the type of semiotic mediating devices emphasized by Vygotsky, representations of their stance toward their projects. Use of these mediating devices solidifies their perspective and orients their subsequent work. Team A members talked about the team as one that was constructed purposively from talented programmers to build "something neat." Their history as a prewired group that they themselves had created was expressed a number of times and acted out in their treatment of several of the course requirements that they considered peripheral to the main task of developing an efficient and aesthetically pleasing program with the functionalities they desired. Team B early on picked up the notion that its project, because it involved a relatively large component of operations analysis, was "different" from many of the projects that other class teams had taken on. The members quickly began to describe their project and their team, both to themselves and others (including the boss/teacher and their client), as "different."

The emergence of collective perspectives is discernible from other studies as well. Carroll et al. (1992), for example, note that "members of design projects sometimes preserve and exchange informal history and rationale: they 'make' a history and rationale for their project by telling stories among themselves." The authors go on to suggest that these perspectives are important for subsequent work, playing "a variety of roles in the design team's problem-solving and group dynamics." Even in such cases as the airport described by Goodwin and Goodwin and Suchman, where the division of labor is fairly rigid and closely specified by the airline companies, the workers develop a group stance toward their work. At least there is a hint that they do. Goodwin and Goodwin refer briefly to an "ethos." Although they stress the tone of relations among workers in the operations room in their discussion of ethos, it is conceivable that ethos could encompass the seriousness with which the workers perform their duties, their evaluation of their work as good and worthwhile, rather than exploitative and boring, and their attitudes toward the company, for example. Ethos is a collective product and could conceivably, as in the case we describe here, affect the way in which work activities are construed and carried out.

The collective nature of team perspectives is especially obvious in cases where there is none. In the case of Team C in our study, powerful figures outside the group seemed to be withholding needed resources, and factions developed within the team over the stance that should be taken toward these figures. During a period of struggle that lasted over a month, as a result of these factions, much of the team's intellectual work was, in effect, devoted to resisting one another (see Merton and Schwartz 1982 for an extended analysis of a similar situation in another work setting; see also Engeström 1992).

ACTIVITY THEORY, "CONTRADICTIONS," AND THE SIGNIFICANCE OF "PERSPECTIVE"

Regardless of where one stands on the issue of joint development, "perspective," or a similar concept, needs to be elaborated in theories of situated cognition. Kuutti (this volume) refers to "contradictions," the conceptual apparatus of activity theory most relevant to the issues raised by our case. Our case reveals the enigmas that result in the absence of a concept such as "contradictions," which directs attention to historical structures and contemporary social struggles and dynamics that, in a sense, lie beyond, but profoundly shape, the institutionally supported activities of the workplace and classroom.[17]

"Contradictions," according to Engeström's (1987, 1991) model of the structuring of activity systems, are the key to understanding shifts in activity systems. The working out of multilevel contradictions, primarily stemming from the opposition between use value and exchange value in capitalist political economies, drives change. Such contradictions are clearly suggestive with respect to the on-the-ground diversity that we found embodied in the different perspectives of the programming teams. Although the third team, with its period of chronic internal struggle over leadership, is difficult to characterize along such a dimension, Team A's perspective could easily be cast as emphasizing the use value of the program it was producing and Team B's as emphasizing exchange value.[18] We also note that Lave and Wenger (1991) employ "contradiction" in analyzing situated learning. They agree with activity theorists such as Engeström who posit "the major contradiction underlying the historical development of learning" in capitalist systems as "that of the commodity" (i.e., between the use value and exchange value of knowledge). In addition, they note an inherent conflict between the interests of old-timers and those of newcomers, a systemic contradiction between continuity and displacement. Especially important for our purposes here, they link this contradiction to viewpoint, or what we have called "perspective": "The different ways in which old-timers and newcomers establish and maintain identities conflict and generate competing viewpoints on the practice and its development" (115).[19]

"Perspective" is a further elaboration of concepts that link activity systems to one another and to structures and dynamics of power and privilege. It allows one to speak more directly to agency in Marx's work, to the capacity of humans to apprehend the conditions of their activity and through their practice change those very conditions. As Lave and Wenger implicitly suggest, "perspective" potentially names a place where systemic contradictions become manifest in persons. We would add that perspective is a place where contradictions and other aspects of self in contexts of action become manifest and elaborated in consciousness.[20] What we have seen, by following teams over the entire course of their projects, is that perspectives are constructed and develop over time through the appropriation of discursive and other cultural resources. "Contradiction" marks out the major and derivative oppositions set in motion by the system; "perspective," as we use it here, points to the understanding that agents (in this case, programming teams) construct about themselves in relation to the contexts of action in which they find themselves. These perspectives, in turn, affect the ways that the teams construe and carry out their projects. The perspectives of the teams we observed were heavily influenced by the members' positions as students and defined by the logic and illogic of the institutional system of instruction and by the cultural resources (e.g., time logs) required of the teams. Still, the perspectives escaped total determination and so were diverse because they were also constructed by the teams contingently, from cultural discourses and symbols specific to their experience.

The efforts by Engeström (see also Engeström 1989) and Lave and Wenger to recognize and to account for the effects of systemic contradictions, social conflict and difference, played out in the outcomes of activities are relatively unusual. Attention to efforts to control and discipline labor in work activities and to attendant resistance is not commonplace among theorists and researchers of situated cognition. This is often true even in the case of those who depend on activity theory, despite its ties to Marxist thought. As recently as the national anthropology meetings of 1992, Terrence Turner, in commenting on a set of research papers on situated cognition, strongly criticized the majority of research in the field for omitting these social forces and dynamics as determinants of the shape of cognitive work.[21]

For the case of intellectual labor, "perspective" highlights and problematizes the relationship between the workers and those who would manage them and/or a system that treats their labor as though it were an abstract entity. "Perspective" draws attention to the likelihood that workers (or students) construct viewpoints on their projects that are somewhat independent of the viewpoint advocated by their bosses (or teachers) and that these perspectives, even though they are sometimes embedded in practice and scarcely developed discursively, may be the basis from which workers and students react to and sometimes resist institutional attempts at disciplining them. "Perspective," at the least, is a hedge against oversimplified views of context that adopt ideological, institutionally given views of the activity at hand, or otherwise ignore the unsettled and conflicted relations of boss to employee, teacher to student, and one team member to another.

Perspective, like activity, is a historical product, and one that develops subject to events that may well be external to the immediate work context. When seen as arising from events in ongoing historical relations among people in different positions of power in fields embedding the workplace, shifts in perspective on activities and the coexistence of a variety of developing perspectives, such as we found in our case, are not surprising. The perspectives of the programming teams we studied strongly resonated with, and sometimes were explicitly linked to, the long-term, ongoing efforts to discipline programming labor to fit the needs of the software industry (Holland and Reeves 1992; see Wertsch 1991 for more general commentary) and to the perennial struggle between teachers and students.[22] Suffice it to say that if what we heard during the course of our project is any indication, there were numerous discourses circulating among the students. Many of these were alternative, if not heretical, to those of efficiency and productivity taught in the software engineering class; they included, for example, stories of heroic and gifted programmers who managed to avoid IBM's efforts to regulate and monitor them. These discourses, along with campus-wide ones on such topics as the pragmatics of making good grades with a minimum of work, competed with class instruction and with the faculty's talk about performance and learning. The students we followed had cultural resources beyond the classroom from which to construct a perspective or point of view on their software project.

As a means to understanding programming and other forms of intelligent behavior, theories of situated cognition, especially activity theory, are outstanding in their refusal to essentialize human cognition, to treat intelligent behavior as though it were simply a manifestation of ahistorical, asocial, individual cognitive potentials. Our study brings home this central point once again: writing programs for computers takes place within socially produced activities by means of historically derived artifacts and technologies. In our case, the point that "programming" is not a stable, essential cognitive task becomes obvious through the comparison across teams. As we have seen, the teams differed radically in their construction of the objects of their intellectual work and so in the place, priority, and shape given to programming tasks, in their activities. These differences afforded us the opportunity not only to point out the value of theories of situated cognition but also to discuss the ways in which social relations, struggle, and conflict affect activities. We suggest that teams of programmers, and the individuals who make them up, bring to and further develop, within the activity of programming, a perspective on their project, a point of view derived in part from the discourses extant in their communities, discourses that may or may not follow institutional ideologies.

ACKNOWLEDGMENTS

The work reported in this chapter is part of a larger study funded by the National Science Foundation (Grant IRI-9015443; PI: John B. Smith; Co-PI, F. Donelson Smith). We thank the members of the teams that we studied, as well as the instructor of the class, for their assistance in this research. We also give credit and thanks to Anne Larme who was the researcher for one of the groups described here; to Phil Agre, Carole Cain, Dana K. Smith, and especially to Bonnie Nardi, William Lachicotte, and two anonymous reviewers who made helpful comments on earlier drafts of the chapter; and Marcy Lansman, John Smith, and Don Smith, who have contributed comments and ideas to our analysis of the study.

NOTES

1. This is a revised version of a paper that appeared in *Mind, Culture and Activity* 1 (Winter–Spring 1994), used with permission of the publisher.

2. We use "theories of situated cognition" as a general term for the three major approaches to the study of cognition in practice: activity theory, situated action models, and distributed cognition. (The labels come from Nardi, chapter 4, this

volume, who also lists key texts and analyzes the implications of the differences among these approaches for practical projects of system design.) Although the historical roots of these theories are quite different and their stances on the structuring of activity, the significance of culturally developed artifacts, and other key issues, disparate, they are similar in two respects that are important for this chapter. First, all three insist on the study of cognition in practice, as opposed to cognition in the head, and so they sometimes provide inspiration for one another. Second, they all have underdeveloped concepts of perspective and say relatively little about issues of social diversity, conflict, and power. Activity theory, which receives more of our attention than the other two, is by far the most developed in this latter regard.

3. Team A consisted of four graduate students in computer science; Team B, one graduate student and two undergraduates; Team C, three graduate students and two undergraduates.

4. There is movement away from these assumptions. See, for example, Flor and Hutchins (1992). For a discussion of coercion, control, and manipulation in the workplace rather than cooperation and efficiency, see Kling (1991) and Kyng (1991). Allen (1992) provides a useful critique of the view of social and organizational reality held by groupware technologists.

5. He concludes that "there is a need to study groups that are doing projects that extend over meaningful periods of time, on which the constituent tasks are viewed as merely one possible set of instrumental activities that can accomplish the project mission" (McGrath 1990, 28).

6. For examples of exception, see Guindon, Krasner, and Curtis (1987), Bendifallah (1989), and Bendifallah and Walt (1989). These studies examine teamwork in the course of work on a project; however, their analyses of organizational "breakdowns" solely in terms of an interruption of the flow of work and productive effort in the team ignore the possibility that teams in fact work on breakdowns.

7. Grudin (1994) felt it necessary to reiterate many of the points from his article of six years before. Many recent empirical studies of programming or design teams continue to restrict their observations to one or two events over the course of a project, make implicit assumptions about what should be considered work (and dictate those assumptions in an experimental protocol), or assume design meetings as the loci of collaboration. See, for example, Guindon (1990), Olson and Olson (1991, 1992), and Olson et al. (1993).

8. Developers may well ignore these issues because they do not view them as being properly defined as "work," and their efforts in system design have been aimed at enhancing or improving work processes, that is, improving productivity. A consequence of not taking into account social, political, and motivational factors of workplaces in designing groupware is that the application can be resisted or outright rejected (see the reception given to Coordinator by some users in Grudin 1988).

9. Making a related point in regard to theories of learning. Lave and Wenger (1991) stress the always present inflection of knowledge according to the social position of its enactor.

10. We use "disciplined" in a Foucauldian sense to indicate a history of institutional attempts to supervise, classify, monitor, and otherwise control works. For Foucault's ideas of discipline see Foucault (1975).

11. All names are pseudonyms.

12. The UNIX utility "word count."

13. We do not mean to imply that the team completely avoided being disciplined to work "in time." As will be seen, possible untoward effects are not the point of focus here.

14. The producer's job was to call meetings and keep the team's production on schedule.

15. The brevity of Team B's program was due in part to the client's change of goal in the middle of the project. Because the team had built good relations with the boss (teacher) and kept him fully apprised of and involved with the project, he was willing to reward their efforts nonetheless. For other teams we saw, which maintained a less extensive and less forthcoming relationship with the boss, the situation could have been a disaster.

16. Through her discussion of the missing ramp episode, Suchman vividly critiques nonpractice orientations along the same lines proposed by Bourdieu (1977, 1990) in his less than vivid discussions of the limitations of structuralism. Structuralist approaches omit point of view. For insistence that point of view is important, see also Kondo (1990), Volosinov (1929/1986), and Goodwin and Goodwin (1994).

17. Activity theory, with its roots in Marxist analyses of capitalism and other historically specific modes of production, works with an explicit social theory not evident in the situated action and distributed cognition approaches. Lave's (1988) attention to "arena" is recognized as an exception to the general focus of situated action models on locally emergent patterns. But the development of "arena" in *Cognition in Practice* is overshadowed by the book's focus on the immediate details of doing arithmetic in the grocery store, an emphasis appropriate to the book's objective of challenging the dominant view of cognition as occurring in the head. See also Nardi (chapter 4, this volume).

18. Connections could also be drawn between the type of contradictions Engeström (1987, 82–92) designates as secondary and quaternary.

19. They write: "Newcomers are caught in a dilemma. On the one hand, they need to engage in existing practice, which has developed over time: to understand it, to participate in it, and to become full members of the community in which it exists. On the other hand, they have a stake in its development as they begin to establish their own identity in its future" (115). It is to this contradiction that they

attribute "the common observation that knowers come in a range of types, from clones to heretics" (116).

20. Delineating an important development in Marxist thought, now placed under the rubric of cultural studies, Stuart Hall (1980) presents a view of the relation of agency, consciousness, culture, and structure that we find helpful here.

21. The session went under the rubric of activity theory and was organized in memory of Sylvia Scribner and her outstanding cognitive studies of work.

22. Some analogize student-teacher relations to those between factory workers who try to do minimum work for maximum salary and owners who try to extract maximize work for the minimum salary (see Foley 1990 for an example). Depending on the class composition of the school, others see the relations as a product of teachers' protecting and working-class students' challenging class relations extant in the larger society (see Willis 1981 for one example).

REFERENCES

Allen, J. (1992). Groupware and social reality. *Computers and Society* 22(1–4):24–28.

Axel, E. (1992). One developmental line in European activity theory. *Quarterly Newsletter of the Laboratory of Comparative Human Cognition* 14(1):8–17.

Bendifallah, S. (1989). Understanding software specification teamwork: An empirical analysis and model. Ph.D. thesis, University of Southern California.

Bendifallah, S., and Walt, S. (1989). Work structures and shifts: An empirical analysis of software specification teamwork. In *Proceedings of the 11th International Conference on Software Engineering*, Pittsburgh, Pennsylvania.

Bourdieu, P. (1977). *Outline of a Theory of Practice*. R. Nice, trans. Cambridge: Cambridge University Press.

Bourdieu, P. (1990). *The Logic of Practice*. R. Nice, trans. Stanford: Stanford University Press. (First published 1980)

Carroll, J. M., Van Deusen, M. S., Karat, J., Alpert, S. R., and Rosson, M. B. (1992). *Raison d'être: Embodying Design History and Rationale in Hypermedia Folklore*. Yorktown Heights, NY: IBM Research Division, T. J. Watson Research Center.

Dreyfus, H. (1984). What expert systems can't do. *Raritan* 3:22–36.

Dreyfus, H., and Dreyfus, S. (1987). *Mind over Machine: The Power and Expertise in the Era of the Computer*. Oxford: Blackwell.

Engeström, Y. (1986). The zone of proximal development as the basic category of educational psychology. *Quarterly Newsletter of the Laboratory of Comparative Human Cognition* 8(1):23–42.

Engeström, Y. (1987). *Learning by Expanding: An Activity-Theoretical Approach to Developmental Research*. Helsinki: Orienta-Konsultit Oy.

Engeström, Y. (1989). The cultural-historical theory of activity and the study of political repression. *International Journal of Mental Health* 17(4):29–41.

Engeström, Y. (1991). Activity theory and individual and social transformation. *Activity Theory* 7(8):6–17.

Engeström, Y. (1992). *Interactive Expertise: Studies in Distributed Working Intelligence*. Research Bulletin 83. Helsinki: University of Helsinki, Department of Education.

Flor, N. V., and Hutchins, E. L. (1992). Analyzing distributed cognition in software teams: A case study of team programming during perfective software maintenance. In J. Koenemann-Belliveau and T. G. Moher, eds., *Empirical Studies of Programmers* (pp. 36–59). Fourth workshop. Norwood, NJ: Ablex Publishing.

Foley, D. E. (1990). *Learning Capitalist Culture: Deep in the Heart of Tejas*. Philadelphia: University of Pennsylvania Press.

Foucault, M. (1975). *Discipline and Punish: The Birth of the Prison*. A. Sheridan, trans. New York: Vintage.

Goodwin, C., and Goodwin, M. H. (1994). Seeing as a situated activity: Formulating planes. In Y. Engeström and D. Middleton, eds., *Cognition and Communication at Work*. Cambridge: Cambridge University Press.

Grudin, J. (1988). Why CSCW applications fail: Problems in the design and evaluation of organizational interfaces. In *Proceedings of the Second Conference on Computer Supported Cooperative Work* (pp. 85–93). New York: ACM.

Grudin, J. (1994). Groupware and social dynamics: Eight challenges for developers. *Communications of the ACM* 37(1):93–105.

Guindon, R. (1990). Designing the design process: Exploiting opportunistic thoughts. *Human-Computer Interaction* 5:305–344.

Guindon, R., Krasner, H., and Curtis, B. (1987). Breakdowns and processes during the early activities of software design by professionals. In G. Olson, S. Sheppard, and E. Soloway, eds., *Empirical Studies of Programmers*, Second workshop. Norwood, NJ: Ablex Publishing Corporation.

Hall, S. (1980). Cultural studies: Two paradigms. *Media, Culture and Society* 2:57–72.

Holland, D. (1992). How cultural systems become desire. In R. G. D'Andrade and C. Strauss, eds., *Human Motives and Cultural Models* (1st ed., pp. 61–89). Cambridge: Cambridge University Press.

Holland, D., and Reeves, J. R. (1992). *Creativity and rationalizability: Beasts in the tarpits of software engineering*. Paper delivered at the annual meeting of the Society for Literature and Science, Atlanta, Georgia, October.

Holland, D., Reeves, J. R., and Larme, A. (1992). *The Constitution of Intellectual Work by Programming Teams.* Technical Report 92-13. Chapel Hill: University of North Carolina, Department of Computer Science.

Kling, R. (1991). Cooperation, coordination and control in computer-supported work. *Communications of the ACM* 34(12):83–87.

Kondo, D. K. (1990). *Crafting Selves: Power, Gender, and Discourses of Identity in a Japanese Workplace.* Chicago: University of Chicago Press.

Kuutti, K. (1991). Activity theory and its applications to information systems research and development. In H. E. Nissen, H. K. Klein, and R. Hirschheim, eds., *Information Systems Research: Contemporary Approaches and Emergent Traditions* (pp. 529–549). Netherlands: Elsevier Science Publishers.

Kyng, M. (1991). Designing for cooperation; cooperating for design. *Communications of the ACM* 34(12):64–73.

Lave, J. (1988). *Cognition in Practice: Mind, Mathematics and Culture in Everyday Life.* Cambridge: Cambridge University Press.

Lave, J., and Wenger, E. (1991). *Situated Learning: Legitimate Peripheral Participation.* Cambridge: Cambridge University Press.

Leont'ev, A. N. (1974/1975). The problem of activity in psychology. *Soviet Psychology* 13(2):4–33. (Original work published in *Voprosy Filosofii*, 1972, 9:95–108)

Leont'ev, A. N. (1978). *Activity, Consciousness, and Personality.* Englewood-Cliffs, NJ: Prentice-Hall.

Leont'ev, A. N. (1981). *Problems of the Development of the Mind.* Moscow: Progress Publishers.

McGrath, J. E. (1990). Time matters in groups. In J. Galeher, R. Kraut, and C. Egido, eds., *Intellectual Teamwork: Social and Technological Foundations of Cooperative Work* (pp. 23–61). Hillsdale, NJ: Lawrence Erlbaum Associates.

Merton, D., and Schwartz, G. (1982). Metaphor and self: Symbolic process in everyday life. *American Anthropologist* 84:796–810.

Middleton, D. (1987). Dance to the music: Conversational remembering and joint activity in learning an English Morris dance. *Quarterly Newsletter of the Laboratory of Comparative Human Cognition* 9(1):23–38.

Olson, G. M., and Olson, J. (1991). User centered design of collaboration technology. *Journal of Organizational Computing* 1:61–83.

Olson, G. M., and Olson, J. (1992). Small group design meetings: An analysis of collaboration. *Human-Computer Interaction* 7:347–374.

Olson, J. S., Olson, G., Storrosten, M., and Carter, M. (1993). Groupwork close up: A comparison of the group design process with and without a simple group editor. *ACM Transactions on Information Systems*. Special Issue on Computer Supported Cooperative Work 11(4):321–348.

Suchman, L. (1994). Constituting shared workspaces. In Y. Engeström and D. Middleton, eds., *Cognition and Communication at Work*. Cambridge: Cambridge University Press.

Volosinov, V. N. (1986). *Marxism and the Philosophy of Language*. Cambridge, MA: Harvard University Press. (Original work published 1929)

Wertsch, J. V. (1991). *Voices of the Mind: A Sociocultural Approach to Mediated Action*. Cambridge, MA: Harvard University Press.

Willis, P. (1981). *Learning to Labor: How Working Class Kids Get Working Class Jobs*. New York: Columbia University Press. (Original work published 1977)

12

Developing Activity Theory: The Zone of Proximal Development and Beyond

Vladimir P. Zinchenko

It is widely acknowledged that machines and technology have profoundly influenced the twentieth century's outlook, perspective, and worldview. What is less evident is that our perspective has been similarly influenced by the human sciences. Psychoanalysis, behaviorism, reflexology, and many other theories have shaped the way we think about the world and ourselves.

Human personal development is mediated by special entities. Mediators are understood as twin entities that have both material and ideal properties simultaneously. Most scientists consider mediators to include such things as signs, words, symbols, myths, and deeds. Human beings open up the material side of a mediator through their activities. And while accomplishing one or another kind of activity, they assimilate the ideal plane of a mediator. Then, while comprehending newly learned (sometimes unconsciously learned) senses, realized through a mediator's ideal plane, humans necessarily recognize new ways of manifesting their activity.

Computers possess unique capabilities to model events, whether natural or artificial. So, it seems quite reasonable to try to model the mediating functions. In fact, such efforts are underway, with many modern software products modeling some of the functions of some mediators. Programs such as games provide an opportunity for training some human sensory-motor functions. Here the mediating function of action is modeled. Still other programs (e.g., databases) make it possible to perfect memory, attention, operational thinking, or understanding; they model some of the mediating functions of signs and words. Other programs (e.g., programs for teaching history) help to understand cultural values. Here we meet models for some mediating functions. There are not, however, any programs that can completely model the mediating functions of symbols, myths, and deeds.

This chapter concerns the proximate and further development of activity theory. It deals with the version of activity theory that has been developed in the Russian psychological tradition and also considers another subject that has emerged in our collapsing empire under the conditions of stagnation and odd-primitive capitalism, which are referred to for some reason, as a "market economy." The subject is related to Vygotsky's (1984) wonderful idea of a child's "zone of proximal development" and appears as an idea of the infinite human development perspective. Some may interpret the idea as merely one more notion from post-Soviet utopian thought. But the very fact of the subject's emergence illustrates the general defectiveness of the Marxist formula claiming that "[social] existence determines one's consciousness." It is the remarkable property of consciousness that it seeks by all available means to reach beyond the bounds of existence and not become destroyed by it or driven into a dead corner.

Science points to a number of oppositions among various forms of activity, such as action-reaction and activity-behavior. Reaction and behavior are often characterized as determined and preordained, involving little or no freedom or free will. On the other side, when describing categories such as activity, action, act, or deed, freedom is usually emphasized—right up to asserting that the forms of activity and freedom are identical. In consequence of this identification, humans are characterized as free creatures and, flowing from that freedom, as active ones. As Schelling (1927) wrote, "It is the internal necessity of comprehensible essence that is freedom ... necessity and freedom exist one within the other as a single entity that is viewed from different sides—and so appears now one, now another."

Not only the identification of act and freedom is interesting here but also the idea that freedom cannot be reduced to necessity, as it was with the stoics, Spinoza, and, to a considerable extent, Kant and Fichte (see Oyzerman 1993). Schelling's notion of freedom means that the differences between action and reaction, and activity and behavior, are not absolute differences. Activity and behavior—like freedom and necessity—can represent the same entity, can exist one in another. When the entity (activity in our case) is viewed from different positions, it appears now as an act, now as a reaction. That is why it is so difficult in psychology to differentiate act and reaction, to provide them with strict definitions. Of course, freedom is related not only to action but also to human consciousness. Still, when we speak of human nature and the genesis of freedom in terms of psychology, it is action—not reaction or reflex—that appears in the first place. Hegel (1959) wrote well about this: "The true being of person ... is their activity; individuality is real in it." Hegel also associated freedom with motion: "Spirit itself is not anything abstract; it is a system of motions, where it distinguishes itself in moments, but stays free while distinguishing." A poetic character from Goethe's *Faust* makes a similar statement: "Act is the basis of existence." These words serve as a kind of touchstone for the great attention that both traditional and modern psychologists have paid to motion, action, and activity, including the construction of general theories of activity, action models, and the study of various aspects of living motion. Many psychologists have proposed action as a basic unit for all psychological analysis. Attempts have been made to derive all psychological functions from action/living motion, and, in some cases, to reduce all psychological functions to these categories. For example, Sherrington not only derived memory and anticipation from action but also localized them in action (and not in the brain):

> While performing actions directed towards a final, completing act ... a possibility arises for elements of memory (even though rudimentary ones) and elements of anticipation (even though insignificant ones), to develop into the psychological ability to "unwrap" the present moment backward to the past and forward to the future, an ability which is considered with higher animals as a token of higher mental development. (Sherrington 1969)

Similar ideas are found in the works of Janet (1929), Rubinshtein (1940), Piaget (1946), and many others (for a more detailed review of these ideas see Zinchenko and Smirnov 1983). Thus, motion, action, and activity appear in psychology not only as objects of observation and sources of psychological data but also as fundamentally generative in their properties and functions. Rubinshtein (1940) observed that "psychological analysis can discover *in activity* the origins of all psychological elements." Activity and action are, then, explanatory principles for all human psychology.

These principles were developed in Soviet psychology by scientists such as Leont'ev (1974) and Rubinshtein (1940), and their colleagues and followers, in the framework of activity theory. In this theory, perception, recognition, attention, memory, imagination, thinking, and emotion are not merely derived from activity *but are themselves interpreted as forms of activity*. That is, these psychological functions are not parts or elements of activity; rather, they are themselves distinct forms of activity. Activity theory introduces a unity, an inseparability, of thought and activity; doing and thinking are no longer polarities. This notion is the most distinctive aspect of the activity approach to the human mind. This approach has been developed and elaborated, beyond the original work of Leont'ev and Rubinshtein, by scholars such as Gal'perin (1966), Davydov (1985), Zaporozhets (1986), P. I. Zinchenko (1979), D. B. El'konin (1989), and others.

Of course the activity approach to the human mind is not universally understood or accepted. Activity theory is closer to the European tradition than to the American one, where cognitive, executive, and activity spheres are studied relatively independently. Activity theory itself is also partly to blame for being less well known than it might be. Its adepts concentrated mostly on its external features rather than its internal ones; its operational-technical properties were more carefully worked out than its intimate-personal aspects. This chapter is aimed at enriching activity theory's basic definitions and suggesting a location for its proximate development zone, especially with respect to the intimate-personal sphere.

BASIC ACTIVITY THEORY NOTIONS

In this section I consider, from scientific, aesthetic, and philosophical viewpoints, two key aspects of activity theory: functional organs and the processes of internalization and externalization.

Functional Organs of an Individual

The notion of the functional organ was introduced in German classical philosophy. Hegel and Marx considered memory, thinking, consciousness, and emotions such as love to be functional organs. Indeed, all phenomena of the individual psychological life were included among such organs. From Marx's point of view, the major property of any living system, individual or social, is its capability to create needed organs in the course of its growth and development. Similar ideas were being developed by the Russian physiologist Ukhtomsky, who defined a dynamic, integral functional organ: "Usually we associate the name 'organ' with the notion of something that has already formed, something static and constant. It is not necessarily so. Any temporary combination of forces which is capable of attaining a definite end can be called an organ" (Ukhtomsky 1978).

Living motion is a sort of motion inherent in all living organisms (though we speak here mostly of humans), in contrast to the kinds of motion inherent in nonanimated objects (a machine, or a falling stone, or a flying bullet when a gun shoots). Living motion is also a functional organ of the individual. It can react (as we react and change our walking depending on whether we on are a parquet floor on in deep snow); it is sensitive to its proper motor abilities, that is, to its own possibilities of performing one or another kind of motion (in the sense that each living organism "feels" its opportunities to perform any given motion). It also possesses "internal motor functions" or "an internal image of its possibilities." The internal image has two aspects and is related to both the operational-technical conditions for reaching a given goal and the motives that the individual has with regard to the motor task to be performed.

The sensitivity to a situation and to one's own possibilities are reciprocal; they alternate with a certain temporal shift. Their comparison in short-term memory constitutes the origin of reflection, as the simplest form of reflection is comparing one's own possibilities to a given situation. This can be illustrated with the following example. A subject in an experiment using the biological feedback technique can be trained to control the tonus of his or her blood vessels. But in order to be able to relax or strain them, the subject should first acquire the ability to feel the current state of blood vessels.

One must keep in mind, however, that defining living motion strictly is just as difficult as defining living substance in general. Bernshtein (1924) reckoned living motion to be a dynamic functional organ. Living motion may be thought of as the raw material of activity; that is, it is distinct from full object-related activity. Bernshtein argued that living motion has evolutionary properties and can react just as morphological organs do. Zaporozhets (1986) added to the notion of living motion the property of perceptibility, and Gordeyeva and Zinchenko (1991) added that of sensitivity. In other words, a human subject perceives and senses his or her own living motion.

These two properties are needed to make living motion a controlled entity. Bernshtein believed that living motion possesses a complex biodynamic tissue (or "the matter of action," as Humboldt 1918/1985 put it) and can be best described not by a metric but by a topological category. In a lovely image, Bernshtein compared living motion with a "web on the wind." The motion possesses some sensitive tissue and bears some sense-related and meaning-related features as it takes part in task solving. So, living motion—just as object-related activity that possesses its proper additional features or properties—is, in fact, a kind of dynamic functional organ.

Thus we may now speak of "neomorphs"—newly formed functional organs—which are a temporal combination of forces capable of accomplishing a certain achievement. Neomorph in this sense is an artificial formation, or an artifact. Newly acquired action, a new image of something, a new human ability or skill: all are examples of neomorphs.

Internal and External Forms in Psychology

One of the earliest, and at the same time perpetually new, themes of psychology is the interrelations between the internal and the external in human life. The problem of the internal and the external takes its origin from outside psychology and long before it. There is a dialog in the apocryphal Gospel according to St. Thomas, where the apostles talk to Christ about infants like those who enter the Kingdom. Jesus said: "Once you make internal like external, and external like internal, and upper like lower; and if you make man and woman to be one thing—so that man wouldn't be man, and woman wouldn't be woman—and when you make eye instead of eyes, hand instead of hands, leg instead of legs, and image instead of images, then you come into the Kingdom" (Apocrypha of Ancient Christians 1989).

The problem of the internal and the external is a traditional subject for aesthetics. Spet (1922) talks about reality in the context of his reflections on aesthetics:

> All of its [true reality's] internal is its external. External can exist without internal: such are illusions, but internal without external cannot be. No one single atom of the internal exists without appearance. Reality, actuality, are only defined by appearance. Only appearance is directly aesthetic. To be aesthetically perceived the internal must be mediated by the external.... The very mediation process is a matter of aesthetic contemplation that comes into being when one touches the external.... All that is aesthetically true must be true in the world. (Spet 1922)

In psychology scientists often concentrate the bulk of their attention on either the external or the internal (e.g., behaviorism, introspectionism). The underlying mediating mechanisms of internalization (Janet 1929; Vygotsky 1984; Piaget 1946; Gal'perin 1966) are still a problem of psychology. Spet's other reflections concerning the internal and the external are relevant here:

> What do we acquire from the strong love of our "near ones," when such a love is only "in the bottom of their hearts"? ... And how much would we acquire if they did not deceive us with the imaginary reality of sincere hearts but instead always behaved like those who love us? What after all is vitally real: good feeling inside or ill breeding from without, "good for humankind" inside or a knife in the hand from without, true caress and attention from without, and from inside ... —who cares what is then "inside"? ... In general, it may be that philosophers and psychologists failed to find the "seat of a soul" merely because they looked for it *inside*, whereas all of the human soul is outside.... All the blows our soul receives we wear on our outer face as wrinkles and scars. All the soul is appearance. Man is alive while he has appearance. And personality is appearance. (Spet 1922)

Here is a true hymn to the external, and yet it is, at the same time, not a negation of the internal. Spet emphasizes the internal to be an idea that is nothing if it cannot be released to the outside. According to him, all real being, down to its very last bit, is without, and all inside is but an ideal entity until realized externally.

The last statement evokes no doubts, but it is too general, for the ideal itself should be decoded, defined in a more complete way, and psychologically interpreted. Psychological interpretation is especially important here because "ideal" categories are often considered in psychology from either a naturalist or a mystical position. As I have noted, many problems in activity theory (and its predecessor, cultural-historical psychology) are far from resolved. Activity theorists have studied the process of internalization—how the external means of activity are transformed into the internal means of the activity realization—but there has been little study of externalization. Spet wrote, "To realize an ideal entity one must accomplish a complex process of uncovering the meaning of its content and bring what is actually real into the empirical level" (1922). But, in fact, the process of externalization implied in this formulation was not studied. Many different points of view concerning the structure of the internal were suggested. Some asserted, for example, that both the internal and the external have in principle the same structure or even that they are identical. The internal was sometimes reduced to various brain mechanisms.

And the very life of the internal—its living forms, its dynamics and capability to generate new forms—was not studied at all. This last reproach might seem a little unjust. Gal'perin's (1966) theory describing the step-by-step formation of mental actions contains the following sequence proposed for the process: material action, loud speech, internal speech, and ideal plane. But in this theory the ideal plane was merely marked. An ideal plane should be present at all these steps; otherwise, there is no place from which it could appear at the last step. Being asked about what is behind "internal speech"—that is, what is actually at the last stage—Leont'ev merely noted that a mighty brain's work stands behind it!

Vygotsky gave primacy to the sociopsychological nature of internalization, the general course of which, he believed, went from the interindividual to the internally individual. In other words, people's relations—culture—are what is internalized. In contrast to Vygotsky, Gal'perin made the object-related aspect of internalization primary. An object-related, material, or materialized action appeared as the first stage of internalization, and the sociopsychological plane served as a loose background for the process. In other words, according to Gal'perin, it was not human relations but the force of *things* that was internalized. In this case, there is no way to understand the nature of the ideal, of spiritual origins.

The course from outside to inside, when led to a logical end, turned out to be not so harmless. It is not only that any conception of internalization in general denies the sacred nature of human experience, but also that culture is made monological and appears as a kind of monotheistic divinity. In this view, culture not only determines development but also makes it hermetic.

Leont'ev saw that the internal plane derives initially from internalization processes. But he did not see how to follow up on its destiny, which depends on both the internal and the external. Internal development has its own rules, which differ from those of external development. Yet our knowledge of the laws of the internal is too modest to stimulate discovering the laws of the external. To a certain extent this can account for the deterministic principles that held sway in Russian psychology during the Soviet period. Only Zaporozhets (1986) spoke of "spontaneous development," that is, development from within, citing Lenin (he happily found the term in Lenin's works).[1]

What then might be another way to study (or at least discuss) the problem of the correlation and interconnection between the external and the internal? I believe it is necessary to reformulate in some way the very positioning of the problem. To do this, I discuss some ideas of internal and external forms that exist in art and science.

Linguists have studied the relation between the external and internal. For example, Humboldt (1918/1985) observed, "The human subject here is both he who observes and what is observed, so he always ... adapts himself to his internal spiritual form.... Language is a *human* organ.... That is why the art of poetry is a duality of external and internal forms, for world and man.... In poetry, external and internal forms are set in a close accordance with each other; they mutually embrace and complement each other."

Spet (1922) discussed the internal and external in detail in his work on the inner form of word. Spet believed that the morphological forms of words—how words are built—are external forms. The ontological forms of the named things are things that are used by people and named by them—things that, according to Spet's conceptualization, are the subject and the object at the same time: "pure" forms. The logical forms that are situated between them are internal forms. But all these forms—morphological, ontological, and logical—are forms of one and the same thing; they are all various kinds of the external form of word. Yet I am not speaking of sense and meaning. Spet (1922) noted, "Logical forms are, in fact, internal forms ... ontological forms are really pure forms of the existing and possible thing-related content."

Similarly, Spet explained that this very thin accordance between logical and ontological properties can serve as a criterion for determining logical validity. One must speak not only of an external form corresponding to its manifold internal forms, but of the possibility of the internal forms being developed and self-developed, transforming themselves and generating new forms—neomorphs. The internal cannot possibly be just a plane on which land cultural conceptions from the outside; otherwise change, creativity, would be impossible.

The advantage of discussing psychological problems in terms of interconnected internal and external forms, as compared to opposing the external to the internal, is that we then deal with a single object of study, discarding the unproductive objective-subjective opposition (see also Kaptelinin, chapter 3, this volume; Kuutti, this volume). When from the very beginning we tear the internal from the external, we can never bind them together again in the framework of any logically homogeneous reasoning, never return to the place where they were fused together.

Figure 12.1 illustrates how the mutual (but not simultaneous) conversion of internal and external forms occurs. Formerly we gave a brief characterization of the internal form of word described by Spet (1922). Later, Austin (1973), who could hardly have known Spet's works, introduced a similar notion of word action that he called "performative." These varied works all consider action as the major component of a word's internal form.

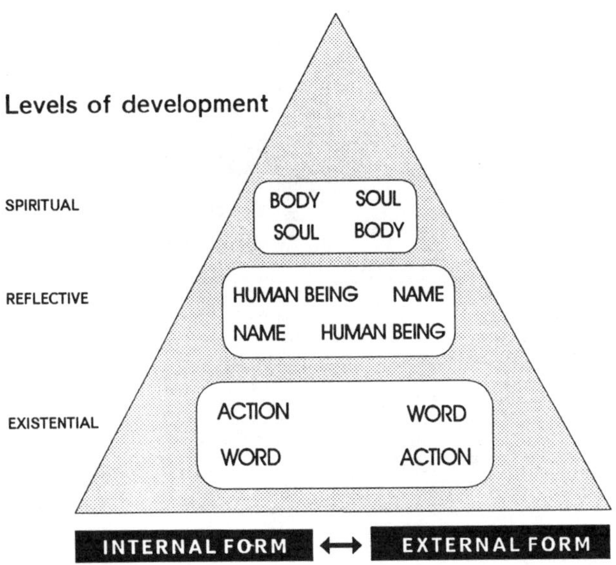

Figure 12.1
Convertibility of the internal and external forms in human subjects.

As for solving the opposite task—to demonstrate word as the internal form of action—there seem to exist some necessary grounds. Along with sensations and imagery, word has been long considered in psychology as a regulator of arbitrary motions and actions. Leont'ev and Zaporozhets (1945) introduced the notion of the internal image of a motion. As in the former case, *word* appears here as one major component of the internal form of *action*.

Figure 12.2 depicts a simple characterization of the interrelation between internal and external forms of action. The arrow, which goes from the past to the present, can bear living motions, object-related actions, and deeds. These are discrete in time and have gaps or breaks between them. The breaks are not empty; one could, in fact, name them "breaks of continuous experience." It is these breaks where fixation of the experience occurs, further motions and actions are anticipated and formed, and dynamic functional organs—artifacts—are originated. Above and below the arrow are depicted "mental clouds" or "mental depths," which embrace the past, the present, and the future with regard to various acts that occur in the time. So at whatever point on the time axis

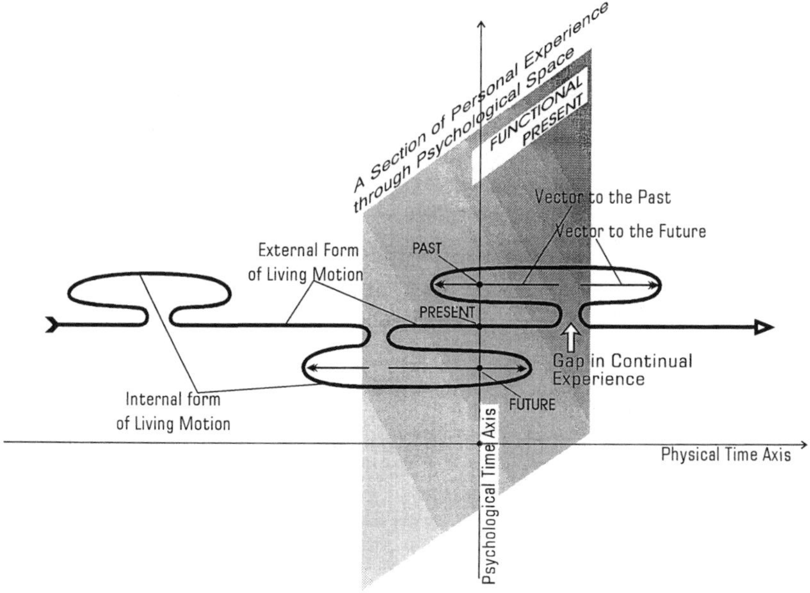

Figure 12.2
Chronotope of living motion. The loops represent the course of personal experience through psychological time.

where some act occurs one draws a secant, it will pass through all three times that together represent a field of the future. The actual future field is perceived by the acting subject as the functional present. It is the way living creatures act, using their past experiences as the means of new activity, uniting the past, the present, and the future in one structure.

The possibility of such structural union explains the wholeness, integrity of actions, and reactions to the environment carried out by living creatures. An envisioned future field may have different temporal perspectives (much like spatial perspectives)—compressed to a point, expanded, reversed, concentrating within itself all living experience.

I call the scheme in question "chronotope" (from the Greek *chronos* and *topos*) to capture the notion that time and space are combined in a single entity (after Ukhtomsky, by way of Bakhtin). Real motion and action occur within objective space and time. "Mental clouds and depths" represent subjective space and time. If these did not exist, no sensible motion or action could occur at all. One can assume that chronotope represents a kind of virtual though elementary particle of eternity, or infinity. One good poetic illustration of chronotope is found in William Blake:

> To see a World in a grain of sand,
> And heaven in a wild flower,
> Hold infinity in the palm of your hand,
> And Eternity in an hour.

Similar images are found in Osip Mandelstam:

> To take this World into the palm of a hand—
> Just as we do with a common apple

and

> In the cradle of little eternity
> a big universe gently sleeps.

These images serve as a demonstration of a virtual reality that is far from being created in modern computer systems. (That may be not so bad, because it leaves us some opportunity to enjoy poetry. For more details, see Zinchenko and Morgunov 1994.)

How might we think about the relationship of the problem of internal and external and the dynamic functional organs that we have been considering? We can observe that at the highest levels of performing object-related activity, the expert level, the object and the art of motion become a single psychophysical or even psychophysiological construct. Together they constitute a living functional organ. A quotation from an interview with the famous cello player Mstislav Rostropovich is illuminating here. Upon being asked by a journalist about his relations with his Stradivarius-Dupor cello, Rostropovich answered:

> There no longer exist relations between us. Some time ago I lost my sense of the border between us. I've got two portraits of myself—one from long ago created by Salvador Dalí, and another one made much later by Glikman, an amazing painter who lives in Germany, in his eighties now. So, in the Dalí there I was with my cello; I held it and all was excellent. In Glikman's portrait, however, there I was—and my cello became just a red spot at my belly, like a dissected peritoneum. And actually, I feel it now in this manner, much

> like a singer seems to feel his vocal cords. I experience no difficulty in playing sounds. Indeed, I give no report to myself on how I speak. Just so, I play music, involuntarily. The cello is my tool no more. Does it not feel itself offended at being so dissolved? Sure, it does! But so be it. (quoted in Chernov 1994)

This is not a unique case of a master's introspection. Among other examples of composite functional organs-artifacts I could mention D'Artagnan with his sword, horseman and horse, surgeon and scalpel, or human and computer. In all of these and similar cases we can observe temporary combinations of wonderfully consonant forces that are joined into a kind of single organism capable of the performance or enactment of a memorable achievement. Such things are possible, however, *only when a human subject inspires an object*, puts his own soul, at least partially, into it and thereby into the performed acts. The opposite is also possible. In the case of Rostropovich, the master imbibed through his cello the soul (or a particle of it) of the cello's creator, Stradivarius. Thus, tools can appear not just as an extension or amplification of human capabilities but also, and much more profoundly, as a continuation of the human soul. In our example, the cello appears to connect and continue the two souls of Stradivarius and Rostropovich.

NAME, WORD, AND SOME EXAMPLES

Now we consider the second pair of notions in figure 12.1: the notions of a human and a name. The relation between them can be understood and accepted only by considering both the human creature and the word-name that denotes it to be a living thing. Such an approach to word in general and name in particular was developed in the twenties by the Russian philosopher Losev. Like Spet, he analyzed the internal life of word, trying to penetrate into it through the sound shell. Losev viewed meaning as an authentic essence of word, pointing out that a phoneme is but an external cue, though it bears some energy of nonphonemic layers of a word. Losev (1993) related the secret of word to its contacts with objects and with other people:

> Word is a way out of the narrow bounds of an enclosed individuality. It is a bridge between "subject" and "object." A living

> word keeps hidden its intimate relation to an object and the essential knowledge of its innermost depths.... An object's name is the ring where the perceiving and the perceived—or more exactly, what cognizes and what is cognized—meet. A name involves some intimate unity of separate dominions of being; it is the kind of unity that leads the dominions to a combined existence in an integral whole consciousness that is not merely a "subjective" or "objective" consciousness.
>
> An object's name is a whole organism of its life in another life, where the other life establishes contacts to the subject's life and tries to reincarnate into it, to become it. "Man without word and name is ... essentially and principally antisocial, unable to communicate, counsel, negotiate, and, therefore, also non-individual, non-existing; he is a pure animal organism, and though still human, mindless." (Losev 1993)

This means, in particular, that humans experience a need of name. Blake notably wrote:

> I have no name,
> I am but two days old.

In one of Mandelstam's verses even a splinter in a gnat pretends to be named:

> Don't forget me, execute me,
> But name me, just give me a name.

Losev (1993) amplifies the sense of *living* word, *living* name:

> Name in a proper sense is always a *proper* name, not nominal. Name is a name for a *living* thing. Name itself is always alive. Name is generated by living interacting personalities. And the name of a thing i.e., what people call various things, serves as a tool to deal with the thing as if it were a living individuality.... The sense and meaning of name—the meaning or sense that each name possesses—is the living and individual sense and meaning of personality. Name is the revelation of a personality, the personality's face, a meaningful energy of the self-affirming individuality. Name is not just what something is called, not just a word, a term or label; it is not a signboard or conventional symbol. Name is the personal symbol, or tool, for individual-personal interaction.

In our terms, name is a functional organ, an artifact that is both product and condition of interpersonal relations. Human and name interinspire each other, reincarnate one into other. According to Losev, name carries a very special function in relation to the external and the internal, it is the demiurge of them:

> All, absolutely all, external and internal, is consecrated, and even created by name. If name did not exist, the world would have turned into a deaf abyss of dark and chaos, where *nothing* and *nobody* could be. Through name, the world and man are illuminated and realized, and self-consciousness comes into being. Mindful and clear understanding, mutual understanding, emerge with name and overcome "the blind night of animal sensation." (Losev, 1993)

And, finally, Losev (1993) gives a very good conceptualization of the sense and principle of the convertibility of external and internal forms, the mechanism that is related to all the pairs represented in figure 12.1:

> It is the antinomial game between essence and name, where both these domains are once and forever identical, where essence disappears in name in order to affirm itself, and where name drowns within essence in order to manifest itself in this eternal and wonderful game of sense; where the absolute plays with itself and with all other-being, where the last secret of naming is hidden. Our everyday fates of naming are essentially but resemblance.

And again two more lines from Mandelstam's verse:

> The name of God like a big bird
> flew out of my bosom.

I hope the reader finds here convincing support for the proposal to study the person and the person's name as convertible internal and external forms. For the convertibility to be realized, the two forms *must* be living forms. In other words, they must be complementary; they cannot exist one without the other. Name can be considered as an artifact; name is a product of interindividual, aggregate activity, a product and condition for interpersonal communication. I clearly understand that the quoted passages from Losev and Bytie need to be psychologically interpreted. I believe this will be done soon, because the development of the philosophical and psychological issues related to name may well result in unexpected turns in the areas of the psychology of personality and interpersonal relations.

Now I turn to the last pair in figure 12.1 in an attempt to consider body and soul as convertible external and internal forms. This is an endless subject; endless ink has been spilled in its pursuit. We know examples where body and soul were identified, set in opposition, reduced one to another, derived one from other, or soul encapsulated within the body or a particular organ such as the heart. In a word, there has been a wide scope for fantasy. What is the most positive in all these reflections concerns their interrelation; soul and spirit not only influence body but also depend on it.

Here we need to make some assumptions or recall some other way of thinking about body and soul with the aim of finding some basis or frame for the mechanisms of convertibility. In other words, the task is to find something that could represent and at the same time consist of the matter of body and soul. In my opinion, this "something" is living motion. Plotin knew about this:

> Why is the beauty of a live face so dazzling, while there is nothing but a trace of it on a dead face? ... A homely but living face is much, much more than a beautiful statue.... If soul rests at the level of reason, it surely sees beautiful and handsome forms. It is then, however, as if there were a face before it that was no doubt beautiful, but did not gladden view, for it had not yet the something that could attract its gaze: a combination of grace and beauty.

Pierre Ado (1991) from whose book these lines are quoted, comments: "A word has been pronounced—it is 'something': it is a motion ... which joined with beauty evokes love; it is grace." Ado (1991) cites Bergson: "It is not often that both the fascination evinced through motion and the act of magnanimity that is a Divine virtue are called with the same word; the two senses of one word 'grace' constitute one thing."

Ado, following Ravesson and Bergson, discusses the ambiguity of the word "grace." It means, on the one hand, motion, life, charm, and, on the other hand, a magnanimity, a blessing. Ado also alludes to Bergson's idea that "beauty is but stiffened grace," recalling Shlegel's definitions of music as "a fluid architecture" and of architecture as "a stiffened music." In a similar vein, Rilke, describing Rodin's works, wrote that the sculptor viewed the human body as a whole thing only while some general (internal or external) action holds all the parts and forces in a unified whole.

Thus we make a smooth shift from soul to body. Motion is a fundamental principle for body just as for soul. In Ranke's reflections we find the likening of the human body to a living wave: "To a naturalist, any form is a motion; any form is caused by motion, and our sensations can represent for us motions only" (Ranke 1901). Ranke's reflection can be compared to Rodin's opinion: "An artist's major task is to model the living muscular system.... For those who can see, the naked body represents a splendid sense" (Rodin 1913). Gorsky (1993) comments on Rodin's idea: "Most of the public and most critics cannot *see*. That is why they seek an *invisible*, bodiless, abstracted-from-the-body, spiritual sense. Actually, every outline, if it is constructive in relation to the organism, i.e., includes the body-building lines, is pregnant thereby with multiple possible subjects and senses whirled around 'flesh' and 'spirits.'" Gorsky dwells on the problem of soul. He cites the definition of soul given by the ancient musician and philosopher Aristoksen, Aristotle's disciple. According to Aristoksen, soul is rhythmically tuned body vibrations (Gorsky 1993). These examples should suffice to show how body and soul have been characterized and defined through various forms of motor activity. By no means do I wish to reduce body or soul completely to motion, but it is important to emphasize that motion is the living substance of both. The fact that the substance is present allows us to consider the interrelation of body and soul as now an internal, now an external, form.

Such a conceptualization does not contradict traditional philosophical approaches such as Spinoza's. He built his system on the concept of God, or nature (*Deus sive natura*). At the same time he identified God with body (*Deus sive corpus*); body appears as an attribute of divine substance, or nature (by extension). Similarly, while taking into account the spiritual plane of the same substance, that is, thinking, Spinoza says: "*Deus sive animus*" ("God is the living origin of human being, its spirit").

Earlier I discussed conceptions in which grace, or living motion, appeared in place of God or nature. Let us view this notion from another side. It is known that leaves concentrate within themselves all of the plant's properties. The early twentieth-century Russian botanist Timiryazev said that the leaf is a plant, even though the plant may also involve trunk, roots, and fruits. Quite similarly, the Russian physiologist Sechenov said that a muscle is an animal, though the latter may have a skeleton, blood vessels, nervous system, and so on. Let us take these notions closer to the question of what the human mind is, while taking into consideration that the body is engaged. Considering all this, one can conclude that mind represents a holistic composition of living substance and living motion.

MEDIATION AND THE MEDIATORS OF DEVELOPMENT

In both cultural-historical psychology (as in Vygotsky's work) and activity theory (especially in the versions of Leont'ev and Rubinshtein) the processes of the mind's functioning and development are understood to involve the availability of appropriate means, either external (objects or things) or internal (mental, ideal). The very development of the mind is treated in these paradigms as an act of internalization—the act of transforming an external means of activity into an internal way of implementing the activity.

In the logic of cultural-historical psychology, mediation of development refers to external means, such as a working tool, a child's toy, a sign, a word, a myth. But a simple and sensible differentiation made on the basis of the concreteness of external means is prevented by one detail. There exist tool-related, sign-related speech and symbolic actions that serve also as mediators of development. This implies that sign, word, and symbol, being first external means, then become internal or personal tools of the person.

Living motion and sign-related action can be considered as raw material—as something that exists and is to be developed and perfected. They can be referred to as means of internal or personal development. These processes do not always necessarily accompany internalization. Many actions simply are not subject to these processes, even though they can be performed mentally, internally. But if the result to be gained is to be an external one, then the actions performed to achieve a goal are naturally also external and object related. And the more the internal form has been elaborated, the more the external action is economical, elegant, and perfect.

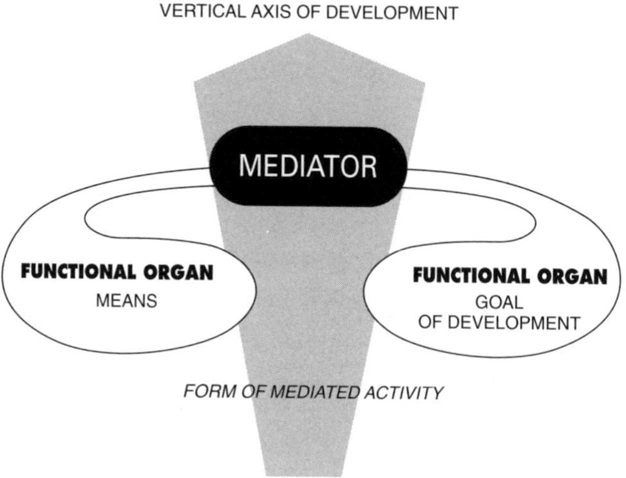

Figure 12.3
One node of development.

External tools act as mediators for actions, but so also do mental tools; let us call them virtual mediators. Among the universal virtual mediators are sign, word, symbol, and myth. Figure 12.3 displays a developmental unit or node of development. It shows how mediators can mediate the transformation of one form into another form, or of one functional organ into another functional organ.

This is a critical point in our discussion. Its complexity consists in the fact that the functional organs actually show a polyfunctional, polyphonic character. Motion and action, for example, may appear as a material of or as a means (various activity forms, or various modes of operation with virtual mediators) of development and as its goal. This applies to both external and internal forms. Once the developmental act has been accomplished, and its goal achieved, with one form transformed into another form, then the other form may become material, or a means for forming a new functional organ in a next act of formation and development. Actually, I am talking here about self-development understood as an open process. It is open toward assimilating more and more new mediators of a variety of kinds. Not just external forms are perfected in the process of development, but also internal forms are enriched. The externalization of internal forms is the necessary condition for development.

The term "node of development" (figure 12.3) comes from Mandelstam's line, "The life node, in which we are recognized and unbound for being." This line seems to characterize an aspect of development for which nodes should be not only "tied up"—in the sense of the Russian expression "a knot for memory," alluding to the old trick of remembering a certain action that you have to do by tying a knot in your handkerchief[2]—but also "untied"—nodes should not merely be properly formed but also properly realized. The latter is of no less importance and often constitutes a much more difficult process. A lack of opportunity to "untie" a node may lead to the cessation of development. Experiencing difficulties in "untying" life nodes implies crises in personal growth and development.

As the careful reader might conclude from the characterization of developmental nodes, true personal development should consist of a series of nodes. As the initial point of thinking about this subject and of searching for the appropriate image of development and its components, I took Dante's conceptualization of the development of poetic matter based on the image of a flying ship. More precisely, I took the image as it was updated by Mandelstam to a flying machine, a fitting image for the zeitgeist of his times in which a rocket symbolized something very progressive:

> Image development can be considered as a kind of development on a relative basis only. Imagine a flying machine that while flying designs and constructs ... another machine and launches it. This other flying machine is very busy with its own motion, but manages nevertheless to construct and launch yet another machine.... I add that the construction and launch of these machines during flight is not a by-product, or a side-function of the former machines, but constitutes the most necessary attribute of, and an integral part of, the very flight. It conditions the flight's possibility and safety in no less a degree than the correct rudder or reliable motor. (Mandelstam 1990)

Mandelstam provided an image of a multistage rocket whose stages are being built while performing a flight. He also noted a property of poetic matter that he called convertibility. Convertibility permits the ongoing transformation of poetical substance; the substance maintains its unity and strives to penetrate into itself. Mandelstam's metaphor is a quite plausible and interesting image of human development.

For our purposes, we replace the notion of poetic matter with the notion of psychological reality. As a result, a new conceptualization of a self-developing human subject, based on a kind of spiritual (vertical) axis (figure 12.4), occurs. I emphasize that it is self-development that we mean here, since Mandelstam spoke of penetrating into oneself. Blake believed that the prophet's role is to facilitate the opening of one's eyes, to be able to look into oneself. Now I turn to the description of the "vertical axis of development" in figure 12.4.

In relation to the horizontal axis, along which a human lifetime goes (the real-time arrow), the scheme represents a hypothesized vertical axis of spiritual growth (or spiritual development), whose (the axis's) existence has been postulated by many scientists. The scheme includes seven nodes—or seven stages of the multistage rocket in Mandelstam's terms—that represent seven stages leading to the human spiritual development (HSD) summits. The scheme is intended to extend the conceptualization (and Vygotsky's dream as well) of the supreme, or acmeist, psychology—one oriented not just to the depths but also to the heights of consciousness and personality development. The magic number of nodes (seven) emphasizes the hypothetical character of the scheme. Theoretically, the number could be bigger or smaller; what is of interest here is not the number itself but rather the possible direction and principles on which HSD is based. In fact, the scheme shows not the necessary HSD nodes but rather desirable or potentially possible ones. Not every human being reaches these summits (for a multitude of reasons).

Critical to the scheme is an understanding of spirituality. Let's agree with Michel Foucault and understand spirituality as "the quest, or practical activity, the experience, through which subjects realize in themselves the transformations needed to reach the truth" (Foucault 1993). Leaving aside the vague notion of "truth," it is important to see that Foucault numbers practical activity among the sources of spirituality. This stands in direct correspondence to the activity theory views we have been exploring. The notion of "experience" is also broad enough to embrace both the practical experience and the contemplative one, including introspection, or mental penetration into oneself. The main thing, I believe,

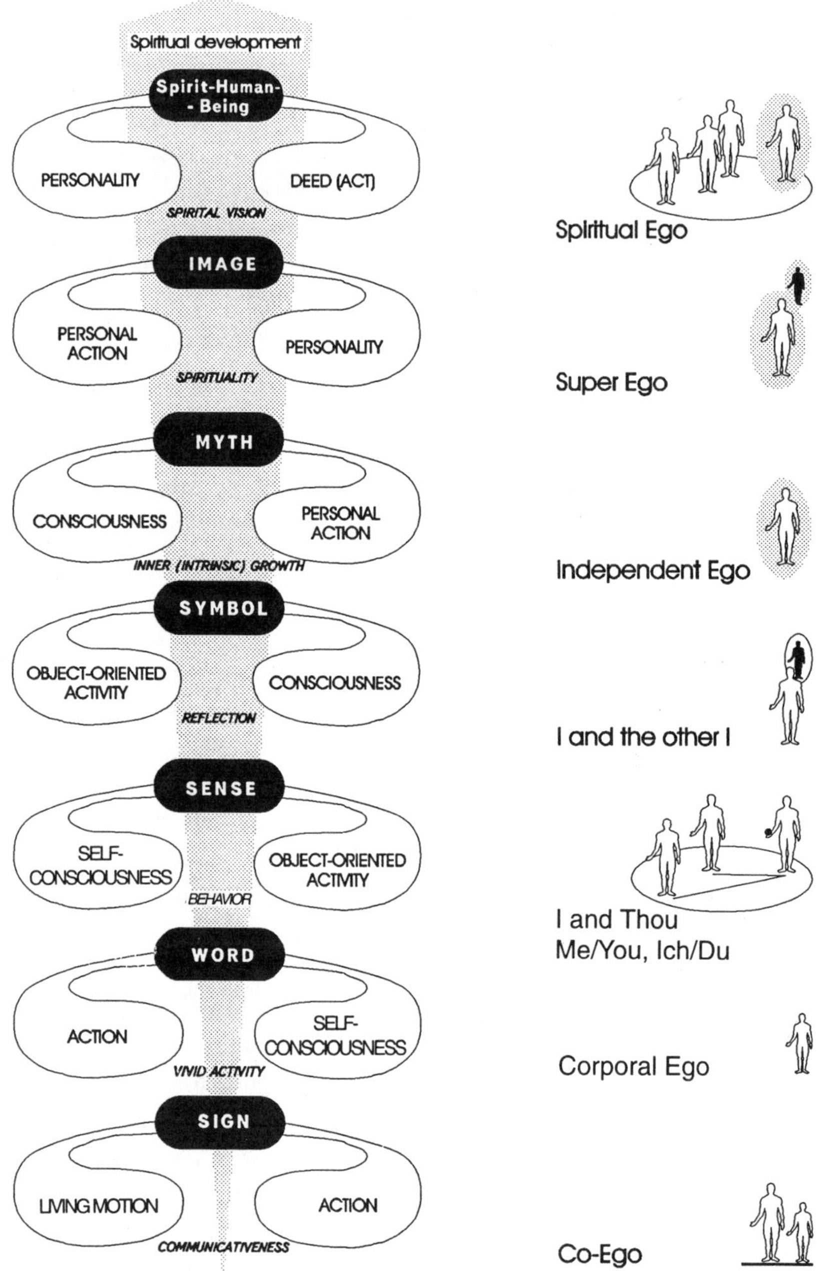

Figure 12.4
The vertical axis of development.

is that spiritual activity is directed toward transformation. In this relation it is similar to object-related activity. It is generally accepted that object-related activity is externally directed and spiritual activity is directed at the human subject, so that it changes the subject and her notion of herself. This differentiation is undoubtedly just; it corresponds to empirical observation or to everyday notions of psychology. But another view would be more useful. When a person assimilates objects, or "cultural things," the person changes as well. And if the person possesses spirituality, then the spirituality is directed also outward and can change surrounding people. Spirituality remaining only inside is equivalent to its complete absence.

As figure 12.4 shows, the ascending path to spirituality is mediated by the various forms of external and internal activity of a subject, such as communication, living activity, behavior, and reflection. Taken together, the activities are the necessary condition, the foundation, on which spiritual experiences arise and grow.

Apart from these activity forms, sign, word, symbol, and myth are critical mediators, as I have argued. All of them appear as a means of individual and social development. The essential feature of these mediators is their twofold nature. Both real and ideal properties are combined in them. A sacred symbol, according to Florensky (1977), is a thing and an idea at the same time, for example, a cross or an icon. The same is true for secular symbols. Mediators possess energy obtained from their creators, users, and worshippers. Communist and fascist symbols acquired such fanatic energy that, like black holes, they nearly devoured the great cultures of Russia and Germany.

That sense, face, and human spirit are also present as mediators requires special argumentation. Indeed the very logic of constructing the scheme as consisting of not four but seven nodes led me to include them in my conceptualization. A void in the scheme's center needed filling. But there are not, in any culture, three more mediators that would possess properties similar to those of sign, symbol, and so forth. Sense, for example, cannot be considered to have material properties, as does symbol. Sense is an ideal and yet living entity. Our hypothesis (and excuse at the same time) is that sense, while being ideal, is, in Spet's words, nevertheless rooted in existence; it carries in it (in the transformed form) some properties of existence and its values. Therefore, sense can perform mediational functions. Furthermore, ideal senses are realized in activity, implemented in its products, and objectified. The talented though not overly modest Russian poet Igor Severyanin once said:

> I am so senselessly marvelous
> That Sense bows down before me.

Various ideals and idols rooted in ideology can stand in place of sense. Though not possessing immediate material properties, sense, like thought, does have its own living energy.

There is also some argument for recognizing face and human spirit as mediators. The first investigator of personal psychology, St. Augustine, called Jesus Christ the mediator between God and human. The idea of mediation runs throughout his writing. His autobiographical work, *The Confessions of St. Augustine*, begins with a discussion of mediation. In the logic of Augustine, a mediator is necessary not only because "all the treasures of wisdom and knowledge," but also truth, speaks through it. Mediators facilitate the awakening of human activity, quest, and strivings. Christ has "humanized" the Word of God, brought it into human voice. Since Christ is identified with God, and Word *is* God, then Christ also can be identified with Word.

No special argument need be made to assume the possibility and reality of identifying Christ as a symbol. Actually He is a symbol, the symbol of faith. Christ is a sign, the sign that God sent to people. According to Losev, personality is a myth and a miracle. Thus, Christ can be identified with myth. As a result we find an interesting situation: all the main mediators—sign, word, symbol, and myth—are not only related to human spirit but concentrated within them. (That is perhaps why Augustine called Christ the "true mediator.") Thus, in the logic of theology, human spirit is a mediator. In secular logic such functions can be ascribed to another person. Since the present text follows a secular logic, I place into our scheme a spiritual human. Moving down one step, face is placed—a hero, a mask, a dictator, a guise, an idol. I leave more to the reader's imagination.

Ascending to spirituality starts with living motion in which external and internal forms are indistinguishable, amalgamated one with the other. It can be suggested that living motion—at least in its initial "shapeless form"—represents a prepsychic formation, a kind of raw material that is used to build functional organs, first elementary and then complex ones. In the course of the development and transformation of living motion, the detachment and differentiation of its external and internal forms occurs, right up to these forms' being transformed into independent external and internal actions, so as to become relatively autonomous.

This implies that there is a special generative logic in the development and functioning of external and internal forms. Action that appears as an external form enriches the related internal forms, which leads to the generation of self-consciousness. The development of self-consciousness, in turn, enriches action, and as a result the latter is transformed into activity. Activity is perfected as an external form and thereby generates the consciousness of a new internal form.

Through a careful analysis of the vertical axis of development, we can see that external and internal forms, or external and internal activities, alternate regularly. External forms such as action, activity, or deed generate internal forms such as self-consciousness, consciousness, and personality. The opposite is also true: internal forms (self-consciousness, consciousness, and personality) generate external forms (action, activity, and deed). These entities do not merely alternate, but they generate each other, remaining (I emphasize it once more) relatively autonomous formations. The external could not generate the internal if it did not contain its origins in itself. The same is true for the internal.

According to both the cultural-historical theory of the mind and activity theory, all human psychological life is mediated by tools, culture, environment, communication, social, and work activity. Such a view of the mind is principally correct, but it is only partially correct with regard to the formation of the mind and its functional organs, however we refer to them—as internal actions, transformed forms, mental functions, artifacts, and so forth. As far as their life, development, and functioning are concerned, such an interpretation of mind needs some modification. Having once emerged, or formed in accordance with the rules of internalization, an internal form keeps only genetic succession in relationship to the parent external form. In its individual existence and development, the functional organ shows independence, losing some similarity to its parent source. The functional organ behaves quite independently. It lives, matures, develops, becomes adult, it looks around no more in the search of its roots and origins, and if it does yet look around for them, then it cannot find or recall them. Such origins can be displaced or immersed into the "depths of unconsciousness" but later can be restored by means of psychoanalysis.

An important feature of the process involved in the conversion of an external form into an internal one is that the process is always a creative act of composing a new form, or deriving a new language for describing the external world, the external form of the action, one's own behavior. Finally, the functional organ acquires generative capabilities; a new form, having emerged as an artifact, becomes autonomous, capable of generating a new artifact that in its turn can have both an external and internal form of existence. And then the new artifact's existence occurs by some laws of externalization. These last are known far less than those of internalization.

Thus, for example, the origins of deed remain unclear today. Deed seems to appear like Aphrodite, from the foam of the sea. The view of deed as something that is generated by consciousness or (more often) as a logical result of a person's previous life can hardly be accepted. For one's consciousness is "exploded" by a deed, and in the event it undergoes a great change. A deed having been accomplished, the (current) difference between the external and the internal is eliminated. A person is realized in a deed as a whole, and, what is more, as a new whole. Therefore, the deed may seem unpreconditioned, inexplicable, unexpected to an outside observer. Equally strange, the deed may seem so even to the very person who has accomplished it. The person's subsequent reflections with regard to the deed give rise to certainty in his or her own forces, change his or her vision of self. In other words, deed gives rise to personality that, having once formed, also manifests itself as a whole in the external domain. Thus, the personality appears not as something separate or individual but rather as a unique entity that is an open and closed whole at the same time. All of a personality's life is a "serial deed"; personality combines in itself both the "deeding thinking" (Bakhtin's term) and deed.

I emphasize once more that the importance of the external and internal forms is not exhausted by the fact that they condition and mediate each other, generate one another. They can exist relatively autonomously, undergo changes, and develop. Such an existence that is both dependent and relatively independent at the same time entails a feature that Gurvich, the Russian evolutionary biologist who studied organic formations, has called "irrepressible ontogenesis." A sociological example is the following: if in a certain society a living human thought is prohibited (in Pyatigorsky's words there is "a bad season for thinking"), thought is still developed, though latently, and then it may emerge "from the depths." (Of course, there are cases when prohibitions are absent, and the season is good, but no thought is seen . . .)

The phenomenon of irrepressible ontogenesis can be described not only as including the development of organic and mental forms. An assumption can be made that the developmental logic of mental forms is similar to a certain degree to that of organic forms; in both cases, one cannot miss a stage. Each stage—or, in our terms, each node—is unique and necessary for full development. Considering this fact, Zaporozhets (1986) recommended following the child development strategy of amplification and enrichment of the child's experience, not the simplification of the experience; do not hurry unwisely or jump steps, he cautioned.

Let us turn again to the problem of mediatedness-spontaneity of the mind, of its artificial or natural character and to facts and artifacts. Here lies one key subject for developmental psychology. Galua, the nineteenth-century French mathematician who suggested a general theory for solving algebra equations, wrote that his results had been given to him long ago, but he did not know when he should yet come to them. An illumination is the same kind of explosion in internal activity as a deed in external activity. Functioning does not replicate development. What was the last in the course of formation and development turns out to be the first in functioning. As an Eastern proverb expresses it "When a caravan turns, the lame camel becomes the first one." All this seems to suggest that the necessity and possibility exist to transform the mediated into the immediate, an artifact into a fact, the artificial into the natural. Generally, from activity theory's point of view, it would be more exact to speak not of artiFACTs, but of artifACTs, that is, of artificially grown actions. I believe that any psychology and, equally, any theology or philosophy (when it is a cultural, not a dogmatic one) should be interested not so much in facts as in acts accomplished by human subjects. Strictly speaking, humans themselves are not facts; they are acts. This last thought belongs to Florensky; Mamardashvili caught it up and said that it is not nature that makes people, for people make them themselves.

CULTURE AS A FUNCTIONAL ORGAN

At this point, my brief characterization of the vertical axis of development could be complete; indeed, its detailed description requires a voluminous monograph. On the other hand, the suggested scheme still has one essential shortcoming that could cause readers to question the scheme's plausibility as a whole. I refer to the fact that the scheme represents one possible development scenario for a separate individual. This may seem a kind of Robinson Crusoesque scenario, obviously diverging from the true situation in the world whereby human development occurs in society, in group activity, in communication with others. I cannot simply assert that communication activity is implied in our scheme. Thus a fundamental question remains unclear: how do society, culture, and civilization take part in an individual's development? Of course, they all provide a general developmental context, but how can we conceptualize the way in which the context participates in the development of a separate person? In fact, the scheme contains an answer to this question, but for the answer to be understood and accepted, the scheme needs to be changed to some degree and explained.

A real rocket—not Mandelstam's, which is technically impossible—overcomes terrestrial attraction and then flies not in emptiness but rather in a vacuum of a complex structure, as modern physicists now describe some vacuums. The image of a complexly organized sociocultural vacuum seems to describe the situation in which human development occurs. A person can be situated in a culture and yet remain outside it, look at it vacantly, pass through it as through emptiness. That is what I mean by the metaphor of being in a culture as in a vacuum. The vacuum may become alive or acquire the properties of an object only by virtue of human efforts. Although such a conceptualization of culture has a somewhat provocative character, it corresponds with Bakhtin's (1973) thought:

> One should not ... think of the cultural domain as a spatial whole that has its limits but also has some internal territory. For the domain of culture does not have any internal territory. All of it is situated on its borders; borders are everywhere in culture, in its every moment; the organized unity of culture reaches into the atoms of cultural life; the unity is reflected in every atom like the sun is reflected in each and every raindrop. Every cultural atom essentially lives on its borders: this is what the earnestness and significance of culture consist in. Being diverted from its borders, the cultural atom loses its ground, becomes empty, arrogant, and dies.

The assumption about the border localization of culture is supported by many scientists, though interpretations vary. Some theorists place culture on the border between the natural, the individual, and the superindividual. Rabinovich (1979), for example, interprets culture as an edge, limit, or frontier that cries for someone to overcome it. Culture, in this view, is a kind of barrier that is a challenging appeal directed at people—a barrier that says, "Overcome me." An attempt has been made to locate culture at the borders of the material and the spiritual (Zinchenko 1989). Perhaps the most interesting version of the border interpretation is one that places culture on the border between life and death: "In the roots of human culture there lies an idea that seeks to overcome death through the accumulation, storage, and processing of data concerning the past.... To a certain extent, all of human culture remains a protest against death and destruction, against growing chaos—or growing uniformity, against entropy" (Ivanov 1973).

Karyakin (1989), a well-known expert on Dostoevsky's works, accepts this concept of culture. He notes, however, that culture not only remains but tends more and more toward protest; culture becomes ever more aware of itself as the only lifesaving force. It seems to me that such ambitious pretensions are not peculiar to culture. What is really important is not that culture recognizes its missionary role but rather that humanity recognize and accept the role of culture in surviving and in keeping humanity itself as a species that has (mistakenly) been called "Homo sapiens." The realization of Homo sapiens will not likely occur anytime soon; we have no grounds for any illusion on that subject, since humankind today listens to the voices of culture and mind with only half an ear. Still, Karyakin cites a consoling thought from Dostoevsky: "Being can be only when it is under the menace of non-being. Being only then comes to be, when non-being threatens it."

The menace of nonbeing—indeed, a kind of holocaust—is palpable. Perhaps its existence will accelerate the awakening of humanity's consciousness, with the help of culture itself. According to the view of human development that I hold to in this chapter, culture is a functional organ that is being created by humanity at the cost of enormous effort and has the purpose of penetrating into itself. Due to this effort, the consciousness of culture gradually becomes that of humanity, which facilitates the overcoming of human immoral arbitrariness, of human unconscious will. Because of the difficulties that culture experiences in the search for sense and truth, it often constructs and imposes on society various (tragic) utopian designs for reconfiguring society. As Nabokov wrote, "Life sometimes meanly mimics artistic fictions." But we have no other, better culture to choose, so let us accept the fact that some mistakes are inherent in culture—just as in people. Having said that, we can note that despite tragedies, culture yields its fruits, produces ideal forms, and fertilizes human development. The presence of culture is a condition for development, and our fruitful existence is a condition for penetrating into culture.

In one of his lectures, Vygotsky (1984), when considering the specificity of mental development and comparing it to other sorts of development (embryonic, geological, historical), said:

> Let's ask ourselves if we can imagine ... that at the time when the first primeval human beings had just appeared on the earth, some much later form of human—the human of the future—already existed simultaneously with them. Could it be that the ideal form immediately influenced the first steps of the primeval human, that the human of the future lived together with and influenced the primeval human? No, it is impossible to imagine.... In not one of those developmental types [embryonic, etc.] do we ever know things that happened so that in the moment when the initial form came into being ... another, highest, ideal form, that usually should appear at the end of development, already existed and immediately interacted with the first [form]. Here is what the greatest specificity of child development consists in as compared to other developmental types: in child development—in the sense of a child's personal development and of the personality's specific human properties—environment

> serves as a source of development, i.e., environment plays the role not of situation, but of a developmental source.

In the light of the quoted argumentation, we can reasonably assume that the most important function of culture consists in the creation of ideal (in both direct and figurative senses) forms. The latter represent the proximate and further (with infinity as a limit) zone of human development. Vygotsky (1984) made the statement more concrete with regard to children's speech: "A child's speech is a personal activity of the child and we make a grave mistake when we try to discuss it separately from ideal forms, i.e., from the speech of adults. Only discussing speech as a part of dialogue, of collaboration, of communication, will help us to understand how it changes.... The ideal form is a source of the child's speech development." The same is true for consciousness, intentionality, and generally subjectivity understood in a broad sense. All of these phenomena represent not only personal qualities but also ontogenetic, superpersonal ones that serve as a source of the former.

The idea that an ideal form exists at the beginning of development is not a new one, but it has been forgotten completely by psychologists. Spranger (cited by Rubinshtein 1940) seems to have been the first psychologist who suggested that the notion of development is not only defined by the relation between the actual and ideal structure, between the ideal and real forms, but also is driven by them. (In my opinion, ideal forms should be considered not as determining or driving forces but rather as inviting forces.) Of course, even earlier sources can be found, for example: "In the beginning was the Word."

We should speak, however, not of where the origin of the notion of the "ideal form" lies, but of its real functions in development. This is not an idle question, since when one ascribes the driving or originating functions of development to culture, ideal form, or environment, one leaves thereby unclear the role that subjects themselves play in their development. But they do not behave passively, and in due course they even become themselves the source and drive that is capable of developing culture and civilization, generating new ideal forms and overcoming older ones. Unfortunately, humans spend too much energy attributing generative, developmental forces to environmental changes. For further discussion I find it useful to quote some reflections by one great poet:

"Nobody, not even an inveterate mechanist, considers an organism's growth to be a result of environmental variability. That would be impossibly insolent. Environment can only invite an organism to growth.... Thus, an organism is to environment a possibility, a desirability, an expectancy. Environment is to an organism an inviting force. Not so much an envelope, but a challenge" (Mandelstam 1990).

If we accept this view, then we should recognize the relations between an organism and environment and between human and culture to be mutually active, communicative, and dialogical. The dialog may be friendly or hostile; it may become aggressive.

A person may accept the challenge of culture or remain indifferent. Culture may invite or repel. In other words, there is a "difference in potentials" between ideal and real forms, which generates the driving forces of development. Thus, the forces are situated not in culture or in the individual but between them, in their interrelations. As to culture's potential, even though it is huge and hardly can be measured, principally it is known and understandable. The nature of proper human potential, however—and a person's measurable characteristics to be included—remains mysterious and enigmatic. The only thing that can be claimed is that human capabilities are apparently commensurate with the potential of culture, and sometimes (in some domains) they exceed it. It is well known that an infant is open to the perception and assimilation of any of more than seven thousand human languages. It is also known that infant twins in a situation of communicational deprivation generate a sort of language that is understandable to them alone; the subsequent task of deciphering it is similar to the one of deciphering the dolphin's language. Not resting further on traditional and fruitless debate about the nature of individual development potential, I cite one poetic image of it:

> And long before I dared to be born
> I was a letter of the alphabet, was a vine's line
> I was the book you dreamed of
> (Mandelstam 1990)

It is the tripled "was" on the poet's "thinking lips"[3] that represents the necessary condition of both growing into an ideal form and also the possibility of overgrowing it.

Let us turn to figure 12.5, which represents the ontological and phenomenological planes of development. It retains the vertical axis of development that we saw in figure 12.4, but is called here the "real form." Next to it, the same vertical axis is shown rotated by 180 degrees and called the "ideal form." The two forms are joined. The link between them illustrates Vygotsky's idea of immediate interaction with a highest, or ideal, form that takes place from the first steps of a child's development.

Of course, circumstances in real life do not always turn out so happily as the picture shows. Chance comes into play, including the chances involved in birth. Actually, the "ideal form" interacting with the first developmental steps of a child may well be far from ideal. Besides, it may turn out that the child's potential is not sufficient to reach high developmental levels (figure 12.6). Thus, it is not only the concrete circumstances of birth, or the nearest environment that determine the situation of personal development, but social conditions as well.

Of course, real people, with their language, their world of meanings and symbols, and other forms that preexist or precede an individual's development, are the true carriers of ideal form. The opportunities that exist for the development of an individual depend on how rich the ideal form is. Ideal form or culture appears as a kind of an inviting force. It exists, it calls for development, but it by no means obtrudes itself (in figure 12.7 we see a fairly successful case). On the other hand, the carriers of ideal form are capable of restricting individual development, preventing realization of the great potential of human development. They can direct a human subject to a channel of their choosing, can form a personality with features of their choosing, or even create a sort of zombie.

Consider figure 12.5 again. With a little imagination, one can perceive some similarity between its structure and the double spiral of genetic code. Thus the represented interaction between ideal form and real form can be characterized as the "genome" of human cultural and spiritual development.

The overall scheme of the figures should be understood as a sphere of comprehension, or a kind of visual space in which a discussion of human development may more conveniently take place. All the schemes entailed in these figures and in this chapter might well be regarded as hypertextual

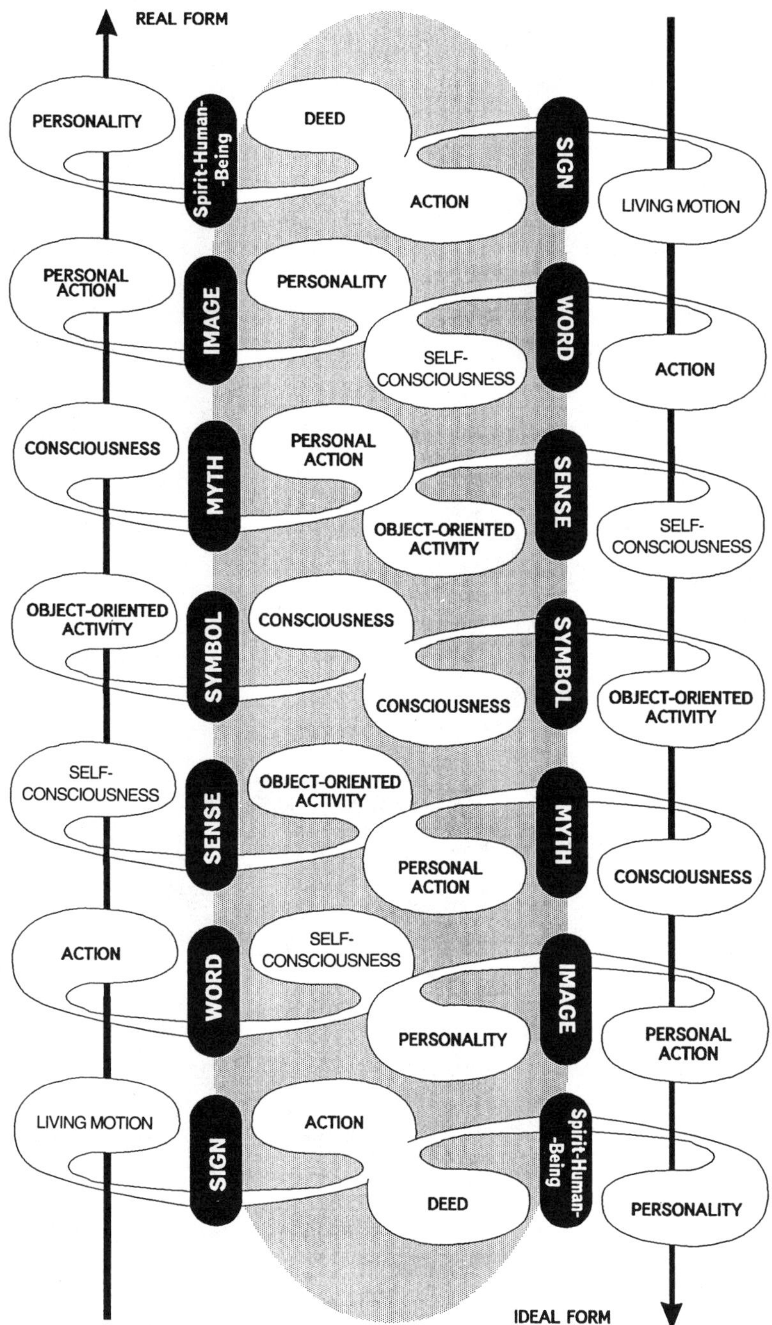

Figure 12.5
Ontological and phenomenological aspects of development.

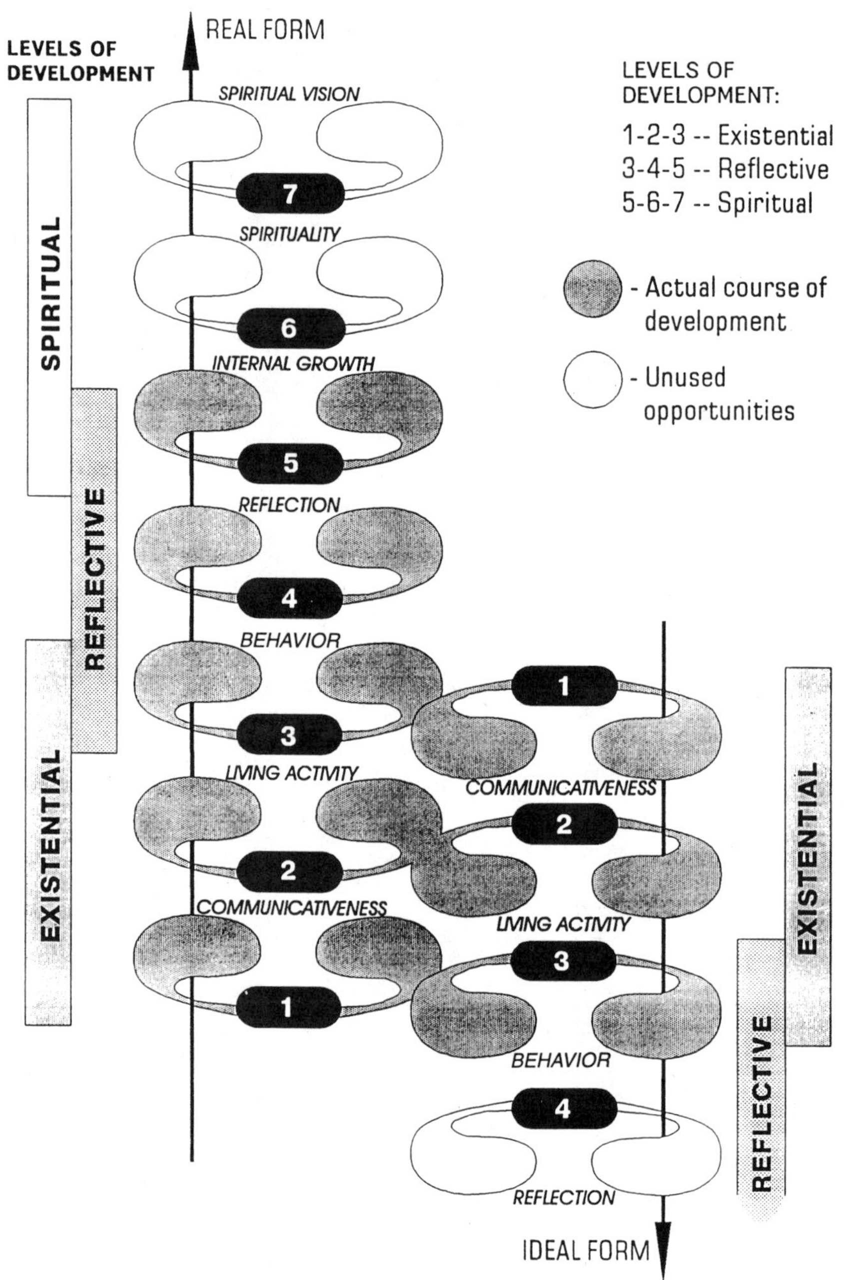

Figure 12.6
Visualization of one possible developmental case.

material. Interested readers may change the conceptual filling, change relations that connect various elements, even change the overall arrangement as well. One thing is important to keep unchanged: the *vertical* axis of development. For the most highly interested and creative readers I provide figure 12.7, a special space for conceptual, constructive efforts stimulated by a general composition bare of details.

AFTERWORD

My intention while writing this chapter was to go beyond the bounds of the zone of proximal development of both cultural-historical psychology and activity theory, while keeping safe at the same time all the valuable achievements accumulated in these trends. At this stage of work I have not completely succeeded in differentiating the ontology of psychological reality from the gnosis involved in studying it. This is a subject for further investigation. Regrettably, the ontology I am trying to understand is not only psychological reality itself but also the social reality in which the theories were developed. The Soviet reality has been very easily and intelligently referred to by Pyatigorsky as a "dead season for thought." Thoughts, however, arose even during that time; besides, they were truly "not seasonal" and therefore the more carefully and attentively these thoughts should be regarded. To the Russian ear, words like *season* and *zone* sound similar and, respectively, are felt to have a similar sense that implies such things as limits, developmental limitations in time, sensitive period, or a special kind of sensitivity to certain phenomena, impacts, interactions. This old and fruitful idea, linked to such names as M. McMillan, M. Montessori, and O. Decroly, has developed thus far primarily in pedagogics and psychology. In Russia, however, the word *zona* also has another spatial-geographical sense. For several generations of Russian people it has become a synonym for a concentration camp (e.g., gulag)—in both a physical and mental sense, beyond the bounds of which I strongly hope to go. Thus the chapter's subtitle, "The Zone of Proximal Development and Beyond," has a double meaning not just from a conscious point of view, but from an ontological one as well.

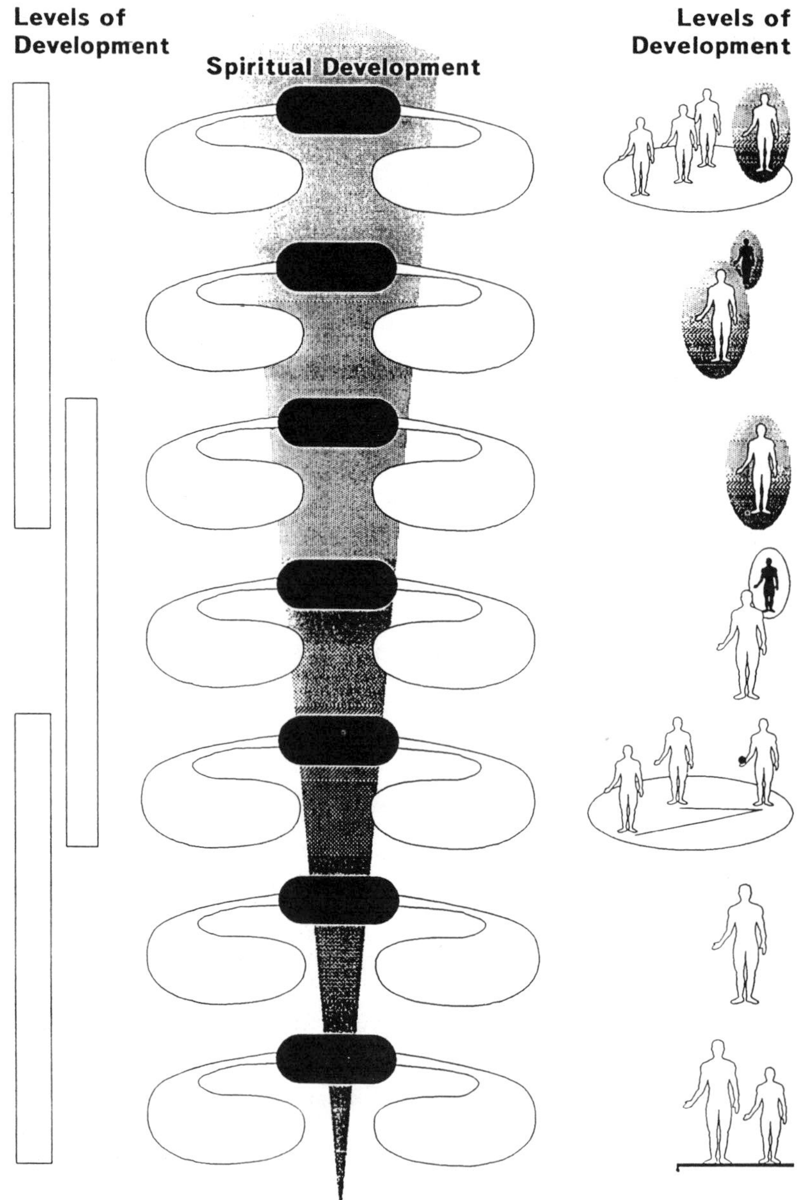

Figure 12.7
Space for the creative conceptual efforts of the most interested readers.

ACKNOWLEDGMENTS

The author expresses his gratitude to M. S. Belokhovskaya, N. D. Gordeyeva, A. I. Nazarov, and B. D. El'konin for their assistance in the visualization of major ideas stated in this chapter, which represents first results obtained in the course of two research programs, the Genome of Cultural and Spiritual Human Development and Deed Location, which obtained support from the Russian Academy of Education, the Cultural Initiative Foundation and the International Foundation for Scientific Research established by George Soros. The author expresses his gratitude to the compiler and editor of this book, Bonnie Nardi, for her proposal to me to prepare a chapter for it and also for her valuable remarks and observations made in the process of preparation. The author expresses his gratitude to Nicolas Yu. Spomior for his translation of this chapter.

NOTES

1. The Bolsheviks forbade Vygotsky and his works for many years, although ironically, it was the internalization principles that served in Soviet ideological practice as a basis for the system for imprinting communist ideology into people's heads. Of course, Vygotsky himself is not to blame in all this. In his last works, published many years after his death, he was making progress on the problems of internal structures and spontaneous development.

2. [Editor's note: The Russian practice of tying a knot in the handkerchief is similar to the Western practice of tying a string around your finger to remember something.]

3. Many poetic images that are very impressive and useful to psychologists come from Mandelstam. The metaphor above characterizes just one potential for development that cannot be realized automatically. Mandelstam also emphasized this in the following metaphor: "I am a gardener, and I am the flower." Now he speaks not so much about self-development but more about the spiritual self-building that in his case was accomplished in a rather dark social context. He continues: "I am not alone in the prison of this world." By "prison of this world" he meant, of course, the Stalinist Soviet Union.

Other interesting images-metaphors can be found in Mandelstam, for example, "Hamlet, thinking with fearful steps." Throughout the tragedy, Hamlet accomplishes no deeds and few actions; the "fearful steps" depict the absence of deed. In his letter to Ophelia, Hamlet writes: "Thine evermore most dear lady, whilst this machine is to him. Hamlet" (Hamlet speaks of himself in the third person.) As Vygotsky noted, "Hamlet's personal tragedy consists in the fact that he is a man, not a machine—and at the same time he does not belong to himself" (Vygotsky 1987). Hamlet accomplishes his human, not mechanical, actions and deeds when beyond the domain of living. At the end of the tragedy, Hamlet acts not in the situation of "to be," but in the situation of "not to be." In contrast to Hamlet, today we do not regard our machinelike aspects of everyday life as a tragedy . . .

There are two more images from Mandelstam I would like to cite here: "the dying body and the thinking immortal mouth" and "the shame of seeing fingers." These images are highly metaphorical but no more metaphorical then the image of a "thinking brain." I believe that Mandelstam's metaphors are closer to activity theory than all the "brain" metaphors, including that recently suggested (but seriously, not as a metaphor) by Francis Crick (Gregory 1994). I refer to Crick's idea of "neurons of awareness" in which an attempt is made to reduce awareness and consciousness to neuronal structures.

REFERENCES

Ado, P. (1991). *Plotin ili Prostota Vzglyada* (Plotin or simplicity of view). Moscow: Grego-Latinskii Cabinet.

Apokrify Drevnih Khristian (Apocrypha of ancient Christians). (1989). Moscow: Mysl' Publishers.

Austin, J. L. (1973). *How to Do Things with Words.* Oxford: Oxford University Press.

Bakhtin, M. M. (1973). *Context.* Annual issue. Moscow: Nauka Publisher.

Bernshtein, N. A. (1924). Biologicheskaya normal' udara (The biological normal of stroke). *Issledovaniya Central'nogo instituta truda* (The research works of the Central Labor Institute) 1(2).

Chernov, V. (1994). Mstislav Rostropovich: Citizen of the world, man of Russia. *Ogon'ok*, no. 8 (February): 12.

Davydov, V. V. (1985). *Problemy razvivayuschego obucheniya* (The problems of development-oriented teaching). Moscow: Pedagogika.

El'konin, D. B. (1989). Zametki o razvitii predmetnyh deistvii v rannem detstve (Notes on the development of object-related actions in early childhood). In V. V. Davydov and V. P. Zinchenko, eds., *Selected Psychological Works.* Moscow: Pedagogika.

Florensky, P. A. (1977). Filosofiya Kul'ta (The philosophy of culture). In *Theological Works* (vol. 17). Moscow: Moscow Patriarchate.

Foucault, M. (1993). Germenevtika sub'ekta (Germenevtics of subject). *Socio-Logos* 1:284–311.

Gal'perin, P. Y. (1966). Psihologiya myshleniya i uchenie o poetapnom razvitii umstvennyh deistvii (Psychology of thinking and the idea of the step-by-step development of mental actions). In *Research in Thinking in Soviet Psychology*. Moscow: Nauka Publisher.

Gordeyeva, N. D., and Zinchenko, V. P. (1991). Model' predmetnogo deistviya: sposoby postroeniya, structura organizacii i sistema funkzionirovaniya (The model of object-related action: Ways of composing, organizational structure, and functional system). In *Sistemnye issledovaniya. Ezhegodnik* (Annual systems research). Moscow.

Gorsky, A. K. (1993). Ogromny ocherk (Enormous essay). *Put' Journal*, no. 4.

Gregory, R. L. (1994). DNA in the mind's eye. Review of Crick's 1994 book. *Nature* 2(3):57.

Hegel, G. W. (1959). *Sochinenija* (Works) (vol. 4). Moscow: SocEcGIz.

Humboldt, W. von (1985). Reflections on the driving forces of world history. In *Language of Culture and Philosophy of Culture: Selected Works and Fragments*. Moscow: Progress Publisher. (First published in 1918)

Ivanov, V. V. (1973). The time category in art and culture of the 20th century. In J. Van Der Eng, ed., *Structure of Texts and Semiotics of Culture*. The Hague: Mouton.

Janet, P. L. (1929). *Evolution psychologique de la personalité* (Psychological evolution of personality). Paris: Presse Université de France.

Karyakin, Y. (1989). *Dostoevsky i kanun XXI veka* (Dostoevsky and the eve of the twenty-first century). Moscow: Soviet Writer Publisher.

Leont'ev, A. (1974). The problem of activity in psychology. *Soviet Psychology* 13(2):4–33.

Losev, A. F. (1993). *Cosmos* (Being, name, cosmos). Moscow: Mysl' Publisher.

Mamardashvili, M. K. (1992). *Kak Ya Ponimayu Philosiphiyu* (How I understand philosophy). Moscow: Progress Publisher.

Mandelshtam, O. (1990). *Sochineniya* v 2-h t.t. (Works. 2 vol. Vol. II]. Moscow: Khudozhestvennaya Literatura Publisher.

Oyzerman, T. I. (1993). Filosofija Hegelya kak uchenie o pervichnosti svobody (Hegel's philosophy as a teaching about the primacy of freedom). *Voprosy filosofii* 11 (Problems in philosophy, 11).

Piaget, J. (1946). *La Psychologie de l'intelligence*. Paris: Presse Université de France.

Rabinovich, P. (1979). *Alhimiya kak fenomen srednevekovoi kul'tury* (Alchemy as a medieval-age phenomenon). Moscow: Nauka Publishers.

Ranke, I. (1901). *Chelovek* (Man) (vol. 1, pp. 3–4). St. Petersburg.

Rodin, O. (1913). *Ryad besed, zapisannyh P. Gsell* (A series of conversations recorded by P. Gsell). St. Petersburg.

Rubinshtein, S. L. (1940). *Osnovy obschei pshychologii* (Basics of general psychology). Moscow: State Teaching-Pedagogical Publishers (UchPedGIz).

Schelling, F. (1927). *Die Werke* (Works). Munich: Beck and Oldenbourg.

Sherrington, C. (1969). *Integrativnaja dejatel'nost' nervnoi sistemy* (The integrating activity of nervous system). Leningrad: Nauka.

Spet, G. G. (1922). *Aestheticheskie fragmenty* (Aesthetic fragments) (pts. 1, 2). St. Petersburg: Knigoizdatel'stvo "Kolos" Publishers.

Ukhtomsky, A. A. (1978). *Izbrannye trudy* (Selected works). Leningrad: Nauka.

Vygotsky, L. S. (1984). *Collected Works* (6 vols.). Moscow: Pedagogika.

Vygotsky, L. S. (1987). *Psyhologiya iskusstva* (The psychology of art). Moscow: Pedagogica.

Zaporozhets, A. V. (1986). *Zbrannye psihologicheskie trudy* v 2-h t.t. (Selected psychological works in 2 vols.). Edited by V. V. Davydov and V. P. Zinchenko. Vol. 2. Moscow: Pedagogika.

Zinchenko, P. I. (1979). Involuntary memory and goal-directed nature of activity. In J. Wertsch, ed., *The Concept of Activity in Soviet Psychology*. Armonk, NY: Sharpe.

Zinchenko, V. P. (1989). Kul'tura i tehnika (Culture and technology). In *Krasnaya kniga kul'tury* (The red book of culture). Moscow: Iskussktvo.

Zinchenko, V. P., and Morgunov, E. B. (1994). *Chelovek razvivayushiisya* (The developing man). Moscow: Trivola Publisher.

Zinchenko, V. P., and Smirnov, S. D. (1983). *Metodologicheskie voprosy psichologii* (Methodological problems of psychology). Moscow: Moscow State University Press.

13

Mundane Tool or Object of Affection? The Rise and Fall of the Postal Buddy

Yrjö Engeström and Virginia Escalante

Studies of human-computer interaction are commonly limited to microlevel interactions between programmers or users and computers. The broader social forces and structures that constrain such interactions and are themselves reproduced and molded by microlevel events are often left unexamined. This contributes to a naive image of human-computer interaction as narrowly technical and as a problem of cognitive optimization. In the HCI literature, computers are also commonly understood only as machines explicitly labeled and used as "computers." The tremendously varied uses of computers as technologies embedded in other artifacts, typically consumer electronics, appliances, and machinery of all kinds, are seldom examined in HCI studies.

This chapter analyzes the rise and fall of a technological innovation, focusing on and interrelating both macro- and microlevel events and interactions. The artifact we analyze, the Postal Buddy kiosk, was not identified as a "computer" by its users, yet its functioning was entirely based on sophisticated computer technology embedded within the artifact.

The Postal Buddy was a free-standing electronic kiosk that was supposed to enable immediate, online change of address as well as easy purchase of customized business cards, address labels, and stamps. The Postal Buddy represents embedded computer systems designed exclusively for consumer use. The manufacturer of the Postal Buddy designed the system to be extremely user friendly and likable, with a touch screen, instructions spoken by a human voice, and a somewhat humanlike external appearance (figure 13.1).

Figure 13.1
Postal Buddy kiosk.

We analyze the Postal Buddy system as an interactive computer artifact at two levels. First, we trace the historical evolution of the Postal Buddy as a technological innovation and as a business venture from its inception in early 1989 to its sudden crisis in the fall of 1993 when the United States Postal Service (USPS) canceled its contract with the manufacturer and the Postal Buddies were abruptly removed from post offices. At this macrolevel of analysis, we examine the formation and stepwise growth of a commercial and technological network of actors around the Postal Buddy, using interviews and documents as our data. At this level, we employ and examine critically the conceptual framework of actor-network theory as a potential source of analytical tools for activity theory.

Although the growth and strengthening of the network around the Postal Buddy was impressive, the macrolevel analysis alone is unable to explain its sudden failure. At the second level of analysis, we first turn to the developers' ways of talking about Postal Buddy, including hesitations and dilemmas in their discourse. After that, we analyze videotapes and transcripts of microinteractions between post office customers and the Postal Buddy. At this level, we will use and elaborate the activity-theoretical concepts of object and artifact as analytical resources. Finally, we will discuss the potential contribution of activity theory to network analyses of technological innovations in the light of the Postal Buddy case.

NARRATIVE OF THE RISE AND FALL OF POSTAL BUDDY

The Postal Buddy was an online, interactive system with a free-standing kiosk that enabled people to change electronically their address with the Postal Service and major mailers, such as magazines and catalogs. In addition to address change, customers could also buy address labels, business cards, postal cards, and stamps from the kiosk.

In a news release produced by Electronic Data Systems (EDS), the technology partner and systems manager of the Postal Buddy Corporation, Postal Buddies were described as "the most advanced multimedia self-service, point-of-sale kiosks in the world":

> The Postal Buddy Kiosk comes to life through a combination of software technologies including object-oriented programming and the integration of 27 peripherals. The development of the Postal Buddy Kiosk marks the first time these advanced technologies have been integrated. The enabling technology which ties it together into a usable, functional whole is an interface methodology popularly known as "multimedia."
>
> True multimedia, as featured in the point-of-sale Postal Buddy Kiosk, integrates audio, digital video, graphics and animation capabilities in an interactive environment. The Postal Buddy Kiosk responds to the customer's request using text, full-motion video and stereo-quality sound initiated by the touch of a screen or a specially-designed, user-friendly keyboard.
>
> The processing platform of the Postal Buddy Kiosk is an 80486/33-based, AT-architecture running the OS/2 operating system. The

> advanced multimedia technology, Intel's i750 DVI (Digital Video Interactive), is integrated directly on the hardware platform's motherboard providing the kiosk with full-motion video. The unique Intel based 486 PC utilizing specially developed operating software controls and monitors 27 separate peripherals which include dual 213 MB hard disc drives, CD-ROM drive, 9600 baud modem, 16-inch color monitor, thermal receipt printer, credit card reader, stamp dispensing units and the first-ever, seven-bin laser printer.
>
> A centralized UNIX-based host system electronically links the Postal Buddy Kiosks providing updated product data and software upgrades in addition to receiving the transmission of daily transactions from the kiosks. The host system will send change-of-address transactions to the United States Postal Service's National Address Information Center on a daily basis. (December 1992)

We encountered Postal Buddies in the spring of 1993 as they appeared in various post offices in the San Diego area. Interactions between customers and the kiosk caught our attention. We began our data collection by observing and videotaping those interactions with the permission of the post office and customers in question. We also interviewed the founder and CEO of the Postal Buddy Corporation, Sidney Goodman, and obtained documents and press releases from the corporation. From Goodman, we obtained a case study that had been made on the early history of Postal Buddy at the Stanford Graduate School of Business (Moriarty 1990).

Our interest was revived in the fall of 1993. Television commercials advertising the Postal Buddy kiosk were broadcast. While the commercials where still run, media carried the news that the United States Postal Service had canceled its contract with the Postal Buddy Corporation and the kiosks were to be withdrawn from post offices shortly. Realizing that we were witnessing the unexpected fall of "the most advanced multimedia kiosks in the world," we decided to study the phenomenon in depth. We initiated a series of interviews with all concerned parties willing to devote their time to our research. Table 13.1 lists the key persons we interviewed in the course of our study.

We gathered news releases, articles, and stories published on the Postal Buddy. We visited and called the headquarters of the Postal Buddy Corporation for many informal conversations with members of the manage-

Table 13.1
Key persons interviewed for the analysis of the Postal Buddy case

Name	Position	Time of interview
Philip R. Baldwin	Acting manager, procurement, U.S. Postal Service	February 1994
Mark Boster	Operations manager, Postal Buddy Corporation	November 1993
Sidney Goodman	President and CEO, Postal Buddy Corporation	April 1993, February 1994
Dan Harden	Vice president, Frog Design	January 1994
Bruce Hurd	Controller, Postal Buddy Corporation	November 1993
Tim May	Project manager, Electronic Data Systems (EDS)	April 1994
Tina Warburton	District representative, Postal Buddy Corporation	February 1994

ment. We had a chance to see and play with representatives of the different generations of the kiosk stored in the corporate headquarters. The following is the (hi)story that emerged.

For fourteen years in the seventies and eighties, Sidney Goodman operated Management Reports, Inc. (MRI), a Cleveland-based computer timesharing company he founded to service the real estate management industry. In 1983, he discovered a technique for two-sided printing of labels and obtained a patent for the label format. In 1985, he sold MRI and moved to San Diego. In 1986, he experimented with marketable uses of label printing technology. In 1987, he and his son created the Welcome Labels Corporation.

The company printed the names and addresses of new residents to local rental property management firms, which sent the labels to the residents as a welcome package. The labels also carried promotions for the apartment property on the backing paper, representing a public relations program for the management companies. By 1988, eighteen months later, the company was generating $10,000 a month in reorders, at an average of $8.50 an order, "an amount that was several times what Goodman expected" (Moriarty 1990, 3). In April 1988, Goodman installed in a drugstore the Label Machine, a cabinet that held a printer from which customers could print labels. This machine was the immediate predecessor of what was to become Postal Buddy.

By midsummer 1988, Goodman decided to draft a business plan for a network of label machines placed in drugstores and other retail outlets throughout the country. In his effort to find a corporate partner, he submitted a proposal to Dennison Manufacturing, which produces stationery, inks, and other office products. In August, he met with the manager of Dennison in Waltham, Massachusetts, and demonstrated the machine. The company liked the idea, but later negotiations slowed because of the reorganization undertaken at Dennison. Goodman traveled to Dennison several times. During one of the trips, he stopped in Washington, D.C., to arrange a meeting with USPS officials.

In December 1988, Goodman met with Tom Berry, a retired AT&T executive who had served as the executive assistant to the previous postmaster general and had begun looking for ways to improve the USPS change-of-address system. Berry had just received funds from a consortium of major mailers for a focus group study to determine if customers would use a terminal in the post office for the change of address. Berry had no prototype, and he asked Goodman to provide a demonstration model for the focus group. This was a turning point: the trajectory shifted from a single-purpose label machine toward the multiproduct Postal Buddy:

> As he talked with Goodman in December 1988, Tom Berry's initial reaction to Goodman's label machine was one of extreme interest. Goodman had naively told Berry that his machine could collect address changes from people buying labels; after all, the company just had to ask the customer if the address was new and then enter it into the computer. Berry recognized that Goodman's label machine would provide an immediate, tangible benefit that would motivate the customer to use the machine. If the machine could somehow be designed to incorporate an address change system as well, Goodman suggested, then the Postal Service and mailers would gain enormous benefit from the nation-wide network of machines. (Moriarty 1990, 7)

Berry's interest was understandable in the light of the fact that at the end of the 1980s, the USPS spent $1.3 billion a year to handle address changes and forwarding of mail to changed addresses. Costs to major mailers, typically the publishing industry, are also large.

The prototype machine was to be demonstrated for the focus group a few weeks later, in January 1989. Goodman agreed to provide the prototype terminal at his own expense. He rushed to develop mock-up address change software for meeting. At his own inspiration, he added features like the vending of preprinted postcards and business cards. The first generation of the actual Postal Buddy was created. "In the process, he redesigned the graphics on the cabinet, got approval to use the USPS logo and created a new name, Postal Buddy. At the same time, he began the application process for another, broader patent, this time on the concept of a self-service print shop" (Moriarty 1990, 7).

Goodman terminated his negotiations with Dennison and focused his efforts on the USPS. In January, the focus group study was conducted with six focus groups in three locations. The study was deemed a success. Goodman set up the prototype machine in Berry's office so that it could be demonstrated to major mailers. Roy Vandegrift, the national accounts manager, brought the postmaster general, Anthony Frank, to see the machine. The postmaster general was enthusiastic, and Goodman began pushing for an agreement with the USPS. Yet in spite of the postmaster general's declared support, the effort met with opposition:

> Over the next several months in early 1989, several significant groups emerged in opposition to the Postal Buddy project. Certain of the most important internal groups resented the external development of a major ground-breaking technology in an area they considered to be rightfully within their domain. In particular, Procurement, a group that in the not too distant past had been the focus of a major scandal, was overly sensitive to the issue of sole-sourcing a project of this magnitude with Postal Buddy [Corporation]. (Moriarty 1990, 8–9)

While negotiating with the USPS, Goodman used other routes to raise support. Vandegrift began to work with the major mailers interested in becoming Postal Buddy subscribers. With the approval of Berry and Vandegrift, Postal Buddy Corporation collected a $500 subscription fee from over 100 large mailers who wanted to participate in a market test.

In August 1989, the Postal Buddy Corporation was established. About the same time, Goodman and the USPS formalized an agreement enabling

Postal Buddy Corporation to develop the software for the change-of-address system for a market test involving thirty Postal Buddy kiosks. The Postal Buddy Corporation was allowed to use the USPS logo and authorization on the machines, with the USPS investing $500,000 in the project. The actual market test contract would be awarded when the operational machine was delivered. In return, the Postal Buddy Corporation agreed to create a fully operational Postal Buddy kiosk at its own expense. This second-generation version of the Postal Buddy was developed in-house by Goodman and his associates. In October 1989, Goodman filed three additional patents, covering the address system, the customized Postal Buddy keyboard, and the printing of the labels, postcards, and business cards. The second-generation Postal Buddy did not yet have a humanlike appearance or a voice.

The development of the second-generation kiosks required cash. Late in 1989, Goodman sold Welcome Labels. The first major investor in the Postal Buddy Corporation was David Hirsch, managing director of a major investment banking firm, who invested over $500,000 in the company. Subsequently Goodman recruited other investors.

In June 1990, an agreement between the Postal Buddy Corporation and the USPS enabled Goodman to launch the market test. From July 1990 to December 1991, the USPS financed the market testing of thirty kiosks in post offices and other sites, such as supermarkets in northern Virginia, outside Washington, D.C.

As the market test was being conducted, the Postal Buddy Corporation began to negotiate with the USPS for a large-scale contract that would put Postal Buddies into post offices around the country. Electronic Data Systems (EDS) entered the picture in June 1991.

> *Interviewer:* Was it easy to recruit EDS?
>
> *Goodman:* No. As a matter of fact, uhm, I had, we had negotiated with almost every major corporation in America. Uhm, and we got turned down by everybody. We went to IBM, Unisys, Bell Atlantic, AT&T, MCI.... Who, you name it: Xerox, Kodak, uh, you know, the who's who of technology companies, uh.
>
> *Interviewer:* Was it simply too risky in their opinion?
>
> *Goodman:* It was, it was, it wasn't so much risky as it was not, uh, a strategic, not a bull's eye hit with their corporate strategy.

> And, uh, so they didn't want to, so they just couldn't get involved with it.
>
> *Interviewer:* What made it click with EDS?
>
> *Goodman:* Well, it was their Government Services Division, and they saw it as a really creative way of, of building a new relationship with the government.... EDS came in, and uh, helped us get the contract with the post office. The money was not in ... they invested uh, uh just under a million dollars, uh, to help us get the engineering design work done and a lot of the long lead time items. But their big investment came, was contingent on our winning the contract. But they helped us put together the proposal because they're very expert at, at putting together proposals for the government. But it was, you know, basically our information which they helped format in the right format, and then they added their stuff to it. So that, that allowed us to produce the winning bid. And, and, as soon as we won the bid their financing took place. (interview with Sidney Goodman, February 1994)

The market test was interpreted as a success. A Postal Buddy Corporation news release in December 1992 states that during the test period, Postal Buddy served over 100,000 people, and "its customers were constantly amazed at how quick and easy it was to enter a change-of-address and print personalized products." In January 1992, Postal Buddy Corporation and the USPS signed an $8\frac{1}{2}$-year license agreement for the production and nationwide deployment of up to 10,000 Postal Buddy kiosks. Soon after the contract was signed, the Postal Buddy Corporation distributed a press release quoting Patricia M. Gibert, vice president for customer service support at USPS: "The introduction of cutting-edge technology is the only solution to updating and improving the Postal Service. Our partnership with Postal Buddy Corporation is ideal as it allows the Postal Service to modernize itself at no additional expense."

Also in January 1992, an agreement was made between the Postal Buddy Corporation and EDS. The USPS contract and the involvement of a giant company like EDS attracted investors, notably Goldman Sachs, a major investment banker in New York, which invested $10 million in February and March 1992:

> *Goodman*: EDS came in, uh, into the picture a couple of months before Goldman. That's all. Once EDS was there, uh, then, uh,

> that, it made the Goldman people much more comf ... confident that we had the resources to deploy this many machines. That was the biggest question everybody always had was: "How, how can you, because you're just a small company, how can you even begin to believe that you can manage a task this large?" (interview with Goodman, February 1994)

Between January and November 1992, EDS and Postal Buddy Corporation developed the third generation of 183 Postal Buddy kiosks. These machines, deployed in San Diego and Washington, D.C., beginning in November 1992, were still very much a child of Sidney Goodman and his son, Martin Goodman. However, the Postal Buddy Corporation hired a leading design firm, Frog Design, to create the overall appearance of the kiosks in accordance with basic parameters given by the Goodmans.

These third-generation kiosks were rounder and less box-like than the previous generations. They had a visually dominant logo that made them appear to have a human face, and they spoke to the customer in a human male voice. In fact, they started talking as soon as someone came near enough, inviting the would-be customer to come and check out the offerings of the kiosk. According to Goodman, "We wanted, we wanted people to become attached to it, to feel like when they were done, uh, that they were saying good-bye to a, to a friend, uh, and, as, you know, like you would to a clerk in a store.... We just tried to use what we thought was, in our estimation, a friendly representation of the character we were trying to portray in the machine, you know, the personality, uhm" (interview with Goodman February 1994).

The vice president of Frog Design, Dan Harden said, "We are seeing the birth of industrial design, or I should say the blossoming of industrial design where products have sensibilities about them. They're friendlier to use, they're more comfortable to use, they're a lot more humane, a lot more driven by emotions and less by physical need" (interview with Dan Harden, March 1994).

In March and April 1993, the Postal Buddy Corporation began advertising the kiosk in television commercials. The campaign was halted between April and September, until the machine was made more reliable. In September, the company launched an advertising campaign, including television commercials and direct mail brochures distributed to homes, called "Demo Days." Customers were offered a coupon good for a $1 rebate if they used the machine.

On September 17, 1993, the USPS canceled its contract with the Postal Buddy Corporation. By that time, there were 200 machines on the assembly line, with parts ordered for another 600 machines. More than 350 enhancements and improvements had been made to the kiosk, though none of them structurally significant. Shipment of these fourth-generation Postal Buddies was scheduled for November 1993. On November 11, 1993, the board of directors of the Postal Buddy Corporation decided not to invest any more money in the project. In February 1994, Bill Bennett, an attorney for the USPS, stated, "Litigation is a certainty" in the Postal Buddy case.

Different parties gave different reasons for the cancellation.

USPS Explanation 1

USPS originally believed processing address changes through Postal Buddy would save between $300 million and $500 million in data-entry labor during the life of the contract. But Sandra Harding, a postal spokeswoman, said this proved not to be the case.

"Postal Buddy sent us the change of address information, and they sent the confirmation notices to the users," Harding said. "But it cost us 39 cents each time." The Postal Service estimated that it would end up paying $4.5 million for address changes each year and another $500,000 for administration, such as renting the real estate and providing electrical set-ups for each Postal Buddy.

Postal officials expected each kiosk to generate revenues from $35 to $55 each day, but the first machines yielded only $15 to $30 a day.

"Postal Buddy Corp. needed to generate at least $42 [a day per unit] before the Postal Service would make something on it," Harding said. "We just weren't getting the money back. So, we decided to cut our losses." (*Government Computer News*, September 1993)

USPS Explanation 2

Functionally, the Postal Buddy system worked quite well. The disappointment was that not as many customers used it as had been predicted.

There was substantial collaboration between the Postal Buddy and the USPS. The problem was not with the system, but with getting customers to make timely use of it. Postal Buddy sent a confirmation letter to each customer that entered a change of address. It cost Postal Buddy 10 cents to print each letter and 29 cents for postage. Early in program development the USPS intended to provide the address change confirmation. Later the USPS found it was unable to do this. Total expenditure was on the order of $45,000.

In 1989 when this program was under consideration the annual cost of mail undeliverable as addressed was $1 billion. It was thought that if customers could be persuaded to make timely use of an electronic system, the cost might eventually be cut in half.

By mid-93 Postal Buddy was suggesting that the number of units it could profitably deploy might be far fewer than originally projected, and revenue by mid-93 was several orders of magnitude less than projected. The USPS decided to cut its losses on ample evidence that the program might well fail.

The USPS has not attempted to itemize or total its investment in the program. The program did not progress far enough for a revenue expectation to emerge.

The only problem of significance created by Postal Buddy in post offices was requests at the counter for refunds when the machine did not give the customer the products purchased. (written answers to our questions by Philip R. Baldwin, acting manager of procurement, USPS, February 1994)

Sidney Goodman's Explanation

Goodman: The revenues we were expecting were dependent upon marketing, advertising and marketing, which we withdrew from because of the technical problems. So we wanted to solve our problems before we asked customers to use our machine. And, uh, but by the time those were solved in September and our advertising started, revenues were right where we wanted them to be. We were quite pleased.

Interviewer: So it's not as if that was the cause of . . . ?

Goodman: Absolutely not. They've fabricated reasons. Somebody, they used the reasons to do what they did and I can't say any more about it, but it's just a fabricated reason. Revenues were just fine. Well, we had, some third of the machines were in the wrong locations, but we were gonna move them. You can't take 185 machines and throw them out there and expect to . . . at every location.

Interviewer: The other reason that has been presented to the public . . . have been implications that the process of the address change would not be saving the money that it was supposed to save.

Goodman: Bullshit.

Interviewer: ... it was presented also in one of the government newspapers.

Goodman: That's smoke....

Interviewer: Did you have any indication ...?

Goodman: None. This was totally out of the blue.

Interviewer: Now, at the level of communication, it strikes me as so odd that there was a network in place, in terms of all the different players were aligned.... Would it be just the tremendous differences in cultures between the government and the private business or something that created a sort of gap in communication, or ...?

Goodman: I know what it is. I just can't say.

Interviewer: Off the record, maybe?

Goodman: No ... you'll find out. It's just one man. He's a maniacal bureaucrat. (Interview with Goodman, February 1994)

EDS Explanation

Interviewer: Do you think that eventually the usage would have increased and it would have been quite profitable if the post office hadn't pulled out?

May: Uh, yeah, it could have been, it would have been probable. We were seeing revenues increase, we were seeing costs decrease. Like any start-up company, is that there is a curve from which it takes to build and create the business. So the answer to that is yes. It would've been profitable, it would've been good business. (Interview with Tim May, February 1994)

There are basically two competing explanations. The USPS claims that not enough people were using Postal Buddies; thus the revenues were too low. The Postal Buddy Corporation and EDS claim that the cancellation was caused by internal politics within USPS; the revenues were increasing and matched the expectations at the time of the cancellation. We might call the first claim the revenue explanation and the second claim the conspiracy explanation. The relative merits of the two explanations will probably be decided in courts of law.

A possible third explanation would claim that the whole concept of a computerized kiosk such as Postal Buddy was an oddball idea, destined to irrelevance and obsolescence from the beginning. However, since

Postal Buddy, a growing wave of similar and apparently successful machines, offering a broad range of services, have been appearing in various sites. For example, in some Arizona courthouses kiosks called QuickCourt and Lawyer Buddy have been deployed. In a large chain of drugstores, a Home Select kiosk was deployed in 1994, characterized as "the automatic seven-minute home finder." Computerized kiosks for producing personally designed greeting cards have become a large-scale business. And there are more examples as well. They all but rule out the "oddball" explanation:

> A specialized workstation called DesignCenter, developed by a Weyerhaeuser subsidiary, Innovis, targets the do-it-yourself market. Home improvement stores install a kiosk containing DesignCenter in their display area. A customer, usually with modest help from a sales clerk, can easily design a home deck by himself or herself using the interactive system. The look and feel is somewhat analogous to a video game. The deck is visually displayed and easily manipulated to meet the customer's wishes concerning size, shape, type of wood, and the like. After the design is finished, a push of a button brings a complete bill of materials with dimensions, costs, and other specifications for all parts. The customer can walk away with a drawing of the finished product and a hard copy of the bill of materials. Using the DesignCenter, do-it-yourselfers created $150 million in projects during the first eight months of operation. Much of this represents a market expansion of projects that home owners would not otherwise have built.
>
> DesignCenter typifies an important new class of applications of information technology in which the customer solves his or her own problem, thereby increasing the primary demand for the product. (Little 1994, 458)

USING ACTOR-NETWORK THEORY TO ANALYZE THE POSTAL BUDDY CASE

The story of the Postal Buddy is one of network building. A techno-economic network was created that embodied and moved forward the innovation called Postal Buddy.

In activity theory, particularly in the tradition of developmental work research (Engeström 1991a, 1991b, 1993), increasing attention is being paid to interactions among multiple activity systems (Saarelma 1993; Miettinen 1993). However, the study of activity networks is only beginning within activity theory. In the sociology of science and technology, the actor-network theory of Latour (1987, 1988b) and Callon (1992), and their colleagues, has produced a rapidly growing number of interesting studies of technological innovations. The decidedly mediational emphasis of actor-network theory (Latour 1993b) makes it particularly promising as a source of ideas for activity theory.

In actor-network theory, innovations are depicted as gradually emerging networks of actors and intermediaries, both human and nonhuman. The theory is based on a principle of symmetry, which maintains that human and nonhuman actors are treated equally in the analysis. An actor is any entity that claims to have authorship over an intermediary. An intermediary is anything that passes from one actor to another: "Technoeconomic networks are composite. They mix humans and non-humans, inscriptions of all sorts, and money in all its forms. Their dynamic can only be understood by way of the translation operation which inscribes the mutual definition of the actors in the intermediaries which are put into circulation" (Callon 1992, 96).

Postal Buddy kiosks could be seen as a prime example of nonhuman actors. They certainly acted much more like humans than most other machines. Much of the function of Postal Buddy kiosks was to send intermediaries, such as address changes, to other actors in the network. Authorship was crucial too. The success of the Postal Buddy was largely dependent on its ability to show to the USPS that it could handle 50 percent or more of all the address changes in the post offices where it was deployed.

In addition to address changes, Postal Buddy sent "self-reflective" intermediaries and completed "self-critical" inscriptions:

> We had such a huge network. I mean, the intelligence in the computer, in the kiosk itself alerted us every time there was a problem. It, it dialed into San Diego and set off an alarm that we could follow up....
>
> You have to remember the Postal Buddy kiosk was so intelligent that anything, we have records of every keystroke of every time somebody walked up to a kiosk, whatever they did, we have that in our database. (Interview with Mark Boster, November 1993)

A key process in the formation of actor networks is irreversibilization, which refers to the normalization, stabilization, and standardization of interactions and relations of the network. Callon (1992) writes, "When a network is strongly convergent and strongly irreversibilized, it can be approximated as a black box, whose behavior can be known and predicted independently of its content. It can then link itself to one or several 'external' actor-networks, with which it exchanges intermediaries, which traverse its border in both directions."

Actor-network theory is above all interested in "the mobilizing of allies and, in general, the transformation of weak into strong associations" (Latour 1988a). There is a strong and open Machiavellian bias in the approach (Callon, Law, and Rip 1986; Latour 1988c). "The problem of the builder of the fact is the same as the builder of the 'objects': How to convince others, how to control their behavior, how to gather sufficient resources in one place, how to have the claim or the object to spread out in time and space. In both cases, it is others who have the power to transform the claim or object into a durable whole" (Latour 1987, 131).

The emphasis in actor-network theory is on processes of gaining power, establishing authority, stabilizing institutions—in short, on winning (Shapin 1988; Radder 1992).

It is tempting to depict Sidney Goodman as a Machiavellian-Latourian "prince of machines and machinations." Indeed, here is a man who, step by step, mobilized nonhuman and human actors and got them to join his network: the USPS, EDS, investment bankers, Frog Design, devoted employees, and, of course, the Postal Buddy kiosks. The story may be read as one of increasing convergence and irreversibilization—and of increasing drawing power: "We were out there just about to land a major commitment for investment dollars" (interview with Bruce Hurd, November 1993).

When Sidney Goodman gained the first agreements with the USPS and with his partners, that is, when he completed the enlisting of actors, the Postal Buddy network was built around an inner circle with access to and responsibility for strategic design and business issues and decisions. The inner circle consisted of the management of the Postal Buddy Corporation itself, EDS, Frog Design, and the key investors. While the interface with the USPS was relatively narrow, one can safely maintain that some people in the postal service management were at least marginally inside the inner circle. The Postal Buddy kiosk itself, the key actant, following the vocabulary of actor-network theory, had a central place in the inner circle of the network. Only the manufacturer and subcontractors were outside the inner circle, as were the end users, who at this stage were mainly regarded as sources of information in focus group studies. In other words, the network was tight and relatively short (figure 13.2).

As the number of kiosks grew, and they were placed in both Washington, D.C., and San Diego, the role of EDS grew bigger and the network grew longer.

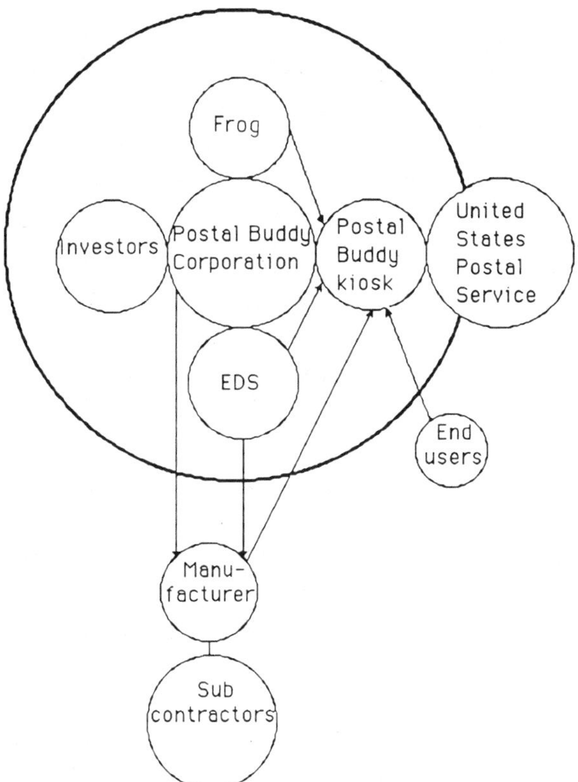

Figure 13.2
Postal Buddy network at the completion of enlisting actors.

> *Boster:* They've been in Herndon [the EDS engineers]. I think that was a major problem, too....
>
> A lot of phone calls, a lot of trips sometimes. And some of that was, is probably okay, and some of the software development is okay to have three, three thousand miles away. It's not a problem of having that so far away. What the problem is, is the interface of, of the requirements to, to the design and, and that interface was a problem of having it all the way to San Diego, I mean all the way in Herndon....
>
> It's a lot more expensive to maintain the kiosks because now you have to have a whole new level of service. You have your maintenance people, but now you also have to have somebody that goes around and collects money and re-stocks the, the thing. (Interview with Boster)

At the same time, the distance between the inner circle and the USPS increased. Said Hurd:

> See, we started the contract with certain people with a certain regime. They then left when the [new postmaster general's] regime came in. Many of them left. Most of our personal contacts left. Our contract was then, uh, put in the hand of someone who was never, from what I've been told, never a proponent of the contract to begin with. And as a result, we became somewhat of a stepchild of the postal service and we never really got the attention.... If we just had some people on their side that knew our project and supported the project, we could've developed a relationship we needed to make it work. (Interview with Hurd)

In other words, as the network grew longer, it also got looser (figure 13.3). The distances between all the actors of the inner circle, including the kiosk itself, grew longer. Frog Design was no longer in the inner circle. More important, the USPS also moved out of the inner circle. The end users remained outside, now regarded as sources of revenue and reclamations.

Was the breakdown of the Postal Buddy network simply a consequence of uncontrolled extension? Such an explanation begs the question. What made the extension uncontrolled? While superficially elegant, this account leaves the sudden cancellation of the project mysterious.

The emphasis of actor-network theory on winning does not preclude interest in failed innovations—after all, losing is the flip side of winning.

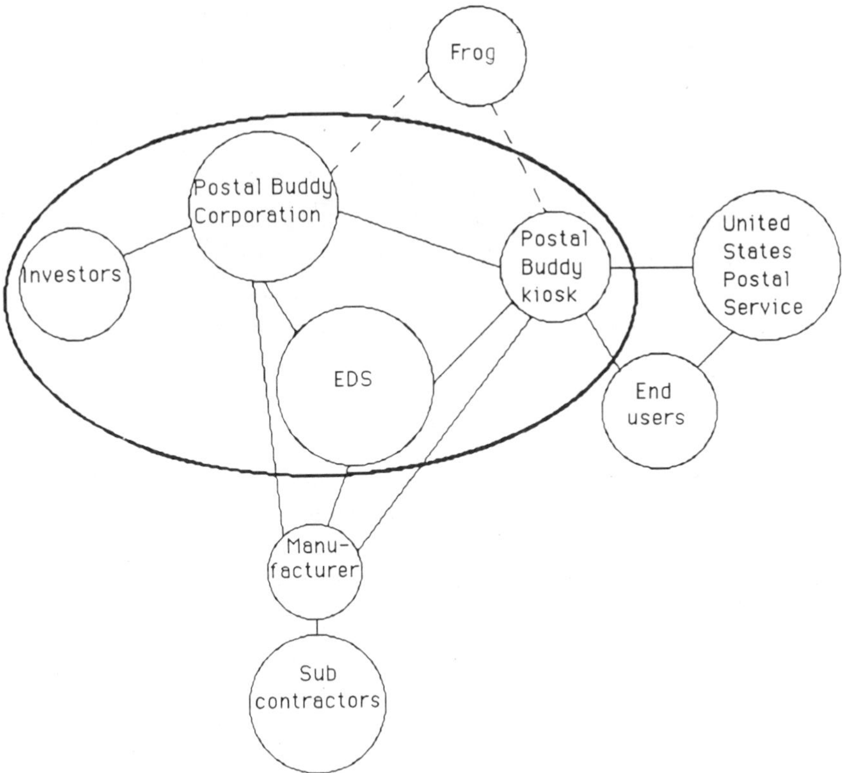

Figure 13.3
Postal Buddy network extended.

For the purpose of analyzing the rise and fall of the Postal Buddy, studies of failure (Akrich 1993; Latour 1993a; Law and Callon 1992) are of particular importance. In his analysis of the failure of Aramis, a revolutionary subway system planned in the south of Paris, Latour identifies the isolation of the technology as a chief cause of its failure:

> It is because Aramis completely isolates the core technical ideas of the project from the rest of the network (exploitation, systems, political vagaries, costs, engineers' skills) that it cannot become an institution and is fated to remain a utopia.... An object cannot come to existence if the range of interests gathered around the project do not intersect. Of course, interests may be modified and so may projects. But, if the two-way movement translating

> interests and modifying the project is interrupted, then the object cannot become real....
>
> The irony of the Aramis case is that the main engineers behind the project really believed in the epistemological myth of a technology fully independent of the rest of society. They maintained the basic specifications of the system for fifteen years without a single modification. (Latour 1993a, 391–392)

In their analysis of the failure of a projected British military aircraft, TSR.2, Law and Callon attribute the failure largely to an inability of the project management to keep the local network sufficiently isolated from the larger global network surrounding it: "Actors in the global network were able to interfere with the structure and shape of the local network, while those in the local network were able to go behind the back of the project management, and consult directly with actors in the global network. The result was that the project management was unable to impose itself as an obligatory point of passage between the two networks, and the troubles that we have detailed followed" (Law and Callon 1992, 42).

So failure can be caused by too much isolation or by too little isolation, too tight a network or too loose a network. However, neither explanation seems to fit the case of the Postal Buddy. The Aramis engineers refused to make modifications, the Postal Buddy engineers made over 350 modifications between April and September 1993. We found no evidence of disloyalty or interference of the kinds found in the TSR.2 case, only a rather clear-cut "us versus them."

This leaves us with the original opposite explanations offered by our informants: revenues and conspiracy. Are we forced to return to square one?

We suspect that this impasse is caused by the very nature of a Machiavellian frame of analysis. In its search for convergence, irreversibilization, and closure, this kind of analysis overlooks the inner dynamics and contradictions of the activities of the various actors in the network. The concrete activities and actions of makers and users—engineers, shop-floor workers, consumers, and others—have received little detailed attention in the actor-network genre of studies. Somehow the networks described do not seem to reach that far. As Button (1993, 24) points out, what is missing is "an account of *the details of the associating*, an account of the interactional work, the particular embodied practices."

The concepts of "trust" and "reciprocity," so central in new theorizing on network organizations (Alter and Hage 1993; Nohria and Eccles 1992; Powell 1990), and the whole contradictory dialectic of cooperation and competition (Bleeke and Ernst 1993), are curiously missing in the vocabulary of actor-network theory. This feature goes along with an emphasis on monologues and a relative absence of dialogical interactions. Network builders' words are often reported, but you will not find dialogs between the various actors, between engineers and workers, or manufacturers and users. Monologism prevails also in the treatment of individual actors' conceptions and interests. Not much attention is paid to hesitations, dilemmas, and shifts in the actors' voices, all relevant when mind is seen in dialogical and argumentational terms (Bakhtin 1982; Billig 1987).

From the perspective of human-computer interaction, a particularly problematic feature of actor-network theory is the elimination of the specificity of the activities and interests of end users. If discussed at all (Akrich 1992 is a rare example), users seem to be treated as just another potential link in the chain of actors to be enlisted and mobilized. Latour (1988c) asks, "To what extremities is a Prince not led in order to interest, please, seduce, capture or imprison consumers? How unreliable and feckless people are, always shifting from one opinion to another, enslaved by fashion and passion. To keep them well aligned, one needs constantly renewed and ever fresher resources" (26).

The possibility that the users might have fundamentally different interests from those of the manufacturers, vendors, and other propagators of technological innovations is not examined. The user is an abstraction constructed by the researcher, not a concrete agent who contributes to the shaping of the innovation, either by making suggestions and alterations or by causing trouble. This neglect of end users as agents is in stark contrast with some of the most interesting recent work in the economics of technological innovations. This research indicates that "lead users" play a much more important part in the different stages of the innovation process of various industries than has been previously realized (von Hippel 1988).

These critical considerations lead us to examine the story of the Postal Buddy from a different angle. We will now focus on the actors' personal ways of relating to Postal Buddy, including hesitations and dilemmas in their discourse. After that, we will look at end users' interactions with the Postal Buddy kiosk. Perhaps these angles will shed new light on the failure of the project.

A LOVE AFFAIR AND ITS DILEMMAS: HOW ACTORS TALKED ABOUT POSTAL BUDDY

We did not have a chance to observe the work practices of the managers and employees of Postal Buddy Corporation and its allies. However, in our interviews they talked about their relationship to Postal Buddy as well as about the customers' relationship to it. We found the dilemmatic and hesitant aspects of our informants' talk to be of special interest:

> The presence of contrary themes in discussions is revealed by the use of qualifications. The unqualified expression of one theme seems to call forth a counter-qualification in the name of the opposing theme. There is a tension in the discourse, which can make even monologue take the form of argumentation and argument occur, even when all participants share similar contrary themes.... The dilemmatic aspects do not only concern contrary ways of talking about the world; they exist in practice as well as in discourse. Above all, the dilemmatic aspects can give rise to actual dilemmas in which choices have to be made. (Billig et al. 1988, 144)

Our corporate informants representing the Postal Buddy network put tremendous emphasis on the positive value of the humanlike characteristics, or 'personality,' of the Postal Buddy kiosk.

> *Goodman:* It's what would the customer endear himself to most? What would he remember the most and wanna come back to use again? And there was a personality that, that did that.....
>
> I think everybody really developed, you know, a fondness for the concept, and the machine, and the personality. (Interview with Goodman, February 1994)

> *Boster:* To this day, we're still getting a bunch of calls every day, "Where can I buy the Postal Buddy?" There was a huge following of people who liked it....
>
> I mean, this company was founded on the fact that the kiosk had personality, and everything we did was a personality....

> I think that's what set it apart. I think that's what drew people to the kiosk and I think it relieved a lot of their anxiety. They made it to be almost personlike. Uh, it was friendly, you know. It was not machinelike. . . .
>
> We had all kinds of stories of people. "Yeah, I was afraid to use it, but my kid did it and you know, now I love it," and so forth. (Interview with Boster)
>
> *Hurd:* Our customers loved our products and got what they'd never been able to buy before in an environment with an interactive kiosk which is where they have all the fun at. . . .
>
> We really saw Postal Buddy as a person. We wanted Postal Buddy to relate. The customers were supposed to be able to relate to him as a person. We wanted people to have fun at the kiosk. Absolutely. . . . And I think we were enormously successful in that. . . .
>
> I think we were all predisposed to become somewhat evangelists for Postal Buddy. Because that was the kind of people that they wanted. They wanted people that could really sink their teeth into this and really fall in love with it and, and act accordingly. And we were very successful in recruiting people like that. . . .
>
> People were telling us that it was friendly and people like it. They're fascinated with what's going on, the products, the interface, and all they have to do is touch a button. People just love that kind of stuff. . . .
>
> Everybody loved Postal Buddy. . . .
>
> When you, once you develop, as a customer and as a part of the team, this relationship with the concept, uh, you know, yeah, it's kind of like having a death in the family. (Interview with Hurd)
>
> *Warburton:* Yeah, I mean everybody kind of, almost had a sense of ownership to him. Uh, just because it was such a unique and new, innovative idea that everybody just loved it and everybody was very positive. . . .
>
> I mean, we all loved it. We just thought it was wonderful. I mean, you know, it's a great machine. It provides a wonderful service. It's a great thing. (Interview with Tina Warburton, February 1994)
>
> *Harden:* Just about everybody that saw it and used it fell in love with it. (Interview with Harden)

The informants repeatedly talked about loving Postal Buddy. They referred to customers as well as to themselves, as employees or developers, essentially assuming that both shared the same affection for Postal

Buddy. Notice also the all-pervasive generality and absoluteness imputed to this love affair: "*everybody* really developed a fondness"; "a *huge* following of people liked it"; "we were *all* predisposed to become evangelists"; "we *all* loved it"; "*everybody* that saw it and used it fell in love with it." There is an interesting mismatch between these proclamations of absolute love and statements given by the same informants registering complaints from customers:

> *Goodman:* We had a lot of people be insulted, uh, and so we were ... you know, before this all hit the fan ... we were in the process of actually trying to make a more direct link for the experienced user so that they didn't have to put up with all the things the inexperienced user had to put up with....
>
> I think we didn't take into consideration the fact that repeat users are annoyed by what.... What they needed on the first and second time, they became annoyed with on the third or fourth and subsequent time. (Interview with Goodman, February 1994)

> *Boster:* I mean, we had, obviously, when you take somebody's credit card and don't give it back, you have a real problem and you're gonna get people upset....
>
> *Interviewer:* What about money cards? Did you have problems with acceptance by the public?
>
> *Boster:* Yes and no. Uhm.
>
> *Interviewer:* What happened?
>
> *Boster:* Uh, some people liked it, some people hated it and some people were really mad. (Interview with Boster)

> *Hurd:* We were very interested to determine whether there was any resistance to the, to the, uh, money cards.... We believe strongly in the idea.... Well, now, now I think that, uh, there was enough resistance on the customers' side and enough technological problems associated with it for us to reconsider their use in the future.... If we get a chance to develop a new machine, I don't think it'll be part of it. (Interview with Hurd)

Instead of universal love, we suddenly hear words like *insulted*, *annoyed*, *upset*, *hated*, *mad*, and *resistance*. These negative responses from customers are duly noted, but that does not seem to have any effect on the overwhelmingly strong belief in universal love toward Postal Buddy. It is as if the image of love and the registration of contrary emotions remained two separate and closed compartments in the discourse and thinking of the informants. (For previous analyses of compartmentalization, see Engeström 1990.)

Another dilemmatic feature of our informants' discourse was qualifications, hedges, hesitations, and doubts. Here are instances we found in our interview transcripts:

> *Goodman:* We were trying to make the interaction like it would be with a person. You're never gonna get that. But, but at least, uhm, that was what the attempt was. I think we went overboard a little bit.
>
> *Interviewer:* Do you?
>
> *Goodman:* Well, yeah, I mean, I think that, uh, no, I'm not sure we did. (Interview with Goodman, February 1994)

> *Harden:* The Postal Buddy to us was too cutesy. We felt, after all, the service that it was providing was not "cute." It was very informative. In other words, you change your address, make business cards, uh, it's for using communication. Those are serious, but everyday events. And we felt that it was a little too cute and cuddly with that logo, so I didn't like that. As far as the industrial design goes, we wouldn't have changed a thing. (Interview with Harden)

> *Hurd:* But, uh, obviously, my point of view is a little painted because we were such a, such a tight team and had such a relationship with the whole concept of what we were doing. So maybe it might be a little difficult for me to tell you whether the customer base really did develop that relationship. (Interview with Hurd)

Hesitations and doubts are important markers for potential self-reflection. However, the examples we found contain nothing that would directly indicate a critical awareness of the dilemma between love and complaint. The hesitations remain momentary and isolated from the rest of our informants' discourse.

A LOVE AFFAIR THAT NEVER HAPPENED: HOW USERS INTERACTED WITH POSTAL BUDDY

In the spring of 1993, we observed and videotaped the interactions of ten randomly chosen customers with a Postal Buddy kiosk in a post office in

San Diego. The average total time spent by the subjects to accomplish what they wanted to do with the Postal Buddy was 14 minutes, of which 7.6 minutes was spent interacting with the machine and 6.4 minutes waiting in line.

The quality of these interactions varied. Customer 1 was obviously an expert. She typed rapidly and accurately, retracting her steps only once to select a style for the labels she wanted. She even interrupted the machine six times to save time: when it started to explain that it did not take coins, that there were many styles to choose from, when it started to say "Hooold on a minute," when it asked if she wanted to buy stamps, when it gave directions to begin a process, and when she retracted a step. Customer 1 completed her task successfully. She would fit Goodman's description of an experienced user who should not "have to put up with all the things the inexperienced user had to put up with."

Two of the subjects did not accomplish their tasks at all. Customer 9 spent less than a minute with the machine and walked away, saying, "I'm stopping because it's not going to give me any change." Customer 2 wanted to buy labels, pecked at the keyboard with one finger, but nonetheless followed every step of the procedure up until it was time to make the payment. Following is our observation of customer 2:

01	*Postal Buddy voice:*	Touch your preferred method of payment. Remember, if you choose to pay with cash, I'll dispense any change due on a money card. If you already have a money card, you can use it for payment even if the amount remaining is less than your purchase price.
02	*Customer 2:*	[Starts looking for money in purse; pulls out wallet.] I didn't know it had tax on it. It only takes ones. [Pulls out wrinkled bills.] I think I need change. [Presses dollar icon.]
03	*Postal Buddy screen:*	[Screen changes; goes to video that shows a dollar bill being inserted into the machine and change being returned on a money card.]

04	*Postal Buddy voice:*	You've chosen to pay with cash. So that I can be a more reliable buddy, I'll dispense your change with a Postal Buddy money card. You can use this card to buy stamps or any product at any Postal Buddy. If you prefer to pay with the exact amount, please pay with a credit card or an ATM card.
05	*Customer 2:*	[Starts to put a dollar bill in but waits for Postal Buddy to finish talking.]
06	*Postal Buddy screen:*	[Video shows coins and a red circle with a line through it to show the machine does not accept coins.]
07	*Customer 2:*	[Tries to insert a dollar bill.]
08	*Postal Buddy:*	[Bill validator rejects the bill.]
09	*Customer 2:*	[Turns, smoothes dollar bill, tries to insert it again.]
10	*Postal Buddy:*	[Bill validator rejects the bill.]
11	*Customer 2:*	[Tries another dollar bill.]
12	*Postal Buddy:*	[Bill validator rejects the bill.]
13	*Customer 2:*	[Tries another dollar bill.]
14	*Postal Buddy:*	[Bill validator rejects the bill.]
15	*Customer 2:*	[Tries another dollar bill.]
16	*Postal Buddy:*	[Bill validator rejects the bill.]
17	*Customer 2:*	[Pauses.]
18	*Postal Buddy voice:*	Hey! Are you still there?
19	*Customer 2:*	[Tries again to insert a dollar bill.]
20	*Postal Buddy:*	[Bill validator rejects the bill.]
21	*Customer 2:*	[Tries again.]
22	*Postal Buddy:*	[Bill validator rejects the bill.]
23	*Customer 2:*	[Tries again.]
24	*Postal Buddy:*	[Bill validator rejects the bill.]
25	*Customer 2:*	It's not gonna take it. [Presses Cancel button; pauses.]

26	*Postal Buddy:*	[Does not respond.]
27	*Customer 2:*	[Presses Cancel button again; pauses.]
28	*Postal Buddy:*	[Does not respond.]
29	*Customer 2:*	[Presses Cancel button again; pauses.]
30	*Postal Buddy:*	[Does not respond.]
31	*Customer 2:*	[Makes an exasperated sound. Presses Cancel button three more consecutive times.]
32	*Customer 2:*	It won't cancel. It didn't take my dollar, so. [Presses Cancel button another three times.]
33	*Postal Buddy:*	[Does not respond.]
34	*Customer 2:*	See, it won't fit. [Presses Cancel button another three times.]
35	*Postal Buddy:*	[Does not respond.]
36	*Customer 2:*	[Tries pressing some keys on the keyboard. Presses green button on the left, which says Go back. Presses button at top center. Presses Cancel button.]
37	*Postal Buddy:*	[The screen clears.]
38	*Customer 2:*	It's weird.
39	*Postal Buddy screen:*	[Screen shows three orange buttons.]
40	*Customer 2:*	[Presses the middle button on screen. Walks away.] It wouldn't take 'em. [Goes to a postal clerk and mails a package.]

What is striking in this sequence is the customer's tenacity. She tried eight times in vain to get her dollar bills accepted and another six times in vain to cancel the interaction. This type of tenacious fixation on an ostensibly unsuccessful response to a problem resembles the "tunnel vision" phenomenon well known from various realms of human-machine interaction: "The operators at Three Mile Island fixed on their first theory, pressure buildup, despite accumulating evidence that the structure and direction had changed. The power of these first impressions persisted well into the first day of the accident" (Hirschhorn 1984, 88).

The other seven users accomplished their tasks with degrees of success varying between the proficient expertise of customer 1 and the frustration of customer 2. In five of those seven cases we observed some problems, typically with money. None of our subjects showed visible or audible signs of fascination or affection toward Postal Buddy.

Perhaps the most interesting example of these interactions was that of customer 3, an obvious novice with Postal Buddy. She wanted to buy custom-made business cards from the machine. This required that she enter the information to be printed on the cards into appropriate lines on the Postal Buddy screen.

On the screen, the line for the fax number looked like this (the first word was printed in yellow, the underlined word was printed in white):

FAX#: Fax:_______

When she entered the fax line, customer 3 first deleted the second word "Fax:" by using the backspace key; then she typed in her fax number. She did not distinguish between the information given as *instruction (tool)* for the user (the first word "FAX #:" in yellow) and the word given as part of the *object* actually to appear on the business card (the second, underlined word "Fax:" in white). The word *fax* was needed as part of the object, to separate the fax number from the telephone number on the card. Three very subtle markers were used by the designers to differentiate between the instruction and object: color (yellow versus white), case (uppercase versus lowercase), # sign, and underlining. These markers did not bring the message home in this case (figure 13.4).

Since the same word appeared twice in a row on the screen, it was an understandable reaction to delete the second word as redundant. Basic similarity overrode subtle markers of difference. This exemplifies a blurring of instructions (tools) and object in a supposedly self-explanatory, stand-alone machine such as Postal Buddy. Instructions seem to disappear by virtue of being merged into the formation of the object. With them disappears a possibility to reflect upon and remediate one's actions. Analyzing the role of instructions in photocopying task, Suchman (1987, 141) points out that "a conflict between the action on an object described by an instruction, and the action required by the object itself, can be a

(a)

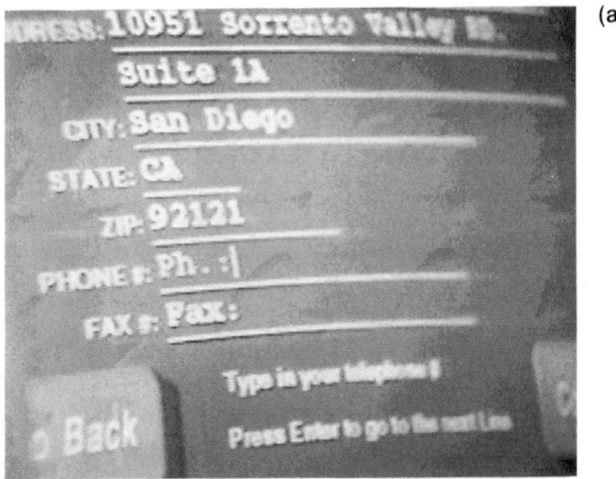

(b)

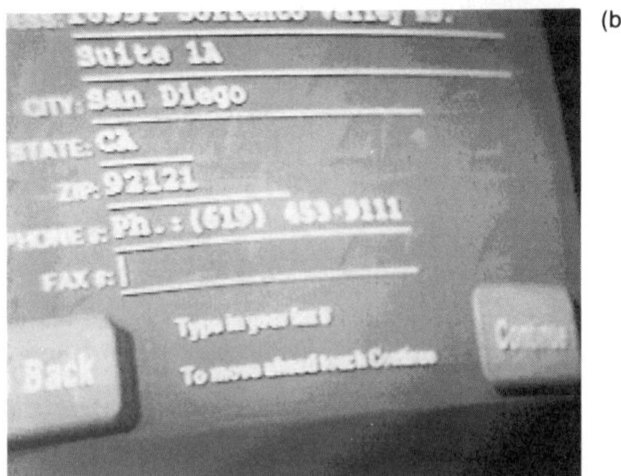

(c)

Figure 13.4
The problem with the fax: (*a*) the initial screen; (*b*) the customer deletes second word "Fax:" (*c*) only the fax number, not the word "Fax:" will appear on the actual business card.

resource for identifying trouble in the interpretation of an instruction, and its resolution." Such a reciprocal and reflective relationship between instructions and actions-on-objects requires that instructions are identified as instructions. The emergence of such a reflective relationship is a precondition for the emergence of the machine itself for the user as a tool rather than as a captivating or debilitating object in itself.

Interestingly enough, customer 3 did not delete the word "Phone:" on the telephone number line just above the fax line, although that word too appeared twice. Apparently the subtle markers of difference were sufficient on that line but not on the next one. This inconsistency indicates that for a novice user, each subtask (each line, in this case) tends to be separate from the other subtasks, so that the logic followed in one subtask does not necessarily stay the same across the subtasks.

After the Postal Buddy screen displayed the business card as it was to be printed, customer 3 decided to review and correct the text on her card. She found and corrected some typing errors. She did not detect the missing word "Fax:" Two problems created uncertainty. In the street address, she had typed *RD.* for *Road*, and in the name of her company she had a small *v* instead of a capital *V* as the first letter. She apparently tried to rectify the second problem but did not succeed.

01	*Customer 3:*	Now it's getting frustrating. [Moves her hand onto the screen; moves her finger along the street address line, then up and along the company name line.]
02	*Customer 4:*	[Man standing in line behind customer 3] It's where the *d* in *Road* is small?
03	*Customer 3:*	Uhm, here they have it capitalized [referring to a model text shown on a previous Postal Buddy screen] so I'm trying to do what is here. But I'm concerned about the *v*, it doesn't show up as a capital, and this comes out as *m*, on the printout.
04	*Customer 4:*	Yeah.
05	*Customer 3:*	[Touches Continue on the screen.]

06 *Postal Buddy screen:* [Screen closes; a new one opens, showing a picture of the finished business card.] [Top of the screen:] Is this how you want your card to look? [Bottom of the screen:] Note: Text may appear to overlap. Printed product will be correct.

07 *Postal Buddy voice:* This is the best I can show your product on my screen. But I assure you . . .

08 *Customer 3:* [Customer 3 moves her finger through the card's text on the screen; text overlaps, the company name begins with a small *v* while the rest of the name is printed in capital letters.]

09 *Customer 3:* A lot of junk, there [mumbling].

10 *Customer 3:* [Presses Continue on the screen.]

11 *Postal Buddy screen:* Please wait.

12 *Customer 3:* They assured me the product will be correct, right? [Laughs slightly, sarcastically.]

This episode is an example of manifest helplessness—or lack of tools—on the part of the customer. For some reason, which remains unexplained to us, she was unable to change the small *v* into a capital *V*. As Suchman (1987, 132) points out, "The premise of a self-explanatory machine is that users will discover its intended use through information found in and on the machine itself, with no need for further instruction." Postal Buddy offered instructions, but they were very closely merged with and embedded in the work the user and the machine did on the object. The machine gave the following voice instruction for the correction of the text on a business card:

Postal Buddy voice: Type in your text and press Enter to go to the next line. To make a correction, just press that line on the screen and use the Backspace key to erase. When you're all done, touch Continue.

At the same time as this voice instruction was given, the screen depicted the lines of the business card text and prompted:

Postal Buddy screen: Type in your company name. Press Enter to go to the next line.

The simultaneity of these two instructions—the general voice instruction and the specifically object-bound screen instruction—created a situation that called for typing, not for reflection. Symptomatically, customer 3 never touched the screen as the voice instruction asked her to do; she used the keyboard only to enter and delete text. Possibly because of this lack of reflective distance (merging of instructions into the task itself), the instructions embedded in the machine did not enable customer 3 to solve her problem with the small *v*. She thus tried to remediate her actions with tools she invented or found outside the machine in the context of the situation. The first tool she invented was her own hand and fingers (lines 01 and 08; figure 13.5), the second tool was the next person waiting in the line (lines 02 to 04; figure 13.6), and finally the third tool was sarcasm (line 12).

The remediation of the human-machine interaction with the help of other humans waiting in line is more pronounced later when customer 3 tries to pay for her business cards and runs into trouble. At the end of her rather prolonged interaction with Postal Buddy, customer 3 waited for the machine to print out her business cards. The following short discussion ensued:

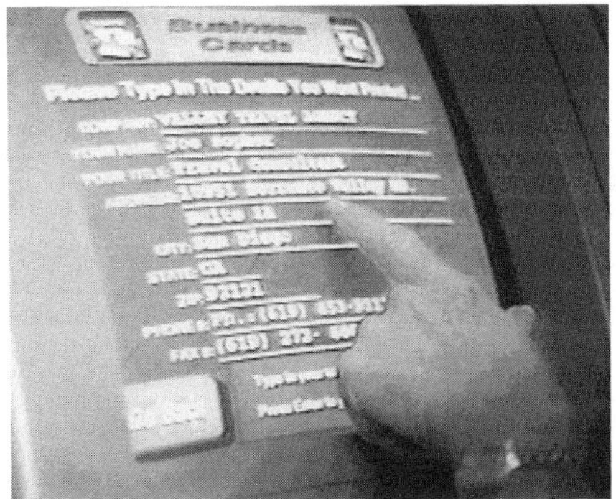

Figure 13.5
The finger used as a remediating tool.

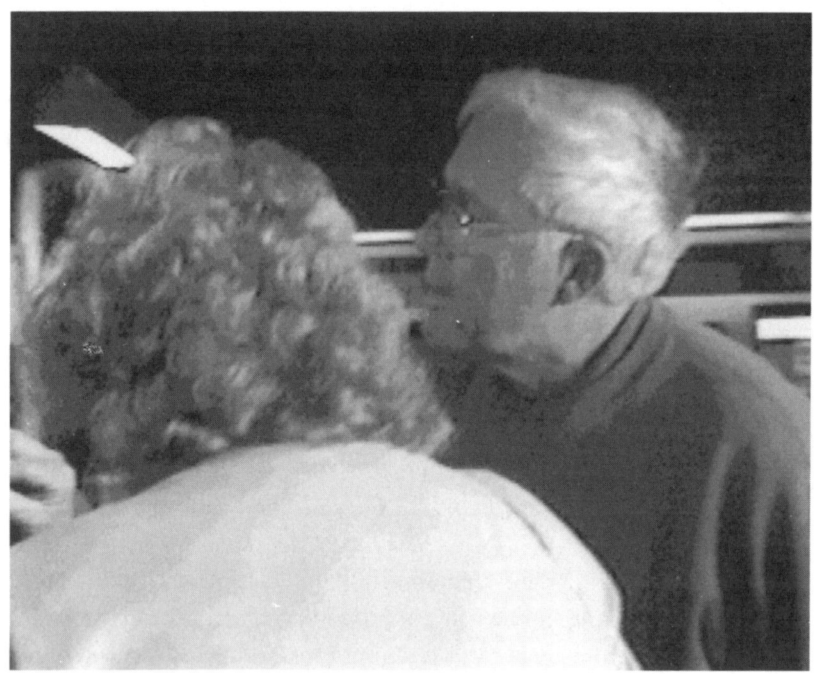

Figure 13.6
Another customer used as a remediating tool.

01	*Customer 4:*	[Points to a sign above Postal Buddy] It says "Quick and easy."
02	*Customer 3:*	I know. It's false ... (inaudible). It would be nice if they had somebody here. I can't even get change in and ...
03	*Customer 5:*	I guess it's blocked so that you can't ... you have to take ... Once you put a dollar in, you get a change deal [refers to the money card] back and they're hoping you'll lose your change deal in your purse and never use it, like, uh ...
04	*Postal Buddy screen:*	[Screen closes; changes to video showing labels being dispensed and a hand retrieving the sheets of labels.] Dispensing products. Please remove your items from the bin. Do not forget your receipt.

05	*Postal Buddy voice:*	Please remove your products from the bin and don't forget your receipt. You're all done! Thanks for using Postal Buddy and have a great day. Come back again soon and be sure to tell your friends.
06	*Customer 3:*	[Retrieves the labels; looks at them.] This came out funny.
07	*Customer 4:*	Didn't print the little *v*.
08	*Customer 3:*	Mmmh ... Well ... Did anybody show up at the window? [Leaves.]

The tone of the exchange here is far from love toward Postal Buddy. In this particular sequence, Postal Buddy emerges more like an object of suspicion than an object of affection. On line 02, customer 3 expresses her frustration over the fact that the post office personnel offer no assistance in dealings with the kiosk. On line 08, she finally gives up on the machine and once more in vain looks for assistance from the post office personnel.

We observed several instances where customers tried to get help from post office personnel. The clerks declined. One of our informants offered an explanation:

> *Boster:* I think, very frankly, the postal people in, uh, in the locations where the kiosk was housed, uh, developed a, you know, an attitude and, uh, that attitude was very difficult to change. Once we turned things around and the reliability was up and so on, you know, there was still this lingering attitude by them, that the thing doesn't work, you know, and so on and so forth. I mean, the reality is that the Postal Service's vending equipment, it never works.... An the only difference is that they had people on site that had a key that can open it and give you your product and clear a jam or fix it. The difference there was that we didn't have the, you know, they didn't have the ability to open up our kiosk. And we couldn't give it to them because of how much value was contained in the kiosk.
>
> *Interviewer:* Did they complain that a lot of people would go to them for help with the machine in using it, or ...?
>
> *Boster:* Not necessarily in using it, but when it didn't dispense correctly or, you know, it malfunctioned, they, they obviously were ... I think there's another issue, too, and that is the postal

> service union. The union was fighting us. And, uh, right before we shut down, right before all this happened, we were told and ordered by the postal service not to sell stamps anymore in their lobbies because the union said it was taking away jobs. (Interview with Boster)

INTERPRETING THE LOVE AFFAIR: OBJECTS AND ARTIFACTS IN ACTIVITY THEORY

The cultural-historical theory of activity is based on the notion of object relatedness or objectiveness of human activity. "The expression 'objectless activity' is devoid of any meaning. Activity may seem objectless, but scientific investigation of activity necessarily requires discovering its object" (Leont'ev 1978, 52).

It is relatively easy to envision the objects of basic material activities such as manual labor. The object of a farmer is the field, transformed time and again from brute earth to crops of grain in the process of work activity. It is much more difficult to envision and define the objects of such activities as trade, administration, play, recreation, or scientific research. A closer look at any such activity reveals the slippery and multifaceted character of its objects. Yet it is clear that those activities are oriented toward something and driven by something. This something—the object—is constantly in transition and under construction, and it manifests itself in different forms for different participants of the activity (Engeström 1990, 107–129).

The object should not be confused with a conscious goal or aim. In activity theory, conscious goals are related to discrete, finite, and individual actions; objects are related to continuous, collective activity systems and their motives. However, as Suchman (1987) has shown, even goals of actions are constantly evolving and situationally negotiated. As Leont'ev (1978, 65) put it, "Isolation and perception of goals by no means occurs automatically, nor is it an instantaneous act but a relatively long process of approbation of the goals by action and by their objective filling."

The slippery and transitional nature of objects sometimes evokes a denial of their very existence. Looking at the trajectory of a failed high-technology innovation, Bruno Latour (1993a) asserts:

> As long as it was a project, it was *not yet* an object. When it was finally realized it was no longer an object but a whole *institution*. So when does a piece of machinery become an object? Never, except when extracted portions of the institution are placed on view inside technical museums! ... It is only once on the scrap heap, when it begins to be dismembered, that a technical object finally becomes an object.... Even there it is an active entity. No, it is an object, a real object, only when it has disappeared beneath the ground, relegated to oblivion and potentially ready to be discovered by future archaeologists.... A high-technology object is a myth. (382)

For activity theory, this animate and transitional nature of objects is their necessary characteristic as objects of activity, that is, integral components of a system of human practice. In classical German philosophy, the object's embeddedness-in-activity was captured by the concept of *Gegenstand*, as distinct from the notion of mere *Objekt*. Latour, too, continues to use the notion of object after denying it. There is no escape.

But objects do not exist for us in themselves, directly and without mediation. We relate to objects *by means* of other objects:

> Thus the implementation of the act of cognition as a specifically human reflection or reproduction of the object's essential characteristics presupposes not only the subject's handling the object but also man's creation ... of a definite system of "artificial" objects mediating the process of reflection and carrying cognitive norms and standards in themselves. These mediating objects, acting as instruments of cognition, have a certain specificity. On the one hand, their purpose is to enable the subject to reflect in cognition the characteristics of objects existing independently of them. On the other hand, the mediators themselves are objects with specific features of their own, possessing internal connections assuming definite modes of operating with them.... But that means that implementation of the cognitive act assumes not only the subject's ability to correlate mediating objects with the object cognized. The subject must also master the modes of handling the specific reality constituted by the socially functioning artificial objects. (Lektorsky 1984, 138–139)

This means that objects appear in two fundamentally different roles: as objects (*Gegenstand*) and as mediating artifacts or tools. There is nothing in the material makeup of an object as such that would determine which one it is: object or tool. The constellation of the activity determines the place and meaning of the object (Engeström 1990, 171–195).

Lektorsky's point about the need to master "the specific reality" constituted by mediating artifacts is crucially important. What is meant to function as a tool is easily turned into an object; an instrument becomes an end in itself. Complex material and symbolic technologies demonstrate this tendency of displacement particularly strongly. Ong (1982) argues that writing systems have captivated and detached whole cultures, creating self-sufficient worlds of reflection and abstract reasoning. Olson (1980) makes essentially the same point about the authority and holding power of school texts; instead of functioning as tools for grasping the world, they tend to replace the world and become substitute objects of learning. Turkle (1984) maintains that computers and programming languages have a similar tremendous holding power, creating closed hacker subcultures characterized by "loving the machine for itself."

Getting immersed in the relatively self-contained "specific reality" of a technology may be compared to dream and play: "Within the dream the dreamer is usually unaware that he is dreaming, and within 'play' he must often be reminded that 'This is play.' Similarly, within dream or fantasy the dreamer does not operate with the concept 'untrue.' He operates with all sorts of statements but with a curious inability to achieve meta-statements. He cannot ... dream a statement referring to (i.e., framing) his dream" (Bateson 1972, 185).

The ability of actors to make metacommunicative statements, that is, to discriminate between tool and object and to play with their relationship, is a vital feature of an activity capable of self-reflection and change. When a tool becomes a closed, self-sufficient substitute object, this ability is lost. Something like this seems to have happened among key actors of the Postal Buddy network. Bruce Hurd recalled, "So, it was important to us to develop this relationship, so that as we changed our product lines, it didn't matter. Their relationship was with Postal Buddy. It had nothing necessarily to do with labels, change of address, stamps, any of that" (interview with Hurd). In other words, the customer's original object—labels, change of address, stamps—is replaced with Postal Buddy as a substitute object of affection. This substitute object is supposed to become independent of the products. The logical outcome is an image of a customer who comes to do business with Postal Buddy regardless of what the machine is selling, for the sake of the machine itself. This image of an absolute, closed, and self-contained love affair seems to have been so strong among some of the key actors that it indeed resembles dreaming. Customers' complaints are registered, but they remain curiously separate from the image of the love affair, as if in a cognitive compartment of their own. The hesitations and hedges are but weak rudiments of metacommunicative statements.

The emergence of a technology as a substitute object has consequences. The self-contained nature of the substitute object implies that it merges and subsumes in itself both the object and mediating artifacts; thus, external tools for the handling of the substitute object are considered unnecessary. This "instrumental impoverishment" (Engeström 1987, 101) may be seen in various examples: you are supposed to learn to read and write by just reading and writing, to use a computer by just using it (manuals are commonly regarded as notoriously useless). The lack of tools means a lack of distance and a lack of critical reflection. You learn school texts by plunging into them, not by comparing and questioning them with the help of other sources. This is the age-old myth of a non-mediated relationship between the cognizing subject and the external world, or the "postulate of directness" (Leont'ev 1978, 47) reborn.

The somewhat dreamlike love affair of corporate actors with Postal Buddy thoroughly molded the machine itself. The kiosk was supposed to be totally self-sufficient and self-explanatory. As our informants put it, Postal Buddy was "a salesman" (interview with Boster, November 1993), "selling a product without a person," "so that even the most computer illiterate folks could use the machine" (interview with May). This tremendous emphasis on self-sufficiency led to a blurring of instructions and objects in the design of the user interface. Instruction manuals or catalogs outside the actual screen and voice of the machine were not offered. Inside the machine, general instructions were typically presented simultaneously with prompts demanding specific object-oriented action, such as entering information by typing, effectively hampering reflective problem solving on the part of the user. The point was well summarized by Sidney Goodman himself when he told us about his ideas of a possible next machine to follow Postal Buddy:

> There's actually going to be a little catalog where you can flip through and see all the different styles that are going to be ... so you're gonna.... The biggest problem we always had was you could never explain to somebody all the wonderful things that are inside this box. And going down a path, by shooting a path, you're excluding all the other paths. Uh, and so what we're gonna do is have all the choices in a catalog this thick. And it'll say "I want business cards and I want this style or that," and then you'll be able to pick a style number and just punch in that number and you won't have to flip through menus. (Interview with Goodman, February 1994)

What do these insights tell us about the causes that led to the sudden fall of the Postal Buddy? How do they alter the dichotomous picture of revenue explanation versus conspiracy explanation?

In the interviews, the conspiracy explanation goes together with the image of universal love toward Postal Buddy. We found no evidence of universal love among the users. There was a wide gap between the proclaimed love affair of the corporate actors and the open frustration of many users. We suggest that this gap was an important ground cause of the failure. If the users had been wildly enthusiastic about Postal Buddy—if they had indeed fallen in love with it—the USPS would surely have thought twice before canceling the project. Had the users really loved the machine, they would surely have used it so much that it would have been very difficult for the USPS conspirators to justify the cancellation financially. Our microlevel analysis thus seriously undermines the conspiracy explanation as the sole cause of the failure. In other words, there may have been a conspiracy, but it would have been ineffective without serious problems among the end users.

As to the revenue explanation, it begs the crucial question of why revenues might have remained unsatisfactory. Our microlevel analysis points toward a very fundamental displacement as explanation: the transformation of a mundane, albeit complex, tool into a substitute object of affection. This displacement is evident not only in the discourse of the corporate actors; it is equally evident in the material design and interactive functioning of Postal Buddy kiosks.

A MISSING LINK IN THE NETWORK

We suggest that there is a viable alternative to Machiavellian analyses of networks. Bruce Hurd's following remark helps concretize the direction of network analysis we are advocating: "Here is a small, dynamic, entrepreneurial company that makes decisions and moves like this [snaps his fingers], dealing with the ultimate in bureaucracies. And we were bound to have our problems with it" (interview with Hurd).

How to analyze systematically the inner dynamics of "a small, dynamic, entrepreneurial company" and those of "the ultimate in bureaucracies"? Activity theory, particularly developmental work research, has developed a conceptual tool kit and a reservoir of empirical case studies suited for that very task. We think that an alternative mode of network analysis begins with the inner dynamics, contradictions, and dialogical interactions *within* the activity systems of each participant of a network. Connections and exchanges *between* the nodes can be adequately characterized only on the basis of historically grounded understanding of the inner workings of the nodes of the network. This requires an articulated conceptual model of the anatomy of an activity system (Engeström 1987, 82–91, 1993; Cole and Engeström 1993; Saarelma 1993).

For a depiction of the management of Postal Buddy Corporation as an activity system, a clear understanding of the overarching mediational artifact of that activity is vitally important. In this case, such a "tertiary artifact" (Wartofsky 1979) consisted of a vision, a collective representation of the computerized kiosk as a substitute human being. This representation is not unique or novel. It is a powerful image that has a history at least as long as the history of artificial intelligence. The initial document of the Strategic Computing Initiative launched by the U.S. military in 1983 formulated the vision succinctly:

> In contrast with previous computers, the new generation will exhibit human-like, "intelligent" capabilities for planning and reasoning. The computers will also have capabilities that enable direct, natural interactions with their users and their environments as, for example, through vision and speech.
>
> Using this new technology, machines will perform complex tasks with little human intervention, or even with complete autonomy. Our citizens will have machines that are "capable associates,"

> which can greatly augment each person's ability to perform tasks that require specialized expertise. (Defense Advanced Research Projects Agency 1983, 1; for an elaboration of the closed world image of computing, see Edwards forthcoming)

The Postal Buddy vision, however, had an important touch of originality: the idea of lovability. The Postal Buddy was not only, not even, primarily a substitute human thinker; it was a substitute object of affection. This ingenious variation of the powerful image of a computer-as-substitute-human dramatically changed the position of the machine in the activity from a tool to an object. We may now depict the activity system of the management of the Postal Buddy Corporation with the help of a diagram (figure 13.7).

In the figure, the component of rules is particularly important. For the Postal Buddy management, the terms of the USPS contract were a rule above all others. Said Bruce Hurd, "I mean, that was put almost above anything else. I mean, I knew that if we screwed up on the postal services contract from an accounting standpoint, if we did something wrong, I knew I would lose my job. And I was never threatened by it, but I just

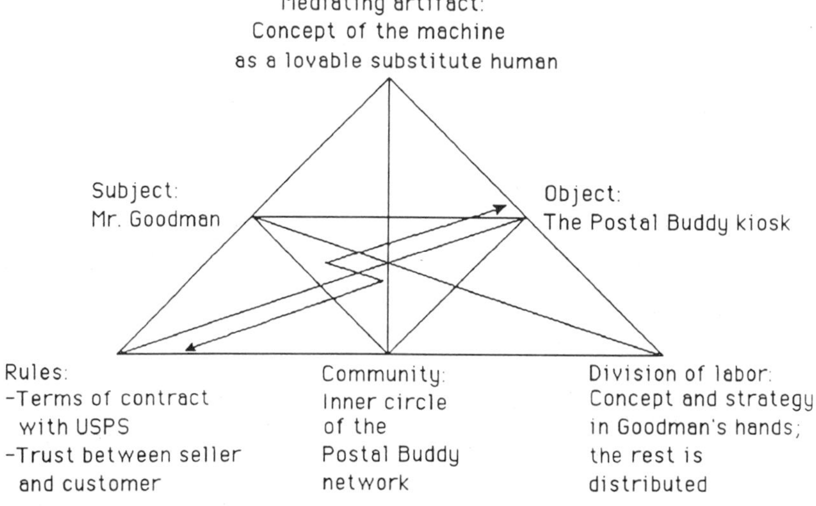

Figure 13.7
Activity system of the management of Postal Buddy Corporation.

knew that that was the kind of emphasis on quality and the reliability that we needed to put into our relationship with it. We took it very, very seriously" (interview with Hurd).

This rule was closely associated with another central rule, demanding trust between the seller (the Postal Buddy Corporation) and the customer (USPS). It seems that the exclusive focusing on the kiosk as object of affection gradually created a tension, suppressing and violating this rule of trust. Hurd reflected, "Unfortunately, I, I don't think we developed a personal relationship with them [in the USPS] that we should've over the years, you know. I think that if we had come to know them better as people, maybe we could've talked to them" (interview with Hurd).

This tension between the *rule* of trust between the seller and the customer and the *object* understood as a lovable stand-alone substitute human is depicted with the help of a lightning-shaped arrow in figure 13.3.

An attempt to turn a machine such as the Postal Buddy into a substitute object of affection is in effect a heroic attempt to turn the actions of buying stamps, labels, or business cards into a long-term activity of dealing with the Postal Buddy for the sake of the kiosk itself. In the case of the computer as a substitute object, a successful displacement is possible due to the inherent flexibility and open-endedness of the machine. The substitute object opens up an expanding horizon of possible actions; there are no limits to what hackers can do. Thus, communities of hackers can and do emerge, giving longevity and social coherence to the activity. In contrast, Postal Buddy allows for a very limited range of actions. A community of Postal Buddy fans is conceivable only as an oddity, even more eccentric than the "imaginary social worlds" of fans obsessed with movie stars and rock idols (Caughey 1984).

The identification of the tool- to substitute-object displacement within the management of the Postal Buddy Corporation as a causative mechanism behind the fall of the Postal Buddy does not close the issue. If the Postal Buddy kiosk was a substitute object, what might have been a more robust and sustainable object? What was the management of Postal Buddy Corporation missing? And why did the USPS first follow suit, then change its orientation?

We have many fewer data on the activity system of the USPS management. Thus, only first tentative steps of analysis can be taken here. Our informant provides a clue for a possible direction of such analysis:

> My own opinion is that the post office [implying the USPS] had very specific ideas as to what they wanted to do in the lobbies of the post offices—a whole retailing merchandising department that they'd created over the last several years. They had developed some plans that involved possibly several vendors providing products. And the Postal Buddy contract itself had, uh, some exclusivity to it that would not allow them to do what they wanted to do from a marketing standpoint. And I think it, uh, was based on that they thought we were just incompatible with the direction they wanted to go from a retailing standpoint. (interview with Hurd)

No matter how speculative, this statement contains the important idea of looking carefully at the recent history and inner dynamics of the activity system of USPS retailing and merchandising. It also directs our attention to the local post office as an activity system.

Elaborating on Hurd's statement as a working hypothesis, it is plausible that the USPS management initially saw the Postal Buddy kiosk as a stand-alone object. As the issue was further studied within the USPS management, the object expanded so as to encompass the entire local post office as a new kind of setting for multiple commercial interactions. A new activity—development of retail and merchandising—emerged with the USPS. The object of this activity is literally a horizon of possible actions, a transitional field between post offices as currently existing material settings and post offices as projected possibilities. The Postal Buddy kiosk became a subordinate, interchangeable, and replaceable tool that might or might not be useful in constructing such an object.

For the Postal Buddy Corporation and its immediate business allies, the object remained the Postal Buddy kiosk itself as a stand-alone generator of affection and revenue. Although Postal Buddy Corporation and EDS made some 350 modifications in the machine, they seem to have had little, if any, interest in reformulating and renegotiating the relationship between the Postal Buddy kiosk and the rest of the local post office activity. The local post office remained a blank space, a missing link in the Postal Buddy network. The Postal Buddy kiosk was to be self-

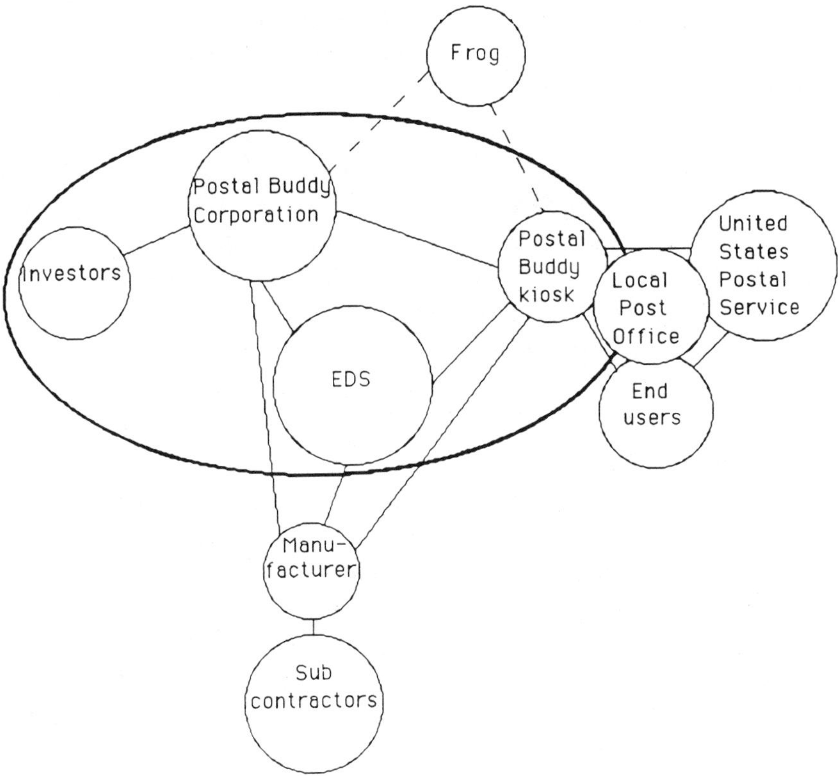

Figure 13.8
The local post office identified as a missing link in the Postal Buddy network.

sufficient and independent of whatever else was going on in a post office. Even the actions of the postal service workers' union against the Postal Buddy (as described by Boster in the interview) did not seem to change this attitude. We can now complete our network depiction by placing the missing link in where it belongs (figure 13.8).

The uncovering of the missing link makes visible a new power concentration in the network, largely outside the inner circle. This concentration consists of the Postal Buddy kiosk, the USPS, and the end users, all three now glued together by a neglected fourth actor, the local post office. The local post office becomes the glue by virtue of being the scene of the moments of truth: the actual microlevel meetings between the machine and the customer, commonly neglected by both corporate managers and by actor-network theorists. Figure 13.8 helps us understand why the management of the USPS may have begun to see its object in a new light—as a complex system of interaction in the local post office rather than as a stand-alone automated kiosk.

This mismatch between the objects as constructed by the USPS on the one hand and by the Postal Buddy inner circle on the other hand was bound to create a rift. To overcome this mismatch of objects, the Postal Buddy Corporation would have needed to retool and reorient its activity, that is, develop concepts for initiating and conducting a dialog on the future of the entire local post office as a retail setting. This would have required serious attention to Postal Buddy customers' problems in which they repeatedly and in vain looked for remediational tools by turning to other customers, post office personnel, and other resources outside the machine itself. Those innovative microlevel attempts of customers to expand their means of reflective problem solving were indications of where the macrolevel network actors should have looked: into the post office activity system surrounding the machine. It is not accidental that the account of the successful DesignCenter kiosk quoted early in this chapter concludes as follows: "In presenting the workstation to retailers, Weyerhaeuser emphasizes the involvement of store sales people in assisting the customer, thereby strengthening relations between manufacturer and retailer as well as ensuring that the customer can obtain any necessary information not contained in the computer program" (Little 1994, 458).

ACKNOWLEDGMENTS

Partial funding for this research was provided by the Academy of Finland (grant to the first author for the project Learning and Expertise in Teams and Networks). We thank our informants and interviewees for their time and willingness to share their experiences and interpretations with us. We thank Phil Agre, Ellen Christiansen, Michael Cole, Adrian Cussins, Charles Goodwin, Dorothy Holland, Reijo Miettinen, and Bonnie Nardi for helpful comments on an earlier version of the chapter.

REFERENCES

Akrich, M. (1992). The description of technical objects. In W. E. Bijker and J. Law, eds., *Shaping Technology/Building Society: Studies in Sociotechnical Change*. Cambridge, MA: MIT Press.

Akrich, M. (1993). A gazogene in Costa Rica: An experiment in technosociology. In P. Lemonnier, ed., *Technological Choices: Transformation in Material Cultures Since the Neolithic*. London: Routledge.

Alter, C., and Hage, J. (1993). *Organizations Working Together*. Newbury Park, CA: Sage.

Bakhtin, M. M. (1982). *The Dialogic Imagination: Four Essays by M. M. Bakhtin*. Edited by M. Holquist. Austin: University of Texas Press.

Bateson, G. (1972). *Steps to an Ecology of Mind*. New York: Ballantine Books.

Billig, M. (1987). *Arguing and Thinking: A Rhetorical Approach to Social Psychology*. Cambridge: Cambridge University Press.

Billig, M., et al. (1988). *Ideological Dilemmas: A Social Psychology of Everyday Thinking*. London: Sage.

Bleeke, J., and Ernst, D., eds. (1993). *Collaborating to Compete: Using Strategic Alliances and Acquisitions in the Global Marketplace*. New York: Wiley.

Button, G. (1993). The curious case of the vanishing technology. In G. Button, ed., *Technology on Working Order: Studies of Work, Interaction, and Technology*. London: Routledge.

Callon, M. (1992). The dynamics of technoeconomic networks. In R. Coombs, P. Saviotti, and V. Walsh, eds., *Technological Change and Company Strategies*. London: Academic Press.

Callon, M., Law, J., and Rip. A. (1986). How to study the force of science. In M. Callon, J. Law, and A. Rip, eds., *Mapping the Dynamics of Science and Technology*. London: Macmillan.

Caughey, J. L. (1984). *Imaginary Social Worlds: A Cultural Approach*. Lincoln: University of Nebraska Press.

Cole, M., and Engeström, Y. (1993). A cultural-historical approach to distributed cognition. In G. Salomon, ed., *Distributed Cognitions: Psychological and Educational Considerations*. Cambridge: Cambridge University Press.

Defense Advanced Research Projects Agency. (1983). *Strategic Computing—New Generation Computing Technology: A Strategic Plan for Its Development and Application to Critical Problems in Defense*. Washington, DC: DARPA.

Edwards, P. N. (forthcoming). *The Closed World: Computers and the Politics of Discourse in Cold War America*. Cambridge, MA: MIT Press.

Engeström, Y. (1987). *Learning by Expanding: An Activity-Theoretical Approach to Developmental Research*. Helsinki: Orienta-Konsultit.

Engeström, Y. (1990). *Learning, Working and Imagining: Twelve Studies in Activity Theory*. Helsinki: Orienta-Konsultit.

Engeström, Y. (1991a). Developmental work research: A paradigm in practice. *Quarterly Newsletter of the Laboratory of Comparative Human Cognition* 13:79–80.

Engeström, Y. (1991b). Developmental work research: Reconstructing expertise through expansive learning. In M. I. Nurminen and G. R. S. Weir, eds., *Human Jobs and Computer Interfaces*. Amsterdam: Elsevier.

Engeström, Y. (1993). Developmental studies of work as a testbench of activity theory: The case of primary care medical practice. In S. Chaiklin and J. Lave, eds., *Understanding Practice: Perspectives on Activity and Context*. Cambridge: Cambridge University Press.

von Hippel, E. (1988). *The Sources of Innovation*. New York: Oxford University Press.

Hirschhorn, L. (1984). *Beyond Mechanization: Work and Technology in a Post-industrial Age*. Cambridge, MA: MIT Press.

Latour, B. (1987). *Science in Action: How to Follow Scientists and Engineers through Society*. Cambridge, MA: Harvard University Press.

Latour, B. (1988a). Drawing things together. In M. Lynch and S. Woolgar, eds., *Representation in Scientific Practice*. Cambridge, MA: MIT Press.

Latour, B. (1988b). *The Pasteurization of France*. Cambridge, MA: Harvard University Press.

Latour, B. (1988c). *The Prince* for machines as well as for machinations. In B. Elliot, ed., *Technology and Social Process*. Edinburgh: Edinburgh University Press.

Latour, B. (1993a). Ethnography of a "high-tech" case: About Aramis. In P. Lemonnier, ed., *Technological Choices: Transformation in Material Cultures Since the Neolithic*. London: Routledge.

Latour, B. (1993b). On technical mediation: Three talks prepared for the Messenges Lectures on the Evolution of Civilization. Cornell University (manuscript).

Law, J., and Callon, M. (1992). The life and death of an aircraft: A network analysis of technical change. In W. E. Bijker and J. Law, eds., *Shaping Technology/Building Society: Studies in Sociotechnical Change*. Cambridge, MA: MIT Press.

Lektorsky, V. A. (1984). *Subject, Object, Cognition*. Moscow: Progress.

Leont'ev, A. N. (1978). *Activity, Consciousness, and Personality*. Englewood Cliffs, NJ: Prentice-Hall.

Little, J. D. C. (1994). Information technology in marketing. In T. J. Allen and M. S. Scott Morton, eds., *Information Technology and the Corporation of the 1990s: Research Studies*. New York: Oxford University Press.

Miettinen, R. (1993). *Methodological Issues of Studying Innovation-Related Networks*. Group for Technology Studies, Working Paper 4. Espoo: Technical Research Center of Finland.

Moriarty, K. E. (1990). Postal Buddy. Unpublished case study. Stanford Graduate School of Business.

Nohria, N., and Eccles, R. G., eds. (1992). *Networks and Organizations: Structure, Form, and Action*. Boston: Harvard Business School Press.

Olson, D. R. (1980). On the language and authority of textbooks. *Journal of Communications* 30:186–196.

Ong, W. J. (1982). *Orality and Literacy: The Technologizing of the Word*. London: Methuen.

Powell, W. W. (1990). Neither market nor hierarchy: Network forms of organization. In L. L. Cummings and B. Staw, eds., *Research in Organizational Behavior*. Greenwich, CT: JAI Press.

Radder, H. (1992). Normative reflections on constructivist approaches to science and technology. *Social Studies of Science* 22:141–173.

Saarelma, O. (1993). Descriptions of subjective networks as a mediator of developmental dialogue. *Quarterly Newsletter of the Laboratory of Comparative Human Cognition* 15:102–112.

Shapin, S. (1988). Following scientists around. Essay review of "Science in action: How to follow the scientists and engineers through society" by Bruno Latour. *Social Studies of Science* 18:533–550.

Suchman, L. A. (1987). *Plans and Situated Actions: The Problem of Human-Machine Communication*. Cambridge: Cambridge University Press.

Turkle, S. (1984). *The Second Self: Computers and the Human Spirit*. New York: Simon and Schuster.

Wartofsky, M. (1979). *Models: Representation and Scientific Understanding*. Dordrecht: Reidel.

14 Epilogue

Bonnie A. Nardi

Activity theory offers substantial tools for a broadly scoped study of "computer-mediated activity" (Kaptelinin, chapter 3, this volume), transcending a more narrowly conceived focus on "human-computer interaction." Efforts in the study of computer-mediated activity will pave the way for an even larger project of understanding "how artifacts are used in individual and cooperative work" (Kuutti, this volume), extending our concerns to technology as a whole, not just computers. The chapters in this book are a step toward a richer understanding of the way computers mediate experience and how the tools and sign systems we create interpenetrate our consciousness and our very existence. Our own practice of trying to understand practice causes us to search, recursively, for new mediating tools and representations, as we see in Bødker (this volume) and Raeithel and Velichkovsky (this volume), who offer new mediating structures for analysis and modeling.

I have found activity theory compelling because it weaves together, in a single coherent framework, so many interesting theoretical constructs crucial to an understanding of human activity: dynamic levels of activity, mediation, contradiction, intentionality, development, history, collaboration, functional organ, the unity of internal and external. Other theoretical frameworks treat these constructs individually, or in less rich form, or not at all. Activity theory as a unified approach obviates the need to construct a theoretical apparatus bricoleur fashion, from a multiplicity of smaller frameworks (if indeed this would even be possible as Kaptelinin, chapter 3, this volume, questions). Activity theory situates itself within a humane matrix in which science is in the service of the everyday, people and things are not the same, and the activity systems of all relevant parties, not just the powerful, are important.

Activity theory is a solid but still partial theoretical framework for handling the difficult questions of technology design we seek to answer. There remain many problems to work out. How do we understand webs of complexly interleaved activities? Are there really only three levels of activity? How are conflicting objects handled within and between subjects? What is the provenance of objects? How does culture relate to activity? And what indeed is culture? It is the work of a minute to provide an enumeration of sticky problems but months and years of effort to make progress on even one of them. Activity theory has the momentum and theoretical underpinnings to yield fresh contributions to the answers to these questions, as many contributions to this book show. In particular, activity theory has provided the conceptual infrastructure to permit the precise formulation and articulation of these problems.

Still, in many areas, activity theory is underdeveloped. As often happens, art provokes our doubts and inflames our questions, and I was struck by a passage in *Middlemarch*, by George Eliot, in which she brilliantly describes an episode in the consciousness of one of her characters, Will Ladislaw. The problems of consciousness are a major theme of *Middlemarch*, and, as it happens, many of the missing pieces of activity theory are laid out with economy and artistry in this single passage to which I refer (not, of course, that that was Eliot's intent!).

Let us consider this passage. Will Ladislaw and Dorothea Casaubon are members of the nineteenth-century English upper class. Dorothea is married to a rich cleric, and Will is an artistic but penniless young man. Will is trying to earn his living as an assistant to Dorothea's uncle, a wealthy landowner named Mr. Brooke, helping him manage his land, tenants, and political activity. Will is in love with Dorothea. We find Will in Mr. Brooke's library, going over some papers. Dorothea enters the library:

> Will, the moment before, had been low in the depths of boredom, and, obliged to help Mr. Brooke in arranging "documents" about hanging sheep-stealers, was exemplifying the power our minds have of riding several horses at once by inwardly arranging measures towards getting a lodging for himself in Middlemarch and cutting

> short his constant residence at the Grange; while there flitted through all these steadier images a tickling vision of a sheep-stealing epic written with Homeric particularity. When Mrs. Casaubon was announced he started up as from an electric shock, and felt a tingling at his finger-ends. Any one observing him would have seen a change in the vividness of his glance, which might have made them imagine that every molecule in his body had passed the message of a magic touch. And so it had. For effective magic is transcendent nature; and who shall measure the subtlety of those touches which convey the quality of soul as well as body, and make a man's passion for one woman differ from his passion for another as joy in the morning light over valley and river and white mountain-top differs from joy among Chinese lanterns and glass panels? Will, too, was made of very impressible stuff. The bow of a violin drawn near him cleverly, would at one stroke change the aspect of the world for him, and his point of view shifted as easily as his mood. Dorothea's entrance was the freshness of morning.

In this short but evocative passage, we find a number of interesting claims about consciousness. Will is somehow thinking of three things at once, and three rather different things: the work of the documents he is desultorily attending to, the entirely practical matter of moving house, and the "tickling vision" by which the tedious content of the documents is being transmuted to a hilariously inappropriate literary form. Will is at once bored, diverted, and planful. Activity theory does not, as far as I know, deal with the mechanics of how one could be in three states of consciousness at once, or feel three different things at once, and yet the passage from Eliot does seem to capture experience. All of this speaks directly to issues of technology design. We must consider how many things a person could reasonably attend to at once and what sorts of things those might be and in what combinations, for example, when we layer visual or auditory cues on top of other actions the user is taking and other information she is being exposed to. We might also consider how we can help users avoid boredom and perhaps even provide some diverting moments at least as good as the sheep-stealing epic!

When Dorothea enters the room, Will has a powerful emotional response that reverberates through his body to his very fingertips. Indeed, Eliot avers that "every molecule in his body" is affected, thereby asserting the primacy of the body in our activity, our responses to events. This part of the passage seems to be very much what Zinchenko (this volume) is getting at in his discussion of "body and soul as convertible external and internal forms." In fact, Eliot tells us precisely what we would see in the "vividness of [Will's] glance," just as Zinchenko directs our attention to Spet's and Plotin's reflections on the human face. Eliot has gone far beyond Cartesian misapprehensions about mind-body duality, though she can articulate the link between "soul as well as body" only by invoking "magic." Still, she tells us that we must consider the body, and its most deeply felt responses, as a fundamental, integral element of human experience. By contrast, although activity theory is not at all Cartesian and has a well-developed notion of functional organ, there is nevertheless a distinctly rational feel to the depiction of an ordered reality regulated through objects, mediators, and goal-directed behavior. Control and regulation are at the heart of activity theory rather than a reality of electrifying bodily shocks of the kind Will experiences.

And then there is the "impressible stuff" of which Will is apparently made. He is extremely responsive to environmental stimuli: the cleverly drawn bow can alter his mood in a flash. More fundamentally, his "point of view" is capable of rapid shift as well. Holland and Reeves (this volume) begin to chip away at this problem, and it is indeed a thorny one. Activity theory excels at describing object-related activity but says little about how we are diverted, distracted, interrupted, seduced away from our objects, subject to serendipity and surprise. Bødker (this volume) takes on the problem of providing methods for describing how attention shifts between objects, but there is still a need for a theoretical concept that defines the relationship of object-related activity to the very real and sometimes substantial impingement of events outside the scope of our object-related activities. What is called for is not a behavioristic account of reaction to stimuli or situation but a way of explaining the articulation and coordination of object-related activity and impinging events external to objects.

I find Eliot's concerns with "impressibility," point of view, and bodily response to be entirely relevant to post-postmodern technology design. As we move toward technologies that play directly to our impressibility (voice, video, cool graphics, virtual reality), suppress, manipulate, or subvert point of view (hypertext, MUDs), and significantly engage body and sensation (virtual reality), even incorporating these technologies into our children's education as Bellamy (this volume) reminds us, and going so far as to fall in love with our technology, as Engeström and Escalante (this volume) recount, we had better be concerned with these things. Why? The fox in *The Little Prince* answered that one. Let us continue the conversation with him that Christiansen (this volume) initiated:

> "It is the time you have wasted on your rose that makes it so precious."
>
> "It is the time I have wasted on my rose—" said the little prince, so that he would be sure to remember.
>
> "Men have forgotten this truth," said the fox. "But you must not forget it. You become responsible, forever, for what you have tamed. You are responsible for your rose."
>
> "I am responsible for my rose," the little prince repeated, so that he would be sure to remember.

Contributors

R. K. E. Bellamy
Learning Technologies
Advanced Technology Group
Apple Computer Inc., MS 301-3E
1 Infinite Loop
Cupertino, CA 95014
United States
rachel@apple.com

Susanne Bødker
Department of Computer Science
Aarhus University
Denmark
bodker@daimi.aau.dk

Ellen Christiansen
Department of Communication
Aalborg University
Langagervej 8
DK-9220 Aalborg
Denmark
ellen@hum.auc.dk

Yrjö Engeström
Laboratory of Comparative Human Cognition
University of California, San Diego
La Jolla, CA 92093
United States
yengestr@weber.ucsd.edu

Virginia Escalante
Communication Department
University of California, San Diego
La Jolla, CA 92093
United States
vescalan@weber.ucsd.edu

Dorothy Holland
Department of Anthropology
University of North Carolina
Chapel Hill, NC 27599
United States
dchollan@isisa.oit.unc.edu

Victor Kaptelinin
Umea University
Department of Informatics
S - 901 87 Umeå
Sweden
Victor.Kaptelinin@informatik.umu.se

Kari Kuutti
Department of Information Processing Science
University of Oulu
Linnanmaa, SF-90570
Oulu
Finland
kuutti@rieska.oulu.fi

Bonnie A. Nardi
Intelligent Systems Program
Advanced Technology Group
Apple Computer, MS 301-3S
1 Infinite Loop
Cupertino, CA 95014
United States
nardi@apple.com

Arne Raeithel
Department of Psychology
University of Hamburg
Hamburg
Germany
raeithel@informatik. uni-hamburg.de

James R. Reeves
Department of Anthropology
University of North Carolina
Chapel Hill, NC 27599
United States

Boris M. Velichkovsky
Unit of Applied Cognitive Research/
Psychology
Technical University of Dresden
D-01062 Dresden
Germany
velich@psy1.psych.tu-dresden.de

Vladimir P. Zinchenko
Moscow Russian Academy of
Education
Department of Psychology and
Developmental Physiology, Room 428
Moscow
Russia
zinch@rae.msk.su

Index

Access in K-12 education, 127, 142
Actions
vs. activities, 25–26, 32
in activity theory, 73–76
and artifacts, 310–311
chains of, 30–31
clusters of, 149
communicative, 35, 58, 221–222
evaluation of, 89–90, 228
examples of, 33
goals of, 30, 80
humans as, 311
internal plane of (IPA), 51–53, 112
mental, 290
operations for, 108
planes of, 209
plans and models for, 31
polymotivated, 58–59
sign-related, 301
and tasks, 219
transformed, 149, 201
word, 292–293
Activities
vs. actions, 25–26, 32
in activity theory, 25–37, 79–83
authentic, 131
as basic units of analysis, 25–26
components of, 73
as consciousness, 7, 11
developmental stages in, 62–63
in Dinosaur Canyon simulation, 132–134
in distributed cognition, 79–83
dynamic nature of, 33–34, 38–40, 75
evaluation of, 228
examples of, 33
history in, 26
levels of, 30–38, 108
limitations of term, 41
for meaning, 177
in Media Fusion, 139, 141
and mind, 285–286
motives for, 30–31
and objects, 34, 360, 362
operations from, 40
and perception, 209–210
of persons-acting in setting, 71
relationships in, 175–176
in situated action model, 79–83
structure of, 27–30
in VIRK system, 158–161
Activity systems, Postal Buddy as, 365–370
Activity theory
activities in, 25–37, 79–83
artifacts and mediation in, 26–27
context in, 37–38, 46, 73–76, 78–88
in design, 127–128
evaluation of, 88–94
functional organs in, 286–288
and HCI, 7–15, 25–41, 110–112
limitations of, 63–64
methodological implications of, 94–96
people and things in, 86–88
perspective in, 107–108, 271–275

Activity theory (cont.)
- position and possibilities of, 37–40
- principles of, 107–110
- vs. situated action model and distributed cognition, 78–88
- social processes in, 37–38, 46, 63–64, 107
- structures in, 83–86

Actor-network theory, 252–253, 338–346
Ado, Pierre, on words, 299
Affection for objects. *See* Postal Buddy
Affordances, 56–57
Agents
- collective, 59
- and consciousness, 12
- in distributed cognition, 86–87

Airport baggage handler study, 260–261
Applications, computer. *See* Computer applications
Aramis subway system, 343–344
Arcimboldo, Giuseppe, painting by, 205–206, 211–212
Arenas in situated action model, 71, 277
Aristoksen, on soul, 300
Artifacts, 7–8
- and actions, 310–311
- activity theory as, 46
- breakdowns and focus shifts in, 149–152, 154–156
- caring about, 193–196
- for children, 130
- in cognitive science, 14, 62
- context of, 46
- contradictions in, 150–152
- design of, 127–128
- in distributed cognition, 77–78, 84–85
- in Flying Squad, 179–182
- history in, 75, 150
- in K-12 education, 126
- mediation by, 26–27, 75–76, 124, 148–149
- names as, 298
- vs. people, 86–88
- in Postal Buddy system, 365–367
- relationships with, 175–176
- role of, 14
- and social processes, 75, 130
- tertiary, 365
- in VIRK system, 158–161

Artifacts-in-use-in-a-certain-practice, 149
AT project. *See* VIRK system
Attention, joint, 204–213
Attentional landscapes, 210
Augustine, Saint, on mediation, 307
Austin, J. L., on performative word actions, 292
Authentic activities, 131
- in Dinosaur Canyon, 132–134
- in Media Fusion, 139, 141

Authentic learning, 130
Automation, 34
Awareness, neurons of, 322
Axel, E., 268–269

Backtracking search strategies, 53
Baggage handler study, 260–261
Bakhtin, M. M., on culture, 311–312
Baldwin, Philip R., in Postal Buddy development, 329, 336
Bannon, Liam J.
- on activity theory in HCI, 147
- cognitive science criticism by, 20–22
- interface design classification by, 24

Bateson, G., on dreams, 362
Behavior, free will in, 284
Belotti, V., software design survey by, 18
Bendifallah, S., teamwork study by, 276
Bennett, Bill, 335
Bergson, on words, 299
Bernshtein, N.
- and development, 111
- on living motion, 287–288

Berry, Tom, 330–331

Bertelsen, O., on Fitts's law, 87–88
Billig, M., on qualified expressions, 346
Biological feedback, 287
Bird watching, evaluating actions in, 89–90
Blake, William
chronotope illustration by, 295
on names, 297
on prophets, 304
Bobrow, D., on programming, 12
Bødker, Susanne
activity theory ideas presented by, 104
on activity theory in HCI, 147–148
on breakdowns, 171
on cultural factors, 107
on design, 218
on flexibility, 75
on focus shifts, 151
on HCI structures, 111
on interfaces, 49–50
on reflection in design, 196
on tools approach, 243
on transformed actions, 201
on VIRK, 160
Body, motion as principle for, 300
Border localization of culture, 312
Boster, Mark, in Postal Buddy development, 329, 339, 342, 346–348, 359–360, 363
Breakdowns, 149–152, 154–156
checklist for, 168–169
in VIRK system, 163–166, 170–172
in WordPerfect, 166–168
Brooks, R.
on HCI purposes, 69–70
on human-factors task analysis, 83
BRS software environment, 185
Bruner, J., on joint attention, 206–207
Button, G., on associating, 344

Callon, M.
on technoeconomic networks, 339–340
on TSR.2 aircraft, 344
Canoeing example in situated action model, 90–91
Canyon simulation, 132–137
Carey, T., on observations, 12–13
Carroll, J. M.
criticism of cognitive science by, 19–20
on group perspectives, 271
on psychology in interface design, 18
and task-artifact cycle, 54
Cartesian ideal of cognitive science, 19, 219
Cartographical design in ESA, 222
Case of the Evaporated Outline, 199–201
Case work, police investigations. *See* Flying Squad
Central cognitive structures, 52
Central information processing subsystems in HCI, 104
Chains of actions, 30–31
Change of address system. *See* Postal Buddy
Christiansen, Ellen, on objects, 74
Chronotope scheme, 294–295
Circular schemes, 229
Civilization in development, 311
Classifications in interface design, 23–24
Clusters
of actions, 149
of tasks, 225
Cockpit system in distributed cognition, 77
Co-construction
rule-guided, 220–225
of task structures, 217–220
Cognitive processes and activities, 33
Cognitive science, 17–18
artifacts in, 14, 62
criticism of, 19–22
in HCI, 13–14, 104–107
human factors in, 20–21

Cole, Michael
 on cognitive psychology, 112
 on cultural context, 124–127
Collaboration, 86
 in Dinosaur Canyon, 134–137
 in education, 131
 joint attention in, 204–213
 in Media Fusion, 137–140
Collaborative manipulation, 84
Collective perspectives, 269–271
Collective subjects, 58–59, 63
Collegial support in K-12 education, 127, 142
Common views in rule-guided co-construction, 220–225
Common vocabulary, 10
Communicative actions, 35
 collective subjects for, 58
 in RepGrids, 221–222
Communities of practice, 131, 148–149, 178
Community. *See also* Society and culture
 in K-12 education, 126
 in subject-object relationships, 27–28, 124–125
 in team programming, 29
Comparisons in situated action model, 92
Competition in actor-network theory, 345
Complexity in HCI research, 37
Composite functional organs, 296
Computer applications
 breakdowns in, 151–152
 changing, 169–170
 ethnographic study of, 238–244
 objects in, 152–155
 task-specific vs. generic, 235–238
 team programming for, 29–30, 257–271
 VIRK. *See* VIRK system
Computerized medical records, 195–196
Computer-mediated activity, 49–54
 development of, 54–57
 group and organizational use, 57–59
 studies on, 85–86
Computers
 caring about, 193–196
 group use of, 57–59
Computer-supported cooperative work (CSCW), 47, 103, 203, 259
Conceptual level in information systems, 24
Conceptual models, 365
Conceptual tools, 8
Conditions in activity theory, 108
Consciousness
 activity as, 7, 11
 in activity theory, 107
 development and function of, 8
 and freedom, 285
 intentionality in, 12–13
 in *Middlemarch*, 376–377
 and operations, 31–32
 self-consciousness, 308
 and transformed actions, 201
Consensual validation, 225
Constructed goals in situated action model, 79–80
Construction
 in Dinosaur Canyon, 134–135
 in education, 131
 joint, 267–271
 in Media Fusion, 138–139
Construct poles, 221–222
Context, 69–70. *See also* Society and culture
 for actions, 26
 in activity theory, 37–38, 46, 73–76, 78–88
 in computer applications, 155
 in design process, 128
 in distributed cognition, 78–88
 in HCI, 47–48, 110
 in K-12 education, 126–127
 in mediation by artifacts, 124–125
 simulated, 132
 in situated action model, 78–88

structures in, 83–86
Context-sensitive help functions, 216–217
Contingency in perspective, 268–269
Contingent situated actions, 84
Contradictions, 34
in activity theory, 271–275
in artifacts, 150–152
in VIRK system, 160–161
Convertibility
of internal and external forms, 298–299, 378
in poetic matter, 303–304
Cooperation in actor-network theory, 345
Cooperative error correction, 85
Cooperative modeling, 225–226
Cooperative work
computer-supported (CSCW), 47, 103, 203, 259
studies on, 86
Cottage cheese story, 71–72
Crick, Francis, on neurons of awareness, 322
Cultural process, growth as, 204
Cultural resources, perspectives from, 274
Cultural science paradigm in HCI, 204
Culture. *See* Society and culture
Culture-specific tools, 109

Dance troupe, joint remembering by, 263, 265
Danish National Labor Inspection Service (NLIS). *See* VIRK system
Danish National Police. *See* Flying Squad
Data collection techniques, 95
Davydov, V. V.
on activities vs. actions, 32
on subjects and objects, 90
Deeding thinking, 309
Deeds, 309
Deixis in natural language, 205–206
Dennison Manufacturing, 330
Depths of unconsciousness, 309
Design, 22–24
activity theory in, 127–128
comparisons for, 92
in ESA, 222
freedom and uncertainty of course in, 201–204
guidelines for, 49–50
in HCI, 22, 69–70
one-way-mirror paradigm in, 210
reflection in, 196
research on, 18
and task structure, 218
users in, 22, 128
DesignCenter workstations, 338, 370
Development
in activities, 26
in activity theory, 109
civilization in, 311
in computer-mediated activity, 55
of consciousness, 8
in HCI, 48, 110–111
of human practices, 38–40
from learning, 195
mediation of, 128–129, 301–311
mental, 313–314
planes of, 316–319
of self-consciousness, 308
speech, 314
spontaneous, 291
Dewey, John, and activity theory, 25
Dilemma of User-Centered Design, 202
Dinosaur Canyon simulation, 132–137
Direct manipulation in cognitive science, 18
Directness, postulate of, 363
Distributed cognition, 76–78
activities in, 79–83
vs. activity theory and situated action model, 78–88
evaluation of, 88–94
people and things in, 86–88
structures in, 83–86

Division of labor
in Flying Squad, 179–182
in K-12 education, 126
in subject, object, and community relationships, 28, 125
in team programming, 29
Documentation in Flying Squad, 179–180, 185, 187, 190, 192
Documents
missing, case of, 199–201
in VIRK system, 158–161
Dostoevsky, Fyodor, on being, 312–313
Dotted menus, 56
Draper, S., on designing for consciousness, 12
Drawing programs for slide preparation, 237
Dwyer, D.
on teacher support, 143
on technology in education, 127
Dynamic nature of activities, 33–34, 38–40, 75

Earth sciences, Dinosaur Canyon for, 132–137
Ecological perspective in activity theory, 107–108
Ecological validity of cognitive psychology, 106
Education
Dinosaur Canyon simulation, 132–137
Media Fusion program, 137–142
mediation in, 125–127
technology in, 123–125, 141–144
Ehn, P., on tools, 183
Eigen-Structure-Analysis (ESA), 222
Electronic Data Systems (EDS) in Postal Buddy development, 327–328, 332–334, 337, 340–341, 369
Elements in personal constructs, 220–221
Eliot, George, 376–378
Ellis, J.
computer-mediated work study by, 85
on distributed cognition, 98
Emergent situated actions, 84
Empirical research, 81, 178
End-to-end task-specificity, 240
Engels, Friedrich, and activity theory, 25
Engeström, Yrjö
activity systemic model by, 27–28
on artifacts, 26–27, 150
on communities of practice, 148
on computerized medical records, 195–196
on conceptual models, 365
on conceptual tools, 8
on contradictions, 160–161, 272–273
on cultural context, 124–127
cycle of developmental work research by, 215
and development research, 338
on group perspective, 57, 269
on instrumental impoverishment, 363
on methods, 93
on objects and activities, 360, 362
on reflection in design, 196
on self-determination in activity theory, 79
and social processes, 63
on task hierarchy, 217
work development model by, 150–151
Environment
in activity theory, 107
and growth, 315
in situated action model, 71
Ethnographic studies
activity theory for, 177
of application software, 238–244
limitations of, 10–11
of programming teams, 257–271
Evidence in videotaping, 97–98
Expansion of HCI, 46–49
Expert-novice collaboration, 140, 204–213
Exploratory data analysis (EDA), 222
External context, 76

External forms
of activities, 32–33
convertibility of, 298–299, 378
names in, 298
in psychology, 288–296
External influences on activities, 34
Externalization in activity theory, 109, 129
External tools as mediators, 302
Eye-tracking studies, 207–208

Failure studies, 343–344, 360–361
Featuritis in programs, 202
Feuerbach, Ludwig, and activity theory, 41
Fichte, Johann, and activity theory, 41
Files, missing, case of, 199–201
Final stage for activities, 62
Financial activities in team programming, 29
Fitts's law, 87–88
Flexibility
in activity theory, 75
in computer-mediated activity, 55
Flor, N.
on distributed cognition, 76–77
on people and artifacts, 87
programmer study by, 78
Florensky, P. A.
on humans as actions, 311
on sacred symbols, 306
Flores, F., on "throwness," 80
Flying Squad, 178–179
artifacts and tools in, 179–182
fraud investigation in, 191–193
homicide investigations in, 183–188
objects in, 179–182
theft notice monitoring in, 188–191
Focus shifts, 149–152, 154–156
in activity theory, 215–216
checklist for, 168–169
from contradictions, 272
in VIRK system, 163–166, 170–172
in WordPerfect, 166–168
Formalization of work procedures, 182–183
Foucault, Michael, on spirituality, 304
Frank, Anthony, 331
Fraud investigation in Flying Squad, 191–193
Freedom
activity as, 284–286
in design, 201–204
Friedman, A., on computer system development, 23
Frog Design firm in Postal Buddy development, 334, 340–342, 369
Functional organs, 50–54, 76, 249
in activity theory, 286–288
composite, 296
culture as, 311–319
generative capabilities of, 309
independence of, 308–309
levels in, 295
mediation of, 302
names as, 297–298
and tool mediation, 109
Functional systems in distributed cognition, 77
Future field in living motion, 294

Gal'perin, P. Ya.
on internalization, 290–291
on mental actions, 290
planes of action by, 209
Galua, on equations, 310
Gantt, M., CAD study by, 85
Gaze direction studies, 207–208
Gear-shifting operations, consciousness in, 31–32, 75, 268
Generalizations in situated action model, 92
Generic application software, 235–239
Gibert, Patricia M., 333
Gibson, J. J., on perception and activity, 209
Global warming studies, 137–141
Goals
of actions, 30, 80
in activity theory, 79–80, 108
changes in, 55
in distributed cognition, 77–80

Goals (cont.)
in GOMS, 60–61
as joint activity, 220
vs. objects, 360
polymotivated, 58–59
in situated action model, 79
tasks for, 219
in team projects, 259–260, 264–266
tool effects on, 53–54
God, philosophical system built on, 300
Goldman Sachs, Postal Buddy investment by, 333
GOMS model, 60–61
Goodman, Martin, 334
Goodman, Sidney, in Postal Buddy development, 328–334, 336–337, 340, 346, 348–349, 364
Goodwin, C. and Goodwin, M. H.
baggage handler study by, 260–261
on ethos, 271
Gordeyeva, N. D., on living motion, 288
Gorsky, A. K., on Rodin, 300
Grace, 299
Graphical data analysis in ESA, 222
Green, T. R. G., CAD study by, 85
Groups and group projects, 29–30
computer use by, 57–59
ethnographic study of, 257–271
situated cognition in, 259–261
task clusters between, 225
Growth
and environment, 315
as social and cultural process, 204
Grudin, Jonathan
on designers, 50
on groups, 259
on phased development, 23–24
on work and benefits, 59, 187
Gurvich, on irrepressible ontogenesis, 310

Hall, Stuart, 278
Hamlet, Mandelstam on, 321–322
Handling aspects of computer applications, 152
Harden, Dan, in Postal Buddy development, 329, 334, 347, 349
Harding, Sandra, 335
Hegel, Georg
and activity theory, 25, 41
on freedom, 285
on functional organs, 286–287
on theory and model, 93
Help functions in programs, 203, 216–218
Henderson, A.
on HCI, 21
on videotaping, 97–98
Hirsch, David, 332
Hirschhorn, L., on first impressions, 352
History
in activities, 26
in artifacts, 75, 150
in perspective, 268–269, 274
Holland, Dorothy
on perspective, 268–269
on teams, 259, 261, 274
Home Select kiosks, 338
Homicide Section in Flying Squad, 179, 183–188
Human-computer interaction (HCI)
and activity theory, 7–15, 25–41, 110–112
benefits of, 69–70
cognitive psychology for, 104–107
complexity in, 37
criticism of, 19–20
expansion of, 46–49
future of, 112–113
laboratory experiments in, 21
levels in, 24
need for theory of, 103–104
perceived problems in, 20–23
research object in, 23–24
views in, 62
VIRK system. *See* VIRK system

Human factors in cognitive science, 20–21
Human-factors task analysis, 83
Human spiritual development (HSD), 304–306
Humboldt, W. von, on internal and external forms, 291
Hunting
activities and actions in, 28–29
as group activity, 259–260
perspectives in, 269
Hurd, Bruce, in Postal Buddy development, 329, 340, 342, 347–349, 362, 365–368
Hutchins, E.
on collaborative manipulation, 84
on distributed cognition, 76–77
error correction study by, 85
on people and artifacts, 87
programmer study by, 78

Ideal forms, 314–318
Ideal planes, 290
Ideological model of work, 259
Image development, 303, 321
Image of motion, 293
Imitative learning, 204
Import/export mechanisms in slide preparation software, 243–244
Impressibility, 378
Improvisatory situated actions, 84
Income tax preparation software, 236–237
Independence of functional organs, 308–309
Individuals in distributed cognition, 77–78
Individual/social dimension of HCI, 48
Informate situations, 34–35
Information processing loops in HCI cognitive model, 105–106
Information systems (IS) research, 24
Information technology
activities in, 34–35
support functions of, 35–37
Initial phase for activities, 62
Inspections, labor. *See* VIRK system
Institutional support in K-12 education, 127, 142
Instrumental impoverishment, 363
Intellectual labor, perspectives in, 273–274
Intentionality
in consciousness, 12–13
in situated action model, 79–80
Interaction analysis
description of, 161, 163
video for, 97–98
Interaction level in cognitive models, 106
Interfaces
in HCI, 111–112
logical consistency in, 50
phased development in, 23–24
psychology in, 18
visualization in, 203
Intermediaries, 339
Intermediate stage for activities, 62
Internal context, 76
Internal forms
of activities, 32–33
convertibility of, 298–299, 378
names in, 298
in psychology, 288–296
Internal images
of motion, 293
of possibilities, 287
Internalization
in activity theory, 109, 129
IPA in, 51–52
and mental processes, 124
of society, 290–291
Internal plane of actions (IPA), 51–53, 112
Internal planes, 291
Interoperable services in software, 244
Inter-subjective mental actions, 109
Interviews
in activity theory, 81–82
in Postal Buddy system study, 328–329
in situated action model, 81

Interviews (cont.)
 in slide preparation software study, 238–239
Intra-subjective mental actions, 109
Investigations, police. *See* Flying Squad
Irrepressible ontogenesis, 310
Irreversibilization in actor networks, 340
Ivanov, V. V., on culture, 312

Joint attention, 204–213
Joint construction, 267–271
Joint perspectives, 269–271
Joint remembering, 263, 265
Jordan, B., on videotaping, 97–98

K-12 education
 Dinosaur Canyon simulation, 132–137
 Media Fusion program, 137–142
 mediation in, 125–127
 technology in, 123–125, 141–144
Kant, Immanuel, and activity theory, 25, 41
Kaptelinin, Victor
 on activity theory and computers, 242–243
 command name recall study by, 55–56
 on development, 111
 on mediation, 75–76
Karyakin, Y., on culture, 312
Kelley, L., on technology in education, 127
Kellogg, W. A., and task-artifact cycle, 54
Kuutti, Kari
 on actions and activities, 241
 on activities and objects, 79
 on activity theory and HCI, 104
 on artifacts, 75
 on context for HCI, 110
 on hunting, 259
 on information technology, 35
 on multidimensional reality of HCI, 48–49
 on transformation of objects, 74

Label machine, 329–330
Laboratory experiments in HCI, 21
Labor inspections. *See* VIRK system
Latour, Bruno
 on Aramis subway system, 343–344
 on consumers, 345
 on high-technology failures, 360–361
 on mobilizing allies, 340
 on tool effects on goals, 53–54
Lave, J.
 on arenas, 277
 on authentic learning, 130
 on cognitive science, 73
 on contradictions, 272–273
 cottage cheese story by, 71–72
 on goals in situated action model, 79–80
 grocery store activity descriptions by, 72
 on institutions, 97
 on intentionality, 79–80
 on interviews, 81
 on learning, 277
 on math, 257–258
 on perspective, 272–273
 on situated action model, 71
Law, J., on TSR.2 aircraft, 344
Lawyer Buddy kiosks, 338
Lead users, 345
Learning. *See also* Education
 authentic, 130
 collaboration in, 204–213
 contradictions in, 272
 cultural, 204
 development from, 195
 by new members, 217–218
 world mediation in, 129
Lektorsky, V. A.
 on objects, 361
 on specific reality, 362

Leont'ev, A. N.
on actions, 73–74
on activities, 73, 176
activity theory development by, 41
on automation, 34
on cognitive processes, 33
on consciousness in manual gear operations, 75, 268
functional organ concept by, 50–51
on goal-directed actions, 80
on goals, 360
hunting example by, 28–29
on internal image of motion, 293
on internalization, 291
on objects and activities, 360
on polymotivated actions, 58–59
on postulate of directness, 363
on tools, 83
on transformations, 32–33
Levels
of activities, 30–38, 108
in cognitive models, 104–106
in computer applications, 155
in cooperative modeling, 225–226
in functional organs, 295
in HCI, 47–48, 110
in information systems, 24
of learning, 205
of performance, 129–130
of social conduct, 213–216
Life nodes, 303
Little, J. D. C., on DesignCenter workstations, 338, 370
Living forms, 298
Living motion, 287–288, 294, 299, 301, 307–308
Living words, 297
Localization of culture, 312
Logical consistency in design, 50
Logical forms as internal, 292
Longitudinal ethnographic observations, 177
Long-term observations
in activity theory, 95
in situated action model, 92
Losev, A. F.
on names, 298
on personality, 307
on words, 296–297
Luria, A. R.
activity theory development by, 41
on cognitive processes, 33

Machines
affection for. *See* Postal Buddy
self-explanatory, 356
Malone, T., on intentionality, 12
Management Reports, Inc., 329
Mandelstam, Osip
chronotope illustration by, 295
on convertibility, 303–304
on growth, 315
on Hamlet, 321–322
on image development, 303, 321
on life nodes, 303
on names, 297–298
Manual gear operations, consciousness in, 31–32, 75, 268
Mapping VIRK system, 161–169
Marx, Karl
and activity theory, 25, 41
on functional organs, 286–287
Matter of action, 288
May, Tim, in Postal Buddy development, 329, 337, 363
McClintock, R., on technology and education, 123
McGrath, J. E., on groups, 259
Mead, G. H., and activity theory, 25
Meaning, activities for, 177
Media Fusion program, 137–142
Media in computer applications, 153–154
Mediating descriptive resources, 220, 227
Mediation, 10, 109
by artifacts, 26–27, 75–76, 124, 148–149
in computer applications, 153–154

Mediation (cont.)
by computers. *See* Computer-mediated activity
culture in, 124–125, 128–130
of development, 128–129, 301–311
in K-12 education, 125–127
in subject, object, and community relationships, 27–28
by systems, 153
by tools, 27–28, 62–63, 83, 109, 302
in VIRK system, 158–161
Medical records, computerized, 195–196
Mental actions, 290
Mental development, 313–314
Mental plane of action, 209
Mental processes, 109, 124
Mental tools as mediators, 302
Menus, 55
dotted, 56
type-ahead, 39–40
Methods in GOMS, 60
Middlemarch (Eliot), 376–377
Middleton, D., on joint remembering, 263
Miller, J., spreadsheet study by, 78, 85
Mind
activity approach to, 285–286
in activity theory, 107
emergence of, 123–124
Missing files case, 199–201
Mobilizing of allies, 340
Model-based communication technology, 137–141
Models
for actions, 31
conceptual, 365
Moran, T., HCI levels proposed by, 106
Moriarty, K. E., on Postal Buddy development, 330–331
Morris dance troupe, joint remembering by, 263, 265
Motion
and freedom, 285
internal image of, 293
living, 287–288, 294, 299, 301, 307–308
as principle for body, 300
Motives
for activities, 30–31
in activity levels, 34
in activity theory, 79–80, 108
changes in, 27
in computer-mediated activity, 55
in distributed cognition, 79–80
objectified, 73, 181
polymotivation, 58–59
in situated action model, 79–80
Motor functions, internal, 287
Motor output subsystems in HCI, 104
Multimedia in Postal Buddy development, 327–328
Muscles as animals, 301
Music, 299
Myths as mediators, 302, 306–307

Nabokov, V., on life, 313
Names, 296–301
Nardi, Bonnie A.
on activity theory and HCI, 104
on collaborative process, 86
on communities of practice, 149
slide preparation software study by, 236, 243
spreadsheet study by, 78, 85
work coordination study by, 86
Natural language, objects in, 205–206
Natural science paradigm, 204
Nature walk, evaluating actions in, 89–90
Neisser, U., on perception and activity, 209
Neomorphs, 288
Networks of actions, 30
Neurons of awareness, 322
Nodes of development, 302–303
Nonbeing, menace of, 313
Norman, D.
and affordances, 56–57
on artifacts, 85

on cognitive artifacts, 62
on Grudin's law, 59

Objectified motives, 73, 181
Objective perspective, 107–108
Objects, 14
and activities, 34, 360, 362
in activity theory, 73–74, 107–108
affection for. *See* Postal Buddy
in computer applications, 152–155
in distributed cognition, 80
in Flying Squad, 179–182
for HCI, 110
in K-12 education, 126
names of, 296–301
in natural language, 205–206
in personal constructs, 220–221
relationships of, 27–28, 32
roles of, 361–362
substitute, 362–363, 366–367
in team programming, 29–30
transformation of, 27, 32–33, 74
in VIRK system, 158–161
Observations
in activity theory, 95
limitations of, 12
longitudinal ethnographic, 177
in situated action model, 92
Olson, D. R., on authority, 362
One-way-mirror paradigm, 210
Ong, W. J., on writing systems, 362
Ontological planes of development, 316–319
OpenDoc framework, 202–203
Operations
for actions, 108
from activities, 40
in activity theory, 73, 75
automation of, 34
development of, 31–32
evaluation of, 228
examples of, 33
Operators in GOMS, 60
Organizations, computer use by, 57–59
Orientation phase for actions, 31

Page numbering in WordPerfect, 165–168, 170
Palme case, 74, 186
Participatory design process, 128
Pattern observations in activity theory, 95
Peer involvement
in Flying Squad software, 185
learning from, 195
in teaching and tutoring, 140
People and things in activity theory, situated action model, and distributed cognition, 86–88
Perception-action cycle, 209
Perception and activities, 209–210
Perceptual plane of action, 209
Performative word actions, 292
Personal construct psychology, 220
Personal views in HCI, 62
Perspectives
in activity theory, 107–108, 271–275
as collective productions, 269–271
as contingent and historical, 268–269
in team projects, 57, 259–260, 267–271
Petre, M., CAD study by, 85
Petrovsky, A. V., and Petrovsky, V. A., on collective subjects, 58
Phased development in interface design, 23–24
Phenomenological planes of development, 316–319
Phylogenetic development, 129
Physical aspects of computer applications, 151–152
Physical device level in cognitive models, 106
Physical plane of action, 209
Planes
of action, 51–53, 112, 209
of development, 316–319
Plans
for actions, 31
as projective accounts of action, 97
in situated action model, 72, 79–81
Plants, 300–301

Plath, Sylvia, on "thinginess of things," 14
Plotin, on living motion, 299
Police investigations. *See* Flying Squad
Polymotivation, 58–59
Ponomarev, Ja. A., on IPA, 51–52
Postal Buddy, 325–327
actor-network theory analysis of, 338–346
affection for, 346–349, 360–364
missing network links in, 365–370
rise and fall of, 327–338
user interaction with, 349–360
Postal Buddy Corporation, 331–333, 365
Postulate of directness, 363
Pragmatism and activity theory, 25
Predictable situated actions, 84
Principle of symmetry, 339
Processing levels in cognitive models, 104–106
Programming, team, 29–30
ethnographic study of, 257–271
joint construction in, 267–271
time log requirement in, 261–267
Projective accounts of action, 97
Psychological factors in K-12 education, 127, 142
Psychology
in interface design, 18
internal and external forms in, 288–296
personal construct, 220
Psychophysiological mechanisms in learning, 205
Purposefulness in activity theory, 79
Pyatigorsky, on season for thinking, 310, 319

Qualified expressions, 346, 349
QuickCourt kiosks, 338

Rabinovich, P., on culture, 312
Raeithel, Arne
on activity theory and HCI, 104
on collaboration management, 204
on ESA, 222
on objects, 74
on similarity horizons, 229
and social processes, 63
Ranke, I., on motion in bodies, 300
Reactions, free will in, 284
Real forms, 314–318
Reciprocity in actor-network theory, 345
Reductionist schemes, 250–251
Reeves, James R., on teams, 259, 261, 274
Reflection in design, 196
Relationships
in activities, 175–176
of subject, object, and community, 27–28, 32, 124–125
Repertory Grid Technique, 220–225
Resources
mediating descriptive, 220, 227
plans and models as, 31
Retrospective reconstructions, 79–81
Rilke, M., on Rodin, 299
Ringstaff, C., on technology in education, 127
Rodin, O., on body, 300
Rogers, Y.
computer-mediated work study by, 85
on distributed cognition, 98
Rosson, M. B., and task-artifact cycle, 54
Rostropovich, Mstislav, relationship to cello, 295–296
Routines in situated action model, 84
Rubinshtein, S. L., on activity, 285
Rule-guided co-construction, 220–225
Rules
in K-12 education, 126
mediation by, 28
in Postal Buddy system, 366–367
in team programming, 29–30
Rusli, M., on observations, 12–13

Sacred symbols, 306
SADT diagrams, 227

Scenario model for design, 218
Schelling, F., on freedom, 284
Schools. *See* Education
Scribner, S., on longitudinal ethnographic observations, 177
Search process histories, 53
Sechenov, on animals, 301
Seifert, C., error correction study by, 85
Self-consciousness, 308
Self-determination, 79
Self-explanatory machines, 356
Self-reflective intermediaries, 339
Semantic knowledge, 205
Semantic level in cognitive models, 106
Sense, mediation by, 306–307
Sensory input subsystems in HCI, 104
Serial deeds, 309
Settings in situated action model, 71
Severyanin, Igor, on sense, 307
Sherrington, C., on action, 285
Shlegel, on music, 299
Shneiderman, B., on type-ahead menus, 39–40
Sign-related actions, 301
Signs as mediators, 302, 306–307
Silver Age of Russian culture, 249–250
Similarity horizons, 229
Simulations, Dinosaur Canyon, 132–137
Situated action models, 71–73
  activities in, 79–83
  vs. activity theory and distributed cognition, 78–88
  design in, 128
  evaluation of, 88–94
  people and things in, 86–88
  structures in, 83–86
Situated cognition and team projects, 259–261
Slice-of-time strategy, 259
Slide preparation software
  ethnographic study of, 238–244
  task-specific vs. generic, 237–238
Social conduct, levels of, 213–216
Society and culture
  in activity theory, 37–38, 46, 63–64, 107
  in artifacts, 75, 130
  and attention, 206
  and consciousness, 7
  in development, 311
  in Flying Squad, 179–182
  as functional organ, 311–319
  growth as, 204
  in HCI, 47–48, 110–112
  in intellectual labor, 273
  internalization of, 290–291
  in K-12 education, 126–127
  in mediation, 124–125, 128–130
  in programming, 29, 275
  tool mediation transmission of, 53
Software. *See* Computer applications
Soul, 300
Specific reality, 362
Speech development, 314
Spet, G. G., on internal and external, 289–290, 292
Spinoza, Baruch, and God, 300
Spiritual development, 304–306
Spontaneous development, 291
Spranger, on ideal forms, 314
Spreadsheets
  as objects, 152
  studies on, 78, 85
Strategic Computing Initiative, 365–366
Structure
  of activities, 27–30
  in activity theory, 83–86
  in distributed cognition, 78, 83–86
  in situated action model, 83–86
  of tasks, 217–220
Strukturlegetechnik, 226–227
Students. *See* Education
Student team programming, 29–30
  ethnographic study of, 257–271
  joint construction in, 267–271
  time log requirement in, 261–267
Subjects
  in activity theory, 73

Subjects (cont.)
collective, 58–59, 63
community relationships with, 124–125
in computer applications, 152, 171
object relationships with, 27–28, 32, 152, 171
in situated action model, 94
in system perspectives, 153
Substitute objects, 362–363, 366–367
Subsystems in HCI, 104
Subtask-specificity, 240–241
Suchman, L.
baggage-handling form analysis by, 72
canoeing example by, 90–91
on cognitive science, 73
on conflicts in instructions, 353, 355
on embodied skills, 80
empirical studies by, 81
on goals, 360
on interaction analysis, 161, 163
on joint activities, 263, 267
on people and things, 88
on plans in situated action model, 79–81
on projective accounts of action, 97
on routine practices, 84
on self-explanatory machines, 356
on situated action model, 71
Support
for CAD software, 85
of information technology, 35–37
in K-12 education, 127, 142–143
Symbolic interactionism, 25
Symbolic tools, 62–63
Symbols as mediators, 302, 306–307
Symmetry, principle of, 339
Symon, G., coordination study by, 85–86
Syntactic level in cognitive models, 106
System goals in distributed cognition, 79
Systems
in computer applications, 153–154
in distributed cognition, 77–78
mediation by, 153
useful, 8
user modifications to, 22
System views in HCI, 62

Tabletop analysis tool, 137–141
Talyzina, N. F.
on activities vs. actions, 32
on subjects and objects, 90
Task analysis, 83
Task-artifact cycle, 54, 110
Task clusters between groups, 225
Tasks, 74
and actions, 219
co-construction of, 217–220
in cognitive models, 106
in slide preparation software study, 240–242
Task-specific application software, 235–241
Teacher development centers (TDCs), 143
Teachers
and Media Fusion, 142
support for, 143
Teaching. *See* Education
Team programming, 29–30
ethnographic study of, 257–271
joint construction in, 267–271
time log requirement in, 261–267
Teamwork in slide preparation process, 242
Technical level in information systems, 24
Technical support in education, 127, 142–143
Technology
and education. *See* Education
as substitute objects, 362–363
Tertiary artifacts, 365
Theft notice monitoring in Flying Squad, 188–191
Thinking
artifacts for, 182
deeding, 309
season for, 310, 319

Throwness in situated action model, 80
Tikhomirov, O., on people in activity theory, 87–88
Time frames, 95
Time log requirement in team programming study, 261–267
Timiryazev, on plants, 300–301
Tools
  activity theory as, 46
  in computer applications, 153–154
  conceptual, 8
  as culture transmitter, 53
  in Flying Squad, 179–183
  formalization of work procedures as, 182–183
  as functional organs, 50–54
  goals affected by, 53–54
  for HCI, 110
  mediation by, 27–28, 62–63, 83, 109, 302
  relationships with, 175–176
  stages in activities mediated by, 62–63
  in team programming, 29–30
  in virtual realities, 64
Total activity systems, 253
Transformation
  of objects, 27, 32–33, 74
  for spiritual development, 306
Transformed actions, 149, 201
Trigg, R.
  baggage-handling form analysis by, 72
  empirical studies by, 81
  on interaction analysis, 161, 163
Trust in actor-network theory, 345
TSR.2 aircraft, 344
Tunnel vision phenomena, 352
Turkle, S., on holding power, 362
Turner, Terrence, on social forces, 273
Tutoring, peer, 140
Type-ahead menus, 39–40

Ukhtomsky, A. A., on functional organs, 287
Uncertainty of course in design, 201–204
United States Postal Service (USPS). *See* Postal Buddy
Unit of analysis
  in activity theory, 73
  in distributed cognition, 77
  in situated action model, 71
Usability labs, 210, 213
Useful systems, 8
User-centered design, 22, 201–204
Users
  in activity theory, 95
  in actor-network theory, 345
  in design process, 22, 128
  in Flying Squad software development, 185
  of Postal Buddy, 349–360, 369
User testing, 210

Validation, consensual, 225
Vandegrift, Roy, 331
Velichkovsky, Boris M.
  on consciousness, 201
  on learning, 205
  on levels of social conduct, 214
  on objects, 74
Vertical axis of development, 304–305
Videotaping
  analysis of, 157–158
  for interaction analysis, 97–98
  of Postal Buddy customers, 328, 349–360
  in situated action model, 81
  of VIRK system, 157
Views in HCI, 62
Virkkunen, J., on information technology as activity enabler, 35
VIRK system, 156–157
  activities in, 158–161
  analysis of, 157–158
  breakdowns and focus shifts in, 163–166, 170–172
  changing, 169–170
  mapping, 161–169
  videotaping of, 157

Virtual mediators, 302
Virtual realities, 64, 295
Visualization in interface design, 203
Vocabulary, 10
von Hippel, E., on lead users, 345
Vygotsky, L. S.
activity theory development by, 41
on consciousness, 11
educational design principles from, 131
on internalization, 290
on learning, 129, 195, 205
on longitudinal ethnographic observations, 177
on mediation, 128–130
on mental development, 313–314
on mental processes, 109
on methods, 93
on mind, 123–124
on socialization of attention, 206
on speech, 314
on zone of proximal development, 130, 204

Walt, S., teamwork study by, 276
Warburton, Tina, in Postal Buddy development, 329, 347
Wartofsky, M., on tertiary artifacts, 365
Welcome Labels Corporation, 329, 332
Wenger, E.
on contradictions, 272–273
on learning, 277
on perspective, 272–273
Whiteside, J., criticism of cognitive science by, 19–20
Wilmore, F., on teacher support, 143
Winograd, T., on throwness, 80
Wixon, D., criticism of cognitive science by, 19–20
Word actions, 292–293
WordPerfect, page numbering in, 165–168, 170
Word processors as objects, 152
Words
as mediators, 302, 306–307
and names, 296–301
Work development model, 150–151
Work procedures as tools, 182–183
Work process level in information systems, 24
World as mediator, 129

Yocam, K., on teacher support, 143

Zaporozhets, A. V.
on child development, 310
on internal image of motion, 293
on living motion, 288
on spontaneous development, 291
Zinchenko, Vladimir P.
on activities vs. actions, 32
eye movement reports by, 222
on subjects and objects, 90
Zone of proximal development, 109, 130, 204, 284, 319
Zuboff, S., on informate situations, 34–35